Enhanced IP Services for Cisco Networks

Donald C. Lee

Cisco Press
201 West 103rd Street
Indianapolis, IN 46290 USA

Enhanced IP Services for Cisco Networks

Donald C. Lee

Copyright © 1999 Donald C. Lee

Cisco Press logo is a trademark of Cisco Systems, Inc.

Published by:
Cisco Press
201 West 103rd Street
Indianapolis, IN 46290 USA

Printed in the United States of America 1 2 3 4 5 6 7 8 9 0

Library of Congress Cataloging-in-Publication Number: 98-86518

ISBN: 1-57870-106-6

Warning and Disclaimer

This book is designed to provide information about enhanced IP services for Cisco networks. Every effort has been made to make this book as complete and as accurate as possible, but no warranty or fitness is implied.

The information is provided on an "as is" basis. The author, Cisco Press, and Cisco Systems, Inc. shall have neither liability nor responsibility to any person or entity with respect to any loss or damages arising from the information contained in this book or from the use of the discs or programs that may accompany it.

The opinions expressed in this book belong to the author and are not necessarily those of Cisco Systems, Inc.

Trademark Acknowledgments

All terms mentioned in this book that are known to be trademarks or service marks have been appropriately capitalized. Cisco Press or Cisco Systems, Inc. cannot attest to the accuracy of this information. Use of a term in this book should not be regarded as affecting the validity of any trademark or service mark.

CERT® and CERT® Coordination Center are registered for Carnegie Mellon University in the U.S. Patent & Trademark Office.

Feedback Information

At Cisco Press, our goal is to create in-depth technical books of the highest quality and value. Each book is crafted with care and precision, undergoing rigorous development that involves the unique expertise of members from the professional technical community.

Readers' feedback is a natural continuation of this process. If you have any comments regarding how we could improve the quality of this book, or otherwise alter it to better suit your needs, you can contact us through email at ciscopress@mcp.com. Please make sure to include the book title and ISBN in your message.

We greatly appreciate your assistance.

Publisher	John Wait
Executive Editor	Alicia Buckley
Cisco Systems Program Manager	Jim LeValley
Managing Editor	Patrick Kanouse
Acquisitions Editor	Lynette Quinn
Development Editor	Katherine Trace
Project Editor	Theresa Wehrle
Copy Editor	Malinda McCain
Technical Reviewers	Erick Mar
	Deepak Munjal
Proofreader	Bob LaRoche
Team Coordinator	Amy Lewis
Book Designer	Gina Rexrode
Cover Designer	Aren Howell
Compositor	Wil Cruz
Indexer	Tim Wright

About the Author

Donald C. Lee (CCIE #3262) is a Senior Systems Engineer at Cisco Systems with more than eight years of networking industry experience and a B.S. degree in Electrical Engineering from UCLA. He has been responsible for designing, implementing, and troubleshooting network solutions for several of Cisco's largest Fortune 500 customers. Prior to Cisco, Donn was an Advisory Systems Engineer at a leading data storage manufacturer and an Information Systems Network Manager/Engineer at a consumer products market leader.

About the Technical Reviewers

Erick Mar is a Senior Systems Engineer at Cisco Systems with CCIE certification in routing and switching (CCIE #3882). As a Systems Engineer for the last seven years for various networking manufacturers, he has provided design and implementation support for large Fortune 500 companies. Erick has an M.B.A. from Santa Clara University and a B.S. in Business Administration from San Francisco State University.

Deepak Munjal (CCIE #4376) has more than 10 years of networking industry experience and a B.S. degree in Computer Science from the University of California, Berkeley. He is currently a Senior Systems Engineer at Cisco Systems and has been actively involved in the design and implementation of end-to-end networking solutions for Cisco's largest Fortune 500 customers. Prior to Cisco, Deepak was a network engineer at a leading computer manufacturing company.

Dedications

To my parents: My parents are great folks and always cheer me up. Now that I'm (mostly) grown-up, I can greatly appreciate all those times they taught, fed, encouraged, and loved me. This book is dedicated to my mom and dad who, I'm proud to say, are the Internet's newest and most distinguished "surfers."

To my wife Shirley: In the age of virtual reality, virtual pets, and virtual offices, Shirley (an incredible human being) experienced a whole new privilege as a result of my book: the *virtual widow*. Despite having to spend some 42 weekends with a keyboard-zombie for a husband, she never stopped her support for the book and she helped me edit many sentences that just wouldn't sit right. This book is also dedicated to her and her enthusiastic support for the Internet (surfing www.gap.com).

Acknowledgments

Kathy Trace deserves extreme kudos and credit for her contribution as the development editor of this book. In addition to being knowledgeable, organized, flexible, and helpful, she's also an exceptionally nice person.

Erick Mar and Deepak Munjal, the technical reviewers, made this book much better than anything I could have written on my own. In addition to being among the best Cisco engineers I know, they are also great friends. Many thanks go to them for their expertise, advice, and editing.

Lynette Quinn did a superb job managing this project from beginning to end. Her positive attitude and receptiveness made my job easy.

Alicia Buckley provided excellent executive leadership, support, and insight. She also listened to all my random ideas for the book. Like everyone else on the Cisco Press team, she's incredibly nice and great to work with.

Julie Fairweather and Kim Lew got me jump-started on the book, provided valuable support, and were always a pleasure to work with.

Amy Lewis is a great team coordinator whose attention to detail and timeliness were crucial to the project.

The Cisco Press team who worked behind-the-scenes is top-notch. I wish to thank everyone in illustration, editorial, layout, and the rest of the production process for their contributions.

Finally, my friends at Cisco were always very positive and supportive of this weekend project. I especially wish to thank my managers Srinivas Ketavarapu, Pasha Quadri, and Rico Sacks. Cisco is a great place to work and it is because of these folks.

Contents at a Glance

Table of Contents

Introduction

Your network should provide more than just connectivity. Successful networking means more than installing hardware and programming it to pass packets of data back and forth. Modern networks have mission-critical applications to support, more users and geographical locations, higher bandwidth requirements, and security threats from inside and outside the network. Furthermore, there's rarely enough money, time, or resources to keep up with these demands.

Requirements and resources are opposing forces and are at odds with each other. To relieve this situation, you must do whatever you can to increase the effectiveness of your network.

Effectiveness is the capability of the network to support your current and future users, applications, locations, and policies. A network that merely provides connectivity between locations might meet the requirement for basic data communication, but it won't have what it takes to deliver reliable service for mission-critical applications, scalability for a growing user population, or security for protecting information. In the end, a highly effective network enables organizations to deploy more services to more users in more locations with greater confidence and security.

Increasing effectiveness means to enhance, optimize, and extend the current capabilities of the network—that is, to make the network more useful, more efficient, and more capable of handling demand. The following are some important network capabilities covered in this book:

- **Routing**—The routing function moves data through the network efficiently and finds new paths when network outages occur. Routing also affects how large the network can grow—that is, the number of users and locations you can support, the complexity of the topology, and the stability of the network as it expands. This ability to grow is called the *scalability* of a network.

- **Intelligence and Quality of Service**—This is the capability of a network to recognize and deliver different types of data based on policies you define. An intelligent network recognizes traffic from different applications and prioritizes them into different qualities of service (also called classes of service). Your policy defines prioritized levels of service and classifies the mix of applications on your network into these levels of service. For example, you might define a high quality of service for mission-critical applications, a medium quality of service for general applications, and a low quality of service for low-priority applications. An intelligent network with quality of service ensures that high-priority traffic is delivered to its destination with the shortest possible delay. Without quality of service, all applications are treated equally. This can adversely affect the deployment and operation of applications requiring short delays and fixed levels of bandwidth.

- **Security**—Security services protect the confidentiality and integrity of information on your network. These services increase the trust users have in the network and make the network suitable for new applications. Some security services protect against attacks that aim to disable or cripple the network service itself. Security countermeasures increase the reliability of the network and are no doubt crucial for a high level of effectiveness. Security services also enable you to extend the network to new locations securely. For example, you might want to extend the network to a telecommuter's home via the public telephone system or to branch-office locations through encrypted tunnels over the public Internet.

Cisco IOS

Cisco's Internetwork Operating System (IOS) software runs in Cisco routers and switches—the devices used to build the Internet and the majority of corporate networks. IOS is packed with so many features in so many technologies that just learning the names of the features and what they do is challenging. A quick look through the documentation, which consumes a good-sized bookshelf, is all you need to realize how comprehensive and daunting the IOS feature set is. However, you do not need to learn the intricacies of every IOS command to build and maintain an effective network for your organization.

Purpose of This Book

This book focuses on *enhanced IOS services* that help you increase the effectiveness of your IP network. You might need these services to help run your network today, or you might need to understand some of these technologies to prepare for the future. This book will help you in either case, by focusing on tasks that give you the most results for your effort. In addition to showing you how to configure each service, this book also provides background on why you might need the service and how it works.

The following list is a sampling of what you will find in this book:

- Getting efficient use of network resources such as addresses and bandwidth
- Optimizing routing services
- Integrating networks with different routing protocols and different addressing architectures
- Gatekeeping the consumption of network bandwidth
- Adding intelligence and quality of service in the network to support new applications
- Setting policies on the network for users and their services
- Extending the network to new places, such as the Internet, securely
- Protecting information and network resources

Study the services and practices in this book. Then analyze the current state of your network. Finally, decide how you might take your network to the next level: to an enhanced network that is scalable, intelligent, and secure.

Audience

This book is intended for networking professionals who are responsible for designing, implementing, and managing IP services in enterprise networks. Although the focus is on Cisco IOS, the principles and strategies covered in this book can readily apply to any IP network. No major background in IOS, TCP/IP, or routing is required, but a familiarity with these topics will get you started right away. For experienced networking professionals such as Cisco Certified Internetwork Experts (CCIEs) and candidate CCIEs, this book aims to provide unique technologies and effective practices that not only deliver value on your network but also provide opportunity for professional growth. For folks completely new to Cisco router configuration, Appendix E, "A Crash Course in Cisco IOS," covers all the basics.

Organization

The eight chapters and five appendixes of this book are organized into four parts.

Part I—Managing Routing

The aim of the first part is to get the most out of IP addressing and routing. Chapter 1 progresses logically from basic addressing to more sophisticated topics such as VLSM, classless addressing, summarization, and NAT. Experienced readers may skip Chapter 2, which covers basic routing protocols and sets up a foundation for Chapter 3. Chapter 3 rounds out Part I with routing services that enhance network flexibility and scalability. These services include route filtering, redistribution, default routing, summarization, and policy routing.

Part II—Managing Quality of Service

The goal for Part II is to understand, implement, and validate quality of service (QoS) on a network. Chapter 4 identifies the driving forces behind QoS and QoS principles and covers basic services such as Priority Queuing, Custom Queuing, and Weighted Fair Queuing. Chapter 5 details IOS's advanced QoS mechanisms, including RSVP, RED, CAR, and Class-Based Weighted Fair Queuing.

Part III—Managing Security

The objective of the third part is to secure the network, protect data and users, and extend connectivity with confidence. Chapter 6 covers access lists, basic router security, AAA services, and some simple commands that enhance network security. Chapter 7 begins a survey of advanced security services and provides details about IPsec—a leading technology for building VPNs. IPsec's building blocks include IKE, transforms, security associations, modes, AH, ESP, and basic cryptography (digital certificates, digital signatures, public key cryptography, Diffie-Hellman, and the like). Finalizing the coverage of advanced security services, Chapter 8 shows you how to use IOS as a stateful firewall and an intrusion detection system. These services protect your organization from malicious attacks.

Part IV—Appendixes

Five appendixes are included in Part IV:

- Appendix A, "Obtaining IETF RFCs," provides instructions on how to obtain IETF RFCs.
- Appendix B, "Retrieving Internet Drafts," explains Internet Drafts and shows you how to get them.
- Appendix C, "Common TCP and UDP Ports," is a reference table of common TCP and UDP port numbers.
- Appendix D, "Password Recovery," is a quick reference for recovering lost or forgotten passwords on Cisco routers.
- Appendix E, "A Crash Course in Cisco IOS," is a quickstart on IOS navigation, configuration, and monitoring. It also furnishes some tips and tricks, so it's worth a skim even if you've worked with IOS for a while.

Conventions and Features

When appropriate, the services covered in this book adopt the following basic content structure:

- **What is it?** A description of the IOS service and why you might need it.
- **How does it work?** Technical information on the underlying mechanism and a look at what's going on behind the scenes.
- **How do you configure it?** Practical instructions and configuration examples.
- **How do you check it?** Some ways of validating, monitoring, and debugging your results.

Within the text, IOS commands are printed in **boldface** for readability. In some cases, boldface is also used as an aid for locating interesting text in IOS outputs. *Italic text*, when used in IOS commands, indicates arguments for which you supply values.

The listings of IOS configurations sometimes include the IOS prompt when it helps illustrate the configuration steps. Otherwise, the prompt is omitted and the relevant portion of the configuration is printed as an output of **show running-config** (or, equivalently, **write term**).

Finally, important concepts are called out from the text as notes, and sidebars offer insight into related concepts or techniques. Tips highlight information that might be helpful as you implement these enhanced services.

Support

Although every effort was made to stamp out errors, documentation bugs sometimes arise from the mass of technical details. In an effort to further customer support, the Cisco Press Web site at www.ciscopress.com is available for clarifications, corrections, and other possible errata related to this book.

Managing Routing

CHAPTER 1

Managing Your IP Address Space

The first step in achieving a scalable and effective IP network is devising a solid addressing plan. Your addressing plan lays down the foundation for the network by portioning your IP address space into smaller, manageable ranges, or *blocks*. The addressing plan also defines the deployment of these blocks into various parts of the network for supporting devices.

Unlike such protocols as IPX or AppleTalk, IP requires a respectable amount of address planning at the outset. This is true for large and small networks alike, because the growth of the Internet has made IP addresses a precious and scarce resource.

The Internet's IP address space is finite. With the growth of the Internet, the number of available addresses is diminishing and addresses are becoming more difficult to obtain. Although addressing is a rather mundane task, a solid addressing plan will save you many headaches in the future (and protect your reputation when others inherit your work). Also, IP networks can—and generally should—have a hierarchical addressing structure. This is achieved by summarizing, or *aggregating*, addresses. Summarization heightens the importance of address planning even more (see "Planning for Address Summarization," later in this chapter).

Devising your address strategy is akin to planning the layout of a house. You are going to spend a lot of time in your house, so a crucial step is spending enough time on the design and allocation of the floor space for now and in the future. Are there enough rooms? Is the size of each room adequate and appropriate? What is the most efficient use of the floor space? Although you cannot guarantee a final house design that meets all future requirements, you need to come up with a plan that makes the most sense. You want a well-thought-out design that will postpone any remodeling efforts until far off in the future. By all means, you want to avoid having to demolish the whole thing and start over with a new floor plan. Like floor plans, IP addressing plans generally do not change for long periods of time and, when they do change, overhauling them can be a major effort.

This chapter covers IP addressing concepts, design techniques, strategies for maximizing efficiency, and services for scaling network addressing.

The main topics of this chapter are

- Review of Traditional IP Addressing
- Subnetting a Classful Address Space

- Subnetting with Variable Length Subnet Masks
- Overview of Classless Addressing
- Planning for Address Summarization
- Conserving Subnets with IP Unnumbered
- Scaling the Address Space with Network Address Translation

Review of Traditional IP Addressing

Traditional IP addressing organizes the entire 32-bit IP address space into blocks called *classes* and further breaks down each class into network numbers. Early Internet standards defined five classes, outlined in Table 1-1.

Table 1-1   *The Original Organization of the 32-bit Address Space*

Class Name	Address Range	# of Addresses per Network	Purpose
A	0.1.0.0 to 126.0.0.0	16,777,216	Unicast; very large networks
B	128.0.0.0 to 191.255.0.0	65,536	Unicast; large networks
C	192.0.1.0 to 223.255.255.0	256	Unicast; small networks
D	224.0.0.0 to 239.255.255.255	N/A	Multicast
E	240.0.0.0 to 247.255.255.255	N/A	Experimental use

NOTE   Network 127.0.0.0 is a special range of addresses reserved for *loopback addresses* (addresses used locally by IP hosts). Such addresses should never appear on a network.

As Table 1-1 illustrates, a 32-bit IP address is written as four *octets* (8-bit groups) separated by periods, with each octet expressed as a decimal number. This is known as *dotted decimal notation*. The following is an example IP address in its binary and dotted decimal forms:

32-bit IP address: 10101100000100000000101000010100
Same address grouped into four octets: 10101100.00010000.00001010.00010100
Same address in dotted decimal notation: 172.16.10.20
Class of the network: B
Network the address belongs to: 172.16.0.0

The class scheme served as a starting point for easy and rapid deployment of the Internet address space. Much like acquiring land for their buildings, organizations obtained network numbers from the three classes (classes A, B, and C) based on the number of IP addresses they needed. Two classes were reserved for special purposes: class D addresses for IP multicast and class E addresses for experimental use.

After an organization secured a class B network, for example, it could autonomously deploy the addresses contained in that range to its computers, or *hosts*. With the additional deployment of internetworking services (*routing*), that class B network could communicate with other class A, class B, and class C networks within the organization and throughout the Internet.

NOTE   This book covers IP version 4, which is the most prevalent form of IP on private networks and the public Internet at the time of this writing. The next version of IP, version 6, has a different addressing format and intends to provide a much larger address space than IP version 4 (IPv6 increases the address space from 32 bits to 128 bits). See the bibliography for sources of IP version 6 information.

To gain more efficient use of the address space, the Internet community adopted a practice of dividing a network into subnetworks called *subnets*. When a network is divided into subnets, its original network number is called the *major network number* or *major net*. Routing is still required to interconnect subnets just as it is required to interconnect major nets.

For most organizations, subnetting is a necessary part of managing an address space—it portions a single major net of limited use into smaller subnets that can be deployed more effectively.

Still, networking professionals are faced with addressing problems that subnetting alone cannot solve. The scarce supply of major nets and pressure from an ever-growing IP population have taken the menial task of addressing to the top of the priority list. Later sections of this chapter offer solutions that will help you get more efficient use of your address space and alleviate the shortage problem.

Subnetting a Classful Address Space

As mentioned previously, the Internet's original address plan was organized into classes: classes A, B, C, D, and E. Networks deployed with this plan are said to be *classful networks* or networks with *classful addressing*. Many privately owned networks still use classful addressing, even though the public Internet has abolished classful addressing in favor of *classless addressing* (covered in "Overview of Classless Addressing" later in this chapter).

In brief, classless addressing discontinues the grouping of addresses into classes A, B, and C and treats the address space as a large, contiguous block of addresses.

NOTE   The Internet community adopted classless addressing to get efficient use of the existing address space and to avoid address depletion. See "Overview of Classless Addressing" later in this chapter.

Why care about classful addressing versus classless addressing? Addresses are addresses, aren't they? The distinction between classful and classless addressing is important when it comes to routing protocols. Some routing protocols—Routing Information Protocol (RIP) and Interior Gateway Routing Protocol (IGRP), for example—were created before the practice of classless addressing and support only the rules defined by traditional classful addressing (these rules are simple, but restrictive). Classful routing protocols, such as RIP, do not support newer and more advanced features developed in classless routing protocols, such as Open Shortest Path First (OSPF) and Enhanced IGRP (EIGRP). These advanced features include variable length masking and summarization and are covered later in this chapter (see "Subnetting with Variable Length Subnet Masks," "Overview of Classless Addressing," and "Planning for Address Summarization"). Routing protocols are also covered in Chapter 2, "Deploying Interior Routing Protocols," and Chapter 3, "Managing Routing Protocols."

Although the Internet has ceased using classful addressing, many organizations need to support networks that were designed with classful networks and classful routing protocols, such as RIP and IGRP. This section covers the basics of subnetting because the technique is crucial for supporting a classful network and is a prerequisite to deploying classless networks. The section includes discussion on

- Major Nets and Subnet Masks
- Classful Subnetting: An Example
- Calculating the Number of Host Addresses in a Subnet
- Finding Subnet Information, Given a Host Address and the Mask
- Disadvantages of Subnetting
- The Rules on Top and Bottom Subnets
- Using Subnet-Zero to Get Around the Rules

Major Nets and Subnet Masks

Every major net has two fields: the *network field*, which uniquely identifies the major net, and the *host field*, which uniquely identifies hosts within the major net. Figure 1-1 illustrates the number of bits in the network and host fields for each class.

As mentioned in the previous section, subnetting is the process of dividing a major net into smaller (and generally more useful) subnets. This is accomplished by "stealing" some bits from the host field of the major net and using those bits to designate the subnet addresses. The host field varies in length, depending on the class of major net being subnetted (see Figure 1-1).

Figure 1-1   *Lengths of the Network and Host Fields by Class*

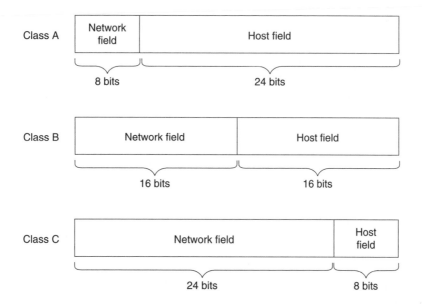

When you consume some of the bits in the host field for subnets, you are left with three fields: the original network field, a newly created subnet field, and a reduced-size host field. Figure 1-2 illustrates the three fields you get after subnetting.

Figure 1-2   *Subnetting Results in Network, Subnet, and Host Fields*

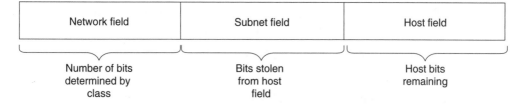

You declare the number of bits you are stealing from the host field with a 32-bit *subnet mask*. The subnet mask contains a contiguous series of ones that start from the left-most bit (also called the *most significant bit*). Where the ones end and the zeros begin is the boundary between the subnet field and the host field. Figure 1-3 describes a subnet mask and provides an example.

Figure 1-3 *Defining the Subnet and Host Fields with a Subnet Mask*

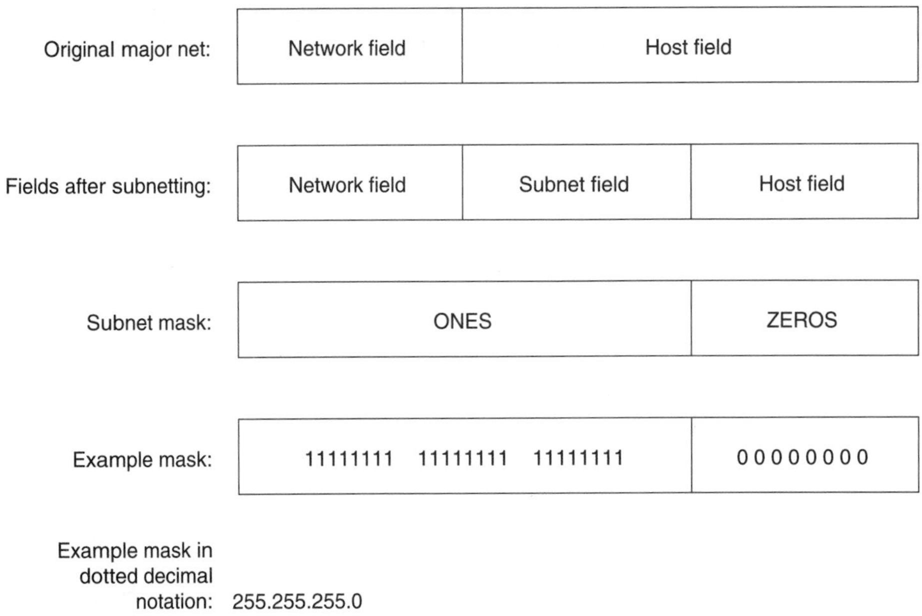

Original major net:	Network field	Host field	

Fields after subnetting:	Network field	Subnet field	Host field

Subnet mask:	ONES		ZEROS

Example mask:	11111111 11111111 11111111		0 0 0 0 0 0 0 0

Example mask in
dotted decimal
notation: 255.255.255.0

The example mask in Figure 1-3 has 24 one bits that start from the far left and 8 zero bits that fill out the remaining bits to the far right. This mask defines a host field of 8 bits because the boundary between the ones and the zeros is between the 24th and 25th bits (bits 25 through 32 are zero and represent the host field). The size of the subnet field depends on whether this mask is applied to a class A, class B, or class C major net. Recall from Figure 1-1 that the network field is defined by the class of the major net.

When you convert the mask from Figure 1-3 into dotted decimal notation, you get 255.255.255.0, because

- The first octet (the first group of 8 bits) is all ones (255 in decimal)
- The second octet is all ones (255 in decimal)
- The third octet is all ones (255 in decimal)
- The last octet is all zeros (0 in decimal)

The example in Figure 1-3 is a rather straightforward example because each octet is either all ones or all zeros. Things get more interesting when the boundary between the ones and zeros falls within an octet. Consider another mask:

```
11111111111111111111111111000000
```

To make this mask easier to read, separate the octets like this:

```
11111111.11111111.11111111.11000000
```

Now, convert each octet into decimal:

```
255.255.255.192
```

The preceding mask defines the subnet-host field boundary between the 26th and 27th bits, resulting in a host field of 6 bits (bits 27 through 32). Again, the size of the subnet field depends on the class of the major net to which you apply this mask. It's time for an example.

Classful Subnetting: An Example

The best way to get familiar with subnetting is to practice. Consider the following example that subnets major net 192.168.1.0 by stealing three bits from the host field to make a three-bit subnet field as shown in Example 1-1.

Example 1-1   *Subnetting a Class C Major Net with a Three-Bit Subnet Mask*

Major net: 192.168.1.0
Class: C
Length of original host field: 8 bits (from Figure 1-1)
Number of host bits to steal for subnet field: 3 bits
Number of host bits remaining after subnetting: 8-3=5 bits

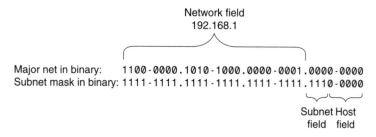

Major net in binary: 1100-0000.1010-1000.0000-0001.0000-0000
Subnet mask in binary: 1111-1111.1111-1111.1111-1111.1110-0000

Subnet mask in
dotted decimal notation: 255.255.255.224

The common way to write a major net together with its subnet mask is by using the shorthand notation of the major net followed by a slash (/) and the number of ones in the mask. The shorthand notation for 192.168.1.0 masked with 255.255.255.224 (see Example 1-1) is 192.168.1.0/27 (there are 27 contiguous ones in 255.255.255.224).

NOTE   Both the dotted decimal and slash notations are acceptable, and both notations are used when working with Cisco routers. For example, configuring an address on a router interface requires the mask in dotted decimal notation, but the output of **show ip route** favors slash notation in most versions of IOS. Also, some people prefer one notation over the other, so a good idea is to be familiar with both.

As you can see from Example 1-1, converting from dotted-decimal notation to binary when subnetting is often convenient. A separator, such as a hyphen, makes it easier to read eight bits in a row.

Example 1-1 uses three bits for the subnet field. This yields eight unique combinations that are used to identify the subnets: 000, 001, 010, 011, 100, 101, 110, and 111. The eight subnets for Example 1-1 are listed in Table 1-2. The three bits that make up the subnet field are printed in boldface to emphasize the distinction between the subnet bits and the host bits.

Table 1-2   *The Eight Subnets for Example 1-1*

Subnet Field	Octet *x* in 192.168.1.*x* (bin)	Octet *x* in 192.168.1.*x* (dec)	Subnet Number
111	**111**0-0000	224	192.168.1.224/27
110	**110**0-0000	192	192.168.1.192/27
101	**101**0-0000	160	192.168.1.160/27
100	**100**0-0000	128	192.168.1.128/27
011	**011**0-0000	96	192.168.1.96/27
010	**010**0-0000	64	192.168.1.64/27
001	**001**0-0000	32	192.168.1.32/27
000	**000**0-0000	0	192.168.1.0/27

In traditional subnetting, you are not allowed to use the so-called *top* and *bottom* subnets. The top subnet has all ones in the subnet field and the bottom subnet contains all zeros. For the preceding example, 192.168.1.224/27 is the top subnet and 192.168.1.0/27 is the bottom subnet. This leaves the middle six subnets available for deployment, but the top and bottom subnets are wasted. The section "Using Subnet-Zero to Get Around the Rules" later in this chapter covers how you can use the bottom subnet.

Calculating the Number of Host Addresses in a Subnet

Calculating the number of hosts that can be addressed per subnet is not difficult. Each bit position can be either a one or a zero, so starting with one bit, there are two possible combinations. The number of possible combinations doubles each time you add an additional bit. Two bits yields four combinations, three bits yields eight combinations, four bits yields 16 combinations, and so on.

The formula for the number of combinations is 2^n, where *n* is the number of bits in the field. Example 1-1 has five bits in the host field after three bits are stolen for the subnet field. This yields $2^5=32$ unique combinations for addressing hosts; however, the all-zeros and all-ones patterns are reserved for the subnet number and subnet broadcast address, respectively. After subtracting these two reserved addresses, 30 addresses per subnet remain for host addresses.

Finding Subnet Information, Given a Host Address and the Mask

Given a host address and the subnet mask, you can determine the subnet on which that host lives. This is another common exercise and is useful anytime you need to track the subnet number for a host (in a routing table, for example). Suppose you are given the following host address and subnet mask:

```
172.16.9.136/22
```

To start the process, convert the host address and mask to binary and write the mask below the host address (for clarity, the host field bits are printed in boldface here):

```
1010-1100.0001-0000.0000-1001.1000-1000 = 172.16.9.136
1111-1111.1111-1111.1111-1100.0000-0000 = /22
```

Now, focus on the boundary defined by the mask (where the ones end and the zeros begin). This is the boundary between the subnet field and the host field and tells you that the last 10 bits of the address make up the host field. An easy way to determine the subnet number is to take the host address and set all of the bits in the *host field* to zero, like this:

```
1010-1100.0001-0000.0000-1000.0000-0000 = 172.16.8.0
```

Thus, host 172.16.9.136/22 is on subnet 172.16.8.0/22.

NOTE You might notice that the subnet number is the result of a binary "AND" operation on the address and mask at each bit position. This is how computers (and routers) calculate the subnet number.

Additionally, you can easily find the IP broadcast address for the subnet. This is done by setting all of the bits in the host field (printed again in boldface) to one, like this:

```
1010-1100.0001-0000.0000-1011.1111-1111 = 172.16.11.255
```

Thus, the broadcast address of subnet 172.16.8.0/22 is 172.16.11.255. Sending a packet (a ping, for example) to 172.16.11.255 is a transmission to every host in the subnet.

Last, you can find the range of valid host addresses for this subnet. The range contains the addresses *between* the subnet number (host field of all zeros) and the broadcast address (host field of all ones), so the host address range for subnet 172.16.8.0/22 is

```
1010-1100.0001-0000.0000-1000.0000-0001 = 172.16.8.1
```

through

```
1010-1100.0001-0000.0000-1011.1111-1110 = 172.16.11.254
```

You can verify that the host address 172.16.9.136, introduced at the start of this section, indeed falls within this address range.

Disadvantages of Subnetting

Note that subnetting is restrictive because the technique forces you to commit to the number of subnets you need now and in the future. You also need to commit to the number of hosts per subnet, because every bit you steal for the subnet field means one less bit you can use for host addresses.

Making matters worse, the technique produces subnets that are all of equal size in the number of hosts that can be supported per subnet. Therefore, you often have to do the sizing based on the largest subnet needed and waste addresses when deploying the remaining subnets to areas with fewer hosts. These issues apply when you're using a routing protocol that only supports a fixed-size mask. "Subnetting with Variable Length Subnet Masks," later in this chapter, covers a method of subnetting that mitigates some of the problems with fixed-size masks.

The Rules on Top and Bottom Subnets

Arguments exist both in theory and in practice for not using the top and bottom subnets in a classful network. Theoretically, a bit field has two special patterns:

- **All-zeros pattern**—usually means "this" as in "this host" or "this network."
- **All-ones pattern**—usually means "all" as in "all hosts" or "all networks."

Early Internet documents said it was a good idea to keep these meanings and apply them to the subnet field, thus disallowing the use of the bottom subnet of all zeros and the top subnet of all ones. As a result, IP software in devices obeyed these rules and checked if users erroneously attempted to configure a device in violation of the rules.

NOTE   The advent of classless addressing abolished the notion of the top and bottom subnets (and subnets in general). In a classless environment, devices can use the address space that the classful world knows as the top and bottom subnets. See "Overview of Classless Addressing" later in this chapter for information on classless addressing.

In practice, using the top or bottom subnet can be problematic, because not all devices, especially legacy devices, allow these to be configured. Although you might be successful at deploying some hosts and routers on these outer subnets, you might find that other devices forbid you to configure an address from the top or bottom subnet. You'll then have to find another subnet for those devices. To avoid problems, a good idea is to be familiar with the diversity of devices in your environment and determine the addressing allowed on those devices.

The root of the controversy lies in the ambiguity of addresses when you're using the top or bottom subnets. Take, for example, a bottom subnet field that contains all zeros (the host field also contains all zeros)—the subnet number is the same as the major net number. This is apparent in Example 1-1, where the bottom subnet 192.168.1.0/27 is the same address as the major net (see Table 1-2). This ambiguity can be a source of confusion for some devices because a reference to the subnet is indistinguishable from a reference to the major net. Similarly, an all-ones broadcast to the top subnet could be interpreted as a broadcast address to all of the major net, because the top subnet and major net broadcasts are also indistinguishable. Looking again at the example in Table 1-2, a broadcast to the upper subnet 192.168.1.224/27 is 192.168.1.255—the same address as a broadcast to the entire class C (192.168.1.0).

Using Subnet-Zero to Get Around the Rules

Keeping in mind the caveats listed in the preceding section, you can configure Cisco routers to use the bottom subnet so that you gain one more subnet out of your subnetting efforts. To enable the use of the bottom subnet, use the **ip subnet-zero** global command:

```
Router#conf t
Router(config)#ip subnet-zero
```

If you forget to configure this, the router will "complain" when it comes time to assign an address to an interface. The following is an attempt to configure an interface with an address from a bottom subnet on a router without the **ip subnet-zero** command (notice the output **Bad mask**):

```
Router(config)#int s0
Router(config-if)#ip address 192.168.1.2 255.255.255.224
Bad mask /27 for address 192.168.1.2
```

Because the broadcast address for the top subnet is the same as the broadcast address to the entire major net, deploying the top subnet with such classful routing protocols as RIP and IGRP is not recommended. This is not a problem for classless routing protocols, such as OSPF and EIGRP.

A Word on Semantics

For the remainder of this book, the term *network* defines a general service of TCP/IP communication, as in the "corporate network" or "enterprise network." This is also known as an organization's *intranet* and is usually built of campus networks and wide-area networks. The term *major net* refers to a specific IP address space that follows classful addressing, and *subnet* refers to an address space that is extracted from the major net with the subnetting procedure covered earlier in "Subnetting a Classful Address Space."

Subnetting with Variable Length Subnet Masks

With Variable Length Subnet Masks (VLSMs), you carve an address space (such as a major net) with masks of varying lengths to design subnets of different sizes. This allows you to deploy subnets that are appropriate in size to the number of hosts you need to support in a given part of the network. As a result, you can gain efficient consumption of your address space and—depending on how you deploy the addresses—flexibility in the future as you adjust the size of each subnet to handle growth.

NOTE   Your routers must be running a routing protocol that supports VLSM, such as OSPF or EIGRP. RIP and IGRP are classful routing protocols and do not support VLSM. Classful routing protocols are limited to a single subnet mask per major net.

Here is the basic technique for variably subnetting a major net:

1   Subnet the space (for example, a major net) into large address blocks based on the large subnets you need in your network.

2   Deploy these large blocks of addresses to support your large subnets.

3   Take any unused large blocks and subnet them further to support smaller subnets with fewer hosts. You can think of this as a second round of subnetting.

4   Deploy the subnets from the second round of subnetting.

5   With additional rounds of subnetting, continue dividing unused blocks of addresses into multiple smaller subnets and deploying them as needed.

Some binary is involved here. Subnetting requires that you understand and visualize binary patterns and apply those patterns to masks. Consider the following example that uses a class C major net.

Using VLSM for Address Space Efficiency: An Example

Suppose Widget, Inc., asks you to subnet one of its class C major nets and tells you it needs the following:

- Two subnets that can support at least 60 hosts
- Four subnets that can support at least 10 hosts
- As many subnets as possible that can support two hosts

The subnets are needed to support some new additions to its network, as summarized in Table 1-3.

Table 1-3   *Subnets Needed by Widget, Inc.*

Subnet Size	Quantity Needed	Purpose
60+ hosts	2	Branch offices
10+ hosts	4	Server farms
2 hosts	As many as possible (use the remaining space)	Point-to-point home offices

First, you should do a quick check of the quantity of addresses needed. The branch offices require at least 120 host addresses (60 addresses times 2 branch offices), and the server farms require at least 40 host addresses (10 addresses times 4 farms). Any remaining addresses will be used for the point-to-point home offices, but this is not a hard requirement, so the basic need is for 160 (120 plus 40) addresses. This seems to be a reasonable request, because a class C has an 8-bit host field (see Figure 1-1), and an 8-bit host field with no subnetting can support up to 254 addresses (see "Calculating the Number of Host Addresses in a Subnet" earlier in this chapter). At least Widget, Inc., is not asking for the impossible; for example, it is not asking you to support 500 addresses with a single class C.

Next, tackle the largest subnets—the subnets for the branch offices. To accommodate the branch offices, you need to subnet the class C address space into chunks of at least 60 host addresses each. This is done in the following section and represents an initial round of subnetting.

Round 1 of Subnetting

To start, you create four subnets that can support 62 hosts each. You can accomplish this by applying a 26-bit subnet mask to Widget's class C. Two of the resulting subnets will be deployed for branch offices, and the other two will be subnetted further to accommodate the other requirements. The following is Widget's class C and mask (the last octet of the mask is expanded into binary to help illustrate what's happening):

Widget, Inc.'s Major Net: 192.168.1.0 (8-bit host field)
Mask for round 1: 255.255.255.**11**00-0000 (/26 mask that supports 62 hosts per subnet)

The two bits printed in boldface represent the bits that were stolen to make a 2-bit subnet field.

Table 1-4 lists the subnets created by the first round of subnetting. The two bits that make up the subnet field are printed in boldface to emphasize the distinction between the subnet bits and the host bits.

Table 1-4   *Subnets Created by the Mask for Round 1*

Name	Subnet Number in Binary (Last Octet)	Subnet Number in Decimal	Proposed Use
Subnet 1	192.168.1.**0000**-0000	192.168.1.0/26	Subnet further; see round 2
Subnet 2	192.168.1.**0100**-0000	192.168.1.64/26	Branch Office A
Subnet 3	192.168.1.**1000**-0000	192.168.1.128/26	Branch Office B
Subnet 4	192.168.1.**1100**-0000	192.168.1.192/26	Subnet further; see round 2

This first round of subnetting is nothing new—it's the same as traditional subnetting covered in "Subnetting a Classful Address Space" earlier in this chapter. Stealing two bits for the subnet field leaves six bits in the host field and yields 2^6, or 64 combinations. Subtracting the two reserved addresses for the subnet and broadcast address leaves 62 addresses for hosts. This meets Widget, Inc.'s requirement for two subnets of at least 60 hosts, so set aside Subnet 2 and Subnet 3 for the two branch offices—they are ready for deployment. Subnet 2 and Subnet 3 are selected because they are middle subnets rather than top or bottom subnets (see "The Rules on Top and Bottom Subnets" earlier in this chapter).

Figure 1-4 depicts the subnets that are set aside and unused after round 1.

Figure 1-4   *Widget, Inc.'s Address Space After Round 1 of Subnetting*

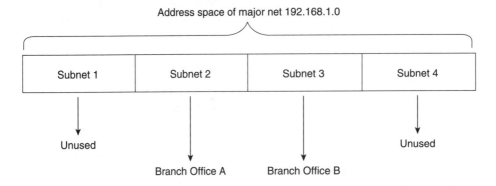

If you were doing traditional subnetting, you would now be finished, and you would have only two subnets remaining after setting aside Subnets 2 and 3. Clearly, this would not meet Widget, Inc.'s requirements, so start a second round of subnetting. This is where VLSM starts. You do not need Subnets 1 and 4 in their full size (62 host addresses), so subnet them further with a second round of subnetting and a new mask.

Round 2 of Subnetting

Perform a second round of subnetting on Subnets 1 and 4 by extending the subnet mask two bits more for a total of four bits in the mask (you are stealing two more bits from the host field and making the subnet field bigger). This further divides Subnets 1 and 4 into multiple smaller subnets.

The following is the second round of subnetting for Subnet 1. The bits printed in boldface represent the expanded subnet field (now a 4-bit field):

> Subnet 1: 192.168.1.0/26 (6-bit host field)
> Mask for round 2: 255.255.255.**1111**-0000 (/28 mask that supports 14 hosts per subnet)

Table 1-5 lists the new subnets created out of Subnet 1 by a second round of subnetting. For clarity, the new subnets are named Subnet 1.*x*, where *x* represents a piece of the original Subnet 1. As before, the bits that make up the subnet field are printed in boldface to emphasize the distinction between the subnet bits and the host bits. The new bits that expanded the subnet field are underlined.

Table 1-5   *Subnets Created by the Mask for Round 2 When Applied to Subnet 1*

Name	Binary (Last Octet)	Decimal	Proposed Use
Subnet 1.1	192.168.1.**0000**-0000	192.168.1.0/28	Subnet further; see round 3
Subnet 1.2	192.168.1.**0001**-0000	192.168.1.16/28	Server Farm A
Subnet 1.3	192.168.1.**0010**-0000	192.168.1.32/28	Server Farm B
Subnet 1.4	192.168.1.**0011**-0000	192.168.1.48/28	Server Farm C

NOTE   Subnet 1's first two subnet bits are 00, as defined by the first round of subnetting. It is very important not to alter these two bits—any change to the 00 bits means you are no longer working with Subnet 1.

Now, perform a second round of subnetting on Subnet 4 with the same /28 mask:

> Subnet 4: 192.168.1.192/26 (6-bit host field)
> Mask for round 2: 255.255.255.**1111**-0000 (/28 mask that supports 14 hosts per subnet)

Table 1-6 lists the new subnets created out of Subnet 4 by a second round of subnetting. For clarity, the new subnets are named Subnet 4.*x*, where *x* represents a piece of the original Subnet 4. The new bits that expanded the subnet field are underlined.

Table 1-6   *Subnets Created by the Mask for Round 2 When Applied to Subnet 4*

Name	Binary (Last Octet)	Decimal	Proposed Use
Subnet 4.1	192.168.1.**1100**-0000	192.168.1.192/28	Server Farm D
Subnet 4.2	192.168.1.**1101**-0000	192.168.1.208/28	Subnet further; see round 3
Subnet 4.3	192.168.1.**1110**-0000	192.168.1.224/28	Subnet further; see round 3
Subnet 4.4	192.168.1.**1111**-0000	192.168.1.240/28	Subnet further; see round 3

This second round of subnetting yields eight more subnets—eight additional subnets for Widget, Inc., out of the same address space. Each of the eight subnets (1.1 through 1.4 and 4.1 through 4.4) can support up to 14 hosts. This meets Widget, Inc.'s requirement for the server farm subnets. Widget, Inc., needs four of these subnets, so set aside Subnets 1.2, 1.3, 1.4, and 4.1 for the four server farms.

Avoid using Subnets 1.1 and 4.4, because they are the bottom and top subnets in the major net. You can deploy them if you are certain that hosts and networking devices in Widget, Inc.'s network are not affected by the caveats about using the top and bottom subnets discussed earlier.

Figure 1-5 depicts the subnets that are set aside and still unused after round 2.

Figure 1-5   *Widget, Inc.'s Address Space After Round 2 of Subnetting*

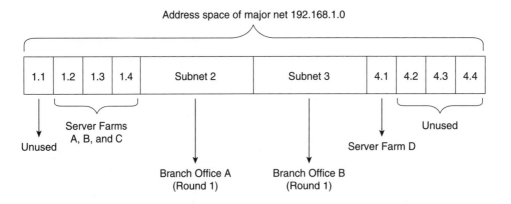

Round 3 of Subnetting

The unused subnets from round 2 can be used to satisfy Widget, Inc.'s requirement for the home office subnets (two hosts each), so now perform a third and final round of subnetting. Extend the mask from the last round by two more bits for a total of 6 bits in the mask. This further divides the unused subnets (1.1, 4.2, 4.3, and 4.4) into smaller, two-host subnets.

The following is the third round of subnetting applied to the unused Subnet 4.2 (from round 2). The bits printed in boldface represent the expanded subnet field (now a 6-bit field):

Subnet 4.2: 192.168.1.208/28 (4-bit host field)
Mask for round 3: 255.255.255.**1111-11**00 (/30 mask that supports two hosts per subnet)

Table 1-7 lists the new subnets created out of Subnet 4.2 by a third round of subnetting. For clarity, the new subnets are named Subnet 4.2.*x*, where *x* represents a piece of the Subnet 4.2. As before, the bits that make up the subnet field are printed in boldface to emphasize the distinction between the subnet bits and the host bits. The new bits that expanded the subnet field are underlined.

Table 1-7   *Subnets Created by the Mask for Round 3 When Applied to Subnet 4.2*

Name	Binary (Last Octet)	Decimal	Proposed Use
Subnet 4.2.1	192.168.1.**1101-00**00	192.168.1.208/30	Home Office
Subnet 4.2.2	192.168.1.**1101-01**00	192.168.1.212/30	Home Office
Subnet 4.2.3	192.168.1.**1101-10**00	192.168.1.216/30	Home Office
Subnet 4.2.4	192.168.1.**1101-11**00	192.168.1.220/30	Home Office

NOTE   Subnet 4.2's first four subnet bits are 1101, as defined by the second round of subnetting. It is very important not to alter these four bits—any change to the 1101 bits means you are no longer working with Subnet 4.2.

This third round of subnetting uses a /30 mask and creates four smaller subnets out of Subnet 4.2. A subnet with a /30 mask can support only two hosts—perfect for Widget, Inc.'s home offices that connect over point-to-point links.

Figure 1-6 depicts the subnets created after subnetting Subnet 4.2 with the mask from round 3 (/30 mask).

Figure 1-6 *Subnet 4.2 After the Third Round of Subnetting*

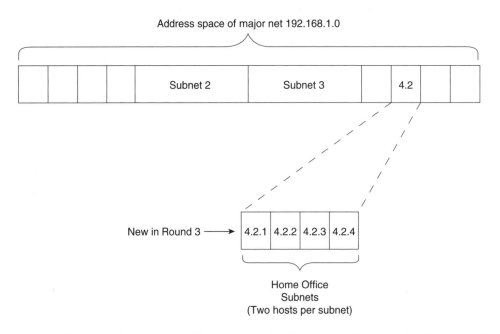

Widget, Inc., wants to use all of the unused address space from round 2 for home offices, so with Subnet 4.2 complete (Table 1-7), simply repeat the third round of subnetting. That is, apply the same /30 mask to the other unused subnets from round 2: Subnets 1.1, 4.3, and 4.4. This results in a total of 16 two-host subnets for home offices, as summarized by Table 1-8.

Table 1-8 *A Summary of the Subnets Created by Round 3*

Name	Binary (Last Octet)	Subnet
1.1.1	192.168.1.**0000-00**00	192.168.1.0/30
1.1.2	192.168.1.**0000-01**00	192.168.1.4/30
1.1.3	192.168.1.**0000-10**00	192.168.1.8/30
1.1.4	192.168.1.**0000-11**00	192.168.1.12/30
4.2.1	192.168.1.**1101-00**00	192.168.1.208/30
4.2.2	192.168.1.**1101-01**00	192.168.1.212/30
4.2.3	192.168.1.**1101-10**00	192.168.1.216/30
4.2.4	192.168.1.**1101-11**00	192.168.1.220/30
4.3.1	192.168.1.**1110-00**00	192.168.1.224/30
4.3.2	192.168.1.**1110-01**00	192.168.1.228/30
4.3.3	192.168.1.**1110-10**00	192.168.1.232/30

Table 1-8   *A Summary of the Subnets Created by Round 3 (Continued)*

Name	Binary (Last Octet)	Subnet
4.3.4	192.168.1.**1110-11**00	192.168.1.236/30
4.4.1	192.168.1.**1111-00**00	192.168.1.240/30
4.4.2	192.168.1.**1111-01**00	192.168.1.244/30
4.4.3	192.168.1.**1111-10**00	192.168.1.248/30
4.4.4	192.168.1.**1111-11**00	192.168.1.252/30

As in the earlier rounds, you still have a top and bottom subnet after round 3; they are 192.168.1.252/30. and 192.168.1.0/30. Although these are generally not deployable, they are small two-host subnets, so you are wasting just a few addresses out of the entire major net space. The third-round VLSM process has effectively reduced the wasted address space from 128 addresses in round 1 (where Subnet 4 and Subnet 1 were the top and bottom subnets) to just 8 addresses in round 3 (where Subnets 4.4.4 and 1.1.1 are the top and bottom subnets). This represents significantly better use of the address space over fixed-length subnet masks.

Final VLSM Results for Widget, Inc.

After the third round of subnetting, you cannot use VLSM to subnet any further—a two-host subnet is the smallest you can make. The totals from all three rounds are listed in Table 1-9.

Table 1-9   *Final Results of Subnetting for Widget, Inc.*

Round	Subnets Created	Subnets Set Aside	Maximum Hosts per Subnet
1	4	2	62
2	8	4	14
3	16	14 (2 wasted)	2

The VLSM process yields a total of 20 deployable subnets of three different sizes and meets the stated requirements of Widget, Inc.

NOTE   RFC 1219 describes a VLSM subnetting strategy that allows subnets to grow in size after they are deployed and also avoids address changes. See Appendix A for information on how to retrieve RFCs.

Overview of Classless Addressing

Classless addressing (described in RFC 1519) abolishes the idea of traditional classes A, B, and C major nets and the notion of a subnet field. Subnets and major nets do not exist in a classless world; instead, there is only a network prefix and a host field. Figure 1-7 describes the difference between classful and classless addressing.

Figure 1-7   *Classful Versus Classless Addressing*

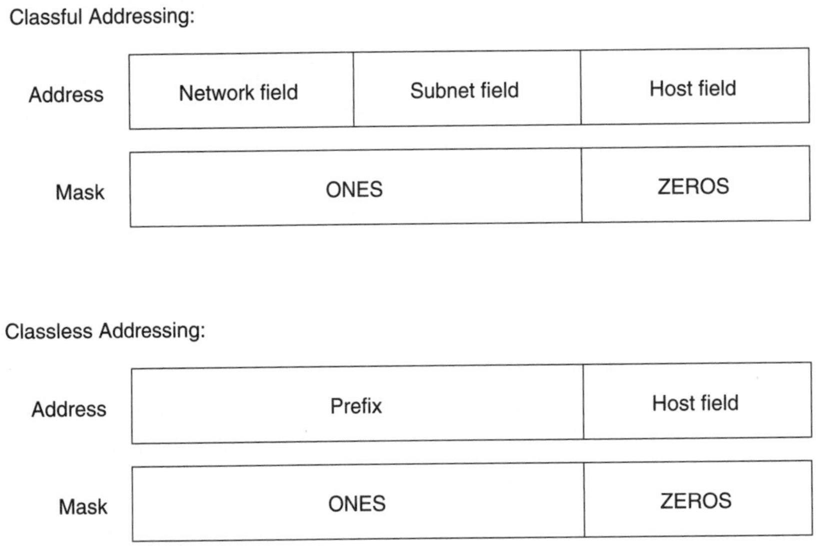

Classful Addressing:

Network field	Subnet field	Host field

Address

ONES	ZEROS

Mask

Classless Addressing:

Prefix	Host field

Address

ONES	ZEROS

Mask

The length of the network prefix is determined by a prefix mask. The prefix mask is a contiguous series of ones that starts with the left-most bit (the most significant bit). Although the prefix mask looks like a subnet mask, it's important to realize that there is no subnet field.

An advantage of classless addressing is the capability to combine what were multiple class C addresses into a contiguous block of addresses called a *supernet* or classless interdomain routing (CIDR) block. Figure 1-8 describes an address space in two ways: as four class C major nets (classful sense) and as one supernet (classless sense).

Figure 1-8   *An Address Space Written as Four Class C Major Nets and as One Supernet*

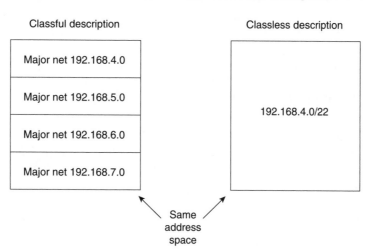

The number after the slash in the classless notation is the prefix length and indicates how many one bits are in the prefix mask. For example, 192.168.4.0/22 represents a prefix of 192.168.4.0 with a mask of 22 contiguous ones. The mask /22 is equivalent to 255.255.252.0 in dotted decimal notation.

With the prefix and the mask, you can determine the addresses covered by the supernet 192.168.4.0/22 (see Example 1-2):

Example 1-2   *Determining the Address Range Covered by 192.168.4.0/22*

```
Prefix: 192.168.4.0  ⟶ 192.168.0000-01|00.0000-0000
Mask: /22            ⟶255.255.1111-11|00.0000-0000
Address: 192.168.0000-0100.0000-0000
              Through
       192.168.0000-0111.1111-1111
              ( or )
       192.168.4.0 through 192.168.7.255
```

In a classless world, the address space depicted in Example 1-2 is one block and, if desired, may be deployed as one "subnet" supporting up to 1022 hosts (2^{10}, subtracting for the network prefix address itself and the all-ones pattern for the network prefix broadcast address). This demonstrates the power of classless addressing. If you had to use classful addressing, you would be stuck with four separate class C major nets—the largest subnet you could make would be 254 hosts. (A class C major net with no subnetting yields 8 bits in the host field, which is $2^8 - 2 = 254$ hosts.)

Using VLSM Techniques with Classless Addressing

Classless addressing doesn't stop there. You can also break up the space any way you choose by using the same techniques of VLSM. (It's now called *variable length network prefixes*; however, the term VLSM is still commonly used, semantics aside). Remember, there are no more subnets by the true definition of the word because there is no subnet field—only a network prefix and its prefix mask. This means there's no such thing as a top or bottom subnet, so in using the techniques of VLSM, you can use all of the possible network prefixes for deployment into the network.

Continuing with Example 1-2, you can use VLSM techniques to divide the 192.168.4.0/22 space into smaller blocks with a longer network prefix. Example 1-3 illustrates the results of applying a /26 mask to 192.168.4.0/22 (this could be the first round of VLSM, for example).

Example 1-3   *Using VLSM to Divide Supernet 192.168.4.0/22 into Smaller Address Blocks*

Original prefix: 192.168.4.0/22

Original prefix
in binary: **192.168.0000-0100.00**|00-0000   (/22)

New mask: 255.255.1111-1111.11|00-0000   (/26)

```
                              Original
                          prefix bits  New prefix
     Result of new mask        ⌒          bits
     applied to the         ⌢⌢⌢⌢⌢⌢⌢  ⌢⌢⌢⌢
     original prefix:    192.168.0000-01xx.xxhh-hhhh
                         ⌣⌣⌣⌣⌣⌣⌣⌣   ⌣⌣⌣⌣
                            Prefix bits    Host bits
```

In Example 1-3, each *x* represents a bit that can be used to create new network prefixes and each *h* represents a host bit.

The new prefix mask /26 yields four bits that divide the original /22 space into 16 (2^4) smaller blocks. Each of these smaller blocks contains 6 bits for host addresses (up to 62 hosts each). Table 1-10 lists the blocks created with the /26 mask. The four new prefix bits resulting from the VLSM operation are printed in boldface for clarity.

Table 1-10   *Listing of the New Prefixes Created from Example 1-3*

Network Prefix (Subnet); *h* Represents Host Bits	Network Prefix (Subnet) in Dotted Decimal Notation
192.168.0000-01**00.00***hh-hhhh*	192.168.4.0/26
192.168.0000-01**00.01***hh-hhhh*	192.168.4.64/26
192.168.0000-01**00.10***hh-hhhh*	192.168.4.128/26
192.168.0000-01**00.11***hh-hhhh*	192.168.4.192/26

Table 1-10   *Listing of the New Prefixes Created from Example 1-3 (Continued)*

Network Prefix (Subnet); *h* Represents Host Bits	Network Prefix (Subnet) in Dotted Decimal Notation
192.168.0000-01**01.00***hh-hhhh*	192.168.5.0/26
192.168.0000-01**01.01***hh-hhhh*	192.168.5.64/26
192.168.0000-01**01.10***hh-hhhh*	192.168.5.128/26
...	...
192.168.0000-01**11.11***hh-hhhh*	192.168.7.192/26

These blocks are equal in meaning to subnets—you deploy them as you would subnets with the same VLSM strategies. Note that the new prefix mask crosses over the traditional class C boundary (the dot after the 24th bit) without concern. This again demonstrates the power and flexibility of classless addressing. Also note that during deployment, you will need to verify that all of your network devices (including hosts) support classless addressing.

NOTE   The terms *subnet* and *network prefix* are often used interchangeably. Many people are familiar with subnet and prefer using it even if they are routing with VLSM and classless routing protocols. This book uses the term *subnet* when it is more descriptive than *network prefix*. Just keep in mind the semantics for any situation in which you have to adhere to strict definitions.

Routing Protocols and Classless Addressing

Having waded through all the theory and binary, consider routing protocols for a moment. To reap the benefits of classless addressing (such as supernetting), you must use a routing protocol that supports classless addressing—perhaps OSPF, EIGRP, or Border Gateway Protocol (BGP). These classless protocols carry both network prefixes and their corresponding prefix masks in routing updates.

RIP and IGRP, on the other hand, do not support classless addressing. RIP and IGRP also do not support variable length masks within a major net, because they do not carry mask information in routing updates as classful routing protocols do. Instead, RIP and IGRP assume there is a fixed subnet mask per major net, and that mask is determined from the mask that was configured on the interface.

NOTE   RIPv2, version 2 of RIP, supports VLSM but is less widely used than OSPF and EIGRP.

Planning for Address Summarization

In a classless world, address *summarization* (also called *aggregation*) allows a router to consolidate multiple network prefixes into a single, less specific prefix. Example 1-2 in this chapter uses a single prefix 192.168.4.0/22 to summarize the address space of four prefixes that resemble class C addresses (192.168.4.0/24, 192.168.5.0/24, 192.168.6.0/24, and 192.168.7.0/24). A router can view the address block as the four /24 prefixes or as the single /22 prefix—it's the same address space, but using the single /22 prefix is more efficient. To extend the idea further, you could summarize all prefixes that start with 192.168 with a single less specific prefix, 192.168.0.0/16. Again, a prefix is equivalent in meaning to a subnet.

Figure 1-9 illustrates an address summarization scenario.

Figure 1-9   *A Router Using Address Summarization*

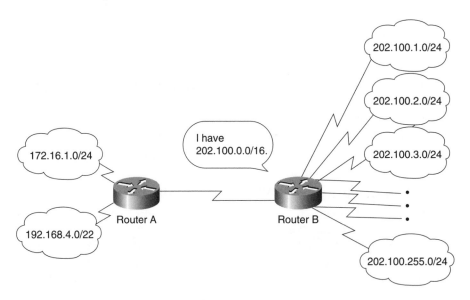

In Figure 1-9, Router B advertises a summary route 202.100.0.0/16 to tell Router A that all prefixes starting with 202.100 are reachable through it. Advertising a single generalized route is more efficient than babbling 255 specific routes with a /24 mask. Router A needs to receive and process only one route—not 255 separate ones.

Summarization reduces the number of network prefixes managed and communicated between routers. With large networks, especially the Internet, managing too many specific prefixes wastes router memory and network bandwidth; therefore, if at all possible, plan for summarization by deploying addresses as contiguous groups. Then, you can use routing protocols, such as OSPF, EIGRP, or BGP, to summarize address blocks and exchange fewer and less specific routes between routers.

Conserving Subnets with IP Unnumbered

Typically, a link between two routers requires a subnet. With classful routing protocols, such as RIP, this is problematic because you waste a multihost subnet for just two routers. Better solutions are to use VLSM and create small, two-host subnets (255.255.255.252 or /30 subnet mask) or to use the IOS *IP unnumbered* feature.

With IP unnumbered, you can save substantial address space by deploying router links without assigned subnets. This feature is applicable to point-to-point networks between router pairs, such as point-to-point leased line, frame relay, and ATM links.

Figure 1-10 illustrates the difference between standard addressing and IP unnumbered.

Figure 1-10 *Standard Addressing Versus IP Unnumbered*

Standard Addressing

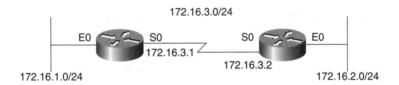

172.16.3.0/24

EO   SO   SO   EO
172.16.3.1
172.16.3.2

172.16.1.0/24   172.16.2.0/24

IP Unnumbered

No subnet assigned

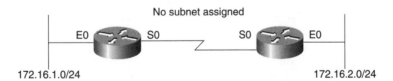

EO   SO   SO   EO

172.16.1.0/24   172.16.2.0/24

In standard addressing, you assign a subnet to each router interface. For Figure 1-10, this means the interfaces Ethernet0 (E0) and Serial0 (S0) on both routers are assigned specific subnets. One subnet, 172.16.3.0/24, exists only to connect the two routers—a waste of addresses. The subnet could be used more effectively; it could support a LAN with clients and servers, for example.

With IP unnumbered, the point-to-point serial interfaces have no assigned addresses and have no subnet between them. This would normally cause problems because a router uses the interface address as the source address for routing updates it sends out that interface. IP unnumbered resolves the problem by borrowing an address from one of the router's *other* interfaces (a LAN interface, for example) and using the borrowed address for the source address of routing updates it generates out of the unnumbered interface.

To configure IP unnumbered and designate the interface from which to borrow an address, use the **ip unnumbered** interface configuration command. The following example starts from enable mode:

```
Router#config terminal
Router(config)#interface s0
Router(config-intf)#ip unnumbered e0
```

The command **ip unnumbered e0** configures Serial0 (**s0**) as an unnumbered interface and designates the address configured on Ethernet0 (**e0**) as the borrowed address (the source address for routing updates going out the unnumbered interface Serial0).

NOTE   You should be familiar with configuring Cisco routers from the IOS command line. For a quick-start tutorial on navigating around IOS and entering commands, refer to Appendix E, "A Crash Course in Cisco IOS."

Scaling the Address Space with Network Address Translation

With Network Address Translation (NAT), you can expand your IP address space by deploying so-called *private addresses* and translating them into publicly registered addresses. NAT can be a viable option in slowing address space depletion, and using it might be more feasible than redesigning the network with VLSM or obtaining new public addresses with your ISP or Internet registry (American Registry for Internet Numbers, if you are in North or South America).

Private addresses are blocks of the IP address space that the Internet community has set aside for use by networks that do not communicate with the public Internet. The address blocks are defined in RFC 1918 and include

- 10.0.0.0 through 10.255.255.255 (10.0.0.0/8)
- 172.16.0.0 through 172.31.255.255 (172.16.0.0/12)
- 192.168.0.0 through 192.168.255.255 (192.168.0.0/16)

Any organization may freely deploy these addresses without notifying the Internet registry. Thus, multiple organizations can use these addresses, each in their private networks, with the understanding that the public Internet does not route traffic to or from these addresses. This might be applicable for hosts that do not need to communicate over the Internet and have no intention to communicate over the Internet in the future (private computer labs are an example). These addresses are deployed within the organization just as any ordinary IP address space, and the same subnetting rules and VLSM techniques apply to these private addresses as to normal public addresses.

Public addresses, on the other hand, are administered by the Internet registry and are routable by the Internet. Every public address is unique (no two hosts on the Internet have the same IP address) and has a registered owner if it's in use. A host addressed with a public address can communicate with hosts both inside the organization and outside on the Internet.

If everyone could have as many public addresses as they want, there would be no need to use private addresses. But the Internet has a finite number of addresses, and getting a share of the public addresses can become difficult as more scrutiny and tighter control are used to determine who gets them. Private addresses are readily available for use, but they come with the big disadvantage that they cannot be used to communicate over the Internet. What you want is the best of both worlds: use of the private address space *and* the ability to communicate over the Internet. This requires a way to translate addresses as they flow between the private and public domains—which is where NAT comes into play.

This section continues with discussions on

- Translating Private Addresses into Public Addresses
- Configuring NAT
- Creating a Pool of Discontiguous Addresses
- Configuring Static NAT
- Special Applications and NAT
- More Important Points on NAT

Translating Private Addresses into Public Addresses

Cisco routers can dynamically translate private addresses into public addresses, allowing hosts with private addresses to communicate with hosts on the Internet without modification. That is, the privately addressed hosts can function as if they are connected to the Internet. You can configure a router to maintain a pool of public addresses that is smaller than the population of privately addressed hosts. The router then manages the pool and dynamically translates private addresses into public addresses as necessary for communicating with the Internet. Hosts on the Internet have no idea they are communicating with a privately addressed host; they communicate with legitimate public addresses from the router's pool. Figure 1-11 shows an example of NAT in action.

Figure 1-11 *Router C Performing NAT for Host A*

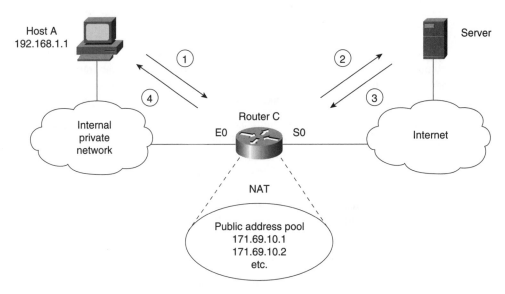

① Packet from Host A: source=192.168.1.1 (private address)
② Packet from Host A: source=171.69.10.1 (public address)
③ Packet to Host A: destination=171.69.10.1 (public address)
④ Packet to Host A: destination=192.168.1.1 (private address)

In Figure 1-11, privately addressed Host A needs to communicate with a server on the
Internet. The following sequence describes a round-trip NAT operation, starting with Host
A's initial packet (refer to the numbered arrows in Figure 1-11):

1 **From Host A (source = 192.168.1.1, private)**—Host A's traffic gets routed through
   the internal network and arrives at the edge router that connects to the Internet, Router
   C. The source address of the packet is 192.168.1.1. Router C detects that Host A's
   packets are sourced from a private address and require address translation. The router
   looks in its pool of public addresses and selects an available address, 171.69.10.1, to
   use for translating packets to and from Host A.

2 **From Host A (source = 171.69.10.1, public)**—Next, the router translates the
   outgoing packets. For the original private source address (192.168.1.1), it substitutes
   public address 171.69.10.1 and sends the modified packets to the Internet. The
   Internet routes Host A's modified packets to the server (Host A's intended destination).

3 **To Host A (destination = 171.69.10.1, public)**—The server responds to 171.69.10.1,
   unaware that Host A's address is really 192.168.1.1. The Internet routes the packets
   from the server to Router C, the keeper and originator of the address 171.69.10.1.

4 **To Host A (destination = 192.168.1.1, private)**—Packets from the server arrive at Router C, which translates 171.69.10.1 (now the destination address) back to 192.168.1.1 and forwards the traffic to the internal network. The internal network routes the traffic to Host A, completing the two-way communication between Host A and the server.

The NAT router (Router C) maintains an idle timer such that if Host A stops sending packets to the Internet for a certain period of time, the router expires the address and returns it to the pool to be used by other hosts. The length of the idle timer is configurable.

Now for some definitions:

- **Inside local address**—The address of the privately addressed host. In the preceding example, 192.168.1.1 is the address of Host A, so it's the inside local address.

- **Inside global addresses**—The pool of legitimate public addresses.

- **Outside global address**—The address of the server on the Internet.

Familiarity with these terms is important when you're configuring and verifying NAT. This will be apparent in the next sections.

Configuring NAT

Consider the following NAT configuration for Router C of Figure 1-11 (for brevity, only the NAT-specific lines are listed):

```
hostname RTC
!
ip nat pool mypool 171.69.10.1 171.69.10.254 prefix-length 24
ip nat inside source list 2 pool mypool overload
!
interface Serial0
ip nat outside
!
interface Ethernet0
ip nat inside
!
access-list 2 permit 192.168.1.0 0.0.0.255
```

The line **ip nat pool mypool 171.69.10.1 171.69.10.254 prefix-length 24** creates the pool of addresses for NAT—the inside global addresses. This pool contains 254 addresses, from 171.69.10.1 to 171.69.10.254. These addresses are legal, public addresses that the router will substitute for the private addresses (inside local addresses).

The line **ip nat inside source list 2 pool mypool overload** configures the router to translate internal private addresses that match access list 2 (configured in a following line), using the pool **mypool** that was created in the preceding line. Internal traffic that does not match access list 2 will not be translated and will be routed normally.

The **overload** keyword means the router may use a single public address to represent multiple privately addressed hosts. This, in effect, multiplexes many private addresses over one public address. Overload might be needed if the public address pool is exhausted of any available addresses because there are many active translations. With overload, the router uses unique TCP and UDP port numbers to differentiate multiple private hosts. Because over 64,000 TCP/UDP port numbers are available per address, you can theoretically support tens of thousands of private hosts with a single IP address; however, you will likely reach practical limits before that.

NOTE   You can create a pool with just one address and use the **overload** keyword. This enables you to translate many private addresses by using a single IP address. That one address in the pool may also be an IP address belonging to one of the router's interfaces.

The line **ip nat outside** is configured in interface configuration mode for the serial interface (Serial0). This tells the router that this interface faces the publicly addressed world. In most cases, this points to the public Internet.

The line **ip nat inside** tells the router that the ethernet interface (Ethernet0) faces the internal network. This is where our privately addressed hosts are: the hosts that need translation to communicate with the Internet.

The line **access-list 2 permit 192.168.1.0 0.0.0.255** creates an access list numbered 2 that defines the hosts that need translation. This access list is used by the previous command, **ip nat inside source list 2 pool mypool**. The router identifies packets to and from inside local addresses by matching the access list criteria, allocates addresses from **mypool**, and translates the addresses as it passes packets between the internal network and the Internet. For information on how to configure access lists and the syntax used, see Chapter 6, "Deploying Basic Security Services."

Instead of using an access list, you can use a route map to trigger translation based on such information as next-hop address and outbound interface. To do this, use the command **ip nat inside source route-map** instead of **ip nat inside source list**. This can be particularly useful if you are connected to two ISPs and want to use different pools for each ISP. See Chapter 3 for information on route maps (covered under policy routing).

Creating a Pool of Discontiguous Addresses

You might need to exclude some addresses from a pool of inside global addresses (for static addresses assigned to hosts or routers, for example). The following example configuration creates a pool of discontiguous addresses:

```
2509(config)#ip nat pool testpool prefix-length 24
2509(config-ipnat-pool)#address 171.69.1.1 171.69.1.4
2509(config-ipnat-pool)#address 171.69.1.6 171.69.1.10
2509(config-ipnat-pool)#exit
```

The preceding commands create a pool called **testpool** that contains addresses 171.69.1.1 through 171.69.1.4 and 171.69.1.6 through 171.69.1.10 (it skips 171.69.1.5). The addresses in the pool have a prefix-length of 24 bits as defined by the keywords **prefix-length 24**.

Configuring Static NAT

You can configure some private addresses for *static* translation, such that they are always translated by using the same public IP address. This could be useful for a privately addressed host that has to be reachable from the Internet with a public address that remains constant. Here is an example configuration of static translation:

```
2509(config)#ip nat inside source static 192.168.1.2 171.69.5.2
```

The preceding command configures a static translation for a private host (192.168.1.2). NAT will translate the private address to and from the public address 171.69.5.2.

Special Applications and NAT

For most traffic, NAT only changes the source and destination addresses in the IP header and does not inspect or modify the data payload contained in the packet. Therefore, applications that carry source or destination IP addresses in the payload of the packet might fail to work because the IP header will be changed by NAT but the payload will be left unchanged. Aware that this could be a problem, Cisco has made and continues to make enhancements to NAT so it can inspect data payloads and support applications that are sensitive to translation. Contact Cisco and get the most recent list of these supported applications (enhancements to NAT occur with each software release). At the time of this writing, H.323, RealAudio, VDOLive, Vxtreme, CuSeeMe (White Pine), NetBIOS over TCP/IP, NFS, rlogin, rsh, rcp, and FTP are supported. Web (http), Telnet, NTP, and other applications that do not carry addresses in the data payload work fine with NAT—they do not require inspection of the data payload.

More Important Points on NAT

The following are some additional notes on NAT of which you should be aware:

- If no available addresses exist in the NAT pool because all are in use, NAT is not able to support any more translations. In this situation, the router drops all packets it cannot translate and sends an Internet Control Message Protocol (ICMP) "Host Unreachable" message back to the privately addressed host. To remedy this, you can try one or more of the following measures:

    — Use the overload option.

    — Increase the size of the NAT pool.

    — Decrease the NAT timers so addresses are returned to the pool more often.

- Privately addressed hosts and publicly addressed hosts can coexist in your network, and you can configure the router to translate addresses for the privately addressed hosts only.

- NAT is not restricted to translating RFC 1918 private addresses. It can also be used to translate IP addresses that were deployed "illegally"—that is, public addresses that are used within an organization but the organization is not the registered owner of those addresses. This might have been done at a time when the organization had never planned to connect to the Internet and probably before reserved private addresses were defined by RFC 1918 in 1996.

- Your organization has the responsibility to filter privately addressed routes so they don't get advertised to the Internet by your routing protocols. Route filtering is covered in Chapter 3.

- If you are translating many concurrent hosts and find NAT causes too much load on your router, you might investigate using dedicated NAT hardware such as Cisco's PIX firewall.

- NAT hides the identity of the internal hosts for which it is translating; therefore, it enhances security to a degree. This in no way substitutes for the security of a full-featured firewall, but it can be a favorable by-product of NAT.

- RFC 1631 also describes NAT.

Summary

This chapter covered a range of IP addressing information from basic definitions to more sophisticated services such as NAT. Developing a plan that makes efficient use of your address space is an important step in building an IP network that meets today's requirements and scales to the future.

The following are the key concepts of this chapter:

- The subnetting procedure divides a major net into smaller subnets by stealing host bits for a new field called the subnet field.

- Traditionally, use of the top and bottom subnets was forbidden. Legacy hosts and networking devices might not let you configure an address from these edge subnets, so be familiar with your organization's installed base if you plan to deploy them.

- The command **ip subnet-zero** enables you to configure a router with an address from the bottom subnet.

- VLSM gives you more flexibility in how you define subnets and more efficient use of your address space.

- Classless routing protocols, such as OSPF and EIGRP, support VLSM.

- Classless addressing abolishes the idea of traditional class A, class B, and class C major nets and the notion of a subnet field.

- A supernet is a contiguous block of addresses that spans the traditional boundaries of classful addressing.

- VLSM techniques also apply to classless address blocks.

- Address summarization improves the scalability of routing protocols by consolidating multiple prefixes into a single, less specific prefix.

- The IP unnumbered feature conserves addresses by enabling point-to-point router links to operate without a subnet.

- RFC 1918 defines three blocks of private addresses that may be used freely without registration. These addresses, however, are not routed on the public Internet.

- NAT can be used to scale your address space by translating private addresses into legitimate public Internet addresses.

CHAPTER 2

Deploying Interior Routing Protocols

A highly effective network must move data through optimal paths and find new paths when outages occur. It should also be expandable and flexible enough to accommodate demands from a growing number of users and geographical locations—not to mention increasing demands for service stability.

Routing is the network service that moves data through your organization. It governs how easily you can grow your network and how stable your service will be. Routing is the circulatory system of your network. When it works, information flows transparently and efficiently—even in very complex networks with many users. However, when routing doesn't work, the flow stops, applications cease working, and a large user population is usually affected.

This chapter covers routing fundamentals and basic configuration for the most widely deployed routing protocols. The main topics of this chapter are

- A Brief Review of Internetworking
- Deploying RIP
- Deploying IGRP
- Deploying Enhanced IGRP
- Deploying OSPF

As you can see from the preceding list, this chapter covers configuration of the most common interior routing protocols: Routing Information Protocol (RIP), Interior Gateway Routing Protocol (IGRP), Enhanced IGRP (EIGRP), and Open Shortest Path First (OSPF). The objective of this chapter is to provide a *baseline* for the routing services covered in Chapter 3, "Managing Routing Protocols." If you are already familiar with configuring the routing protocols found in this chapter, you might want to skip ahead to Chapter 3.

A Brief Review of Internetworking

Internetworking is the practice of connecting multiple individual networks so they function as a single large network (called an *internetwork* or *internet*). The public Internet (spelled with a capital *I*) is an example of an internetwork: It is a collection of many diverse networks, yet it functions as one large network.

Ideally, from any point on the Internet, you can reach any other point on the Internet (assuming the destination you are trying to reach is open to you). Such extensive connectivity is a powerful feature of the Internet. Before internetworking, networks were islands of connectivity: They typically had a local reach, they were locally administered, and they served a specific purpose. Imagine connecting to a network in New York just to exchange e-mail with your friends who live there, or connecting to another network in California to do file transfers with an office in Los Angeles. Although it sounds ridiculous, that was networking before *inter*networking.

Internetworking is made possible by a service called *routing*. Routing is the process of finding a path through an internetwork to a destination (see Figure 2-1).

Figure 2-1   *Routing Is the Process of Finding a Path to a Destination*

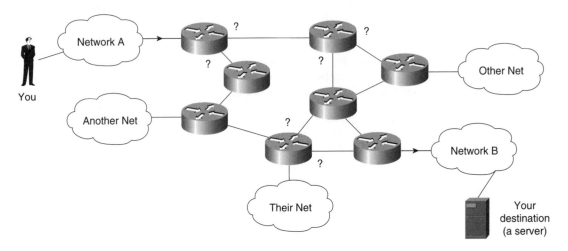

Figure 2-1 depicts multiple individual networks intertwined with routers to form one cohesive internetwork. Now, suppose you are in Network A and you need to send something to a server in Network B. How does your data get there and what path will it take? The **?** symbols in the figure represent some of the possible paths or forks in the road your data can follow. Ultimately, decisions must be made on how your data will weave its way to the destination. The routing service within the internetwork makes these decisions and determines the best path to the destination. With a routing service in place, you don't have to worry about the details of the internetwork itself; instead, you can focus on your application and the reason you need to talk to the server in Network B.

NOTE   A classic application example is the World Wide Web and Web browsing. When you click a link in your Web browser, you don't want to hassle with how your request gets routed through the maze of the Internet; you simply want the Web page you requested to pop up on your screen.

Routing is like mapping a road trip from your hometown to a city far away in another part of the country. What is the shortest path? Is the shortest path necessarily the fastest path? If a highway is closed, what is a good alternate path? In the case of the road trip, your brain performs a routing task, calculating a path based on data gathered from maps, directions from people, and highway advisories. On an internetwork, algorithms programmed in routers (and similar networking devices) perform the routing task. Routers calculate paths based on their software configuration and network "directions and advisories" exchanged with other routers through a routing protocol.

A *routing protocol* is a language for routers. It is what routers use to exchange information about the topology and health of the internetwork. Based on routing information gathered from other routers, a router can calculate a suitable path to a destination. You can think of a routing protocol as a management or system protocol—overhead traffic (extremely vital overhead traffic) that routers use to keep each other informed. Routers can then ensure that data flows the right way through the internetwork.

NOTE   There is a distinction between a routing protocol and a *routed* protocol. A routing protocol is a management protocol used by routers that carries information about the topology and status of the network. A routed protocol is used by hosts (client and servers) and carries data for user applications. TCP/IP, Novell IPX, AppleTalk, and DECnet are examples of routed protocols. The word *routed* means the protocol supports internetworking: It supports interconnecting multiple networks with routers. In contrast, *non-routed* protocols (such as NetBIOS and DEC LAT) were designed to support only one network, typically a LAN, and do not natively support internetworking.

There are two major classes of routing protocols: interior routing protocols and exterior routing protocols. Interior routing protocols (also called interior gateway protocols or IGPs) are used within an *autonomous system*: an internetwork typically under the control of one organization (a company, university, or ISP, for example). Exterior routing protocols (also called exterior gateway protocols or EGPs) are used to interconnect autonomous systems. That is, they are typically used to connect an organization to an ISP, an organization to another organization, or an ISP to another ISP.

NOTE   As mentioned earlier, this book focuses on interior routing protocols (RIP, IGRP, OSPF, and EIGRP). At the time of this writing, Border Gateway Protocol (BGP) is the single most predominant exterior routing protocol in use. See the Bibliography for a BGP resource.

It is not the intention of this book to cover routing theory in depth nor to contrast in detail one routing protocol to another—plenty of good books have done this (see the Bibliography for some of them). Where appropriate, the following sections provide pointers to documents on Cisco's Web site that offer background on selected routing concepts.

If you are unfamiliar with basic routing concepts (metrics, next hop, convergence, distance vector versus link-state protocols, and so on), you can find a brief routing tutorial at http://www.cisco.com/univercd/cc/td/doc/cisintwk/ito_doc/55171.htm. This tutorial, however, is not as thorough as the books listed in the Bibliography. If this URL has changed, search the Cisco Web site for the keywords *routing basics*.

This chapter also assumes that you know how to perform basic configuration tasks such as activating router interfaces and assigning IP addresses to them. See Appendix E, "A Crash Course in Cisco IOS," for a tutorial on how to perform these and other common tasks.

Deploying RIP

RIP is one of the oldest and simplest routing protocols. The following is a list of some key points for RIP:

- RIP is a simple, distance vector routing protocol. A RIP router periodically (roughly every 30 seconds) sends the contents of its routing table to neighboring routers. This periodic activity is common to distance vector protocols. Link-state protocols on the other hand, typically send small advertisements everywhere, and only when network changes occur. Link-state advertisements contain the status about a router's directly connected links (networks) rather than the router's entire routing table.

- RIP is a classful routing protocol and does not support VLSM. The exception is RIP version 2, which supports VLSM but is not deployed as widely as RIP, OSPF or EIGRP. See Chapter 1, "Managing Your IP Address Space," for more information on VLSM.

- As a consequence of not supporting VLSM, RIP requires subnets to be contiguous. That is, subnets of a major net must not be separated from each other by a different, intermediary major net.

- RIP uses a hop count for its metric. With RIP, the maximum distance any network can be is 15 hops—this is called the *network diameter*. A destination more than 15 hops (15 routers) away is considered unreachable.

- RIP converges slowly compared to routing protocols such as OSPF and EIGRP. This means users are more likely to experience temporary outages when network changes occur. Slower convergence is a typical trait of distance vector protocols.

- RIP internetworks are simple, but flat: They generally cannot be organized into hierarchies like internetworks built with OSPF and EIGRP. RIP is generally unaware of autonomous systems and address summarization.

- RIP is easy to implement, and compatibility of RIP among diverse devices is good.

- Because of its limitations and simplicity, RIP does not scale well in large internetworks.
- The RIP standard is defined in RFC 1058.

The following sections describe RIP configuration, beginning with a brief coverage of directly connected networks and their significance to a router.

Directly Connected Networks

When you connect networks to a router and assign IP addresses to each of the router's interfaces, the router immediately knows some basic routing information: It knows how to route to its directly connected networks. Before jumping to RIP configuration, consider the network topology in Figure 2-2 initially without RIP (and then later with RIP).

Figure 2-2   *An Example for RIP Configuration*

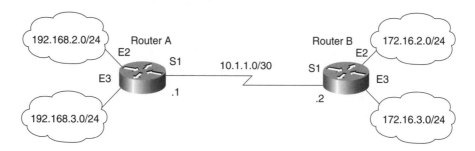

In Figure 2-2, Router A is connected to major nets 192.168.2.0 and 192.168.3.0. Each of these has a /24 mask, and for class C networks this mask means the major net is not subnetted (there is no subnet field). Router A is also attached to major net 10.0.0.0, a class A network that is subnetted with a /30 mask and joins Router A to Router B (10.1.1.0/30 is a subnet of major net 10.0.0.0). Router B also connects to two subnets, 172.16.2.0 and 172.16.3.0. These are subnets from major net 172.16.0.0 (a class B subnetted with a /24 mask).

Without RIP, Router A has no idea that 172.16.0.0 exists, because it knows only its directly attached networks. The routing table displayed with **show ip route** validates this:

```
RTA#sh ip route
Codes: C - connected, S - static, I - IGRP, R - RIP, M - mobile, B - BGP
    D - EIGRP, EX - EIGRP external, O - OSPF, IA - OSPF inter area
    N1 - OSPF NSSA external type 1, N2 - OSPF NSSA external type 2
    E1 - OSPF external type 1, E2 - OSPF external type 2, E - EGP
    i - IS-IS, L1 - IS-IS level-1, L2 - IS-IS level-2, * - candidate default
    U - per-user static route, o - ODR
    T - traffic engineered route

Gateway of last resort is not set

   10.0.0.0/30 is subnetted, 1 subnet
```

continues

```
C    10.1.1.0 is directly connected, Serial1
C  192.168.2.0/24 is directly connected, Ethernet2
C  192.168.3.0/24 is directly connected, Ethernet3
```

In the preceding output, Router A has routes (paths) to three destinations: 10.1.1.0/30, 192.168.2.0/24, and 192.168.3.0/24. These routes are highlighted in boldface. From Figure 2-2, you can verify that these three routes are Router A's directly connected networks. This means Router A can route packets that flow among these three networks.

Missing from the preceding output is a route to the 172.16.0.0 subnets connected to Router B. Router A does not know how to reach 172.16.0.0 because RIP has not been configured yet. As it stands now, Router A is not able to forward any packets destined for major net 172.16.0.0.

The letter at the beginning of a line in **show ip route** is a code and tells you how the route was learned. In the case of Router A's three routes, code **C** indicates the routes are known because they are directly connected to the router. The key at the top of the **show ip route** output provides the meaning of other codes. You will see code **R** (for RIP) shortly.

The following shows the output of **show ip route** for Router B (also not yet configured with RIP):

```
RTB#sh ip ro
Codes: C - connected, S - static, I - IGRP, R - RIP, M - mobile, B - BGP
       D - EIGRP, EX - EIGRP external, O - OSPF, IA - OSPF inter area
       N1 - OSPF NSSA external type 1, N2 - OSPF NSSA external type 2
       E1 - OSPF external type 1, E2 - OSPF external type 2, E - EGP
       i - IS-IS, L1 - IS-IS level-1, L2 - IS-IS level-2, * - candidate default
       U - per-user static route, o - ODR
       T - traffic engineered route

Gateway of last resort is not set

     172.16.0.0/24 is subnetted, 2 subnets
C       172.16.2.0 is directly connected, Ethernet2
C       172.16.3.0 is directly connected, Ethernet3
     10.0.0.0/30 is subnetted, 1 subnet
C       10.1.1.0 is directly connected, Serial1
```

The preceding output confirms the expected result: Router B knows only its directly connected subnets (the routes printed in boldface).

Configuring RIP

Configuring RIP is easy and requires a knowledge of just two IOS commands: **router rip** and **network**. Starting with Router A, here's how you configure the example network from the previous section (Figure 2-2) with RIP:

```
RTA#conf t
Enter configuration commands, one per line. End with CNTL/Z.
RTA(config)#router rip
RTA(config-router)#network 192.168.2.0
RTA(config-router)#network 192.168.3.0
RTA(config-router)#network 10.0.0.0
```

The command **router rip** activates the RIP routing service on the router and changes the prompt to router configuration mode as indicated by the prompt **config-router**.

The command **network 192.168.2.0** tells the router to enable RIP processing on major net 192.168.2.0. This means the router will send and receive RIP messages on all interfaces that are part of this major net—in this case, just one interface, Ethernet2. The command also tells the router to advertise this network, 192.168.2.0, to other routers.

NOTE   With the **network** command you must always specify a major net number, not a subnet number.

The commands **network 192.168.3.0** and **network 10.0.0.0** enable RIP processing for Router A's other two directly connected major nets.

Similarly, configure Router B with RIP and configure the major nets connected to Router B that should run RIP:

```
RTB#conf t
Enter configuration commands, one per line. End with CNTL/Z.
RTB(config)#router rip
RTB(config-router)#network 172.16.0.0
RTB(config-router)#network 10.0.0.0
```

The commands are equal in meaning to the commands used to configure Router A, except the major net numbers are consistent with Router B's directly connected networks. You should note that only one command, **network 172.16.0.0**, is entered to enable RIP for both subnets 172.16.2.0 and 172.16.3.0. This is because the network command specifies the major net (not subnets) that should run RIP—with this command, all interfaces that are part of the major net are RIP-enabled.

As mentioned earlier in "A Brief Review of Internetworking," routing protocols are the languages of routers. Routers talk to each other over routing protocols and exchange information about the internetwork. In the case of RIP, a RIP router sends to its neighboring routers a list of all the networks it knows about. The list includes its directly attached networks and any networks it has learned about from other routers. In the current example (Figure 2-2), Router B must tell Router A about 172.16.0.0 and Router A must tell Router B about 192.168.2.0 and 192.168.3.0. This communication is accomplished with RIP messages called *updates* or *advertisements*.

Verifying RIP Configuration

With RIP enabled on both routers, you can issue **show ip route**, examine the routing tables again, and verify RIP is working. Here is the output for Router A in Figure 2-2:

```
RTA#sh ip ro
Codes: C - connected, S - static, I - IGRP, R - RIP, M - mobile, B - BGP
       D - EIGRP, EX - EIGRP external, O - OSPF, IA - OSPF inter area
```

continues

```
      N1 - OSPF NSSA external type 1, N2 - OSPF NSSA external type 2
      E1 - OSPF external type 1, E2 - OSPF external type 2, E - EGP
      i - IS-IS, L1 - IS-IS level-1, L2 - IS-IS level-2, * - candidate default
      U - per-user static route, o - ODR
      T - traffic engineered route

Gateway of last resort is not set

R    172.16.0.0/16 [120/1] via 10.1.1.2, 00:00:13, Serial1
     10.0.0.0/30 is subnetted, 1 subnet
C       10.1.1.0 is directly connected, Serial1
C    192.168.2.0/24 is directly connected, Ethernet2
C    192.168.3.0/24 is directly connected, Ethernet3
```

The first line of the routing table (shown in boldface) is new and is a route to major net 172.16.0.0. This is the major net advertised by Router B to Router A with the RIP routing protocol (as indicated by the code **R** at the beginning of the line). The output shows that Router A now knows how to reach 172.16.0.0: It has a route to that destination. When Router A receives a packet destined for 172.16.0.0 (perhaps a packet originated by someone in network 192.168.2.0), it can now properly forward it.

The output **[120/1]** provides the *administrative distance* (120) and metric (1 hop) for the route. The administrative distance (covered in Chapter 3) is the priority level of a route and is used to prioritize routes when they are learned from multiple routing protocols. The metric for RIP is a simple hop count and in this example tells you that 172.16.0.0 is one hop (one router) away.

The output **via 10.1.1.2** specifies the address of the neighboring router that is in the direction of the destination (Router B). This is called the *next hop router* or *next hop address*. Packets destined for 172.16.0.0 are sent to this address.

The output **00:00:13** tells you the age of the route: 13 seconds ago, Router A received an advertisement for this route. Because RIP advertises approximately every 30 seconds, this number should stay between 00:00:00 and 00:00:30 under normal circumstances. When a destination becomes unreachable because of an outage or other reason, the age of the route increases until it reaches a maximum age (240 seconds for RIP), at which time it is removed from the routing table.

NOTE   OSPF and EIGRP send routing updates only when changes occur in the network. For these routing protocols, it is perfectly valid to have routes that are many hours old.

The output **Serial1** tells you Router A's Serial1 interface points to the destination network. You can think of this as the exit interface: All packets to 172.16.0.0 are sent out this interface.

Similarly, issuing **show ip route** on Router B confirms that Router B is receiving RIP advertisements from Router A:

```
RTB#sh ip ro
Codes: C - connected, S - static, I - IGRP, R - RIP, M - mobile, B - BGP
       D - EIGRP, EX - EIGRP external, O - OSPF, IA - OSPF inter area
       N1 - OSPF NSSA external type 1, N2 - OSPF NSSA external type 2
       E1 - OSPF external type 1, E2 - OSPF external type 2, E - EGP
       i - IS-IS, L1 - IS-IS level-1, L2 - IS-IS level-2, * - candidate default
       U - per-user static route, o - ODR
       T - traffic engineered route

Gateway of last resort is not set

     172.16.0.0/24 is subnetted, 2 subnets
C       172.16.2.0 is directly connected, Ethernet2
C       172.16.3.0 is directly connected, Ethernet3
     10.0.0.0/30 is subnetted, 1 subnet
C       10.1.1.0 is directly connected, Serial1
R    192.168.2.0/24 [120/1] via 10.1.1.1, 00:00:11, Serial1
R    192.168.3.0/24 [120/1] via 10.1.1.1, 00:00:11, Serial1
```

The two RIP routes shown in boldface in the preceding output are advertised by Router A. Router B now has routes to 192.168.2.0 and 192.168.3.0 and can forward packets destined for them.

Deploying IGRP

IGRP is a routing protocol invented by Cisco that addresses some of the scaling problems with RIP. The following is a list of some key points on IGRP:

- Like RIP, IGRP is a distance vector routing protocol.

- Like RIP, IGRP is a classful routing protocol.

- Unlike RIP, IGRP can support large internetworks and is not limited to a 15-hop network diameter. An IGRP internetwork can have a maximum diameter of 255 hops.

- Instead of a hop count, IGRP uses a sophisticated metric (called a *composite* metric) to select optimal routes through an internetwork. The path characteristics included in the metric are bandwidth, delay, load, and reliability. Optionally, you may adjust the weighting of each characteristic for a user-defined formula. See http://www.cisco.com/warp/public/103/index.shtml for more information.

- IGRP can send traffic to a destination over multiple paths in a load-balancing fashion, even if the paths have different metrics. This is called *unequal-cost load balancing*. By default, RIP, IGRP, EIGRP, and OSPF all support equal-cost load balancing, although IGRP and EIGRP support both equal- and unequal-cost load balancing. This is configured with the **variance** router configuration mode command (see the IOS Configuration Guide for IP Routing Protocols or search the Cisco Web site for *variance*).

- IGRP supports autonomous systems (identified by an autonomous system number). An internetwork can support multiple IGRP autonomous systems, and a router can run multiple IGRP processes with one process for each autonomous system. See "A Brief Review of Internetworking" earlier in this chapter for more on autonomous systems.

- IGRP is a Cisco proprietary routing protocol, so you need to use Cisco routers or, for interoperability with RIP and other protocols, routing protocol redistribution (covered in Chapter 3).

- IGRP sends routing updates less frequently than RIP and thus creates less overhead traffic than RIP. But because IGRP has longer timers, it can sometimes converge more slowly than RIP.

The following sections describe IGRP configuration for the example topology introduced earlier in "Deploying RIP."

Configuring IGRP

Configuring IGRP is just as easy as configuring RIP. The two basic IOS commands are **router igrp** and **network**. Starting with Router A, here's how you use IGRP to configure the example network shown in Figure 2-2:

```
RTA#conf t
Enter configuration commands, one per line. End with CNTL/Z.
RTA(config)#router igrp 100
RTA(config-router)#network 192.168.2.0
RTA(config-router)#network 192.168.3.0
RTA(config-router)#network 10.0.0.0
```

The command **router igrp 100** activates the IGRP routing service on the router and changes the prompt to router configuration mode as indicated by the prompt **config-router**. The number **100** is the autonomous system number and is a required parameter of the **router igrp** command. Instead of 100, you may use any number between 1 and 65535 to identify the autonomous system. Routers within the same autonomous system exchange routing protocol information with each other.

The command **network 192.168.2.0** tells the router to enable RIP processing on major net 192.168.2.0. The meaning is the same as when using the **network** command with RIP: It means the router will send and receive IGRP messages on all interfaces that are part of 192.168.2.0. The command also tells the router to advertise this network, 192.168.2.0, to other routers. Like RIP, the **network** command specifies a major net number, not a subnet.

The commands **network 192.168.3.0** and **network 10.0.0.0** enable IGRP processing for Router A's other two connected networks.

Similarly, configure Router B with IGRP and configure the major nets connected to Router B that should run IGRP:

```
RTB(config)#router igrp 100
RTB(config-router)#network 172.16.0.0
RTB(config-router)#network 10.0.0.0
```

The preceding commands are equal in meaning to the commands used to configure Router A. The autonomous system number (100) in **router igrp 100** must match Router A; otherwise, Router A and Router B will not exchange routing updates—they will be in separate autonomous systems.

Verifying IGRP Configuration

With IGRP enabled on both routers, you can issue **show ip route** to verify its operation. Here is the output for Router A:

```
RTA#sh ip ro
Codes: C - connected, S - static, I - IGRP, R - RIP, M - mobile, B - BGP
       D - EIGRP, EX - EIGRP external, O - OSPF, IA - OSPF inter area
       N1 - OSPF NSSA external type 1, N2 - OSPF NSSA external type 2
       E1 - OSPF external type 1, E2 - OSPF external type 2, E - EGP
       i - IS-IS, L1 - IS-IS level-1, L2 - IS-IS level-2, * - candidate default
       U - per-user static route, o - ODR
       T - traffic engineered route

Gateway of last resort is not set

I   172.16.0.0/16 [100/7500] via 10.1.1.2, 00:00:08, Serial1
       10.0.0.0/30 is subnetted, 1 subnet
C       10.1.1.0 is directly connected, Serial1
C   192.168.2.0/24 is directly connected, Ethernet2
C   192.168.3.0/24 is directly connected, Ethernet3
```

The first line of the routing table (shown in boldface) is a route to major net 172.16.0.0. This route was advertised by Router B to Router A with IGRP (as indicated by the code **I** at the beginning of the line).

The output **[100/7500]** provides the administrative distance (100) and IGRP metric (7500) for the route. As mentioned earlier, the administrative distance is a priority level the router uses to rank routes it receives from multiple routing protocols (covered in Chapter 3). The metric is a composite of bandwidth and delay by default. By tweaking IGRP with the **metric** command, you can incorporate reliability and load into the metric. See the following resources for more information on IGRP metric details:

- IGRP information: http://www.cisco.com/warp/public/103/index.shtml
- IOS Documentation, Configuration Guides:
  http://www.cisco.com/univercd/cc/td/doc/product/software/index.htm

The output **via 10.1.1.2, 00:00:08, Serial1** is just like the output seen earlier with RIP. It specifies the next hop router (**10.1.1.2**), the age of the route (**00:00:08**), and the exit interface (**Serial1**).

Similarly, issuing **show ip route** on Router B confirms that Router B is receiving IGRP advertisements from Router A:

```
RTB#sh ip ro
Codes: C - connected, S - static, I - IGRP, R - RIP, M - mobile, B - BGP
       D - EIGRP, EX - EIGRP external, O - OSPF, IA - OSPF inter area
       N1 - OSPF NSSA external type 1, N2 - OSPF NSSA external type 2
       E1 - OSPF external type 1, E2 - OSPF external type 2, E - EGP
       i - IS-IS, L1 - IS-IS level-1, L2 - IS-IS level-2, * - candidate default
       U - per-user static route, o - ODR
       T - traffic engineered route

Gateway of last resort is not set

     172.16.0.0/24 is subnetted, 2 subnets
C       172.16.2.0 is directly connected, Ethernet2
C       172.16.3.0 is directly connected, Ethernet3
     10.0.0.0/30 is subnetted, 1 subnet
C       10.1.1.0 is directly connected, Serial1
I    192.168.2.0/24 [100/7500] via 10.1.1.1, 00:00:33, Serial1
I    192.168.3.0/24 [100/7500] via 10.1.1.1, 00:00:34, Serial1
```

In the preceding output, the IGRP routes (**192.168.2.0/24** and **192.168.3.0/24**) advertised by Router A are shown in boldface.

Deploying Enhanced IGRP

EIGRP is an advanced routing protocol invented by Cisco that provides scaling for large internetworks, fast convergence, classless routing features, and low overhead.

EIGRP is a hybrid routing protocol. Fundamentally, it's a distance vector protocol, but it has characteristics of a link-state protocol. EIGRP combines the advantages found in both distance vector protocols and link-state protocols, and does away with many of their respective disadvantages.

The following is a list of key points for EIGRP:

- Although its name implies a close relation to IGRP, EIGRP shares little in common with IGRP.
- Like distance vector protocols, EIGRP is generally easy to deploy.
- Unlike distance vector protocols, EIGRP converges quickly and has low overhead. These are advantages often found in link-state protocols such as OSPF (the most popular link-state protocol). EIGRP sends partial updates instead of its entire routing table—and only when changes occur. Also, EIGRP sends an update to only the neighbors that need it.
- Unlike RIP and IGRP, EIGRP is a classless routing protocol and supports VLSM, supernetting, and route summarization. See Chapter 1 for more information on VLSM, supernetting, and summarization.

- Related to VLSM, EIGRP supports discontiguous subnets. This means subnets of a major net can be separated from each other by different, intermediary major nets.

- Like most link-state protocols, EIGRP scales well in large networks and supports multiple autonomous systems.

- EIGRP internetworks are flexible for changes in topology and reengineering. On the contrary, OSPF internetworks are generally more difficult to reengineer because of the OSPF rules on backbones and areas (see "Deploying OSPF," later in this chapter).

- EIGRP uses the same composite metric as IGRP, except it differs by a factor of 256. Multiply an IGRP metric by 256 and you get the equivalent EIGRP metric.

- Like IGRP, EIGRP is a Cisco proprietary routing protocol, so you need to use Cisco routers or—for interoperability with other protocols—routing protocol redistribution (covered in Chapter 3).

- Like IGRP, EIGRP supports unequal-cost load balancing with the **variance** command.

- EIGRP supports route authentication for enhanced security. This means you can configure a router to accept routing updates only from trusted sources. See the IOS Configuration Guide for IP Routing Protocols for more information.

- In addition to IP, EIGRP supports Novell IPX and AppleTalk. You can use EIGRP instead of IPX-RIP or AppleTalk RTMP (Routing Table Maintenance Protocol) and leverage the advanced features of EIGRP.

The following sections describe EIGRP configuration for the example topology shown in Figure 2-2.

Configuring EIGRP

Configuring EIGRP is just as easy as configuring RIP or IGRP. You use the familiar **router** and **network** commands. Starting with Router A, here's how you configure the example network (Figure 2-2) with EIGRP. Notice that the configuration is almost identical to that of IGRP:

```
RTA(config)#router eigrp 100
RTA(config-router)#network 192.168.2.0
RTA(config-router)#network 192.168.3.0
RTA(config-router)#network 10.0.0.0
```

The command **router eigrp 100** activates the EIGRP routing service on the router and changes the prompt to router configuration mode as indicated by the prompt **config-router**. The number **100** is the autonomous system number and is a required parameter of the command.

As with the RIP and IGRP configurations, the commands **network 192.168.2.0**, **network 192.168.3.0**, and **network 10.0.0.0** enable EIGRP processing for Router A's three connected major nets.

Similarly, you can configure Router B with EIGRP and configure the major nets connected to Router B that should run EIGRP:

```
RTB(config)#router eigrp 100
RTB(config-router)#network 172.16.0.0
RTB(config-router)#network 10.0.0.0
```

The preceding commands are equal in meaning to the commands used to configure Router A. The autonomous system number (100) in **router eigrp 100** must match Router A; otherwise, Router A and Router B will not exchange routing updates.

Verifying EIGRP Configuration

Use the command **show ip route** to verify EIGRP operation. Here is the output for Router A:

```
RTA#sh ip ro
Codes: C - connected, S - static, I - IGRP, R - RIP, M - mobile, B - BGP
       D - EIGRP, EX - EIGRP external, O - OSPF, IA - OSPF inter area
       N1 - OSPF NSSA external type 1, N2 - OSPF NSSA external type 2
       E1 - OSPF external type 1, E2 - OSPF external type 2, E - EGP
       i - IS-IS, L1 - IS-IS level-1, L2 - IS-IS level-2, * - candidate default
       U - per-user static route, o - ODR
       T - traffic engineered route

Gateway of last resort is not set

D    172.16.0.0/16 [90/1920000] via 10.1.1.2, 00:09:27, Serial1
     10.0.0.0/8 is variably subnetted, 2 subnets, 2 masks
D       10.0.0.0/8 is a summary, 00:09:29, Null0
C       10.1.1.0/30 is directly connected, Serial1
C    192.168.2.0/24 is directly connected, Ethernet2
C    192.168.3.0/24 is directly connected, Ethernet3
```

The first line of the routing table (shown in boldface) is a route to major net 172.16.0.0. This route was advertised by Router B to Router A with EIGRP (as indicated by the code **D** at the beginning of the line).

Other information you can extract from the output are the route's administrative distance (**90**), EIGRP metric (**1920000**), next hop address (**10.1.1.2**), age of the route (**00:09:27**), and exit interface (**Serial1**).

NOTE   The EIGRP metric differs from the IGRP metric by a factor of 256. The output of **show ip route** in the example proves this: The EIGRP metric (1920000) divided by 256 equals the IGRP metric (7500) from "Verifying IGRP Configuration" earlier in this chapter.

The other EIGRP route printed in boldface, **10.0.0.0/8,** is called a *summary route*. As the name implies, this route summarizes all of the routes in major net 10.0.0.0 with a single, general route—notice the broad **/8** mask, appropriate for generalizing an entire class A network. By default, EIGRP creates a summary route at every major net boundary (a place where two or more major nets meet). Router A is a major net boundary because three major nets meet there: 192.168.2.0, 192.168.3.0, and 10.0.0.0. EIGRP auto-summarization is covered in Chapter 3.

It might seem weird that the summary route points to the **Null0** interface (a logical interface). The Null0 interface is like a trash can or *bit bucket* that leads to nowhere: A packet sent to Null0 is simply discarded by the router. So why have it? This route to Null0 is used to originate a summary route and advertise it to other routers. Router A tells other routers (in the example, just Router B) that it knows how to reach major net 10.0.0.0—that is, it advertises 10.0.0.0/8. When Router A receives a packet destined for 10.0.0.0, it doesn't actually use the summary route to forward the packet. Instead, it uses a route within 10.0.0.0 that describes the destination more exactly. This is called *using the most specific route*. The router uses the most specific route when selecting a route to a destination. If the router doesn't have a specific route to a particular destination, the summary route is the only choice—and in that case, the packet does indeed go to Null0 (it's discarded). This could happen when a client erroneously sends a packet to an unknown destination or when there are routing problems on the network.

For completeness, the following is the output of **show ip route** for Router B:

```
RTB#sh ip ro
Codes: C - connected, S - static, I - IGRP, R - RIP, M - mobile, B - BGP
    D - EIGRP, EX - EIGRP external, O - OSPF, IA - OSPF inter area
    N1 - OSPF NSSA external type 1, N2 - OSPF NSSA external type 2
    E1 - OSPF external type 1, E2 - OSPF external type 2, E - EGP
    i - IS-IS, L1 - IS-IS level-1, L2 - IS-IS level-2, * - candidate default
    U - per-user static route, o - ODR
    T - traffic engineered route

Gateway of last resort is not set

     172.16.0.0/16 is variably subnetted, 3 subnets, 2 masks
D    172.16.0.0/16 is a summary, 01:30:35, Null0
C    172.16.2.0/24 is directly connected, Ethernet2
C    172.16.3.0/24 is directly connected, Ethernet3
     10.0.0.0/8 is variably subnetted, 2 subnets, 2 masks
D    10.0.0.0/8 is a summary, 01:30:35, Null0
C    10.1.1.0/30 is directly connected, Serial1
D    192.168.2.0/24 [90/1920000] via 10.1.1.1, 01:30:08, Serial1
D    192.168.3.0/24 [90/1920000] via 10.1.1.1, 01:30:08, Serial1
```

The boldface routes (**192.168.2.0/24** and **192.168.3.0/24**) are the EIGRP routes advertised by Router A. The other EIGRP routes (**172.16.0.0/16** and **10.0.0.0/8**) are summary routes generated by Router B.

Deploying OSPF

OSPF is a standards-based, link-state routing protocol defined by RFC 2328. The following is a list of some key points for OSPF:

- OSPF is a link-state routing protocol. An OSPF router sends small updates (called *link-state advertisements*, or LSAs) that include information for its attached links only, not for all known routes. These updates propagate a portion of the internetwork called an *area*. Each router in an area builds a database from all of the LSAs it receives. From the database, a router can calculate a shortest (least-cost) path to every known destination by using the *Dijkstra algorithm*.

- Like EIGRP, OSPF is a classless protocol that supports VLSM, supernetting, summarization, and discontiguous subnets.

- OSPF converges quickly and creates low overhead over network links (updates are sent only when they are necessary). However, the LSA database and Dijkstra algorithm require more memory and CPU resources than other routing protocols, resulting in more system resource overhead at the router level.

- OSPF's metric is *cost*. By default, the cost across a link is 10^8 divided by the link bandwidth (10^8/BW). You can set the cost on an interface with the **ip osfp cost** interface configuration command.

- An OSPF autonomous system is built of areas joined in a hierarchical fashion. One area, called *area 0* ("area zero") or the *backbone area*, is required. Inter-area traffic must traverse area 0. Figure 2-3 illustrates a simple arrangement of areas and routers with a couple of user-defined areas (areas 100 and 200) connected to area 0.

Figure 2-3   *A Basic OSPF Hierarchy with Area 0 and Two Non-Backbone Areas*

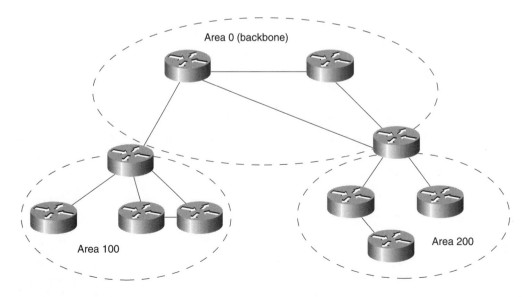

- All OSPF areas must connect to area 0. If, for some reason, an area cannot be directly connected to area 0, a *virtual link* may be configured. A virtual link joins the stray area to area 0 via a transit area (another non-backbone area).

- OSPF generally scales well because of its fast convergence, low overhead, and hierarchical design.

- OSPF generally requires more initial planning and design than other protocols. Very few real-world networks fit into nice hierarchical OSPF areas. A thoughtfully defined area plan that considers growth, router sizing, and area sizing will lead to a more stable and manageable internetwork. It is recommended that you seek the advice of an experienced consultant or Cisco engineer before swinging an OSPF design into action.

- Depending on the original design and the degree of changes on your network, OSPF might be less flexible to topological changes and network reengineering. Select and size your areas wisely. Use the Bibliography resources and recommendations from experienced OSPF engineers. Nothing beats real-world experience when it comes to OSPF network design.

- OSPF supports equal-cost load balancing but not unequal-cost load balancing.

- OSPF supports route authentication for enhanced security.

- More complete information on OSPF can be found in Cisco's *OSPF Design Guide* at http://www.cisco.com/warp/public/104/1.html and in the resources listed in the Bibliography.

Configuring OSPF

For the purpose of illustrating basic OSPF configuration, consider the example topology depicted in Figure 2-4.

Figure 2-4 consists of an area 0 and two non-backbone areas, area 100 and area 200. Router A is called an *area border router (ABR)* because it attaches to both area 0 and area 100. Router B is also an ABR because it connects to area 0 and area 200. Router C is completely contained within area 200 and is called an *internal router.*

Figure 2-4 illustrates a key point for OSPF configuration: You assign *links*, not routers themselves, to areas. Router B, for example, has three links: one in area 0 (Serial1) and two in area 200 (Serial2 and Serial0). The importance of keeping this perspective will be apparent during configuration.

Figure 2-4 *An Example Internetwork for OSPF Configuration*

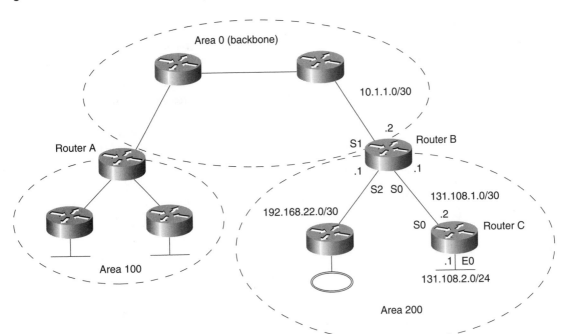

For the purpose of illustrating basic OSPF configuration, consider Router B and Router C. Router C is a good router to start with because it's an internal router in area 200. The following commands configure OSPF on Router C:

```
RTC(config)#router ospf 10
RTC(config-router)#network 131.108.2.0 0.0.0.255 area 200
RTC(config-router)#network 131.108.1.0 0.0.0.3 area 200
```

The command **router ospf 10** starts the OSPF software process on the router. The number **10** denotes a process identification number (*process ID*, for short). Unlike IGRP and EIGRP, this is not an autonomous system number. The process ID uniquely identifies an OSPF routing process when there are multiple OSPF processes running on the router (typically, you configure only one OSPF process per router). The OSPF process ID is locally significant and is not shared with other routers—Router C's process ID does not have to match process IDs on other routers—but if you use a consistent process ID across all routers, you'll probably make configuration maintenance a little easier. Therefore, pick any number that looks good to you.

The command **network 131.108.2.0 0.0.0.255 area 200** assigns Router C's Ethernet0 interface to area 200. This is not readily apparent until you break up the command.

The **network** command has two main pieces:

* The matching criteria: **131.108.2.0 0.0.0.255**
* The area assignment: **area 200**

The area assignment is straightforward: Whatever is matched by the matching criteria is placed into area 200.

The matching criteria requires a look at the IP addresses on the router. As depicted in Figure 2-4, the IP address of Ethernet0 is 131.108.2.1/24. The **network** command contains an address pattern to match 131.108.2.0 and a *wildcard mask* 0.0.0.255. The wildcard mask looks like the inverse of a subnet mask, and that is indeed the case for this example (but it does not have to be). The wildcard mask defines the bits in the address pattern that the router must match when comparing the pattern to its interface addresses. Any interfaces that match the criteria are put into area 200. A zero bit in the mask means to match the corresponding bit of the pattern. A one bit in the mask is a "don't care" bit and means the corresponding bit of the pattern is ignored.

NOTE   Recall from Chapter 1 that there are 32 bits in an IP address but the address is written in dotted decimal notation.

The criteria **131.108.2.0 0.0.0.255** means *match the interfaces that start with 131.108.2 and the last octet (the last 8 bits) can be anything*. This criteria matches Router C's Ethernet0; therefore, Ethernet0 is a link in area 200 (the area assignment). The criteria does not match Serial0, whose address is 131.108.1.2/30, so another command is needed.

NOTE   OSPF's **network** command is a logical assignment rather than a physical one. This means the router's hardware interfaces can change without affecting the assignment of areas as long as the addressing stays intact.

The second **network** command, **network 131.108.1.0 0.0.0.3 area 200**, means all interfaces that match the criteria **131.108.1.0 0.0.0.3** are assigned to area 200. The mask 0.0.0.3 means the first 30 bits of the pattern 131.108.1.0 are matched—convert 0.0.0.3 to binary and you will see 30 zeros followed by two ones. This criteria matches Router C's Serial0; therefore, the link between Router C and Router B is assigned to area 200.

Instead of entering two **network** commands, you could enter a single **network** command that matches all interfaces on Router C and puts them in area 200, like this:

```
RTC(config)#router ospf 10
RTC(config-router)#network 0.0.0.0 255.255.255.255 area 200
```

where **0.0.0.0 255.255.255.255** matches all addresses because the wildcard mask is all ones—instead of 0.0.0.0, you could type any address and get the same result. This works fine for the example because Router C has only two interfaces and both of them are in area 200; however, such a broad match provides the least amount of control over your area assignments. This could be a factor if you add new interfaces to a router or change specific area assignments.

Router B is an ABR (refer to Figure 2-4). The following commands configure OSPF on Router B:

```
RTB(config)#router ospf 10
RTB(config-router)#network 131.108.1.0 0.0.0.3 area 200
RTB(config-router)#network 10.1.1.0 0.0.0.3 area 0
RTB(config-router)#network 192.168.22.0 0.0.0.3 area 200
```

The command **router ospf 10** starts the OSPF process on Router B with a process ID of 10.

The command **network 131.108.1.0 0.0.0.3 area 200** assigns Router B's Serial0 interface to area 200. This agrees with Router C's configuration; that is, both routers agree that the link between them is in area 200. If the routers do not agree, they will not become OSPF neighbors and will not exchange LSAs.

The command **network 10.1.1.0 0.0.0.3 area 0** assigns Router B's Serial1 interface to area 0, the backbone area. This makes Router B an ABR: It's connected to area 0 and at least one other non-backbone area.

The command **network 192.168.22.0 0.0.0.3 area 200** assigns Router B's Serial2 interface to area 200. This agrees with the design described in Figure 2-4.

NOTE   When configuring OSPF on so-called nonbroadcast multiaccess (NBMA) networks such as frame relay and ATM, you might need to configure the **ip ospf network** interface command or **neighbor** router configuration command. Consult the sources in the Bibliography for more information.

Verifying OSPF Configuration

Several good **show** commands exist for verifying OSPF operation. One of the first you should enter is **show ip ospf neighbors**:

```
RTC#sh ip ospf nei

Neighbor ID   Pri  State      Dead Time  Address       Interface
172.16.3.1    1    FULL/ -    0:00:33    131.108.1.1   Serial0
```

The preceding output is a list of OSPF routers neighboring Router C. The key field to examine is **State**. When OSPF is functioning properly, the neighbor state is **FULL**.

The **Neighbor ID** 172.16.3.1 is the OSPF router ID of Router B. 172.16.3.1 is an address assigned to a *loopback interface* on Router B. A loopback interface is a virtual, software interface on the router from which OSPF borrows an address to use for an ID. This is configured with the **interface loopback***N* command, where *N* represents a user-defined number:

```
RTB(config)#int loopback0
RTB(config-if)#ip address 172.16.3.1 255.255.255.255
```

Configuring a loopback interface is optional. The benefit of using a loopback interface is that the router's interface is always up—the network on a loopback interface never goes down unless you force it down with the **shutdown** interface command. Because the loopback is always up, the OSPF router ID never changes (unless you add a new loopback with a higher address). Having a constant router ID is important for some OSPF features, such as virtual links, that must be configured with explicit router IDs. Consistent router IDs also make OSPF troubleshooting easier.

Another good **show** command for validating OSPF configuration is **show ip ospf interface**:

```
RTB#sh ip ospf int
Serial0 is up, line protocol is up
 Internet Address 131.108.1.1/30, Area 200
 Process ID 10, Router ID 172.16.3.1, Network Type POINT_TO_POINT, Cost: 64
 Transmit Delay is 1 sec, State POINT_TO_POINT,
 Timer intervals configured, Hello 10, Dead 40, Wait 40, Retransmit 5
  Hello due in 00:00:07
 Neighbor Count is 1, Adjacent neighbor count is 1
  Adjacent with neighbor 131.108.2.1
 Suppress hello for 0 neighbor(s)
Serial1 is up, line protocol is up
 Internet Address 10.1.1.2/30, Area 0
 Process ID 10, Router ID 172.16.3.1, Network Type POINT_TO_POINT, Cost: 50
 Transmit Delay is 1 sec, State POINT_TO_POINT,
 Timer intervals configured, Hello 10, Dead 40, Wait 40, Retransmit 5
  Hello due in 00:00:08
 Neighbor Count is 1, Adjacent neighbor count is 1
  Adjacent with neighbor 171.70.240.253
 Suppress hello for 0 neighbor(s)
<lines deleted for brevity>
```

With the preceding output, you can check that your OSPF **network** commands with the wildcard masks are assigning interfaces to the expected areas (see the lines in boldface).

Finally, you want to ensure that routers are receiving and registering the OSPF routes. The familiar **show ip route** command does this. The following is a partial listing:

```
RTB#sh ip ro
Codes: C - connected, S - static, I - IGRP, R - RIP, M - mobile, B - BGP
       D - EIGRP, EX - EIGRP external, O - OSPF, IA - OSPF inter area
       N1 - OSPF NSSA external type 1, N2 - OSPF NSSA external type 2
       E1 - OSPF external type 1, E2 - OSPF external type 2, E - EGP
       i - IS-IS, L1 - IS-IS level-1, L2 - IS-IS level-2, * - candidate default
       U - per-user static route, o - ODR
       T - traffic engineered route

Gateway of last resort is not set

     10.0.0.0/30 is subnetted, 1 subnet
C       10.1.1.0 is directly connected, Serial1
     131.108.0.0/16 is variably subnetted, 2 subnets, 2 masks
O       131.108.2.0/24 [110/74] via 131.108.1.2, 05:06:36, Serial0
C       131.108.1.0/30 is directly connected, Serial0
     192.168.2.0/24 is subnetted, 1 subnet
O IA    192.168.2.0 [110/51] via 10.1.1.1, 05:06:26, Serial1
<lines deleted for brevity>
```

The preceding output for Router B contains two OSPF routes shown in boldface. Route 131.108.2.0/24 is coded with a lone letter **O**. This means the route is an intra-area route: The route and Router B are part of the same area. Route 192.168.2.0/24, on the other hand, is coded with **O IA**. This means the route is an inter-area route: The route is from a different area, not attached to this router. The inter-area route originated from another area and arrived at Router B through the backbone area, area 0.

NOTE   You might notice from the key at the top of the **show ip route** output that there are other kinds of OSPF routes. External routes are routes redistributed into OSPF (see Chapter 3). For information on Not-So-Stubby-Area routes, see the IOS Configuration Guide for IP Routing Protocols.

Summary

This chapter covered basic theory and configuration for the most common interior routing protocols: RIP, IGRP, EIGRP, and OSPF. The next chapter, Chapter 3, builds on this baseline study and focuses on how to manage these routing protocols.

The following are the key concepts of this chapter:

- Internetworking is the practice of connecting multiple individual networks so they function as a single large internetwork or internet.

- Routing, which is the process of finding a path to a destination, makes internetworking possible. It is the crucial network service that governs the flow of traffic through your organization.

- A routing protocol is a language for routers. Routers use routing protocols to exchange information about the topology and health of the internetwork.

- RIP, one of the oldest and simplest of routing protocols, is a classful, distance vector protocol limited to a 15-hop metric. RIP generally does not scale well in large internets.

- IGRP, a routing protocol invented by Cisco, is a classful, distance vector protocol with a composite metric. IGRP supports autonomous systems and is designed to scale to larger internets than RIP.

- EIGRP, another routing protocol invented by Cisco, is a classless, hybrid protocol with a composite metric. EIGRP converges quickly, generates low traffic overhead, and scales well in large internets.

- Enabling RIP, IGRP, or EIGRP is fairly simple. To establish one of these services you need two fundamental commands: **router** and **network**. For example, **router eigrp 100** and **network 172.16.0.0**.

- OSPF is a classless, link-state protocol with a cost metric. OSPF converges quickly, generates low traffic overhead, and scales well in large internets. It requires more system resources and more up-front planning than the other protocols.

CHAPTER 3

Managing Routing Protocols

Routing, introduced in Chapter 2, "Deploying Interior Routing Protocols," is crucial to the proper operation of your network. The routing function of a network is like the circulatory system of the human body: It is responsible for moving vital elements (data or blood cells) through a network efficiently. When those vital elements fail to reach their intended destinations, you can expect the systems that feed off the network to suffer (this applies to both internetworks and humans).

Chapter 2 covered basic routing configuration, but routing involves much more than simply enabling RIP, IGRP, OSPF, and EIGRP and letting them run. In a real-world network, routing protocols must be managed, extended, and optimized to promote overall network stability, flexibility, and efficiency. This chapter covers the key techniques that help you achieve these objectives.

The main topics of this chapter are

- Configuring Passive Interfaces
- Filtering Routing Updates
- Managing Redistribution
- Resolving Issues with VLSM and Classful Routing Protocols
- Leveraging Default Routing
- Configuring Route Summarization
- Deploying Policy Routing with Route Maps

Configuring Passive Interfaces

A common way of controlling routing information is to make an interface passive. A passive interface is a silenced interface: an interface on which you deliberately suppress the advertising of routing updates. You might want to do this in certain situations. For example, for security reasons you might have to block routing updates sent to a particular department or company because the updates reveal the topology of your network. In another case, when redistributing from one routing protocol to another, passive interfaces localize updates for efficiency and stability (see "Managing Redistribution," later in this chapter). Also, in dial-on-demand routing setups, passive interfaces prevent routing updates from triggering dial-up lines that are billed per minute—this controls operational costs.

A simple use of a passive interface is for silencing chatty protocols such as RIP on networks that do not require routing updates. Figure 3-1 illustrates such a scenario.

Figure 3-1 *Using a Passive Interface to Block Routing Information*

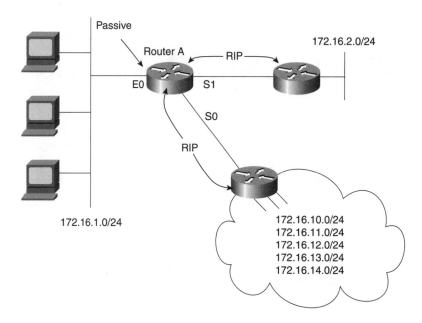

As depicted in Figure 3-1, Router A is using RIP to learn and advertise the subnets in major net 172.16.0.0. However, Router A is the only RIP device on the Ethernet LAN 172.16.1.0 (assume the clients are not RIP-enabled). Therefore, it is unnecessary and wasteful for Router A to send RIP updates out its Ethernet0 interface—no other routers are on the LAN and none of the clients care to receive any RIP information. By configuring Ethernet0 as passive, you can prevent all RIP advertisements from being sent out the interface and to the clients. The IOS command that does this is **passive-interface**, a router configuration mode command. The following is Router A's RIP configuration with the enhancement:

```
router rip
  network 172.16.0.0
  passive-interface Ethernet0
```

Router A is running RIP—it just isn't sending any RIP packets out Ethernet0. In fact, Router A still listens to RIP on the passive interface and would not block any RIP updates arriving on it. To prevent the router from listening to RIP, you must use route filters (see the following section, "Filtering Routing Updates").

To verify that the **passive-interface** command is working, you can look at the debugging messages for the routing protocol. Here's an output of **debug ip rip** for the scenario in Figure 3-1:

```
RTA#debug ip rip
RIP protocol debugging is on

RIP: sending v1 update to 255.255.255.255 via Serial0 (172.16.100.1)
     subnet  172.16.1.0, metric 1
     subnet  172.16.2.0, metric 2
     subnet  172.16.101.0, metric 1
RIP: sending v1 update to 255.255.255.255 via Serial1 (172.16.101.1)
     subnet  172.16.1.0, metric 1
     subnet  172.16.10.0, metric 3
     subnet  172.16.11.0, metric 3
     subnet  172.16.12.0, metric 4
     subnet  172.16.13.0, metric 4
     subnet  172.16.14.0, metric 4
     subnet  172.16.100.0, metric 1
```

The preceding output is one of Router A's periodic waves of RIP updates. The output confirms that Router A is sending updates from Serial0 and Serial1, but not from Ethernet0. Ethernet0 is noticeably absent from the debug output.

Filtering Routing Updates

Route filters give you granular control over the routes sent and received by your router. Unlike the **passive-interface** command that blocks all routes sent out an interface, a route filter can selectively block some updates and let others through. Route filters can also block incoming routes—something the **passive-interface** command cannot do. Filtering incoming routes is like filtering e-mail spam. It rejects routes that are unwanted or unnecessary (for example, improperly sourced default routes that might confuse your router).

Like the passive interface, route filtering is a building block for routing protocol redistribution (which is why it is covered in this chapter before the section on redistribution). The technique is also useful for filtering and sanitizing routes received from a router outside of your control— a router managed by another department or organization, for example.

Suppose you need to control the dispersion of routing updates in the network depicted in Figure 3-2 (the routing protocol is IGRP).

Figure 3-2   *A Scenario for Configuring Route Filters*

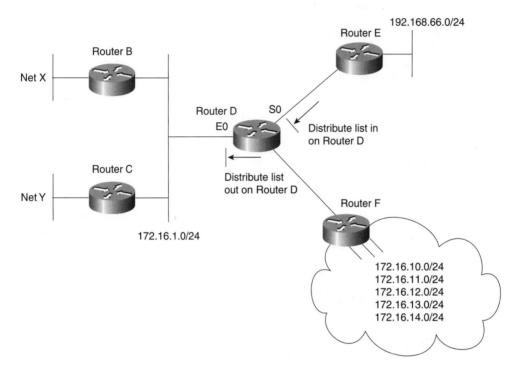

The situation you face is the following:

*   You manage all routers except Router E. Router E is owned by another group who often reconfigure, or rather misconfigure, their router. This sometimes causes problems for your router, Router D, because it gets confused when it receives illegal routes from Router E. You know that one route, 192.168.66.0/24, should be accepted by Router D. All other routes from Router E are noise and should be filtered.

*   For security reasons, Router B and Router C should not have a route to subnet 172.16.13.0/24. This prevents users in Net X and Net Y from accessing that particular subnet. Subsequently, Router D needs to filter 172.16.13.0/24 from its updates to Router B and Router C.

To accomplish these objectives, configure route filters on Router D with the **distribute-list** router mode command. The following is Router D's configuration:

```
router igrp 100
 network 172.16.0.0
 distribute-list 1 in Serial0
 distribute-list 2 out Ethernet0
!
access-list 1 permit 192.168.66.0 0.0.0.255
access-list 2 deny   172.16.13.0 0.0.0.255
access-list 2 permit any
```

The command **distribute-list 1 in Serial0** tells Router D to filter all IGRP updates inbound on Serial0 based on the criteria defined by access list 1, which permits route 192.168.66.0/24 only. This is the only route Router D will accept from Router E. All other routes entering Serial0 (sent from Router E) are ignored.

The command **distribute-list 2 out Ethernet0** tells the router to filter all IGRP updates outbound on Ethernet0, based on the criteria defined by access list 2. Access list 2 denies route 172.16.13.0/24 and permits all other routes—thus meeting the stated requirement to prevent Router B and Router C from learning route 172.16.13.0/24.

The remaining **access-list** commands define the access lists, 1 and 2, that are referenced by the **distribute-list** commands. You don't have to configure a **deny** rule for access list 1 because of the invisible deny-any rule at the end of every access list. Access lists and their syntax are covered in Chapter 6, "Deploying Basic Security Services."

After configuring the route filters, you should verify that they are delivering the expected results. You can issue **show ip route** on Router D to ensure that Router D is accepting only route 192.168.66.0/24 from Router E. Likewise, you can issue **show ip route** on Router B and Router C and verify that those routers have all routes except 172.16.13.0/24.

You can also verify route filtering with debugging commands. The following is an output with **debug ip igrp transactions** enabled on Router D:

```
RTD#deb ip igrp tr
IGRP protocol debugging is on

IGRP: sending update to 255.255.255.255 via Ethernet0 (172.16.1.1)
      subnet 172.16.2.0, metric=501
      subnet 172.16.3.0, metric=501
      subnet 172.16.10.0, metric=9675
      subnet 172.16.11.0, metric=9675
      subnet 172.16.12.0, metric=10255
      subnet 172.16.14.0, metric=9675
      network 192.168.66.0, metric=8576
```

The preceding output shows the IGRP updates sent by Router D out its Ethernet0 interface. Noticeably absent from the list is route 172.16.13.0/24, the route blocked by the route filter (**distribute-list 2 out Ethernet0**). Subnets 172.16.2.0 and 172.16.3.0 are the links joining Router D to Routers E and F (refer to Figure 3-2).

NOTE OSPF complicates the use of route filters somewhat and, in general, you should avoid OSPF route filtering whenever possible. With OSPF, you cannot use **distribute-list out** and specify an interface; however, when redistributing with OSPF, you can specify an external routing protocol with **distribute-list out**. You can prevent a router from entering a route in its routing table with **distribute-list in**, but this does not stop the router from forwarding the LSA to other routers in the network. Because OSPF is a link-state protocol and requires extensive propagation of LSAs, it cannot be route filtered like RIP, IGRP, and EIGRP.

Managing Redistribution

Ideally, all routers in your organization should run the same routing protocol. In reality, however, doing so can be difficult, especially when you are faced with any of the following situations:

- Various groups are managing their own routers and must use different routing protocols for one reason or another. Yet everyone must be internetworked together.

- You are migrating a large network of routers to a new routing protocol but you don't want to convert all routers at once. Instead, you want to migrate sections of the network in phases. During the migration, routers using the new protocol must still interoperate with routers using the old protocol.

- You have just acquired or merged with another organization and it doesn't use the same routing protocol. You need to establish connectivity between the organizations now. Later on, you might consider migrating the unified network to a single routing protocol.

- You run multiple autonomous systems or processes of the same routing protocol for administrative purposes and you need to share routing information across these routing domain boundaries.

- You need to exchange routing information with your Internet Service Provider, who runs a different routing protocol than you do.

Routing protocol redistribution resolves these issues. It is a translation service that allows different routing protocols to interoperate. Consider, for example, an organization's network depicted in Figure 3-3.

As shown in Figure 3-3, this organization has deployed EIGRP (OSPF works equally well) on a core group of routers to take advantage of such varied features as VLSM, fast convergence, better scalability, and route summarization. Off to the lower left is a legacy RIP network—these might be routers that can run only RIP or they might be routers that haven't yet migrated from RIP to EIGRP. To the lower right is a newly acquired company that needs connectivity to the rest of the organization. It also uses RIP.

Figure 3-3   *A Scenario for Routing Protocol Redistribution*

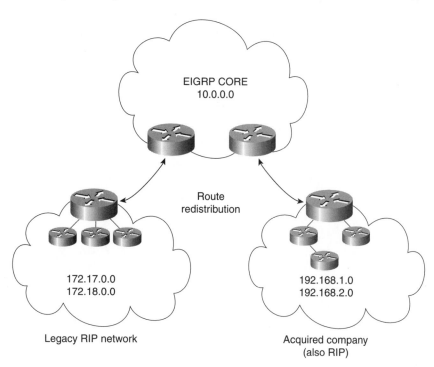

Legacy RIP network   Acquired company
                                      (also RIP)

Redistribution is a service that allows the sharing of routes across the various RIP and EIGRP routing domains. It transfers routes from the RIP domain to the EIGRP domain, and vice versa, so that every route is propagated and full connectivity is achieved (assuming there are no route filters in place). For illustration purposes, consider the propagation of the routes in the legacy RIP network (refer to Figure 3-3):

1 Routes from the legacy RIP network (172.17.0.0 and 172.18.0.0) are redistributed into EIGRP. The routes are converted from the RIP format to an EIGRP format and injected into the core.

2 The routes propagate through the core as EIGRP routes until they reach the boundary between the core and the acquisition network (right side of Figure 3-3).

3 Routes 172.17.0.0 and 172.18.0.0 are redistributed again, but this time from EIGRP into RIP. As the routes are injected into the acquisition network, they are converted from EIGRP to RIP.

4 Routes 172.17.0.0 and 172.18.0.0 are accepted and propagated through the acquisition network as RIP routes.

5 The result: Routers in the core and in the acquisition network now know how to reach 172.17.0.0 and 172.18.0.0 because of redistribution. A similar exercise can be done for tracing the redistribution of routes sourced by the acquisition network.

Configuring Redistribution—RIP and OSPF

Redistribution requires you to configure a router with the **redistribute** router mode command and the two protocols between which you want to redistribute. Consider the example network in Figure 3-4.

Figure 3-4   *A Network for Configuring Mutual Redistribution*

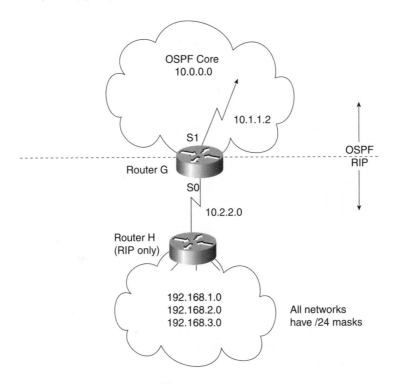

In the example, Router H is a RIP-only router with RIP routes 192.168.x.0 (where x ranges from 1 to 3). Router G is the redistribution router: It must run both RIP and OSPF.

The routing configuration for Router H is nothing new:

```
router rip
 network 10.0.0.0
 network 192.168.1.0
 network 192.168.2.0
 network 192.168.3.0
```

Router G, on the other hand, is a redistribution router. The following is Router G's RIP configuration:

```
router rip
 redistribute ospf 10 metric 3
 passive-interface Serial1
 network 10.0.0.0
```

The command **redistribute ospf 10 metric 3** redistributes the routes Router G learned from its OSPF process 10 into its RIP process with a default metric of 3 hops. Because OSPF has a different metric than RIP, you must assign a starting metric for the redistributed routes (keywords **metric 3**). The **redistribute** command injects a lot of routes into RIP—you can imagine there are many routes up there in that OSPF core. It's as though the router has two "brains": one that knows everything about the OSPF world and another that knows everything about the RIP world. When you redistribute from OSPF into RIP with **redistribute ospf 10 metric 3** (a subcommand of **router rip**), you copy all of the contents of the OSPF brain into the RIP brain. Subsequently, this provides RIP with all of the information learned from OSPF, and that information is a bunch of routes. Router G then advertises the combined database of routes to Router H. This, in turn, provides Router H (a RIP-only router) with all of the routes originated by the OSPF world.

The command **passive-interface Serial1** disables the transmission of RIP out Router G's Serial1 interface. Because only OSPF routers are in the core, there is no need to send RIP advertisements out this interface—disable it for less overhead and more efficiency (see "Configuring Passive Interfaces," earlier in this chapter).

The command **network 10.0.0.0** is the basic RIP command that enables RIP processing on major net 10.0.0.0.

Router G also needs to redistribute routes the other way: from RIP into OSPF. This is called two-way or *mutual redistribution*. The following is Router G's OSPF configuration:

```
router ospf 10
 redistribute rip metric 50 metric-type 1 subnets
 network 10.1.1.0 0.0.0.255 area 0
```

The command **redistribute rip metric 50 metric-type 1 subnets** redistributes the routes learned by the RIP process into OSPF process 10. Break up the command by keywords and you get the following:

- **rip**: The source for the redistribution is the RIP process. Notice that this time **redistribute** is a subcommand of **router ospf 10**. When you want to redistribute into a routing protocol, you put the **redistribute** command under the **router** command for that protocol.

- **metric 50**: Because RIP uses hop count and OSPF uses cost, you have to specify a starting (or default) metric for the routes redistributed into OSPF. Here, the default metric is a cost of 50.

- **metric-type 1**: This sets the redistributed routes to OSPF external type 1 routes. This applies only when you redistribute into OSPF. Basically, two types of external (redistributed) routes exist in OSPF: type 1 and type 2. The metric for type 1 routes is the sum of the cost to reach the redistribution router and the default metric. The metric for type 2 routes is simply the default metric—the OSPF cost is not added because the route propagates the OSPF domain. If you want to include the OSPF cost to reach the redistribution point, use external type 1 routes.

- **subnets**: This tells the router to redistribute both major nets and their subnets. If you exclude this, only major nets are redistributed. This applies only when redistributing into OSPF. A common error is to forget the **subnets** keyword when redistributing into OSPF.

Router G's OSPF configuration does not need the **passive-interface** command because only Serial1 is assigned to an OSPF area. Serial0 is not in an area, and therefore, does not send any OSPF updates. Consult Chapter 2 for OSPF configuration.

A look at the routing table of a core OSPF router (a router somewhere in the OSPF cloud in Figure 3-4) proves that the RIP routes are being redistributed into OSPF:

```
CoreRouter#sh ip ro
Codes: C - connected, S - static, I - IGRP, R - RIP, M - mobile, B - BGP
       D - EIGRP, EX - EIGRP external, O - OSPF, IA - OSPF inter area
       N1 - OSPF NSSA external type 1, N2 - OSPF NSSA external type 2
       E1 - OSPF external type 1, E2 - OSPF external type 2, E - EGP
       i - IS-IS, L1 - IS-IS level-1, L2 - IS-IS level-2, * - candidate default
       U - per-user static route, o - ODR
       T - traffic engineered route

Gateway of last resort is not set

     192.168.11.0/24 is subnetted, 1 subnets
O IA    192.168.11.1 [110/51] via 10.3.3.2, 00:30:40, Serial1
     10.0.0.0/24 is subnetted, 2 subnets
O E1    10.2.2.0 [110/320] via 10.3.3.2, 00:30:40, Serial1
C       10.3.3.0 is directly connected, Serial1
O E1 192.168.1.0/24 [110/400] via 10.3.3.2, 00:30:40, Serial1
O E1 192.168.2.0/24 [110/400] via 10.3.3.2, 00:29:54, Serial1
O E1 192.168.3.0/24 [110/460] via 10.3.3.2, 00:29:54, Serial1
<lines deleted for brevity>
```

In the preceding output, the lines highlighted in boldface are the routes originally sourced from the RIP domain and redistributed into OSPF by Router G. The code **O E1** designates an OSPF type 1 external route. An external route is simply a route that was redistributed into OSPF.

Redistributing into IGRP and EIGRP

Redistributing into IGRP and EIGRP is similar to redistributing into RIP and OSPF except you must define each variable of the composite metric to arrive at the default metric:

```
router eigrp 100
 redistribute rip metric 1544 100 255 1 1500
 network 172.16.0.0
```

where the numbers in the **redistribute** command after the keyword **metric** specify:

- **Bandwidth**—In kilobits per second.

- **Delay**—In tens of microseconds. That is, **100** equals a hundred "tens" or 1,000 microseconds.

- **Reliability**—A number from 0 to 255, where 255 is most reliable.
- **Loading**—A number from 0 to 255, where 255 is a fully loaded (100% saturated) link.
- **MTU (Maximum Transmission Unit)**—In bytes.

For more information on IGRP and EIGRP metrics, see the sources listed in the Bibliography and at http://www.cisco.com/warp/public/103/index.shtml (or search for "igrp metric" on the Cisco Web site).

NOTE   IOS automatically redistributes between IGRP and EIGRP when the autonomous system numbers are the same. You don't have to enter the **redistribute** command. It also adjusts the metrics as it redistributes, because the EIGRP metric is simply 256 multiplied by the IGRP metric (EIGRP metric = IGRP metric × 256).

Understanding Administrative Distance

When you use more than one routing protocol—for example, when you redistribute—you need to be aware of *administrative distances*. An administrative distance is a priority assigned to a route based on its routing protocol. When a router receives the same route from more than one protocol, which one should it use? Should it, for example, use the route heard from RIP or the one heard from OSPF? Because RIP and OSPF have completely different metrics, the router cannot decide by comparing metrics, so another value, the administrative distance, is used. Consider the diagram in Figure 3-5.

Figure 3-5   *Selecting Routes with Administrative Distance*

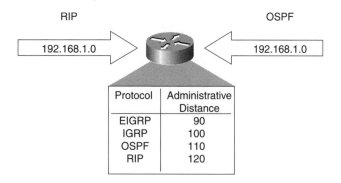

The router in Figure 3-5 has learned the same network, 192.168.1.0, on two different interfaces and from two different protocols: RIP and OSPF. To determine the route that should be used, the router looks at its preprogrammed ranking of protocols by administrative distance. The route learned by the protocol with the lowest administrative distance is preferred. It is the route installed in the routing table and used to reach the destination. For the situation depicted in Figure 3-5, the router prefers the OSPF route to the RIP route because OSPF has a lower administrative distance (110 for OSPF versus 120 for RIP).

NOTE   Administrative distances are locally significant: They are not communicated across routers.

The default administrative distance for each routing protocol is listed in Table 3-1. By default, all routes learned from a protocol have the same administrative distance—for example, all OSPF routes have an administrative distance of 110.

Table 3-1   *Default Administrative Distances by Routing Protocol*

Type of Route	Administrative Distance
Connected interface	0
Static route	1
EIGRP summary route	5
External BGP	20
EIGRP	90
IGRP	100
OSPF	110
IS-IS	115
RIP	120
External EIGRP	170
Internal BGP	200
Unknown/Route ignored	255

External EIGRP routes (see Table 3-1) are routes redistributed into EIGRP. For example, RIP routes redistributed into EIGRP are marked as external routes and carry this distinction as they are routed by EIGRP.

To change the administrative distance of a routing protocol, issue the **distance** router mode command:

```
router ospf 10
  distance 125
```

The preceding configuration changes the administrative distance of OSPF routes from 110 to 125. This is higher than RIP's administrative distance and means the router will prefer RIP routes to OSPF routes (RIP has a default distance of 120). Altering the default distances like this is often done during a migration to a new routing protocol—that is, you make the new routing protocol a higher distance than the old protocol until the new protocol is stable. After the new protocol is in place, you can return the distances to their original values and then disable the old protocol.

NOTE   The administrative distance of a route is sometimes called a measure of the route's *believability.* A router considers a route more believable than another if it has a lower administrative distance.

Administrative distances can cause problems when you redistribute. Consider the network in Figure 3-6.

Figure 3-6   *Problems with Administrative Distance and Redistribution*

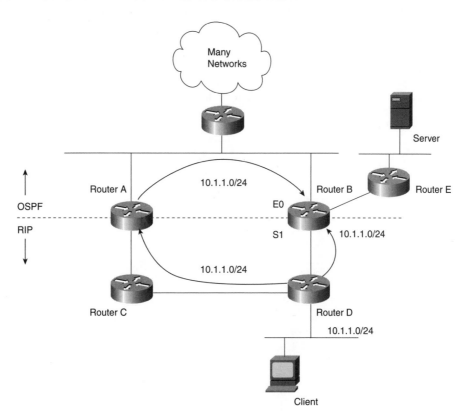

In Figure 3-6, Router A and Router B are doing mutual redistribution between the OSPF and RIP domains. Router D sends RIP advertisements for its directly connected network 10.1.1.0/24. Router C forwards the route to Router A, which redistributes it into OSPF. The route then travels over OSPF to Router B (Router B accepts the route through its Ethernet0 interface). Router B has just learned the route 10.1.1.0/24 through OSPF. Now, Router B also learns of 10.1.1.0/24 on its Serial1 interface through RIP—the route is sent by Router D, as depicted by the arrow from Router D to Router B in Figure 3-6.

Of the two routes received, Router B uses the route learned through OSPF because it has a lower administrative distance than RIP. Subsequently, all traffic from Router B to 10.1.1.0/24 follows a roundabout path (B→A→C→D) instead of the more direct path from Router B to Router D. When the server near Router E (refer to Figure 3-6) sends data to the client below Router D, the traffic flows along the suboptimal path because Router B selects Router A as the next hop. This is an undesirable consequence of redistribution. One way to solve the problem is to apply an inbound route filter on Router B such that Router B does not install the OSPF route for 10.1.1.0/24 in its routing table, thus forcing Router B to use the RIP route to reach the destination. However, this solution does not stop Router B from forwarding the route to other OSPF routers, because OSPF is a link-state protocol and must broadly propagate LSAs. The following section looks at route filters and redistribution in more detail.

Controlling Redistribution Loops with Route Filters

When you combine redundant paths with mutual redistribution, you can encounter problems with redistribution loops. Take for example, the situation in Figure 3-7.

Figure 3-7   *A Redistribution Loop (Route Feedback)*

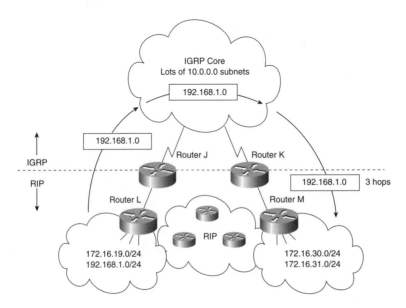

Figure 3-7 shows two points along the IGRP-RIP boundary where redistribution is occurring. Both Router J and Router K are performing mutual redistribution between RIP and IGRP.

Care must be taken to ensure that a route redistributed from RIP into IGRP at Router J does not get redistributed into RIP at Router K—an effect called *route feedback*. Route feedback is represented by the propagation of route 192.168.1.0/24 in Figure 3-7. Here's the sequence:

1   Route 192.168.1.0/24 originates from the RIP cloud behind Router L, propagates up to Router J, and is redistributed into IGRP by Router J.

2   In the IGRP domain, the route propagates via IGRP to Router K, where it is redistributed into RIP (Router K sees 192.168.1.0/24 as just another IGRP update) with a low default metric. Suppose the metric is 3 hops.

3   In turn, Router K forwards the route to Router M with a hop count of 3 (a low default metric), effectively telling Router M that the way to 192.168.1.0/24 is through Router K.

4   The undesirable result: Router M thinks the path to 192.168.1.0/24 is through Router K— a suboptimal route caused by the feedback of the route at Router K. Instead, Router K should reach the destination via the RIP cloud between it and Router L.

Using the same logic, you can deduce that IGRP routes are equally susceptible to route feedback. That is, an IGRP route can be redistributed into RIP, traverse the RIP domain, and get redistributed into IGRP at another redistribution point.

In addition to suboptimal routing, route feedback can also cause such problems as routing loops and loss of reachability. Therefore, it's highly recommended (or better yet *required*) that you always control mutual redistribution with route filters. The basics of route filters are covered in the earlier section "Filtering Routing Updates."

To prevent route feedback, both Router J and Router K in Figure 3-7 should have filters to ensure that routes within the IGRP domain are learned only through IGRP and routes within the RIP domain are learned only through RIP. The filters must ensure a RIP destination is not learned via IGRP and vice versa.

The following is Router K's configuration (Router J's configuration follows a similar strategy):

```
router igrp 100
 redistribute rip metric 1544 2000 255 1 1500
 network 10.0.0.0
 distribute-list 1 in
!
router rip
 redistribute igrp 100 metric 3
 network 172.16.0.0
 distribute-list 2 in
!
access-list 1 permit 10.0.0.0 0.255.255.255
access-list 2 permit 192.168.1.0 0.0.0.255
access-list 2 permit 172.16.0.0 0.0.255.255
```

In the preceding configuration, Router K is redistributing RIP into IGRP and IGRP into RIP (mutual redistribution). This is defined by the two **redistribute** commands.

The command **distribute-list 1 in** is a subcommand of the IGRP routing process activated by **router igrp 100**. It tells the router to filter all routes it receives through IGRP with access list 1. Access list 1 permits routes 10.*x*.*x*.*x* (where *x* denotes any octet) and blocks all other routes. This stops the feedback loop: Router K accepts only 10.0.0.0 routes (native IGRP routes) via IGRP and rejects any non-10.0.0.0 routes it learns via IGRP—routes that have been redistributed from RIP into IGRP.

NOTE   In a real-world network, you typically have many more routes to permit in the access list than a single, contiguous 10.0.0.0. Ensure that your access list includes all routes on one side of the redistribution boundary. Otherwise, those routes will not be redistributed and users on the other side of the boundary will not be able to reach those destinations.

The command **distribute-list 2 in** (a subcommand of **router rip**) tells the router to filter all routes it receives through RIP with access list 2. Access list 2 permits routes 192.168.1.*x* and 172.16.*x*.*x* (where *x* denotes any octet) and blocks all other routes. Like the **distribute-list** command under IGRP, this prevents route feedback: Router K filters and accepts only native RIP routes via the RIP protocol.

The remaining commands, starting with **access-list**, define access lists 1 and 2. Access lists are covered in Chapter 6.

Resolving Issues with VLSM and Classful Routing Protocols

As mentioned in Chapter 1, "Managing Your IP Address Space," classful routing protocols such as RIP and IGRP do not support VLSM, but sometimes you are forced to resolve VLSM and classful routing incompatibilities in a real-world network. Especially when you redistribute, routes might get lost between the parts of your network that use VLSM and the other parts that are classful. Figure 3-8 illustrates a typical scenario.

Figure 3-8   *Issues with VLSM and Redistribution: An Example Network*

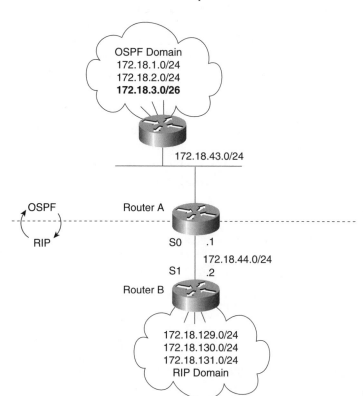

In Figure 3-8, Router A is performing mutual redistribution between OSPF and RIP, and Router B is a RIP-only router. Because RIP is classful and does not support VLSM, all networks in the RIP domain are properly deployed with the same mask, /24. The OSPF domain contains subnets from the same major net and uses VLSM. Subnet 172.18.3.0 has a /26 mask (highlighted in boldface) and all the other subnets in the OSPF domain have a /24 mask.

When Router A redistributes the routes from the OSPF domain into RIP, RIP advertises all of the routes out Serial0 except 172.18.3.0/26. It doesn't forward 172.18.3.0/26 because the mask for that route is not what Router A's RIP process expects. Router A examines the major net and mask configured on Serial0 *before* it advertises a route through it. If the route is part of the *same* major net as the interface but has a different mask, RIP does not advertise it out the interface (this rule applies to IGRP also).

NOTE   If the route is from a *different* major net than the interface, the major net of the route is
advertised out the interface (172.18.0.0/16, for example). In a classful world, the existence of a
different major net means the router sits on a boundary between major nets. One major net does
not need to know the internal subnets of another because subnets are contained within a major
net. As mentioned in Chapter 2, classful protocols do not support discontiguous subnets.

Because Router A does not forward the VLSM route 172.18.3.0/26, Router B never receives
it and no one in the RIP half of the network can reach subnet 172.18.3.0/26. The route is lost
because it is redistributed into a classful routing protocol.

The following output of Router B's routing table shows the problem:

```
RTB#sh ip ro
Codes: C - connected, S - static, I - IGRP, R - RIP, M - mobile, B - BGP
       D - EIGRP, EX - EIGRP external, O - OSPF, IA - OSPF inter area
       E1 - OSPF external type 1, E2 - OSPF external type 2, E - EGP
       i - IS-IS, L1 - IS-IS level-1, L2 - IS-IS level-2, * - candidate default

Gateway of last resort is not set

     172.18.0.0 is subnetted, 7 subnets
C       172.18.44.0/24 is directly connected, Serial1
R       172.18.43.0/24 [120/1] via 172.18.44.1, 00:00:08, Serial1
R       172.18.1.0/24 [120/2] via 172.18.44.1, 00:00:08, Serial1
R       172.18.2.0/24 [120/2] via 172.18.44.1, 00:00:08, Serial1
C       172.18.129.0/24 is directly connected, Ethernet0
R       172.18.130.0/24 [120/4] via 172.18.129.2, 00:00:23, Ethernet0
R       172.18.131.0/24 [120/5] via 172.18.129.2, 00:00:23, Ethernet0
```

The two routes highlighted in boldface in the preceding output are the routes that Router A
redistributes from the OSPF domain into RIP. Notice that route 172.18.3.0/26 is absent from
the table because Router A is not forwarding it to Router B.

To fix the problem of the missing route, you can configure a static route on Router B that tells
the router how to reach the lost subnet:

```
RTB#conf t
Enter configuration commands, one per line.  End with CNTL/Z.
RTB(config)#ip route 172.18.3.0 255.255.255.192 172.18.44.1
```

The command **ip route 172.18.3.0 255.255.255.192 172.18.44.1** installs a static route in Router
B. It tells the router to reach 172.18.3.0/26 through the next hop router, 172.18.44.1 (Router A).
This fixes the problem for Router B, but it does not help other RIP routers in the RIP domain.
You would have to install static routes on the other RIP routers—a laborious task when there
are many routers or many destinations, so consider the next approach.

An alternate solution is to create a static route on Router A that is agreeable to RIP and then redistribute it into the RIP domain. The following is Router A's configuration with this approach (boldface highlights the new commands):

```
router rip
 redistribute static
 redistribute ospf 10 metric 3
 passive-interface Ethernet0
 network 172.18.0.0
 !
 ip route 172.18.3.0 255.255.255.0 Null0
```

where **redistribute static** tells the router to redistribute all static routes configured on the router into RIP. This is like redistributing OSPF into RIP except the source of the redistribution is static routing instead of OSPF.

The command **ip route 172.18.3.0 255.255.255.0 Null0** configures a static route in Router A. This and other existing static routes are redistributed into RIP by **redistribute static**. Notice a couple of things about the route:

- The route is cleverly crafted with a /24 mask—the same mask as Router A's Serial0 interface and the rest of the RIP domain. This route matches the mask that is consistent throughout the RIP domain, so it can be redistributed and circulated by RIP without any problems.

- The route points to the router's Null0 interface—a bit bucket that leads to nowhere. The section on "Verifying EIGRP Configuration" in Chapter 2 explains the strategy behind the Null0 interface. Briefly, Router A doesn't use this route to reach 172.18.3.0/26 because it uses the most specific route: the one it learned through OSPF (172.18.3.0/26 is more specific than 172.18.3.0/24). You create this static so that Router A can redistribute it and make it known to other routers. This is called *originating a static route*.

When Router A redistributes the static route into RIP, RIP sends it out Serial0 (it matches Serial0's /24 mask). Router B learns that it can reach 172.18.3.0/24 through Router A and then propagates the route as a normal RIP route to the rest of the RIP domain. Router B and other RIP routers can now reach 172.18.3.0/26 via the route you fabricated, 172.18.3.0/24.

A caveat of this approach is the generalization (or summarization) of 172.18.3.0/26 by 172.18.3.0/24. The actual subnet (/26 mask) is a subset of the larger address block defined by the static with the /24 mask. This is fine if all addresses in the larger block are in the OSPF domain and reachable from the RIP domain via Router A. However, if portions of 172.18.3.0/24 other than 172.18.3.0/26 (for example, 172.18.3.128/26) are not advertised into RIP by Router A, this approach could cause reachability problems.

NOTE	You can see that there's quite a bit of subnetting and masking in this section. Refer to Chapter 1 if necessary.

Instead of originating a static route, an alternate solution is to use OSPF's summarization capabilities. With this approach, you use the OSPF **area range** command to summarize 172.18.3.0/26 with 172.18.3.0/24 (see "Configuring OSPF Summarization Between Areas" later in this chapter for use of this command). This gives you the same route 172.18.3.0/24, which you can then redistribute into RIP without a fuss.

Sometimes, there is no perfect solution for resolving VLSM issues with classful routing protocols. If your network does not lend itself to a clean solution because the classless space is heavy with VLSM, you might have to use a combination of the approaches presented in this section. You might, for example, have to originate a static route and then fill in missing information by configuring static routes on some selected RIP routers. Alternatively, you might find a reasonable opportunity to renumber some subnets so you can originate a static route as in the example. Finally, you always have the option to migrate off the classful protocol or at least reduce its coverage.

Leveraging Default Routing

Default routing scales the network, conserves resources, and simplifies routing information. A *default route* is a special route that tells the router how to reach unknown destinations—that is, destinations that are absent from the routing table because they are neither learned through a routing protocol nor manually configured with static routes. A default route is a catchall: When the router doesn't know how to forward a packet (because the packet is destined for an unknown network), the router sends it to the next hop defined by the default route. Without the default route, the packet is dropped because the router has no idea how to forward it.

It might sound as though default routes exist to cover up routing mistakes, but that is not the case. With default routing, you purposely withhold routing information from the router so that its routing task is reduced and simplified. This reduces the size of the routing table and conserves router resources (memory and CPU). To make up for the missing routes (the missing information), you provide the router with a simple default route. It's like taking a burden off the router and simplifying its view of the world to only what it needs to know. Default routes can substantially reduce the overhead of routing protocols, and they are a necessity when you connect to the public Internet. Figure 3-9 describes the typical uses for default routing.

Figure 3-9 *Default Routing and the Network of Widget, Inc.*

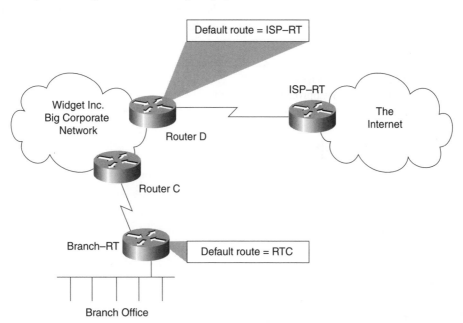

In Figure 3-9, Router D at Widget, Inc., is connected to the Internet through an ISP router, ISP-RT. Because Widget has only one connection to the Internet, Router D doesn't need to hold and manage a full Internet routing table—that's a lot of routes. Router D has only one way to get to the Internet: through ISP-RT. Router D already knows how to reach everything inside of Widget through the interior routing protocol, so traffic going anywhere else must be destined for the Internet. Widget configures a default route on Router D that points to ISP-RT (the IOS configuration of default routes follows in later sections). When Router D receives a packet destined for a non-Widget network, it uses the default route and sends it to ISP-RT.

NOTE   Even if Router D maintains a full Internet table because it's directly connected to the ISP, it's not practical for *all* routers in the big corporate network to also maintain all Internet routes. Eventually, routers in the corporate network downstream of Router D will require default routing to reach the Internet.

Figure 3-9 includes another default routing situation. The branch office router, Branch-RT, has a locally attached LAN and one path out to the big corporate network. Branch-RT doesn't need a full-size routing table with thousands of routes from the big corporate network because two choices suffice: Either packets go to the branch office LAN or they go somewhere else in the world via Router C. Therefore, Widget, Inc., configures a default route on Branch-RT that points to Router C as the next hop. Subsequently, Router C does not need to send Branch-RT any routing updates—Router C can have a passive interface or route filter on its link to Branch-RT, reducing overhead on the link between Branch-RT and Router C.

NOTE   Router C still needs to know how to reach the branch office LAN, so Branch-RT needs to send a single route upstream to Router C.

Propagation of Default Routes

Usually, it is not enough to configure a default route on one router and be done with it. The default route must be shared with other routers, as depicted in Figure 3-10.

Figure 3-10   *Propagation of a Default Route*

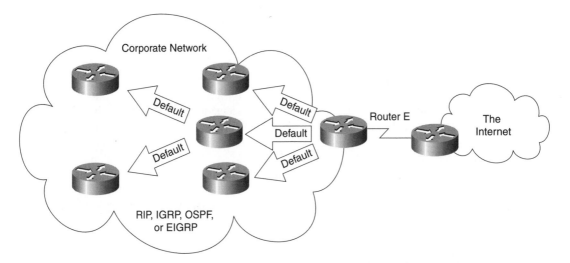

In Figure 3-10, Router E is the exit point for traffic leaving the corporate network and heading out to the Internet. Router E is configured with a default route so that it doesn't have to hold the entire Internet routing table. This satisfies Router E's requirement to reach points on the Internet, but what about the other routers in the corporate network? They must also learn about this default route or they will not know how to forward a packet destined to the Internet (they will drop the packet). To inform others of the default route, Router E propagates the default route with the interior routing protocol. In the same way that it carries normal routes, the routing protocol carries the default route to all parts of the corporate network. As each router receives the default route, it can then forward traffic destined for the Internet. This process is called *originating* (or *advertising*) *a default route*. Because Router E starts it all, E is the *originator*.

Originating a Default Route with RIP

It's easy, sometimes dangerously easy, to configure a router to originate a default route with RIP. All you need to do is configure the default route itself and RIP takes care of the rest. RIP automatically advertises the default out all RIP-enabled interfaces. Consider the example network depicted in Figure 3-11.

Figure 3-11 *RIP and Default Routing*

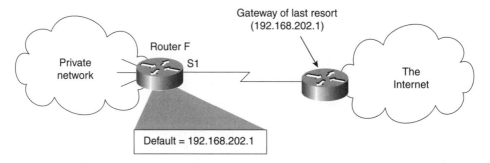

In the network in Figure 3-11, Router F has a default route to the Internet. The following is Router F's RIP configuration:

```
router rip
 network 172.18.0.0
!
ip route 0.0.0.0 0.0.0.0 192.168.202.1
```

The command **ip route 0.0.0.0 0.0.0.0 192.168.202.1** configures a default route in the router. It's a static route with a special network number **0.0.0.0** and mask **0.0.0.0**. The router with address **192.168.202.1** is called the *gateway of last resort*. The gateway of last resort is the target for all destinations Router F does not know how to reach (to which it does not have a route).

To verify that the default route is in effect, issue the **show ip route** command and take note of the following lines highlighted in boldface:

```
RTF#sh ip ro
Codes: C - connected, S - static, I - IGRP, R - RIP, M - mobile, B - BGP
       D - EIGRP, EX - EIGRP external, O - OSPF, IA - OSPF inter area
       E1 - OSPF external type 1, E2 - OSPF external type 2, E - EGP
       i - IS-IS, L1 - IS-IS level-1, L2 - IS-IS level-2, * - candidate default

Gateway of last resort is 192.168.202.1 to network 0.0.0.0

C    192.168.202.0 is directly connected, Serial1
     172.18.0.0 255.255.255.0 is subnetted, 5 subnets
C       172.18.10.0 is directly connected, Ethernet0
R       172.18.11.0 [120/2] via 172.18.10.1, 00:00:17, Ethernet0
```

```
R       172.18.12.0 [120/1] via 172.18.10.1, 00:00:17, Ethernet0
C       172.18.44.0 is directly connected, Serial0
R       172.18.1.0 [120/3] via 172.18.44.1, 00:00:02, Serial0
S*      0.0.0.0 0.0.0.0 [1/0] via 192.168.202.1
```

The line beginning with **Gateway of last resort** confirms that the default route is active and consistent with the configuration.

The last line of the output displays the default route itself. It has a code of **S***, meaning it is a static route and a default route (the asterisk signifies a default route).

Immediately after you configure the default route, RIP starts advertising it to other routers, as shown in the following debug output:

```
RTF#deb ip rip
RIP protocol debugging is on

RIP: sending update to 255.255.255.255 via Serial0 (172.18.44.2)
     subnet 172.18.10.0, metric 1
     subnet 172.18.11.0, metric 3
     subnet 172.18.12.0, metric 2
     default 0.0.0.0, metric 1
```

The boldface line in the preceding output shows that Router F is advertising the default route out its Serial0 interface. The result is a bit surprising because a default route is inherently a static route and you usually have to redistribute statics into RIP before they are advertised (see the use of the **redistribute static** command in "Resolving Issues with VLSM and Classful Routing Protocols" earlier in this chapter). But in this case, 0.0.0.0 is the exception: It is advertised by RIP even if **redistribute static** is missing.

NOTE   Because originating a default route with RIP is so easy, care must be taken to avoid the accidental propagation of default routes. Someone might configure a default route on a RIP router, thinking that the default is for that router only and not realizing that his or her router is sending 0.0.0.0 to the rest of the network. When routers hear multiple default routes, the wrong one might be trusted (if it has a lower hop count). This leads to reachability problems.

Originating a Default Route with IGRP

As with RIP, you can configure a default route on an IGRP router like this:

```
router igrp
 network 172.18.0.0
!
ip route 0.0.0.0 0.0.0.0 192.168.202.1
```

The default route 0.0.0.0 is used locally by the router; however, it cannot be advertised to any other router with IGRP. IGRP does not propagate 0.0.0.0 even if you redistribute it into IGRP with the **redistribute static** command.

To make IGRP originate a default route and advertise it to others, configure IGRP as follows (this also works for EIGRP):

```
router igrp 100
 redistribute static
 network 172.18.0.0
 !
ip route 30.0.0.0 255.0.0.0 192.168.202.1
ip default-network 30.0.0.0
```

where **ip route 30.0.0.0 255.0.0.0 192.168.202.1** creates a static route to a fictitious network 30.0.0.0 (a major net). This network does not actually exist in the organization. It's just a placeholder and a substitute for **ip route 0.0.0.0 0.0.0.0 192.168.202.1**.

The command **ip default-network 30.0.0.0** declares that 30.0.0.0, the fictitious network, is to be treated as a gateway of last resort. Traffic with an unknown destination is sent to this network. The router knows the route to this network is through 192.168.202.1 because of the previous command, **ip route 30.0.0.0 255.0.0.0 192.168.202.1**.

The command **redistribute static** is necessary to redistribute the static route, 30.0.0.0, into IGRP so that it can be advertised to other IGRP routers. Upon receiving 30.0.0.0, other routers will use it as a default route. This is equivalent to a RIP router receiving 0.0.0.0.

To verify the configuration of the originator of the default, issue **show ip route**:

```
IGRP-Router#sh ip ro
Codes: C - connected, S - static, I - IGRP, R - RIP, M - mobile, B - BGP
       D - EIGRP, EX - EIGRP external, O - OSPF, IA - OSPF inter area
       N1 - OSPF NSSA external type 1, N2 - OSPF NSSA external type 2
       E1 - OSPF external type 1, E2 - OSPF external type 2, E - EGP
       i - IS-IS, L1 - IS-IS level-1, L2 - IS-IS level-2, * - candidate default
       U - per-user static route, o - ODR
       T - traffic engineered route

Gateway of last resort is 192.168.202.1 to network 30.0.0.0

S*   30.0.0.0/8 [1/0] via 192.168.202.1
     172.16.0.0/24 is subnetted, 2 subnets
C       172.16.13.0 is directly connected, Serial0
C       172.16.2.0 is directly connected, Serial1
<lines deleted for brevity>
```

The preceding output agrees with the configuration: **Gateway of last resort** is correct, and network 30.0.0.0 is coded with **S***, indicating it is a default route. If you forget to configure the **ip default-network** command, the asterisk (*) will not appear and the static will not be a default route.

Originating a Default Route with EIGRP

To originate a default route with EIGRP, you can use the same method described in "Originating a Default Route with IGRP." Alternatively, you can configure 0.0.0.0 and redistribute it into EIGRP like this:

```
router eigrp 100
 redistribute static
 network 172.18.0.0
 default-metric 1544 2000 255 1 1500
 !
ip route 0.0.0.0 0.0.0.0 192.168.202.1
```

The command **ip route 0.0.0.0 0.0.0.0 192.168.202.1** creates a default route, with 192.168.202.1 as the gateway of last resort.

The command **redistribute static** redistributes 0.0.0.0 (and any other statics) into EIGRP so that it can be advertised to other routers.

The command **default-metric 1544 2000 255 1 1500** defines the starting EIGRP metric for the static routes that are redistributed into EIGRP. In order, the elements of the metric are:

- **Bandwidth**—In kilobits per second.
- **Delay**—In tens of microseconds.
- **Reliability**—A number from 0 to 255, where 255 is most reliable.
- **Loading**—A number from 0 to 255, where 255 is a fully loaded (100% saturated) link.
- **MTU (Maximum Transmission Unit)**—In bytes.

Originating a Default Route with OSPF

Like IGRP and EIGRP, OSPF does not automatically propagate a default route. To originate a default route with OSPF, configure OSPF with the **default-information originate** command:

```
router ospf 10
 network 172.18.43.0 0.0.0.255 area 0
 <other network commands>
 default-information originate metric 20 metric-type 1
 !
ip route 0.0.0.0 0.0.0.0 172.18.44.2
```

where **ip route 0.0.0.0 0.0.0.0 172.18.44.2** configures the default route and gateway of last resort.

The command **default-information originate metric 20 metric-type 1** tells OSPF to propagate 0.0.0.0 with a starting metric of 20. This behaves like the **redistribute** command except it only redistributes the default route. The parameter **metric-type 1** tells OSPF to advertise the route as an external type 1 route. External type 1 and type 2 routes are covered in "Configuring Redistribution," earlier in this chapter.

When an OSPF router receives the default route from the originator, you will see 0.0.0.0 in the table, as shown in the following output of **show ip route**:

```
OSPF-Router#sh ip ro
Codes: C - connected, S - static, I - IGRP, R - RIP, M - mobile, B - BGP
       D - EIGRP, EX - EIGRP external, O - OSPF, IA - OSPF inter area
       N1 - OSPF NSSA external type 1, N2 - OSPF NSSA external type 2
       E1 - OSPF external type 1, E2 - OSPF external type 2, E - EGP
       i - IS-IS, L1 - IS-IS level-1, L2 - IS-IS level-2, * - candidate default
       U - per-user static route, o - ODR
       T - traffic engineered route

Gateway of last resort is 172.18.43.2 to network 0.0.0.0

     172.18.0.0/16 is variably subnetted, 5 subnets, 2 masks
O E2    172.18.200.0/24 [110/10] via 172.18.43.2, 01:39:39, Serial1
O E2    172.18.44.0/24 [110/10] via 172.18.43.2, 01:44:42, Serial1
C       172.18.43.0/24 is directly connected, Serial1
C       172.18.4.0/22 is directly connected, Ethernet0
C       172.18.1.0/24 is directly connected, Serial0
O*E1 0.0.0.0/0 [110/45] via 172.18.43.2, 00:01:12, Serial1
```

In the preceding output, the two lines highlighted in boldface confirm that this router received the default route. It came from 172.18.43.2; therefore, 172.18.43.2 is this router's gateway of last resort.

Default Routing and Classful Behavior

When you use a default route to reach a subnet of a connected major net, you must ensure that the router is configured with the **ip classless** global config command. Without **ip classless**, the router takes a classful posture and problems might surface. Consider the scenario depicted in Figure 3-12.

In the network pictured in Figure 3-12, Router A is classful (configured with **no ip classless**) and has a default route pointing to Router B as the gateway of last resort. Everything in Router A's routing table looks acceptable:

```
RTA#sh ip ro
Codes: C - connected, S - static, I - IGRP, R - RIP, M - mobile, B - BGP
       D - EIGRP, EX - EIGRP external, O - OSPF, IA - OSPF inter area
       E1 - OSPF external type 1, E2 - OSPF external type 2, E - EGP
       i - IS-IS, L1 - IS-IS level-1, L2 - IS-IS level-2, * - candidate default

Gateway of last resort is 172.18.202.1 to network 0.0.0.0

C    172.18.202.0 is directly connected, Serial0
     172.18.0.0/24 is subnetted, 3 subnets
C       172.18.1.0 is directly connected, Ethernet0
C       172.18.2.0 is directly connected, Ethernet1
C       172.18.3.0 is directly connected, Serial1
S*   0.0.0.0 0.0.0.0 [1/0] via 172.18.202.1
```

Figure 3-12 *Problems with Default Routing and Classful Behavior*

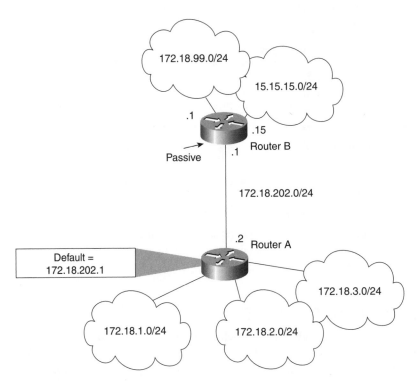

As shown in the preceding output, Router A lacks routes to 172.18.99.0/24 and 15.15.15.0/24, but it has a default route to Router B for all unknown destinations. Will the default route let Router A reach *both* 172.18.99.0/24 and 15.15.15.0/24? The answer is no, as shown by the following ping tests.

Issuing a ping to 15.15.15.15 gives:

```
RTA#ping 15.15.15.15
Type escape sequence to abort.
Sending 5, 100-byte ICMP Echos to 15.15.15.15, timeout is 2 seconds:
!!!!!
Success rate is 100 percent (5/5), round-trip min/avg/max = 4/4/8 ms
```

As shown in the preceding output, Router A can reach 15.15.15.0/24 through the default route (exclamation points signify successful receipt of ping reply packets).

But issuing a ping to 172.18.99.1 gives:

```
RTA#ping 172.18.99.1
Type escape sequence to abort.
Sending 5, 100-byte ICMP Echos to 172.18.99.1, timeout is 2 seconds:
.....
Success rate is 0 percent (0/5)
```

The preceding output shows that Router A *cannot* reach 172.18.99.0/24 (dots indicate ping timeouts). So, what's the difference?

As a classful router, Router A checks for a direct connection to the major net before it forwards a packet. If the packet is destined to a directly connected major net (called a *local domain*), the router ignores the default route and looks in its routing table for a route to the destination. If a route does not exist, the packet is dropped.

Destination 172.18.99.1 is part of Router A's local domain. Subsequently, Router A does not use the default route and it drops the ping packets in the absence of a route to 172.18.99.0/24.

Packets to 15.15.15.0/24, on the other hand, are forwarded to the gateway of last resort because it is outside Router A's local domain and no routes exist for that destination.

To disable classful behavior (checking of the local domain), issue the **ip classless** global config command, like so:

```
RTA#conf t
Enter configuration commands, one per line.  End with CNTL/Z.
RTA(config)#ip classless
```

The **ip classless** command toggles the router from classful mode to classless mode. With this command, the router has no notion of traditional classful addressing nor major nets. It simply looks at network prefixes. If Router A doesn't have a route to a destination, it uses the default route. The local domain check is skipped.

Issuing a ping to 172.18.99.1 with **ip classless** configured gives:

```
RTA#ping 172.18.99.1
Type escape sequence to abort.
Sending 5, 100-byte ICMP Echos to 172.18.99.1, timeout is 2 seconds:
!!!!!
Success rate is 100 percent (5/5), round-trip min/avg/max = 4/4/8 ms
```

The preceding output shows that **ip classless** has resolved the problem of reaching the unknown destination 172.18.99.0/24.

NOTE   An alternate way to resolve the problem with default routing and classful behavior is to configure a static route that points the major net to default route 0.0.0.0. Looking back to the initial problem in Figure 3-12, you can configure **ip route 172.18.0.0 255.255.0.0 0.0.0.0** in Router A. This allows classful Router A to reach unknown subnets of 172.18.0.0 through 0.0.0.0 (**no ip classless** is configured).

Configuring Route Summarization

As mentioned in Chapter 1, route summarization (also called aggregation) is the consolidation of multiple, contiguous routes into a single generalized route. It is recommended that you use summarization whenever you can, as your network addressing allows, to promote efficient and stable routing. If you are deploying a network from scratch, definitely plan your addressing so you can leverage summarization.

Summarization typically applies to classless routing protocols such as EIGRP and OSPF. RIP and IGRP are more primitive and do not have the summarization capabilities covered in this chapter.

NOTE   BGP is a popular exterior routing protocol with rich summarization capabilities. Consult the Bibliography for sources of BGP information. Additionally, a good BGP primer is freely available at http://www.cisco.com/univercd/cc/td/doc/cisintwk/ics/index.htm on Cisco's Web site. The primer can also be found by searching the Cisco Web site for *internetworking case studies*.

Understanding EIGRP Auto-Summarization

By default, EIGRP automatically summarizes across major net boundaries. Often, this is nothing to worry about; however, when you deploy discontiguous subnets, as EIGRP supports, you might have to disable EIGRP auto-summarization. Consider the following scenario with auto-summarization enabled (see Figure 3-13). Assume EIGRP is the only routing protocol.

Figure 3-13   *EIGRP Auto-Summarization*

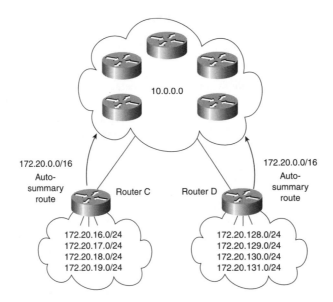

In the network depicted in Figure 3-13, major net 172.20.0.0 is broken up and separated by major net 10.0.0.0—in other words, the subnets of 172.20.0.0 are discontiguous. Router C thinks it's sitting on a major net boundary because it has direct connections to both 10.0.0.0 and 172.20.0.0.

With EIGRP auto-summarization enabled, Router C sends a summary route for all of 172.20.0.0 into 10.0.0.0 because it is a major net boundary. It has no need to tell the routers in 10.0.0.0 about the internal subnets of 172.20.0.0—or so it thinks.

NOTE   Classful protocols RIP and IGRP also automatically summarize across major net boundaries. They are classful, so they naturally assume all subnets of a major net are contiguous. You cannot disable auto-summarization in RIP or IGRP.

After Router C sends 172.20.0.0/16 upstream, the details of the subnets beneath Router C are now lost. The summary route generalizes the four subnets with a single route.

Router D is also an EIGRP router and automatically summarizes its subnets into 10.0.0.0. Router D sends 172.20.0.0/16 into the 10.0.0.0 network. This is the same route advertised by Router C.

In this scenario, you can identify the following problems caused by EIGRP auto-summarization:

- Router D never learns the details of the subnets beneath Router C. Router C's summary route throws away the specific routes to 172.20.16.0/24, 172.20.17.0/24, 172.20.18.0/24, and 172.20.19.0/24.

- In the same way, Router C never learns the details of the subnets beneath Router D.

- Routers in the 10.0.0.0 cloud receive a summary route for 172.20.0.0 but from different directions. When they choose the route with the lowest metric, that route reaches the destinations beneath either Router C or Router D, but not both.

To solve the problems with auto-summarization and discontiguous subnets, disable auto-summarization with the EIGRP **no auto-summary** command. The following is Router C's configuration:

```
router eigrp 100
  network 172.20.0.0
  network 10.0.0.0
  no auto-summary
```

where the command **no auto-summary** disables EIGRP auto-summarization and forces the router to advertise specific routes.

Configuring EIGRP Summarization

EIGRP allows you to manually summarize multiple contiguous routes into a more simplified and generalized route. Summarization is key for network scalability, routing efficiency, and router resource conservation. Consider the application for route summarization shown in Figure 3-14.

Figure 3-14 *Applying EIGRP Route Summarization*

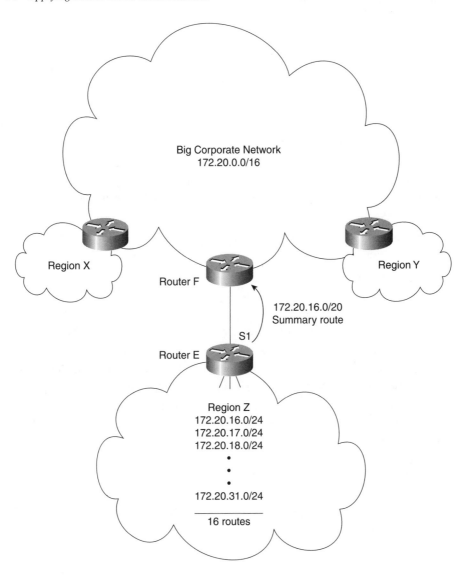

In Figure 3-14, Router E is responsible for advertising Region Z's routes to the big corporate network. Normally, Router E advertises each /24 route separately and injects 16 routes into the big corporate network—this is the default behavior.

Due to some good address planning, the routes in Region Z are contiguous. Subsequently, Router E can summarize and reduce the number of routes it advertises—that is, it can advertise a single route that covers all of Region Z's address space. The rest of the organization, such as Regions X and Y, can still reach everything in Region Z, and every router benefits from sending and maintaining fewer routes.

The following is Router E's configuration with summarization applied:

```
interface Serial1
 ip address 172.20.77.2 255.255.255.0
 ip summary-address eigrp 100 172.20.16.0 255.255.240.0
!
router eigrp 100
 network 172.20.0.0
 no auto-summary
```

where **ip summary-address eigrp 100 172.20.16.0 255.255.240.0** is the key command and summarizes all 16 routes inside Region Z with 172.20.16.0/20 (mask 255.255.240.0 equals /20). Interface Serial1 gets this command because it is the interface pointing to the big corporate network—the summary route exits out this interface. Keywords **eigrp 100** define the associated EIGRP autonomous system (necessary because a router might route for more than one autonomous system).

The command **no auto-summary** might not be necessary. If major net 172.20.0.0 has discontiguous subnets, the command is needed. See "Understanding EIGRP Auto-Summarization," earlier in this chapter.

NOTE   EIGRP route summarization is performed at the interface level. Although OSPF has separate summarization commands for internal (area-to-area) and external (redistributed) routes, EIGRP summarizes both internal and external routes with **ip summary-address eigrp** at the interface.

To understand why 172.20.16.0/20 adequately describes all 16 routes in Region Z, examine the octet where the mask falls (the third octet). Expand the third octet (decimal 16) into binary and apply the /20 mask, as shown in Example 3-1.

Example 3-1 *Analysis of Summarization with 172.20.16.0/20*

```
Third octet = Decimal 16 = 0001-0000
Third octet of /20 mask   = 1111-0000
```
```
Route summarizes:        0001-xxxx
                       (where x is 0 or 1)
```

As shown in Example 3-1, the /20 mask sets the third octet to 0001-*xxxx*, where *x* can be a zero or a one. This means all possible combinations for the third octet are 0001-0000 through 0001-1111 (decimal 16 through 31). Putting the range of the third octet into the rest of the address yields an address range of 172.20.16.0 through 172.20.31.255 (the last octet can be anything from 0 to 255). This equals the address space of the subnets in Region Z; therefore, 172.20.16/20 is the correct summary route for Region Z.

A look at Router E's routing table shows that the summary route is installed:

```
RTE#sh ip ro
Codes: C - connected, S - static, I - IGRP, R - RIP, M - mobile, B - BGP
       D - EIGRP, EX - EIGRP external, O - OSPF, IA - OSPF inter area
       N1 - OSPF NSSA external type 1, N2 - OSPF NSSA external type 2
       E1 - OSPF external type 1, E2 - OSPF external type 2, E - EGP
       i - IS-IS, L1 - IS-IS level-1, L2 - IS-IS level-2, * - candidate default
       U - per-user static route, o - ODR
       T - traffic engineered route

Gateway of last resort is not set

D        172.20.16.0/20 is a summary, 00:06:31, Null0
C        172.20.16.0/24 is directly connected, Serial0.1
C        172.20.17.0/24 is directly connected, Serial0.2
C        172.20.18.0/24 is directly connected, Serial0.3
C        172.20.19.0/24 is directly connected, Serial0.4
<lines deleted for brevity>
```

The entry shown in boldface in the preceding output is the EIGRP summary route for Region Z. Because this router is the originator, the summary route points to Null0.

Likewise, Router F receives and installs the summary route:

```
RTF#sh ip ro
Codes: C - connected, S - static, I - IGRP, R - RIP, M - mobile, B - BGP
       D - EIGRP, EX - EIGRP external, O - OSPF, IA - OSPF inter area
       N1 - OSPF NSSA external type 1, N2 - OSPF NSSA external type 2
       E1 - OSPF external type 1, E2 - OSPF external type 2, E - EGP
       i - IS-IS, L1 - IS-IS level-1, L2 - IS-IS level-2, * - candidate default
       U - per-user static route, o - ODR
       T - traffic engineered route
```

```
Gateway of last resort is not set

     172.20.0.0/16 is variably subnetted, 2 subnets, 2 masks
D        172.20.16.0/20 [90/1920000] via 172.20.77.2, 00:16:48, Serial1
C        172.20.77.0/30 is directly connected, Serial1
<lines deleted for brevity>
```

The boldface entry in the preceding output is the summary route sent to this router (Router F) by Router E.

Configuring OSPF Summarization Between Areas

OSPF also supports manual summarization of routes on area border routers (ABRs). Consider the following topology (Figure 3-15).

Figure 3-15 *Summarizing OSPF Routes Between Areas*

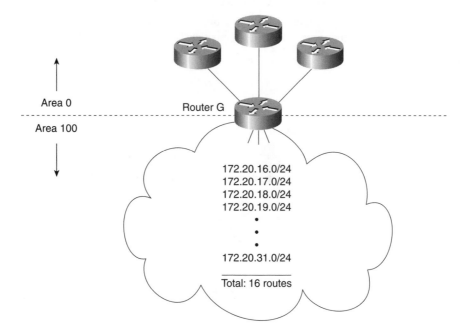

In Figure 3-15, Router G is an ABR between area 0 and area 100 and is responsible for advertising the 16 routes in area 100 to area 0 (the backbone area). Normally, it does not summarize but simply injects 16 routes into area 0. This is another opportunity to summarize because the 16 routes are contiguous. Again, good address planning makes this possible.

To summarize the routes in area 100 with a single summary route, configure Router G with the OSPF **area range** command, like this:

```
router ospf 25
  network 172.20.16.0 0.0.15.255 area 100
  network 172.20.0.0 0.0.3.255 area 0
  area 100 range 172.20.16.0 255.255.240.0
```

where **area 100 range 172.20.16.0 255.255.240.0** is the key command that summarizes the routes in area 100 with a single route 172.20.16.0/20. For an explanation of why 172.20.16.0/20 summarizes the 16 routes inside area 100, see the preceding section "Configuring EIGRP Summarization," which has the same summary route.

The other commands configure OSPF routing (see Chapter 2).

Configuring OSPF Summarization During Redistribution

Unlike EIGRP, OSPF maintains a separate process for summarizing redistributed routes. This is called *external route summarization*. Consider the scenario depicted in Figure 3-16.

Figure 3-16   *OSPF External Route Summarization*

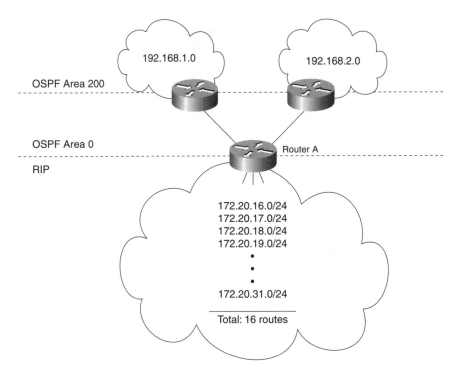

Router A redistributes RIP into OSPF. Normally, the redistribution injects 16 routes, each with a /24 mask, into area 0. Instead of doing that, Router A can summarize the 16 routes and inject just a single route 172.20.16.0/20 into area 0. The following is Router A's OSPF configuration:

```
router ospf 25
  network 172.20.0.0 0.0.3.255 area 0
  summary-address 172.20.16.0 255.255.240.0
```

where **summary-address 172.20.16.0 255.255.240.0** is the key command that summarizes all 16 RIP routes into a single route 172.20.16.0/20. Router A then advertises this summary route to area 0 so that the other OSPF backbone routers learn the route to the RIP destinations.

Deploying Policy Routing with Route Maps

Policy routing enables you to direct traffic over user-defined paths based on the flexible syntax of access lists. With policy routing, you use enhanced filters called *route maps* to override normal forwarding decisions like those based on dynamic routing protocols. Route maps contain your criteria for identifying traffic and your instructions on how that traffic should be forwarded. You might want to do this to support certain routing policies, such as these:

- You want different applications (Web, e-mail, Telnet) to travel over different paths. That is, you want some applications to travel over normal paths determined by routing protocols, but you need other applications to travel over alternate paths—perhaps for performance or bandwidth allocation reasons.

- For legal, contractual, or security reasons, certain types of traffic must go over a different path than other types of traffic.

- You need to assign links to different groups of people for billing purposes. Each group uses and pays for its own bandwidth pipe.

In addition to directing traffic over different paths, policy routing enables you to set IP precedence values in packets. This marks (or *classifies*) packets with a certain quality of service (QoS) level that queuing and discarding services might use to prioritize traffic in the network. Another IOS service, Committed Access Rate (CAR), also classifies packets by setting IP precedence values. CAR and other advanced QoS features are covered in Chapter 5, "Deploying Advanced Quality of Service Features." Chapter 4, "Deploying Basic Quality of Service Features," covers IP precedence, QoS concepts, and basic QoS features.

This section covers both forms of policy routing: forwarding traffic over user-defined paths and classifying traffic with IP precedence.

NOTE   This section requires familiarity with the access list syntax. Consult Chapter 6 as needed.

Forwarding Traffic with Route Maps

Route maps define criteria for matching packets and instructions for what to do with them. In the case of packet forwarding, the instructions define the next hop router to which the packet should be sent or the interface by which the packet should exit. This function is similar to static routing (see "Configuring a Static Route" in Appendix E), but with more control: You can control exactly which packets get forwarded and which do not by using the flexible syntax of access lists.

Route maps are built of one or more entry declarations that each contain so-called *match* and *set* statements. For example, the following commands configure a route map called TESTMAP:

```
route-map TESTMAP permit 20
 match ip address 100
 set ip next-hop 192.168.10.130
```

The command **route-map TESTMAP permit 20** creates a route map entry with a sequence of 20. A route map might contain multiple entries to support multiple policy-routing instructions. The sequence number identifies each entry so you can edit or delete entries without disturbing the rest of the route map. The keyword **permit** tells the router that packets matching the entry, as specified by **match** commands in the entry, should be processed by the instructions (**set** commands) found in the entry—this is the default behavior. If the entry is marked **deny** instead of **permit**, the packets matching the entry are *not* policy routed: They are sent back through the normal forwarding channel.

NOTE   Space out your route map sequence numbers so you have the flexibility to insert new sequences between the entries as needed. When policy-routing a packet, the router compares the packet to each entry in the route map in order of sequence. The entry with the lowest sequence number is examined first.

The command **match ip address 100** defines the matching criteria of the entry. Here, access list 100—configured elsewhere in the router—defines the subset of packets that are policy-routed by the entry. Access lists are covered in Chapter 6.

The command **set ip next-hop 192.168.10.130** defines the action performed on packets that meet the criteria defined by the previous **match** statement. Here, the action is to send the matching packets to the next hop router, 192.168.10.130.

In the TESTMAP example, the first entry is given a sequence number of 20, enabling you to insert new entries before or after the initial entry. This is useful because packets are processed against a route map one entry at a time in order of sequence until a match is found. When a matching entry is found, the router processes the packet according to **set** commands in the entry and restarts the policy-routing procedure with the next packet.

NOTE	A packet that does not match a route map entry is routed (forwarded) normally.

Policy Routing: An Example

To demonstrate the use and configuration of route maps, consider the scenario depicted in Figure 3-17.

Figure 3-17 *An Example for Policy Routing (Route Maps)*

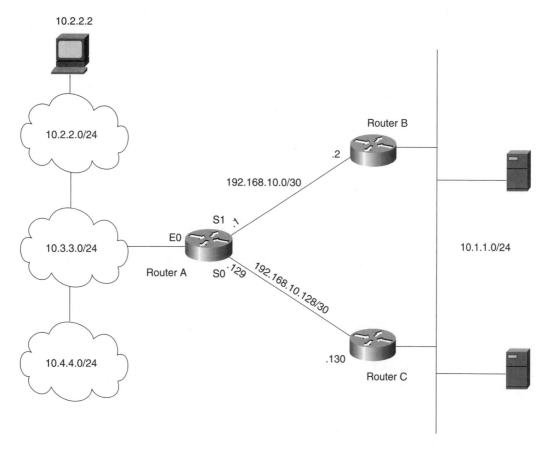

Router A has two paths to subnet 10.1.1.0/24: one through Router B and another through Router C. Dynamic routing protocols such as OSPF, RIP, EIGRP, and the like might dictate to Router A that the preferred path to 10.1.1.0/24 is through either Router B or Router C, or both—*both* being equal-cost load balancing. The client 10.2.2.2 represents a node that is used for validating the policy-routing configuration (see "Validating Policy Routing Configuration," later in this chapter).

Now, suppose you must support the following policy on Router A:

- All traffic from subnet 10.4.4.0/24 to subnet 10.1.1.0/24 should travel over the link between Router A and Router C.

- Telnet sessions from clients in 10.2.2.0/24 to servers in 10.1.1.0/24 should also travel over the link between Router A and Router C.

- All other traffic passing through Router A to 10.1.1.0/24 should use the link between Router A and Router B.

This policy overrides the forwarding decisions determined by routing protocols. In this example, the policy covers all conceivable traffic from Router A to 10.1.1.0/24, but that does not have to be the case. When packets do not match the policy defined by a route map, the packets are forwarded normally as if the route map never existed.

To assist configuration, the policy for Router A is summarized in Table 3-2.

Table 3-1   *Policies to be Implemented on Router A in Figure 3-17*

Source	Destination	Next Hop Router
10.4.4.0/24	10.1.1.0/24	RTC
10.2.2.0/24	10.1.1.0/24 port 23 (Telnet)	RTC
All other traffic	10.1.1.0/24	RTB

Identifying the Traffic for Policy Routing

To begin the policy-routing configuration on Router A, define two access lists: one that defines the traffic that should go to Router C and another that defines the traffic that should go to Router B.

Here is the first access list:

```
access-list 101 permit ip 10.4.4.0 0.0.0.255 10.1.1.0 0.0.0.255
access-list 101 permit tcp 10.2.2.0 0.0.0.255 10.1.1.0 0.0.0.255 eq telnet
```

Access list 101 consists of two rules. The first rule matches all traffic from 10.4.4.0/24 destined to 10.1.1.0/24. The second rule matches all traffic from 10.2.2.0/24 to just the Telnet ports in 10.1.1.0/24. This access list will be used to direct traffic to Router C.

Now, here's the second access list:

```
access-list 102 permit ip 10.3.3.0 0.0.0.255 10.1.1.0 0.0.0.255
access-list 102 permit ip 10.2.2.0 0.0.0.255 10.1.1.0 0.0.0.255
```

Access list 102 consists of two rules, also. The first rule matches all traffic from 10.3.3.0/24 to 10.1.1.0/24. The second rule matches all traffic from 10.2.2.0/24 to 10.1.1.0/24. This access list will be used to direct traffic to Router B.

NOTE	Chapter 6 covers access list fundamentals and configuration.

Access list 102 matches *all* traffic from 10.2.2.0/24 to 10.1.1.0/24, including Telnet packets that are also matched by access list 101. This means for the intended policy to work, the route map must be configured to process packets against access list 101 before access list 102.

Creating the Route Map Entries

Next, create Router A's route map. The first entry of the route map forwards traffic to Router C. This coincides with the desired policy. Here's the first entry:

```
route-map MYMAP permit 20
 match ip address 101
 set ip next-hop 192.168.10.130
```

The command **route-map MYMAP permit 20** creates a route map called MYMAP with an initial entry whose sequence is 20.

The command **match ip address 101** defines the matching criteria of the entry. Here, all packets that match access list 101 are subject to the **set** commands of the entry. Recall that access list 101 encompasses the packets that need to be sent to Router C according to the policy.

The command **set ip next-hop 192.168.10.130** defines the action taken when packets meet the **match** criteria. The action is to forward the packets to neighboring Router C, whose address is 192.168.10.130 (refer to Figure 3-17).

Now, configure a second entry to MYMAP. This entry matches packets that need to be directed to Router B and sets the next hop to 192.168.10.2, Router B's address.

```
route-map MYMAP permit 40
 match ip address 102
 set ip next-hop 192.168.10.2
```

The command **route-map MYMAP permit 40** creates a second entry in MYMAP with a sequence of 40. This entry has a higher sequence number than the previous entry, **route-map MYMAP permit 20**. This means packets are checked against sequence 40, only if they do not match sequence 20. As mentioned earlier, a packet that does not match any sequence is routed normally.

The command **match ip address 102** configures the matching criteria of this entry to the rules in access list 102. Recall that access list 102 encompasses the packets that need to be sent to Router B.

The command **set ip next-hop 192.168.10.2** defines the action taken when packets meet the criteria in the **match** statement. The action is to forward the packets to Router B whose address is 192.168.10.2 (refer to Figure 3-17).

Apply the Route Map to the Proper Interface

With the route map configuration complete, all that remains is to apply the route map to an interface. Route maps do not do anything until you apply them to an interface.

When you apply a route map to an interface, the interface you select is important. Route maps inspect and process packets as they enter the router; therefore, you must apply the route map to the interface that *receives* the traffic to be policy routed.

In the example depicted in Figure 3-17, the proper place to apply MYMAP is interface Ethernet0 because that is the interface on Router A that receives the traffic requiring policy routing.

The following commands apply MYMAP to Ethernet0 on Router A:

```
interface Ethernet0
  ip address 10.3.3.1 255.255.255.0
  ip policy route-map MYMAP
  ip route-cache policy
```

The command **ip policy route-map MYMAP** applies MYMAP to interface Ethernet0. All traffic that enters Router A through this interface is subject to the policies defined in MYMAP.

The command **ip route-cache policy** enables a feature called *fast-switched policy routing*. This feature, available in IOS 11.3 and later, substantially increases the performance of policy routing by caching information so the CPU doesn't have to process every policy-routed packet.

Validating Policy-Routing Configuration

According to the policy, in the example in Figure 3-17, Telnet packets from 10.2.2.0/24 to 10.1.1.0/24 should go over the link between Router A and Router C, but all other traffic from 10.2.2.0/24 to 10.1.1.0/24 should go over the link between Router A and Router B. To test that the route map is indeed making this happen, you can initiate a Telnet session from a client on 10.2.2.0/24 to a server on 10.1.1.0/24. This client is depicted in Figure 3-17 with the address 10.2.2.2.

After you successfully establish the Telnet session, use the command **show ip cache policy** to verify policy routing:

```
RTA#sh ip cac pol
Total adds 1, total deletes 0

Type Routemap/sequence     Age       Interface      Next Hop
NH   MYMAP/20              00:00:04  Serial0        192.168.10.130
```

The preceding output shows one entry in the policy-routing cache. The following list explains the data:

- **NH** stands for next hop. This means the route map is forwarding in response to the **set ip next-hop** command. The other possible keyword in the **Type** column is **Int**, which indicates forwarding by the **set interface** command (see "Other Policy-Routing Commands," later in this chapter).

- **MYMAP/20** is the name of the route map and the sequence number of the route map entry.

- **00:00:04** is the age of the cache entry. Four seconds ago, a packet matched the policy defined by MYMAP's sequence number 20 and caused the router to create an entry in the policy-routing cache. Only the first packet creates the entry and starts the timer. Subsequent packets that match MYMAP sequence 20 are cache hits and do not restart the timer.

- **Serial0** is the output interface for the policy-routed packets.

- **192.168.10.130** is the address of the next hop router (Router C).

NOTE

The command **show ip cache policy** works only when you configure fast-switched policy routing with the **ip route-cache policy** interface command.

The preceding data is a good indication that policy routing is working as expected. An additional test is to have the client 10.2.2.2 send non-Telnet packets—for example, ping packets—to 10.1.1.0/24. According to the policy defined by MYMAP, such packets are forwarded to Router B (192.168.10.2).

After 10.2.2.2 issues the pings, check the policy-routing cache again:

```
RTA#sh ip cac pol
Total adds 2, total deletes 0

Type Routemap/sequence    Age       Interface    Next Hop
NH   MYMAP/20             00:18:32  Serial0      192.168.10.130
NH   MYMAP/40             00:00:27  Serial1      192.168.10.2
```

The last line in the preceding output indicates that the other entry in MYMAP, sequence 40, is actively forwarding packets to Router B, whose address is 192.168.10.2.

Another way of verifying policy routing is to watch the flow of packets through the router with packet-level debugging. This proves to be a more definitive test than checking the policy-routing cache but requires that you disable fast-switched policy routing.

Before you enable packet-level debugging with the **debug ip packet** command, you should create a simple access list that filters the debugging down to the specific source you are interested in watching. Otherwise, you might overload the router with too many debugging messages.

To watch packets sourced by 10.2.2.2, create an access list on Router A that permits only source address 10.2.2.2 (refer to Figure 3-17):

```
RTA#conf t
RTA(config)#access-list 10 permit 10.2.2.2
```

Next, disable fast-switched policy routing on the interface. This forces the router's CPU to examine every packet during policy routing so that debug messages per packet are displayed.

```
RTA(config)#int e0
RTA(config-if)#no ip route-cache policy
RTA(config-if)#end
```

Then, enable packet-level debugging with access list 10 as the filter:

```
RTA#deb ip packet detail 10
IP packet debugging is on (detailed) for access list 10
```

Have the client 10.2.2.2 initiate a Telnet connection to 10.1.1.1 and watch the router's debugging messages:

```
IP: s=10.2.2.2 (Ethernet0), d=10.1.1.1 (Serial0), g=192.168.10.130, len 44, forward
    TCP src=1025, dst=23, seq=3268019581, ack=0, win=512 SYN
IP: s=10.2.2.2 (Ethernet0), d=10.1.1.1 (Serial0), g=192.168.10.130, len 40, forward
    TCP src=1025, dst=23, seq=3268019582, ack=2048489389, win=32120 ACK
IP: s=10.2.2.2 (Ethernet0), d=10.1.1.1 (Serial0), g=192.168.10.130, len 64, forward
    TCP src=1025, dst=23, seq=3268019582, ack=2048489389, win=32248 ACK PSH
IP: s=10.2.2.2 (Ethernet0), d=10.1.1.1 (Serial0), g=192.168.10.130, len 52, forward
    TCP src=1025, dst=23, seq=3268019606, ack=2048489407, win=32248 ACK PSH
```

The preceding debugging output confirms that Router A is properly forwarding Telnet packets from 10.2.2.2 to 10.1.1.1. That is, policy routing is sending those packets to the next-hop router 192.168.10.130 (Router C). This agrees with the policy defined by entry 20 in MYMAP. The next-hop address is highlighted in boldface and has the output **g=192.168.10.130**. The output **dst=23** confirms that the packets belong to Telnet.

When the same client does a ping to 10.1.1.1, the following debugging messages appear:

```
RTA#
IP: s=10.2.2.2 (Ethernet0), d=10.1.1.1 (Serial1), g=192.168.10.2, len 84, forward
    ICMP type=8, code=0
IP: s=10.2.2.2 (Ethernet0), d=10.1.1.1 (Serial1), g=192.168.10.2, len 84, forward
    ICMP type=8, code=0
IP: s=10.2.2.2 (Ethernet0), d=10.1.1.1 (Serial1), g=192.168.10.2, len 84, forward
    ICMP type=8, code=0
```

```
IP: s=10.2.2.2 (Ethernet0), d=10.1.1.1 (Serial1), g=192.168.10.2, len 84, forward
    ICMP type=8, code=0
IP: s=10.2.2.2 (Ethernet0), d=10.1.1.1 (Serial1), g=192.168.10.2, len 84, forward
    ICMP type=8, code=0
```

The preceding output confirms that Router A is properly forwarding non-Telnet packets from 10.2.2.2 to 10.1.1.1. The output **g=192.168.10.2** (highlighted in boldface) indicates that the next-hop router is 192.168.10.2, Router B. This agrees with the policy defined by entry 40 in MYMAP. The output **ICMP** confirms that the packets are ping packets.

Classifying Packets with Route Maps

In addition to directing traffic over certain paths, policy routing can also classify or mark packets with a user-defined quality of service (QoS). This is accomplished with route maps that set the IP precedence value in packets as they enter the router. QoS mechanisms in the router and in the rest of the network can then read the precedence value of a packet and prioritize it relative to other packets. For a complete discussion on QoS and IP precedence, see Chapter 4.

NOTE   Another IOS service, Committed Access Rate (CAR), also classifies packets by setting IP precedence values. CAR is covered in Chapter 5.

Route maps that classify traffic are just like the route maps covered previously in the "Forwarding Traffic with Route Maps" section except they implement the command **set ip precedence** instead of the command **set ip next-hop**. The following is an example:

```
interface Ethernet0
 ip address 10.2.2.1 255.255.255.0
 ip policy route-map QOSMAP
 ip route-cache policy
!
route-map QOSMAP permit 20
 match ip address 101
 set ip precedence critical
!
route-map QOSMAP permit 40
 match ip address 102
 set ip precedence flash
```

In the preceding configuration, the command **ip policy route-map QOSMAP** applies the route map called QOSMAP to interface Ethernet0. As mentioned previously, route maps inspect and apply policies to packets as they enter the router; therefore, route maps must be applied to the interface that receives the packets to be classified. In other words, route maps set precedence as packets enter the router.

The command **ip route-cache policy** enables fast-switched policy routing on the interface. See "Apply the Route Map to the Proper Interface" earlier in this chapter for more on fast-switched policy routing.

The command **route-map QOSMAP permit 20** defines the first entry in the route map named QOSMAP. The following are the subcommands that define the match-set criteria of this entry:

- **match ip address 101**: This is the matching criteria of entry 20. Packets that match access list 101 are subject to the **set** commands of the entry.

- **set ip precedence critical**: This defines the action taken when packets meet the **match** criteria. The action is to set the precedence value in the packet to **critical**, which is equivalent to decimal value 5.

Similarly, the command **route-map QOSMAP permit 40** defines the second and final entry in the route map. In this entry, the matching criteria are defined by access list 102 and the action is to set the precedence of the matching packets to **flash** (decimal value 3).

When you issue the **set ip precedence** command, you can specify precedence values by name or by decimal value—if you specify the decimal value, IOS automatically converts it to the name when you view the configuration. To see a mapping of names to decimal values, use the context-level help feature built into IOS, like this:

```
RTA(config-route-map)#set ip precedence ?
  <0-7>           Precedence value
  critical        Set critical precedence (5)
  flash           Set flash precedence (3)
  flash-override  Set flash override precedence (4)
  immediate       Set immediate precedence (2)
  internet        Set internetwork control precedence (6)
  network         Set network control precedence (7)
  priority        Set priority precedence (1)
  routine         Set routine precedence (0)
```

The preceding output displays a list of precedence levels by name, with their decimal values shown in parentheses.

NOTE   It is highly recommended that you avoid using precedence levels 6 and 7. These are reserved for network control packets such as those belonging to routing protocols. This leaves you with six user-definable precedence levels, 0 through 5.

Setting Next-Hop and Precedence in Tandem

If needed, you can create route map entries that combine the two **set** operations, **set ip next-hop** and **set ip precedence**. The following is an example:

```
route-map COMBO permit 20
 match ip address 103
 set ip precedence critical
 set ip next-hop 192.168.10.130
```

The preceding entry for route map COMBO applies two **set** operations to the packets matching access list 103: The router sets the precedence to **critical** (decimal 5) and then forwards the packets to next-hop router 192.168.10.130.

Other Policy-Routing Commands

The following is a list of other match and set statements for policy routing:

- **match length** *min max*—Matches the length (in bytes) of the packet instead of using an access list. The parameters *min* and *max* specify the minimum and maximum length criteria.

- **set interface** *type number* [*...type number*]—Tells the router where to output the packets meeting the matching criteria. Instead of specifying a next-hop address, this specifies an exit interface on the router (**Serial0**, for example).

- **set default interface** *type number* [*...type number*]—Routes to the interface specified by this **set** command only if there is no explicit route for the destination address in the routing table. Use this to provide an alternate default route for packets meeting the match criteria.

- **set ip default next-hop** *ip-address* [*...ip-address*]—Routes to the next-hop address specified by this **set** command only if there is no explicit route for the destination address in the routing table. Use this to provide an alternate default route for packets meeting the match criteria.

- **set ip tos** *type-of-service*—Sets the type of service (ToS) bits instead of IP precedence.

TIP   When using the **match length** command, ensure that routing protocol packets are not accidentally policy routed to the wrong neighboring routers. Otherwise, routing adjacency problems might occur.

By default, packets that are generated by the router are not policy routed. To change this, issue the global command **ip local policy route-map**, like this:

```
RTA(config)#ip local policy route-map TESTMAP
```

where the keyword **TESTMAP** in the preceding command identifies the route map to use for policy routing locally generated packets.

Summary

As you extend, enhance, and optimize the capabilities of your network, you must deal with the crucial function of routing. This chapter covered some important routing services that help you manage network scalability, complexity, and stability. These services (and your mastery of them) directly impact the number of users and locations you can support, your ability to integrate new networks and topologies, and the stability of the network as it expands.

The following are the key concepts of this chapter:

- A passive interface is an interface on which you deliberately suppress the advertising of routing updates. Use the **passive-interface** command to make an interface passive.

- Route filters give you granular control over the routes sent and received by your router. To filter routes, use access lists and the **distribute-list** router config mode command.

- Redistribution is a service that allows the sharing of routes across different routing domains—for example, between RIP and OSPF. It transfers routes between distinct domains and makes connectivity possible across them. Enable this service with the **redistribute** router config mode command.

- When redistributing routes into OSPF, don't forget to use the **subnets** keyword if you need to redistribute both major nets and their subnets.

- The **administrative distance** is a priority assigned to a route based on its routing protocol. A route with a lower administrative distance is preferred over a route with a higher administrative distance.

- To prevent route feedback caused by mutual redistribution, you should always control redistribution with route filters.

- Although classful routing protocols do not support VLSM, sometimes you are forced to redistribute from a classless domain into a classful one, and routes might be lost in the process. As a workaround, you might be able to originate and redistribute static routes that are agreeable to the classful domain.

- A **default route** is a special route that tells the router how to reach unknown destinations. How you originate and propagate a default route depends on the routing protocol.

- Be careful when you configure a default route on a RIP router. RIP automatically advertises the default route out all RIP-enabled interfaces. Watch out for accidental propagation of default routes on the network.

- When you use a default route to reach a subnet of a connected major net, you must ensure that the router is configured with the **ip classless** global config command.

- EIGRP and OSPF support route summarization: the consolidation of multiple contiguous routes into a single generalized route to promote efficient and stable routing.

- EIGRP automatically summarizes across major net boundaries. When you deploy discontiguous subnets, you might have to disable EIGRP auto-summarization.

- Use the **ip summary-address** interface command to configure EIGRP route summarization.

- To summarize OSPF routes between areas, use the **area range** router config mode command. To summarize routes as they are redistributed into OSPF, use the **summary-address** router config mode command.

- Policy routing allows you to override normal forwarding decisions with route maps. Route maps are built of one or more entries that are created with the **route-map** global config command. Each entry contains **match** and **set** statements that define the routing policy.

- You can also use policy routing to set IP precedence and classify packets for QoS.

CHAPTER 4

Deploying Basic Quality of Service Features

An effective network provides more than just connectivity between endpoints. As you add applications and leverage the convenience of networking, your network must be intelligent enough to recognize and prioritize mission-critical and delay-sensitive traffic. This ability to deliver data based on such policies as importance and time is called the *quality of service* (QoS) capability of the network.

This chapter explains basic QoS principles and the configuration of IOS queuing services that deliver QoS. These are the main topics of this chapter:

- The Case for QoS
- Queuing in a Router
- Priority Queuing
- Custom Queuing
- Understanding IP Precedence
- Weighted Fair Queuing

The Case for QoS

The network serves a wide range of applications for your organization—many more applications than the mere file and printer sharing of the past. In addition to standard IP traffic such as web (HTTP), File Transfer Protocol (FTP), Telnet, and Simple Mail Transfer Protocol (SMTP), networks are carrying:

- **Real-time, mission-critical corporate data**—financial transactions, customer orders, warehouse and shipping records, manufacturing statistics and control data, research and development CAD/code files, and so on

- **Delay-sensitive data**—interactive applications such as server and mainframe logins, packetized voice, video conferences, and data collaboration such as electronic whiteboard and client GUI sharing

- **Bulk data transfers**—system backups, overnight data synchronization and delivery

- **Unknown data**—Uncontrolled or unknown traffic such as user-initiated applications (networked games and shareware, for example)

Despite the broad range of users and applications, many networks give equal access to all users and the same delivery priority to all applications. They do not inspect or care about the contents of the data.

With an ever-increasing number of new applications on the network, the idea of equal priority to all applications becomes a problem. The problem is that applications *vary* by how they use the network, how they behave during network congestion, and how important they are to your organization.

Not all applications are equal. Applications that are mission-critical to your organization deserve preferential and speedy delivery. Some applications may be delay-sensitive and need low delay through the network in order to function properly. Yet other applications may be low priority and should yield network resources to high-priority applications.

After all, your network is a valuable resource that is shared and finite in capacity.

A network that can vary performance based on application type is said to have classes, or *qualities of service*. A QoS is a grade of performance the network provides and differentiates from other grades of performance in the network. A high QoS provides faster delivery and less delay than a low QoS. By assigning applications to different QoS levels, you can vary the performance of applications to reflect your organization's objectives.

NOTE   The actual number of QoS levels you can use depends on the underlying network and queuing technology. Because the focus of this book is on IOS, the sections that follow in this chapter and Chapter 5, "Deploying Advanced Quality of Service Features," explain the QoS levels available in IOS services.

Organizations consider many factors when defining the QoS for an application. The most common criteria are as follows:

- **Mission-critical versus non–mission-critical**—Does this application directly affect my organization's profits and sales? How will my customers perceive the delays in this application, and what is the impact? Does this application affect how quickly I can bring my product to market?

- **Delay-sensitive versus delay-insensitive**—How easily does the user of the application perceive delay? Even if an application is not mission-critical, it may require minimal delay because a human is interacting with it in real time. Login applications such as Telnet are delay-sensitive because typing is difficult when there is a perceptible delay between keystrokes and the display of those keystrokes. On the other hand, non-interactive applications (such as file system backup or FTP) may be triggered and completed with minimal or no user intervention.

Applications such as voice and video over IP are delay-sensitive. These applications need consistent, predictable bandwidth and low delay; otherwise, the transmission may appear garbled or choppy. This does not necessarily mean that *all* users of voice and video should be given high priority, as it might be desirable to set policies (in conjunction with QoS) to limit these applications to certain users.

- **Political versus apolitical**—Whose data is this? What users should get better service from the network?

Cisco offers several IOS services for delivering QoS. As we cover each service in the following sections, keep in mind that each service has its own behavior, purpose, and place in the network. It is not enough to know how to configure these services, but rather, to know how they work, when they might be needed, and where they should be placed in the network. This is covered in the following sections as well as in Chapter 5.

Queuing in a Router

Queuing is used by a router to hold outbound packets when a communications link is congested. When a router receives and processes packets faster than the output link can handle, it temporarily stores those packets in a *queue* (a block of router memory) assigned to the output interface. After the congestion clears, the router removes packets from the queue and sends them out the interface.

How does congestion happen? If the speed of the output link is slower than the traffic coming into the router, there is certain to be a traffic jam of packets because data is coming in faster than it can exit. (The speed of a link is known as its *bandwidth*.) This is analogous to pouring water through a funnel. When you pour slowly, the amount of water going in is equal to the amount exiting, so the funnel does not fill up. However, when you pour quickly and the amount of water entering *exceeds* the amount exiting, there is congestion at the drain, so the water queues (fills up) in the funnel.

NOTE   Queuing a packet is generally more desirable than dropping it (the alternative) because queuing saves the client from having to retransmit the packet.

Dropping a packet means to discard it, or simply throw it away. In certain situations, it is necessary, even desirable, to drop packets from a queue. Random Early Detection (RED), covered in Chapter 5, is an example of a QoS drop strategy.

First-In, First-Out Queuing

When the router removes the oldest packet in the queue first, it's called *first-in, first-out (FIFO) queuing*. FIFO is the most basic form of queuing. It does not offer multiple levels of QoS and is illustrated in Figure 4-1.

Figure 4-1 *FIFO Queuing Is the Most Basic Form of Queuing*

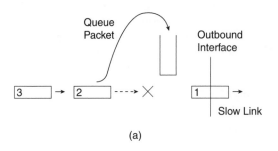

(a)

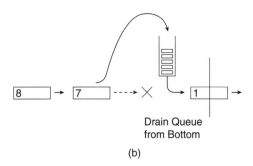

(b)

The first half of Figure 4-1 depicts a situation where the outbound link is congested: Packet 1 is only midway through the Outbound Interface. Another packet, Packet 2, arrives and needs to go out of the interface. Instead of dropping the packet because the outbound interface is congested, the router puts it in the queue so that it can be dispatched after Packet 1 passes through the link. You can think of the queue as a container that temporarily stores packets that are headed out the interface.

NOTE   The time it takes for a packet to pass through an interface is called the *serialization delay.*

The second half of Figure 4-1 depicts a traffic burst situation. That means the rate of packets into the router and processed by the router exceeds the bandwidth of the outbound link. The link is congested and packets are piling up in the queue. Because this is a FIFO queue, the packets are drained from the queue in the order they were placed into the queue. The packets are stacked in the queue so that the oldest packet in the queue is at the bottom.

NOTE   If the burst of packets is too big, it's possible for the queue to fill to its maximum capacity. When this happens, the router drops subsequent packets until there's more room in the queue. This is called a *tail drop condition*. In a well-designed network this should not happen often; if it does, you should investigate the activity and the type of traffic entering the router. Should your investigation prove that nothing is amiss, you may have to control the traffic sources or increase the bandwidth of the output link so that packets can drain from the queue at a faster rate.

FIFO: An Example

Figure 4-2 shows a sample network with a router forwarding packets from two LANs out to a WAN link.

Figure 4-2   *Traffic from LANs May Saturate and Congest Low Bandwidth WAN Links*

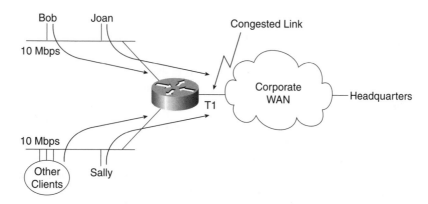

This illustration shows various clients—Bob, Joan, Sally, and Other Clients—attached to the LAN interfaces of a router. There is significantly less bandwidth on the T1 (1.544 Mbps) WAN link than on the 10 Mbps Ethernet LAN links. If there is a significant amount of traffic generated by the clients that's destined to go out the WAN link (as is common in many branch offices), the link can easily fill to its maximum capacity. This congestion triggers the router to queue packets and delay the packets for delivery.

A snapshot in time of the queue for the outbound T1 interface might look something like Figure 4-3.

Figure 4-3   *FIFO Queuing May Cause Undesirable Delays for Some Applications*

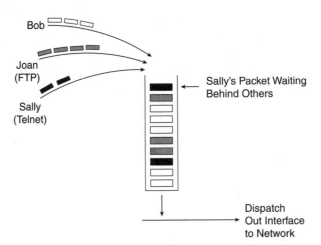

Figure 4-3 shows some packets belonging to Bob, Joan, and Sally sitting in a FIFO queue as more packets from those three are being added to the queue. Although Figure 4-3 shows all packets as the same size (for simplicity), this is probably not the case—Joan's packets are from an FTP transfer and, thus, are probably larger (in bytes) than packets from Sally's Telnet session.

With a FIFO queue on the outbound interface, as shown in Figure 4-1, packets are dispatched on a first-come, first-served basis. As such, Sally's packets (though smaller and fewer in number) will have to wait behind packets from Joan and the other clients. If Sally's packets have to wait too long, Sally will notice delays in her Telnet session. And if this happens too often, Sally may find the application too frustrating to work with and render the application unusable.

Priority Queuing

By using *priority queuing* instead of FIFO queuing, you can configure the router to dispatch packets at different priorities based on a flexible criteria scheme.

Under priority queuing, the router dispatches packets defined with high priority before packets defined with lower priorities. This only happens when the outbound interface is congested and packets need to be queued. When there is no congestion, the router simply forwards packets as fast as it can process them regardless of priority level (for there is no need to purposely delay a packet if the outbound link is not congested).

Also, priority queuing and custom queuing (which is covered later in this chapter) are designed to prioritize traffic on low bandwidth WAN links—not high-speed WAN or LAN links. This is because priority queuing and custom queuing are overhead tasks that can adversely impact the router's CPU at high speeds. Depending on the model of your router, links lower than 1 Mbps or lower than 512 kbps may be good candidates for this service.

NOTE   Some QoS services, such as weighted fair queuing (WFQ), can run on Versatile Interface Processor (VIP) modules for the 7500 family of routers. This distributed form of QoS processing does not negatively impact the main CPU of the router. (For more information, see the "Weighted Fair Queuing" section later in this chapter.)

This section covers:

- Queuing and Classifying Packets with Priority Queuing
- Priority Queuing Strategy
- Configuring Priority Queuing
- Verifying the Priority Queuing Configuration
- Adjusting the Queue Size in Priority Queuing

Queuing and Classifying Packets with Priority Queuing

In priority queuing, there are four queues per interface:

- High-priority queue
- Medium-priority queue
- Normal-priority queue
- Low-priority queue

Figure 4-4 illustrates the mechanics of priority queuing on a router's interface.

Figure 4-4   *With Priority Queuing, the Router Classifies Packets into Four Distinct QoS Levels*

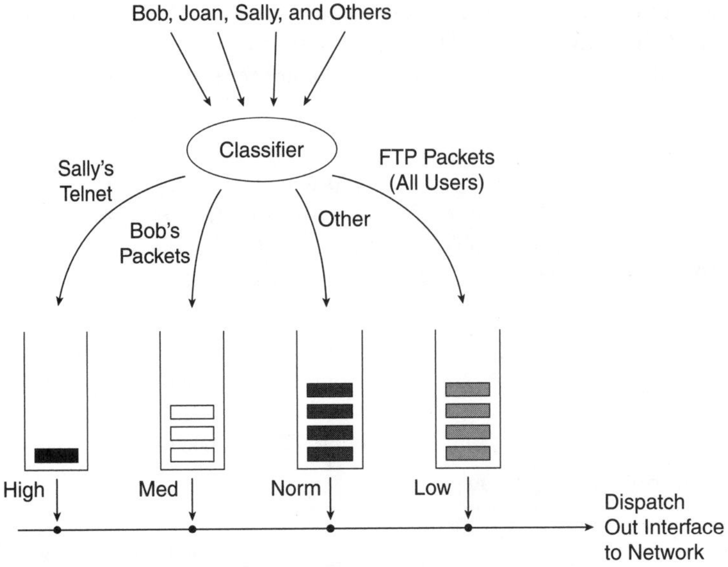

The classifier is a software task on the router that categorizes or (preferably) *classifies* packets into one of four QoS levels (high, medium, normal, or low) based on user-defined criteria. Once the router has identified the proper QoS for a packet, it places the packet in the appropriate queue of the outbound interface. (If the queue happens to be full, the router drops the packet.)

In Figure 4-4, the router is configured to put Sally's Telnet traffic in the high queue, Bob's traffic in the medium queue, FTP traffic from all users in the low queue, and all other traffic in the normal queue.

NOTE   The normal queue is always the default queue. Any packets the router cannot classify and assign to a specific queue are placed into this queue.

You can configure the router to classify the packets based on several criteria:

- Packet size in bytes
- TCP or UDP port number
- Interface the packet arrived on
- Whether the packet is an IP fragment

- Anything that can be described by a standard or extended access list (source/destination IP address, TCP/UDP port number, IP precedence value, and so on)
- Non-IP traffic (IPX and AppleTalk, for example)
- Any packets that do not match the defined criteria (a default catchall)

See "Configuring Priority Queuing" later in this section for information on how to apply these criteria.

Priority Queuing Strategy

The strategy used to drain the queues and dispatch the packets to the outbound interface is the following: Always drain the high-priority queue before the medium-priority queue, the medium-priority queue before the normal-priority queue, and the normal-priority queue before the low-priority queue. This means, as long as there is a packet in the high-priority queue, the medium-priority queue (and lower queues) cannot drain. Likewise, as long as there is a packet in the medium-priority queue, the normal-priority queue (and low-priority queue) cannot drain.

NOTE   Or to put it another way, the medium-priority queue can drain only when the high-priority queue is empty. If a new packet enters the high-priority queue, service to the medium-priority queue stops and the high-priority queue is serviced again until it is empty. The router applies the same rule when it compares the medium-priority queue to the normal-priority queue, and the normal-priority queue to the low-priority queue.

As you can see, priority queuing is a strict guarantee that the router will always service high-priority packets before other packets. Keep in mind that the policy is so strict that it is possible for lower queues to be denied service for long periods of time when there is a constant, steady stream of high-priority traffic.

When the lower queues are denied service for an undesirable length of time, it's called *queue starvation*. Thus, it is important that you carefully monitor the service of lower-priority traffic and its applications when deploying priority queuing. "Custom Queuing," a section later in this chapter, introduces another queuing strategy that avoids queue starvation.

NOTE   The possibility of queue starvation doesn't mean you should dismiss priority queuing as a viable service. Your policies and applications may require a strict queuing policy that priority queuing provides. As long as your high-priority applications provide enough quiet intervals for lower queues to drain, the service can serve those very important packets and still provide acceptable performance for other traffic.

Configuring Priority Queuing

Configuring priority queuing starts by defining a *priority list* with the priority level for each type of packet you wish to classify. For example, you could configure a list like this:

```
priority-list 1 protocol ip medium list 101
priority-list 1 protocol ip high tcp telnet
priority-list 1 interface Ethernet0 low
priority-list 1 default normal
```

The preceding lines are all global configuration commands. See Appendix E, "A Crash Course in Cisco IOS," for more information about global configuration mode and other router modes.

The command **priority-list 1 protocol ip medium list 101** tells the router to classify packets that match extended-access list 101 as medium-priority traffic.

The command **priority-list 1 protocol ip high tcp telnet** tells the router to classify Telnet packets as high-priority traffic.

The command **priority-list 1 interface Ethernet0 low** tells the router to classify packets that arrive on the Ethernet0 interface as low-priority traffic.

The command **priority-list 1 default normal** is a catchall rule that tells the router to classify packets that do not match any of the preceding rules as normal-priority traffic. (This is the default.)

As you add new classification rules to the priority list, they are placed at the bottom of the list. During classification, the router compares packets to the list starting with the first classification rule; and if there is a match, it places the packet in the appropriate queue. If the packet does not match the first rule, the next rule in the list is compared, and so on. The last rule in the list is always the default catchall. (If you do not configure this, the default is to use the normal queue.) Note that the last line in the preceding example may not be displayed when you issue the **show running-config** command, because it is the IOS default.

After a priority list is defined, you must assign it to an interface to activate priority queuing. The following example assigns priority list number 1 to interface Serial1:

```
interface Serial1
 priority-group 1
```

NOTE   The priority list is a simple table of QoS rules. The router won't do any priority queuing of outbound traffic until you bind that list to an interface with the **priority-group** command.

Verifying the Priority Queuing Configuration

To verify that priority queuing is enabled, issue the **show queuing priority** and **show interfaces** commands.

The following sample output validates the rules in priority list 1 and confirms the list is active on Serial1. The output, **high 0/20/0**, tells you information about the high priority queue. The three numbers between the slashes tell you that there are no packets currently in the high queue, the high queue can hold a maximum of 20 packets, and no packets have been dropped from the high queue since the counters were last reset (that is, the last reboot or the last issuing of the **clear counters** command).

```
2503#sh queuing pri
Current priority queue configuration:

List   Queue  Args
1      medium protocol ip         list 101
1      high   protocol ip         tcp port telnet
1      low    interface Ethernet0

2503#sh int s1
Serial1 is up, line protocol is up
  Hardware is HD64570
  Internet address is 192.168.1.2/24
  MTU 1500 bytes, BW 2000 Kbit, DLY 20000 usec, rely 255/255, load 1/255
  Encapsulation HDLC, loopback not set, keepalive set (10 sec)
  Last input 00:00:06, output 00:00:06, output hang never
  Last clearing of "show interface" counters 1d03h
  Input queue: 0/75/0 (size/max/drops); Total output drops: 0
  Queuing strategy: priority-list 1
  Output queue: high 0/20/0, medium 0/40/0, normal 0/60/0, low 0/80/0
  30 second input rate 0 bits/sec, 0 packets/sec
  30 second output rate 0 bits/sec, 0 packets/sec
     41434 packets input, 8446024 bytes, 0 no buffer
     Received 15069 broadcasts, 0 runts, 0 giants, 0 throttles
     0 input errors, 0 CRC, 0 frame, 0 overrun, 0 ignored, 0 abort
     32492 packets output, 15305170 bytes, 0 underruns
     0 output errors, 0 collisions, 0 interface resets
     0 output buffer failures, 0 output buffers swapped out
     0 carrier transitions
     DCD=up  DSR=up  DTR=up  RTS=up  CTS=up
```

Adjusting the Queue Sizes in Priority Queuing

If you need to adjust the depth of a queue (the maximum number of packets that can be held in a queue), configure the list with the **priority-list queue-limit** command:

```
priority-list 1 queue-limit 20 50 70 85
```

The preceding global command sets the depth of the high, medium, normal, and low queues of list 1 to 20, 50, 70, and 85 packets, respectively.

When should you adjust the depth of a queue? In general, try to avoid changing the Cisco defaults for the queue depths, especially if priority queuing is working to your satisfaction. That is, the service is providing enhanced performance for your high-priority applications and acceptable performance for other applications.

Depending on many factors (such as your mix of applications, your queuing criteria, the speed of the link, the load on the network, and so on), some queues may fill to their maximum capacity and drop packets. Either an occasional burst or a constant flow of high-priority traffic could cause this. As mentioned earlier, you can find the drop statistics in the output of the **show interfaces** command.

If the lower queues drop packets at a continuous rate, it's a good sign that you have a constant flow of high-priority traffic monopolizing the link. In such a case, increasing the size of the lower priority queues might not remedy the problem. Extra-large queues might also fill up (they just take a little longer). The approach, then, is to reengineer your priority queuing list so fewer packets flow through the high-priority queue or to try a different queuing service, such as custom queuing (see the section "Custom Queuing" later in this chapter).

If a lower queue needs only a little more headroom so that it can endure the occasional burst of high-priority packets, then increasing the queue depth slightly (by 5 to 10 packets, for example) may help.

In general, *tune* the queue depths and avoid creating huge, deep queues. Deep queues may hold packets for excessive lengths of time and adversely affect applications.

Priority queuing is generally a good fit for those locations requiring just two levels of QoS: a high QoS for just a few mission-critical applications and a normal QoS for all the other traffic. You can scale to more levels of QoS and more high-priority applications as your traffic flows dictate. There is no hard-and-fast rule. It depends on how much traffic your high-priority applications generate and how much delay the lower-priority applications can tolerate. A good approach is to start with a simple QoS policy and add to it as your environment allows. Finally, seeking consultative advice from Cisco is always an option.

Custom Queuing

Custom queuing differs from priority queuing in the following ways:

- In custom queuing, you can define up to 16 queues per interface. You are not limited to 4 queues as you are with priority queuing.

- Instead of naming the queues (*high*, *medium*, *normal*, and *low*), custom queuing simply numbers the queues from 1 to 16.

- Custom queuing is not as strict as priority queuing and is less prone to queue starvation problems.

Although Cisco IOS does let you configure 16 queues, it is probably too much micro-management to do this in practice and make everything work well. Try to configure only as many queues as you need to meet your QoS objective. This will simplify the classification criteria and improve network performance.

The biggest difference between custom and priority queuing is how they service their queues. As mentioned earlier, queue starvation in priority queuing may occur when the high-priority queue contains one or more packets for long periods of time. However, unlike priority queuing, custom queuing serves each queue in a *round-robin fashion*. This means the router serves each queue one-by-one, draining a configurable number of bytes from each queue. After the last queue is served, the cycle repeats, starting again with the first queue. This prevents one queue from monopolizing the link while the other queues starve. Of course, the trade-off is a less strict queuing policy and, possibly, lower performance for high-priority applications as compared to priority queuing.

Figure 4-5 illustrates the operation of custom queuing. As in priority queuing, a classifier sorts packets based on a user-defined profile and places them into the appropriate queue. High-priority queues are allowed to drain more bytes per cycle than lower-priority queues. (The amounts are user-defined.) Thus, each queue is allotted a share of the bandwidth on the link.

Figure 4-5   *Custom Queuing Drains a Configurable Number of Bytes from Each Queue per Round-Robin Cycle*

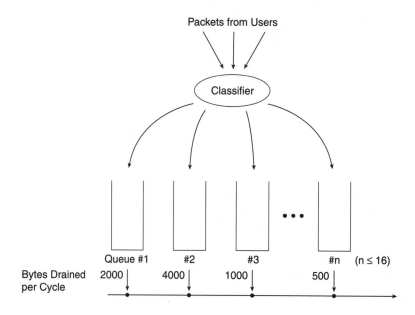

The same criteria (packet size, TCP/UDP port number, access list, and so on) used in priority queuing to classify packets can be used in custom queuing. Much like the priority queuing configuration, you create a classification list and subsequently assign it to an interface.

NOTE   Custom queuing, like priority queuing, is most effective on low-speed WAN links where delay and contention for bandwidth are issues. Depending on the model of your router, links lower than 1 Mbps or lower than 512 kbps may be good candidates for this service.

This section covers:

- Configuring Custom Queuing
- Verifying the Custom Queuing Configuration
- Adjusting the Queue Size in Custom Queuing

Configuring Custom Queuing

To configure custom queuing, you use the **queue-list** command at the global configuration prompt. Here is a portion of a configuration from a sample router configured with custom queuing:

```
queue-list 5 protocol ip 1 list 101
queue-list 5 protocol ip 2 tcp telnet
queue-list 5 protocol ip 3
queue-list 5 interface Ethernet0 4
queue-list 5 default 3
```

This configuration defines a custom queue list 5 with four queues numbered 1 through 4. Packets matching extended-access list 101 are placed in queue 1. Telnet packets are placed in queue 2. IP packets, other than those matching access list 101 and Telnet, are placed in queue 3. Packets arriving on interface Ethernet0 are placed in queue 4. And finally, traffic not matching any of the preceding criteria is placed in queue 3 (along with the general IP traffic defined in the third line, which is also using queue 3).

NOTE   If you do not configure a default catchall queue as shown in the preceding example, the router will use queue 1 as the default queue.

As with priority queuing, the classification rules are checked in order. When a match is made, the packet is placed in the appropriate queue.

Without further configuration, all four queues in the example have an equal number of bytes that they are allowed to drain per cycle (a default of 1500 bytes per cycle).

Defining a Queue's QoS

After you define the packet types and the queues they go into, you need to configure the number of bytes that the router may drain from each queue per round-robin cycle. This is where you define the QoS for each queue:

```
queue-list 5 queue 1 byte-count 1000
queue-list 5 queue 2 byte-count 2000
queue-list 5 queue 3 byte-count 4000
queue-list 5 queue 4 byte-count 500
```

In the preceding lines, we have configured the router to drain 4,000 bytes from queue 3 per cycle—twice the number of bytes that the router will drain from queue 2 per cycle. Thus, users who are serviced by queue 3 will experience roughly twice as much bandwidth as users who are serviced by queue 2. (You can apply the same logic to the service the router will provide to the other queues.) It's roughly twice as much, because the router doesn't enforce a strict policy that it will drain *exactly* 4,000 bytes from queue 3 each cycle. If the 4,000[th] byte is in the middle of a packet, the router will proceed to drain more than 4,000 bytes so that it can drain (and subsequently transmit) a whole packet. It's important to keep this rule in mind, because if you make byte-counts too small (such that they are less than the size of the packets), only one packet per cycle will be serviced from the queues. This could lead to undesirable QoS on the network.

It is usually undesirable to make the byte-count values very large as well. If the router spends a long time draining lots of bytes from each queue before proceeding to the next queue, it can take a long time for the round-robin cycle to complete. This could cause an irregular pattern of bursts when a queue is serviced followed by a long period of no service as a queue waits for its next turn.

Defining Byte-Count Values

What should your byte-count values be? There are no hard and fast rules for byte-count values because it depends on many factors such as the average packet size for each application, the performance you are trying to achieve for each application, the number of queues you are using, and so on. A reasonable plan is to allow the lowest-priority queue to transmit a few, perhaps 2 to 4, *packets* (not bytes!) per cycle and scale the higher-priority queues up from there. The approach looks something like this:

- Do some basic traffic analysis, and find the average packet size of the low-priority traffic.

- Multiply the packet size by the number of packets (2 to 4) to transmit each cycle. The result is your byte-count value for the low-priority queue.

- For a higher-priority queue, determine how many bytes need to be transmitted in relation to the low-priority queue to achieve the target QoS. For example, if a queue should have twice as much bandwidth as the low queue, multiply the low queue's byte-count by 2. The result is the byte-count for the higher-priority queue.

- Apply the custom queue list to the intended interface, observe the applications, and tune the configuration as needed.

In general, avoid making the byte-count values huge in comparison to the packet sizes. For example, avoid making the byte counts of three queues 15,000 bytes, 20,000 bytes, and 30,000 bytes if the packet sizes are around 500 bytes. Also, try not to use too many queues, but just enough queues to define the QoS you need.

These guidelines should work for most cases. However, it's best to understand the mechanics of custom queuing in combination with your traffic and QoS policy to determine the right formula for your particular situation. Also, consider getting Cisco involved to look at your particular case.

Look again at the previous example and the byte-count values configured for each queue. Queue 4 holds the lowest-priority traffic. Although this queue is drained at only 500 bytes per cycle, it is nonetheless guaranteed *some* service each cycle and, therefore, is not at risk of queue starvation. This demonstrates the fundamental difference between custom queuing and priority queuing stated earlier. With priority queuing, you are telling the router to drain the high-priority queue at all costs, even if it means starvation of the other queues. With custom queuing, you are telling the router to give each queue a turn per cycle but specifying that some queues get drained faster than others.

Assigning a Custom Queue List to an Interface

Once the custom queue list is finished, assign it to the intended interface with the **custom-queue-list** command:

```
2503#conf t
Enter configuration commands, one per line.  End with CNTL/Z.
2503(config)#int s1
2503(config-if)#custom-queue-list 5
2503(config-if)#^Z
```

The preceding lines assign custom queue list 5 to interface Serial 1.

Again, queuing only happens when there is congestion on the outbound link. If there is no congestion, the router simply forwards the traffic as fast as it can. That is, on a first-come, first-served basis.

Verifying the Custom Queuing Configuration

To verify that custom queuing is active, issue the **show queuing custom** and **show interfaces** commands:

```
2503#sh queuing cust
Current custom queue configuration:

List    Queue   Args
5       3       default
5       1       protocol ip         list 101
5       2       protocol ip         tcp port telnet
5       3       protocol ip
5       4       interface Ethernet0
5       1       byte-count 1000
5       2       byte-count 2000
5       3       byte-count 4000
5       4       byte-count 500

2503#sh int s1
Serial1 is up, line protocol is up
  Hardware is HD64570
  Internet address is 192.168.1.2/24
  MTU 1500 bytes, BW 2000 Kbit, DLY 20000 usec, rely 255/255, load 1/255
  Encapsulation HDLC, loopback not set, keepalive set (10 sec)
  Last input 00:00:05, output 00:00:07, output hang never
  Last clearing of "show interface" counters 1d05h
  Input queue: 0/75/0 (size/max/drops); Total output drops: 19
  Queuing strategy: custom-list 5
```

continues

```
Output queues: (queue #: size/max/drops)
  0: 0/20/0 1: 9/20/0 2: 0/20/0 3: 0/20/0 4: 0/20/0
  5: 0/20/0 6: 0/20/0 7: 0/20/0 8: 0/20/0 9: 0/20/0
  10: 0/20/0 11: 0/20/0 12: 0/20/0 13: 0/20/0 14: 0/20/0
  15: 0/20/0 16: 0/20/0
30 second input rate 2000 bits/sec, 5 packets/sec
30 second output rate 68000 bits/sec, 6 packets/sec
  48615 packets input, 10064652 bytes, 0 no buffer
  Received 16330 broadcasts, 0 runts, 0 giants, 0 throttles
  0 input errors, 0 CRC, 0 frame, 0 overrun, 0 ignored, 0 abort
  39632 packets output, 22379609 bytes, 0 underruns
  0 output errors, 0 collisions, 0 interface resets
  0 output buffer failures, 0 output buffers swapped out
  0 carrier transitions
  DCD=up  DSR=up  DTR=up  RTS=up  CTS=up
```

The preceding output shows that custom queuing is active on interface Serial1 and that there are 16 queues numbered 1 through 16. Since this example does not assign any packets to queues other than 1 through 4, the other queues are not used.

The output **1: 9/20/0** tells you information about queue 1. The three numbers between the slashes tell you that there were 9 packets in this queue when the **show interface** command was issued, the maximum number of packets this queue can hold is 20 (the default), and no packets have been dropped from this queue since the counters were last reset.

You may notice that there is a 17th queue called queue 0. This is called the *system queue* and is reserved for maintenance packets such as routing protocol control packets. The system queue is served before all other queues.

Adjusting the Queue Sizes in Custom Queuing

If you need to change the default queue depth of 20 packets, configure the list with the **queue-list queue limit** command:

```
queue-list 5 queue 1 limit 30
```

The preceding global command sets the maximum number of packets that can be held in queue number 1 to 30 packets. This is called the *queue limit*.

As mentioned earlier in the section on priority queuing, there are no absolute rules on queue limits. In general, try to avoid changing the Cisco defaults for the queue depths, especially if custom queuing is working to your satisfaction. If you find that packets occasionally drop from lower queues, experiment with increasing the queue limit a small amount (perhaps 5 to 10 packets). Refer to "Adjusting the Queue Sizes in Priority Queuing" earlier in this chapter for more on queue sizing.

Understanding IP Precedence

In the header of every IP packet is a field called the *TOS*, or *Type of Service*, field that contains three bits called the *IP precedence*. These precedence bits can be set by a router to tell other routers the level of QoS the packet requires.

NOTE   The TOS field (a total of eight bits) follows the header length field and precedes the total length field.

With three bits, the possible decimal values for IP precedence are 0 through 7 (000 through 111 in binary). Weighted fair queuing (WFQ), Committed Access Rate (CAR), and Random Early Detect (RED) services (covered later in this chapter and Chapter 5) use these values to give certain packets better QoS than others.

This section covers:

- Setting IP Precedence
- QoS Benefits of IP Precedence
- Diffserv Redefines IP Precedence

Setting IP Precedence

IP precedence bits can be set with policy routing (as discussed in Chapter 3, "Managing Routing Protocols"), CAR, and other services like those found in Voice over IP and H.323 enabled routers. Chapter 5 examines CAR in detail. The following is an example that uses policy routing to set IP precedence:

```
2503#conf t
Enter configuration commands, one per line.  End with Ctrl-Z.
2503(config)#route-map MYPOLICY permit 10
2503(config-route-map)#match ip address 101
2503(config-route-map)#set ip precedence ?
  <0-7>          Precedence value
  critical       Set critical precedence (5)
  flash          Set flash precedence (3)
  flash-override Set flash override precedence (4)
  immediate      Set immediate precedence (2)
  internet       Set internetwork control precedence (6)
  network        Set network control precedence (7)
  priority       Set priority precedence (1)
  routine        Set routine precedence (0)
  <cr>

2503(config-route-map)#set ip precedence 5
```

You can then apply the route map MYPOLICY to an interface (see Chapter 3 for more on policy routing). The router will set the IP precedence of all packets matching extended access list 101 to the decimal value 5.

NOTE   Each IP precedence value has a name such as *routine, priority, intermediate*, and so on. You can use these names instead of their decimal values if it is more convenient.

The highest precedence levels, 6 and 7, are usually reserved for network control traffic such as routing updates. Therefore, you should limit user applications to levels 0 through 5.

QoS Benefits of IP Precedence

Setting IP precedence bits is a convenient way to differentiate traffic into eight classes. Once you set a packet's precedence, it stays with the packet as it gets routed through the network to its destination. At each hop along the path to the destination, a router can inspect the packet's IP precedence and take a prescribed action (give it high-priority service, drop it, or change its precedence, for example). If a router does not support any QoS based on precedence, packets are simply forwarded with no regard of class and the precedence is left intact for the next router to use.

IP precedence is a fundamental QoS building block. A growing number of Cisco services are precedence-aware and leverage the information in precedence bits to deliver QoS. The most important of these services (WFQ, RED, and CAR) are covered later in this chapter and Chapter 5.

As QoS-sensitive applications such as packetized voice and video over IP continue to grow, it is likely that IP precedence and similar strategies (like diffserv) will remain important as ways of delivering QoS on a per-packet basis.

Additionally, by storing QoS information in each individual packet with precedence bits instead of in criteria lists programmed on every router, it is possible to scale end-to-end QoS across larger networks and more applications.

Diffserv Redefines IP Precedence

A follow-on to IP precedence, called *differentiated services* (*diffserv* for short), redefines the entire TOS field, including the three IP precedence bits. The differentiated services field (*DS field* for short) replaces the TOS field and consists of 8 bits: 6 bits called the *DS codepoint* (DSCP) that define the QoS for the packet and 2 bits that are reserved for future use. The 6-bit DSCP allows a packet to contain more QoS information than with IP precedence. This enables the development of more advanced services that can leverage the additional information.

NOTE	For IPv6, the DS field maps to the Traffic Class octet.

As with IP precedence, the DSCP is set based on a user-defined policy and carried within packets through a network of diffserv-capable devices (such as routers). Network devices then inspect those DSCP values, translate the QoS level for the packet, and forward the packet according to a QoS policy called a *per-hop behavior (PHB)*. A PHB can be a particular queuing mechanism, for example, weighted fair queuing. A network device may also change DSCP values and reclassify packets. This is common at network boundaries such as where two organizations interconnect.

NOTE	DSCPs are simply ignored or interpreted as TOS fields (containing IP precedence) on non-diffserv devices.

A goal of diffserv is to maintain some backward compatibility to IP precedence by preserving the meaning of precedence bits that map to the first three bits of the DSCP. This way, a packet marked by a router using precedence will have similar meaning when routed through diffserv-capable devices.

Although only the DS field is mentioned here, diffserv itself is a rather large framework for defining, implementing, and managing QoS over large networks such as the Internet. It is designed to be scalable and flexible enough to handle the complex needs of private organizations and Internet service providers alike. Consult RFC 2475 for more information on diffserv. Also, check with Cisco on current support for diffserv in the QoS features covered in this chapter and in Chapter 5.

Weighted Fair Queuing

Weighted fair queuing (WFQ) is a sophisticated queuing process that requires very little configuration, because it dynamically detects traffic flows between applications and automatically manages separate queues for those flows. In WFQ terms, these application flows are called *conversations*. A conversation could be a Telnet session, an FTP transfer, a video stream over IP, a transmission of a web page, or some other TCP or UDP flow between a client and a server. Specifically, WFQ considers a set of packets part of the same conversation if they contain the same source and destination addresses, source and destination TCP (or UDP) port numbers, and some other packet header information.

When WFQ detects a conversation and determines that packets belonging to that conversation need to be queued, it automatically creates a queue for that conversation. In the presence of many conversations passing through the interface, WFQ manages multiple conversation queues, one for each unique conversation and sorts packets into their appropriate queues based on the conversations. Because WFQ creates queues and sorts packets into these queues automatically, you do not have to manually configure classification lists to identify various traffic types as in priority queuing and custom queuing configuration. Thus, WFQ is much easier to configure.

NOTE   Like other queuing services, WFQ is invoked only when an outbound link is congested.

This section covers:

- Configuring Weighted Fair Queuing
- Fair Queuing in Action
- Fair Queuing Versus FIFO
- Weighting and IP Precedence
- Weighted Fair Queuing on a Network

Configuring Weighted Fair Queuing

To enable WFQ on an interface, simply configure the following:

```
2503#conf t
Enter configuration commands, one per line.  End with Ctrl-Z.
2503(config)#int s1
2503(config-if)#fair-queue
2503(config-if)#^Z
```

In fact, you may not have to type these commands at all, because WFQ is already enabled by default on Cisco router interfaces running at 2.048 Mbps and lower. You might have to configure WFQ if, for example, WFQ was previously disabled for some reason with the command **no fair-queue**.

NOTE   You won't see the command **fair-queue** when you display the router's configuration with the **show running-config** command if WFQ is the default for that interface.

To confirm that WFQ is enabled on the interface, simply issue a **show interfaces** command:

```
2503#sh int s1
Serial1 is up, line protocol is up
  Hardware is HD64570
  Internet address is 192.168.1.2/24
  MTU 1500 bytes, BW 2000 Kbit, DLY 20000 usec, rely 255/255, load 1/255
```

```
Encapsulation HDLC, loopback not set, keepalive set (10 sec)
Last input 00:00:01, output 00:00:00, output hang never
Last clearing of "show interface" counters 6d05h
Input queue: 1/75/0 (size/max/drops); Total output drops: 0
Queuing strategy: weighted fair
Output queue: 11/1000/0 (size/max total/drops)
    Conversations  4/14/64 (active/max active/threshold)
    Reserved Conversations 0/0 (allocated/max allocated)
<lines deleted for brevity>
```

The preceding configuration shows that WFQ is enabled on interface Serial1. If you configure the interface with the command **no fair-queue** (and configure no other queuing process like priority or custom queuing), then the queuing strategy will read **FIFO**.

Fair Queuing in Action

To understand what's going on inside the router, first look at *fair queuing*, which is a basic form of WFQ. Figure 4-6 shows fair queuing in action on an interface.

Figure 4-6   *Fair Queuing Creates a Separate Queue for Each Conversation*

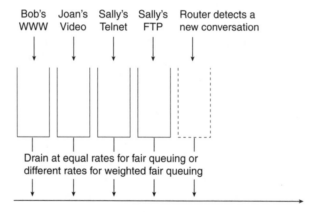

Figure 4-6 shows four active conversations flowing through a router's interface and a new conversation that the router has just detected. Notice that each conversation has its own queue and the router *dynamically* creates a new queue for the conversation it has just detected. The router puts all packets belonging to one conversation into the same conversation queue. For example, the router puts all packets belonging to Sally's Telnet session into the third queue. If Sally decides to do an FTP transfer while she's also doing her Telnet session, as shown in Figure 4-6, then the router will put the packets belonging to her FTP transfer into a queue separate from her Telnet queue. The router does this because Sally's FTP transfer is a separate conversation from her Telnet session (IOS uses a combination of source and destination addresses, port numbers, protocol numbers, and TOS values to identify distinct conversations).

> **NOTE**
> By default, the maximum number of dynamic queues an interface can have at any given time is 256. You can change this parameter using the **fair-queue** interface command. For example, **fair-queue 64 128** sets the maximum to 128 queues (**64** is the default value of the congestive discard threshold, which limits the number of packets held in any one queue).

What's so great about this? If each conversation has its own queue, no one conversation can disrupt the other queues by sending lots of traffic: It will only hurt itself by congesting its own queue.

Additionally, if all the queues are drained at equal rates, then each queue is given an equal share of the bandwidth available on the link. This means no one conversation can monopolize the bandwidth on the interface with a high volume of data: It will be confined to its fair share of bandwidth, and that is all the router will give it. Meanwhile, other conversations that might have low volumes of traffic will get their own share of bandwidth and will not have to compete against high-volume conversations.

> **NOTE**
> You don't have to worry about how to configure fair queuing. Fair queuing is simply WFQ without the use of IP precedence. The section "Weighting and IP Precedence" later in this chapter describes what weighting is and how to enable it to get *weighted* fair queuing.

Fair Queuing Versus FIFO

To illustrate the effects of fair queuing on high- and low-volume traffic, consider the differences between FIFO queuing and fair queuing in the example depicted in Figure 4-7.

Figure 4-7   *A FIFO Queuing Example with Telnet (1, 2) and FTP (A through D) Packets*

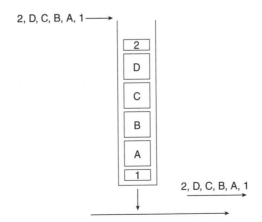

The example illustrated in Figure 4-7 has packets from a Telnet session (low volume conversation) and an FTP transfer (high volume conversation) flowing through a router and destined out an interface with FIFO queuing. Packets 1 and 2 are from the Telnet session, and Packets A through D are from the FTP transfer. Assume that the outbound link is congested prior to the arrival of these packets and remains congested as each packet arrives so that all six packets are in the queue at the same time. Packet 1 arrives first and the router places it in the queue. Suddenly, four large packets (A through D) from the FTP transfer arrive in quick succession; the router adds them to the queue behind Packet 1. Finally, Packet 2 arrives and the router adds it to the queue behind Packet D.

Now consider what happens when the congestion clears and de-queuing begins. Because it's FIFO queuing, the router simply sends the packets in the order they arrived: Packet 1 is sent first, followed by A, B, C, D, and 2. If the outbound interface is a low-bandwidth link, it will take some time for large packets (A, B, C, and D) to pass through the interface. This will delay Packet 2, which is stuck behind those large packets. And if the delay is too long, the Telnet user (whose packets are 1 and 2) may see significant delay between when a key is typed and when it is displayed on the screen—an annoying situation, especially when it is chronic.

You can also imagine that the user's Telnet experience will be worse if instead of just four FTP packets, many more packets get in front of Packet 2 (which can easily happen on a real network).

Now consider the same situation with fair queuing instead of FIFO queuing (see Figure 4-8).

Figure 4-8   *Fair Queuing Example with Telnet (1, 2) and FTP (A through D) Packets*

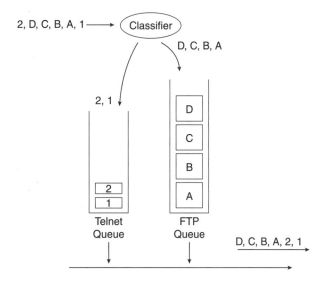

In this scenario, packets arrive at the router in the same order as in the earlier FIFO example. The router receives and queues Packet 1, but this time puts the next packets (A through D) into a different queue, because they are part of a different conversation than Packet 1. Next, Packet 2 arrives and the router puts that into the same queue as Packet 1. (It is part of the same conversation as Packet 1, the Telnet session.) Now when the router starts de-queuing, it will give each queue an equal share of the bandwidth available on the interface. This means the router will drain an equal number of bytes from each queue (in effect, alternating between the two queues as it dispatches the packets).

If Packets 1 and 2 are small packets compared to the large Packets A through D, then draining an equal number of bytes from each queue means multiple small packets will be drained for each large packet that is drained. This results in Packets 1 and 2 being drained one after another, before any packets are drained from the FTP queue.

After Packets 1 and 2 are dispatched, the router drains and dispatches Packet A. If there were more packets waiting in the Telnet queue, for example, Packets 3, 4, 5, and so on, some of these would be drained after Packet A and before Packet B. Again, it's because multiple small packets are drained for every large packet that is drained. However, this is not the case in the example. So, because there are no more packets in the Telnet queue, the router simply finishes draining the FTP queue. When you look at the entire sequence, you see that the order of transmission using fair queuing is: Packet 1 first, followed by 2, A, B, C, and finally D.

This simple example shows that with fair queuing enabled on the interface, low-volume conversations like Telnet do not get stuck behind series of packets from high-volume conversations like FTP. In fact, even if those high-volume conversations send packets at a very aggressive rate, they do not affect the queues belonging to low-volume conversations. All conversation queues are separate from each other, and the router drains each queue fairly. This gives each conversation an equal share of the bandwidth.

NOTE   It is common to use the term *weighted fair queuing* to describe both fair queuing and weighted fair queuing. This is because fair queuing is simply weighted fair queuing with equal weights. See the next section on "Weighting and IP Precedence."

Weighting and IP Precedence

Instead of giving each conversation queue an equal share of the bandwidth, you can give some queues (and their associated conversations) more bandwidth than others. When you do this, you activate the *weighting* factor in WFQ. This is where IP precedence comes into play.

WFQ inspects the IP precedence value of a packet to calculate a number called a *weight* for that packet. WFQ then uses this weight to determine how fast that packet will drain out of a conversation queue.

Weights are simple numbers, typically ranging from 512 to 4096, that only have meaning relative to other weights. The lower the weight, the faster the packet will drain. For example, a conversation queue containing packets of weight 2048 drains roughly twice as many bytes per second as a queue containing packets of weight 4096, regardless of packet size. This means you only need to tag packets with the right precedence value to identify the QoS that should be applied to those packets.

NOTE   The formula for calculating the weight from the precedence value is Weight = 4096 / (Precedence + 1). The weight of a packet of precedence 0 is 4096 and the weight of a packet of precedence 2 is 1365, for example.

For example, if you want to give video packets better QoS than FTP packets, simply set the IP precedence of all video packets to a higher value than the FTP packets.

WFQ will inspect the precedence contained in those video packets, and calculate the appropriate weight to use when draining the video queue relative to the FTP queue. For information on how to use a router to set IP precedence, see "Understanding IP Precedence" earlier in this chapter and "Committed Access Rate" in Chapter 5.

NOTE   If you don't set the packet's precedence value with a router, the precedence will be the value set by the source of the packet and is usually zero by default.

Distributed WFQ (DWFQ)

WFQ can also run in a distributed mode on routers such as the Cisco 7500 with VIP modules. This queuing strategy, known as *Distributed WFQ (DWFQ)*, can handle higher bandwidth upwards of 45 Mbps (and even 155 Mbps, depending on the router and other factors). In DWFQ, fair queuing is called *flow-based WFQ*, while weighting with precedence (and other options) is called *class-based WFQ*. DWFQ includes a few more IOS commands, so consult the IOS documentation if you plan to configure it.

Weighted Fair Queuing on a Network

IP precedence combined with WFQ simplifies QoS configuration on a large network. When each packet contains precedence bits, each packet also carries with it QoS information. Routers along a packet's path from a source to a destination need to inspect only the precedence to learn the QoS that should be applied to the packet.

To illustrate the powerful combination of WFQ and IP precedence, consider the following example of WFQ at work on a WAN (see Figure 4-9).

Figure 4-9 *Setting Precedence at the Edges of a WFQ-Enabled Router Network*

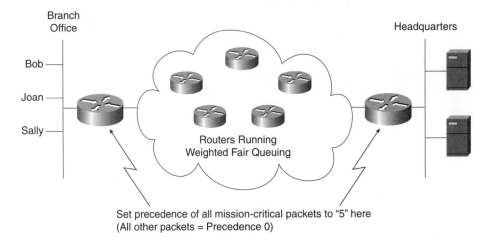

In Figure 4-9, there is a WAN represented by a cloud and two offices connected to it on opposite sides. In the branch office, there are people using a mix of applications that communicate with servers at the headquarters office. To prioritize the mission-critical conversations running between the two offices, the routers on opposite sides of the cloud set the precedence of mission-critical packets to a high value of 5. All other packets are set to a precedence of zero.

Once in the cloud, packets flow from router to router toward their destination with their precedence values never changing. Note that any router along the path may be configured to change the precedence values based on another criteria (for the sake of simplicity, this won't happen in this example). When there is congestion in the cloud on any link along the path, WFQ on the router interface connected to that link creates a queue for each conversation and drains each queue based on the precedence of the packets contained in the queue. In this example, the router drains the queues containing the mission-critical packets of precedence 5 faster than the queues that contain packets of precedence zero. Thus, the network cloud between the two offices is favoring our mission-critical traffic with higher QoS, which was the goal.

In the example, we classify and set precedence only on the two edge routers—the cloud routers in the middle simply have WFQ enabled on their interfaces. This is considerably easier than configuring custom queuing (or priority queuing) on every router that is along the path from the branch office to the headquarters office.

Summary

This chapter covered some basic QoS principles and four queuing techniques: FIFO, priority queuing, custom queuing, and WFQ. The following are the central concepts of the chapter:

- Applications on the network have grown in number and organizations have compelling reasons for delivering QoS for mission-critical and delay-sensitive applications.

- Queuing on a router is necessary to temporarily store packets when a link is congested. The most basic form of queuing is FIFO, which does not offer multiple levels of QoS.

- For a strict QoS policy, you can configure priority queuing on a router. This allows you to identify high-priority applications and give them preferential QoS.

- Custom queuing is an alternative to priority queuing and drains queues in a round-robin fashion to avoid the chance of queue starvation.

- Every IP packet has three precedence bits that can be used to convey QoS information. Precedence is a fundamental building block for scaling QoS over large networks and is leveraged in IOS services such as WFQ, CAR, and RED.

- Diffserv's DS field replaces the TOS field, extends the range of QoS information carried in a packet, and allows for the development of more advanced QoS systems.

- WFQ is a dynamic queuing strategy that separates conversations into distinct queues and allows for fair sharing of bandwidth. WFQ supports IP precedence and uses precedence information to set the QoS for an application.

CHAPTER 5

Deploying Advanced Quality of Service Features

As mentioned in Chapter 4, "Deploying Basic Quality of Service Features," queuing services, such as weighted fair queuing (WFQ), are important functions of the network to recognize and prioritize applications. However, queuing alone might not be sufficient for achieving quality of service (QoS) in all parts of the network. As an example, WFQ might suffice for most parts of the network, but not at the point where the network connects to the Internet—where a form of rate control is also needed.

This chapter explains the operation and deployment of three advanced services for QoS: Resource Reservation Protocol (RSVP), Random Early Detection (RED), and Committed Access Rate (CAR).

Building on the QoS concepts in Chapter 4, these enhanced services introduce subjects such as admission control, QoS signaling, global synchronization, and rate limiting.

As you read this chapter, you will notice an emphasis on the mechanics of the services (and the reasons they exist) rather than on the IOS configuration. This is because the configuration tasks are fairly short, and an explanation of each service's behavior is more important than the commands that activate them.

The main topics of this chapter are

- Resource Reservation Protocol
- Random Early Detection
- Committed Access Rate
- Class-Based WFQ

Resource Reservation Protocol

Resource Reservation Protocol (RSVP), specified in RFC 2205, is a signaling protocol for delivering guaranteed quality of service on a network. Clients use RSVP to request QoS guarantees (called *reservations*) from routers, and routers use RSVP to deliver requests and information about the reservations to other routers. An RSVP client might be embedded in a router instead of the typical workstation; for example, a router could be delivering voice from a private branch exchange (PBX) over the IP network and might use RSVP to request a reservation that guarantees successful delivery of the real-time traffic across the network.

An RSVP reservation guarantees QoS for an application flow, called a *session*. A session is equivalent to any TCP or UDP flow, such as a packetized video or audio stream or even a simple FTP transfer. A session might be a unicast transmission, such as a private audio stream from one client to another, or it might be a multicast transmission, such as a broadcast from a video server to an IP multicast address viewed by members of a multicast group. Again, the content of the session does not have to be multimedia in nature: It can be any TCP or UDP flow. However, RSVP was clearly created with real-time applications such as packetized video and audio in mind.

This section covers

- RSVP Admission Control
- RSVP Signaling Versus Bulk Data
- The RSVP Signaling Process
- RSVP and Weighted Fair Queuing
- Configuring RSVP
- Verifying RSVP Configuration
- Configuring IOS as a Proxy for Path and Resv Messages
- RSVP Scaling Considerations

RSVP Admission Control

Reservations are commitments from routers that a session's bandwidth and delay characteristics will be delivered consistently for the life of the session. This means routers will ensure that reserved sessions get the bandwidth and queuing priorities they need and will protect them from any ill effects of sharing network resources with nonreserved sessions. If a router cannot commit to the QoS required by a session, it sends a reservation rejection to the RSVP client—similar to an "all circuits are busy" message in the telephone world. Such a message signals to the client that the current state of the network does not have enough resources to support the requested QoS. The client can retry the request at a later time, change the request to something with lower QoS parameters, or send its data without any reservation as "best-effort" traffic.

A router's capability to accept and reject reservation requests is known as *admission control* and is key to delivering QoS on a network. Figure 5-1 illustrates RSVP admission control at work on a network.

Figure 5-1   *RSVP Provides Admission Control on a Network*

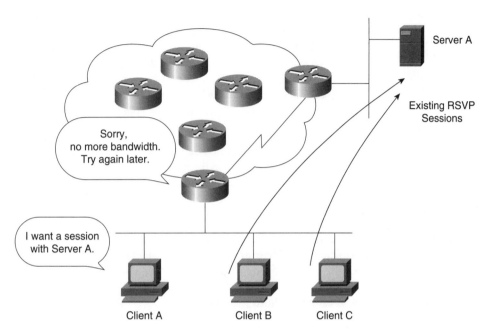

Client A in Figure 5-1 wants a guaranteed level of QoS (a reservation) with the network for a session with Server A. Using the RSVP protocol, Client A sends a request to the network for the desired QoS; unfortunately, active RSVP reservations owned by Clients B and C prevent the routers from guaranteeing Client A's request. Client A's request exceeds the network resources available, so one of the routers sends an RSVP message back to Client A, denying the request. To communicate with Server A, Client A can send another request and ask for less resources (less bandwidth, for example), can resubmit the original request when more resources are available, or can simply communicate with Server A with no reservation (no guaranteed QoS).

Without admission control, you have to rely on prioritizing traffic alone (high, medium, and low classification) for QoS. Traffic prioritization is a necessary part of QoS but is not always sufficient. The problem with traffic prioritization is that incoming traffic is always accepted. You can classify the traffic as high priority, low priority, and everything in between, but you cannot stop the *volume* of incoming traffic. What if there is too much traffic and *all* of the traffic is classified as high priority? The problem is that high priority doesn't mean much anymore. With too much high-priority traffic and unacceptable service, all high-priority sessions suffer equally and are equally useless. It would be better to let a lower number of high-priority sessions get the QoS they need instead of admitting many high-priority sessions that are all useless. With admission control, you can limit your commitment to a realistic volume of traffic and use traffic prioritization to ensure that high-priority sessions (the reservations) get the QoS they expect.

RSVP Signaling Versus Bulk Data

An important note about RSVP is that session data, such as the packets that make up a video stream, does not flow over RSVP. RSVP is a signaling protocol (or a *control protocol*) that is used to set up reservations in a network and communicate the QoS of a session *before* any data starts flowing. RSVP does not carry the bulk data of the session itself. As an analogy, you use the signaling protocol of dialing an area code and phone number and waiting for the other phone to answer before you start sending the bulk content of your call—your actual speech. RSVP is like the dialing protocol, whereas the video stream is the actual content carried over the network in its own format.

In RSVP, senders and receivers of data are distinct. Senders use RSVP to tell routers about the bandwidth their sessions require, and receivers make reservation requests to routers for those sessions. QoS for the session is not established until the receiver's request is accepted by all routers in the path from receiver to sender—thus, RSVP is a receiver-initiated signaling protocol.

RSVP reservations are *unidirectional*, meaning they guarantee QoS only for traffic flowing in one direction: from a sender to a receiver. If you want to guarantee QoS for bidirectional applications—for example, a two-way audio session—you need to establish two reservations, one for each direction of data flow. Each client will be the sender for one reservation and a receiver of the other reservation, as illustrated in Figure 5-2.

Figure 5-2   *Establishing Two RSVP Reservations for Bidirectional Sessions*

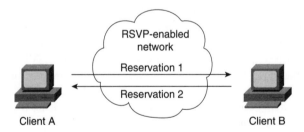

In Figure 5-2, Client A is the sender for Reservation 1 as well as the receiver for Reservation 2. Meanwhile, Client B is the sender for Reservation 2 and the receiver for Reservation 1.

Having covered the general concepts of RSVP, the next section looks at the details of how the protocol works.

The RSVP Signaling Process

Prior to any RSVP signaling, the sender and receiver might have identified each other through their application and agreed to start a session. A conferencing application, for example, might offer a directory service that Client A can use to check if Client B is online and available for a call. The steps before RSVP signaling might look something like this:

- When Client A calls Client B, Client A simply selects Client B's name in the directory list and clicks a button to initiate the call.

- Client B receives a ringing alarm, indicating that Client A is calling, and clicks a button to accept the call.

- The clients negotiate the type of conferencing they will do—for example, audio only or audio plus video.

- After negotiating such conferencing parameters, they know how much bandwidth their session needs.

- At this point, the clients have progressed far enough to move to the RSVP reservation process:

    — They know with whom they are having a session.

    — They know that the other side is ready to accept data.

    — They know the kind of data they will exchange.

    — They know the QoS needed for the data of the session.

NOTE   The preceding steps are a simplistic view of an H.323 conference initialization between Client A and Client B.

RSVP Signaling Details: A Video Streaming Example

Consider the signaling between two clients and a router network, and assume that Client A is going to send Client B a packetized video stream. In other words, RSVP will be used to establish a reservation for the packets flowing from Client A (sender) to Client B (receiver). The RSVP terms *sender* and *receiver* are used to generalize the discussion for this example.

Sending Path Messages

The following steps describe the signaling flow from sender to receiver (see Figure 5-3):

Figure 5-3   *RSVP Path Messages Flow Downstream Along the Normal Routed Path*

Client A
(sender)

Path

RSVP database (path messages)

To	From	Previous hop	Bandwidth
Client B	Client A	Client A	10 Kbps

Path

Path

Path

Client B
(receiver)

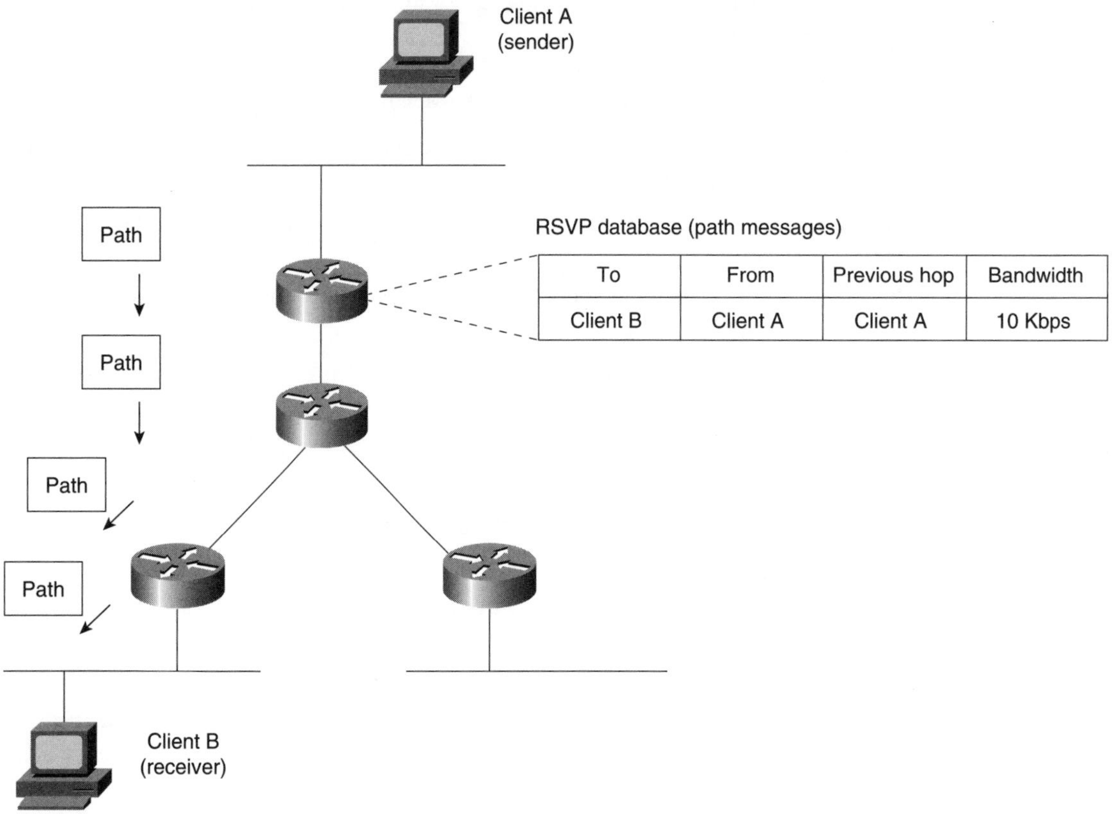

- To start the RSVP process, a sender sends special RSVP packets called *Path messages* to the network. In its Path messages, the sender includes information that describes, by using various QoS metrics, the traffic it intends to send.

- The Path messages flow through the network along the normal routed path of data from the sender's IP address to the receiver's IP address. This routed path from the sender to the receiver is the *downstream* direction of a session. Because RSVP uses the normal routed path to send Path messages, it depends on routing protocols such as EIGRP, OSPF, and RIP (RSVP is not a routing protocol). Path messages are sourced by the sender and propagated through the network on a periodic basis.

- If the receiver's address is an IP multicast group address, the Path message flows down the normal multicast distribution tree as any normal packet sent to the group address.

- When an RSVP-enabled router receives the Path message, it keeps a record of the information contained in the message, as well as some other information such as the previous hop from which the message came. After storing this information in its memory (an RSVP database), the router forwards the message to the next router along the path to the receiver.

Sending Resv Messages

The following steps describe the signaling flow from receiver to sender (see Figure 5-4):

Figure 5-4   *RSVP Resv Messages Propagate Upstream Along the Reverse Route of the Path Messages*

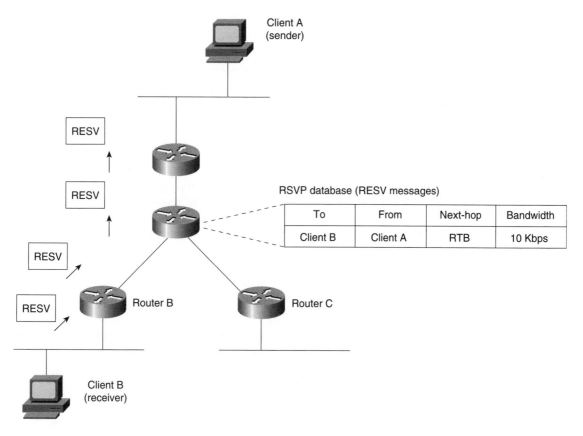

- After the sender's Path message propagates downstream through all router hops and arrives at the receiver, the receiver inspects the Path message and uses the information in the Path message to formulate an RSVP reservation request to the network. A reservation request message, called a *Resv message*, is sent by the receiver and propagates upstream along the exact reverse route of the Path message. The Resv message is a request to a router for a guaranteed level of QoS for the session.

- When the first upstream router receives the Resv message, it accepts or rejects the request based on the availability of its resources. These resources could be bandwidth, queuing, and memory capacity, whose availability depends on the number of active RSVP reservations already in the router.

- If the router rejects the request, it sends an error message to the receiver and does not send the Resv message upstream.

- If the router accepts the reservation, it sets aside router resources for the session, based on the data contained in the Resv message, and forwards the Resv message to the next upstream hop. If the next upstream hop is another router (not the sender), the admission process is repeated. Assuming that no routers along the upstream path reject the request, the Resv message eventually reaches the sender. Resv messages are sourced by the receiver on a periodic basis for the life of the session.

Knowing When QoS Is In Place

The sender, upon receiving the Resv message, now knows that an end-to-end QoS is in place for the session and can start sending its session data to the receiver along the same route as the Path messages. Because each router has accepted the reservation via the upstream propagation of Resv messages, the data from the sender is sent downstream with a guaranteed QoS (see Figure 5-5).

NOTE   Again, RSVP does not transport any of the session data itself. Senders, receivers, and routers use RSVP to manage QoS for a session. After an RSVP reservation is established, the sender simply sends its data to the receiver as it would normally in a non-RSVP situation. The benefit of having the reservation is that all routers in the path know of the session and have committed to a QoS guarantee for the session *before* any data starts flowing.

Figure 5-5   *Downstream Flow of Data over an Established RSVP Reservation*

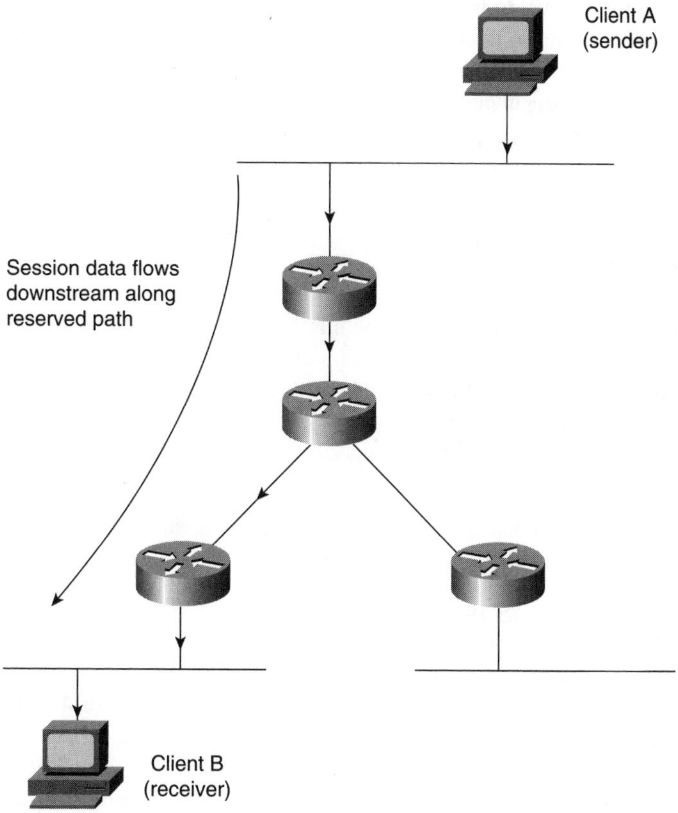

Tear-Down Messages

Finally, like any good signaling protocol, RSVP contains a tear-down message so that either endpoint (sender or receiver) can remove the reservation from the network. A router can also remove a reservation if it detects through a timeout process that the reservation is no longer active. RSVP requires both the sender and the receiver to refresh the state of a reservation by periodically sending Path and Resv messages. If one of the endpoints falls off of the network unexpectedly or if routing changes occur in the network, routers themselves can remove reservations to free up their resources.

NOTE	RSVP signaling is designed to work through an intervening non-RSVP router or a group of intervening non-RSVP routers. This means you do not have to enable RSVP on every router in your network to support RSVP clients. However, to *guarantee* QoS along the entire path from sender to receiver, RSVP must be enabled on all routers in the path. Non-RSVP routers forward Path and Resv messages just fine, but they do not know about any RSVP reservations and therefore cannot perform QoS techniques on sessions associated with those reservations.

RSVP and Weighted Fair Queuing

Just as RSVP is a signaling protocol that does not transport data for a session, RSVP itself is not responsible for queuing and dispatching packets for a session after the reservation is made. RSVP in a Cisco router depends on weighted fair queuing (WFQ), as discussed in Chapter 4, to carry out the queuing and dispatching of packets at the link layer (Layer 2) that ultimately delivers the QoS for a session.

NOTE	You can think of RSVP as the decision-maker for reservations and WFQ as the workhorse that processes the packets for those reservations.

Inside a Cisco router, RSVP communicates with WFQ and informs WFQ of the reservations and the QoS promised in those reservations. Recall from Chapter 4 that in WFQ terminology, session's application flows (TCP/UDP flows, for instance) are called *conversations*. RSVP reservations for sessions have a direct one-for-one relationship to WFQ conversations. RSVP also informs WFQ of a conversation queue number (which uniquely identifies a WFQ queue to use for RSVP) and the weight to use on that queue when it establishes a reservation, as illustrated in Figure 5-6.

NOTE	The communication between RSVP and WFQ happens within a router (not over the network). It's a dialog between two software processes within the router, so although you cannot easily observe the exchange, you can verify that it is enabled (see "Configuring RSVP" later in this chapter).

Figure 5-6   *After RSVP Establishes a Reservation, It Forwards QoS Information to WFQ*

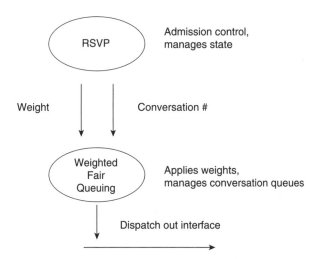

When a reservation is established along a path of routers, WFQ (under the instruction of RSVP) ensures that session data is delivered with the service promised by RSVP. This is done on the output interfaces of the routers when the data is flowing downstream from the sender to the receiver, as shown in Figure 5-7.

NOTE   The actual mechanics of WFQ with RSVP are the same as described in Chapter 4; that is, each conversation has its own queue, and the weight determines QoS for the queue. The difference here is that RSVP, rather than IP precedence, determines the weight for a queue.

Configuring RSVP

Configuring RSVP is simple—so simple, in fact, that the temptation is to enable RSVP without fully understanding how it works. This is not a good idea, which is why this chapter covers the mechanics before it discusses the configuration.

RSVP is enabled on router interfaces, not on the router as a whole. This gives you the flexibility to enable RSVP on some interfaces but leave other interfaces alone.

Figure 5-7 *WFQ on Outbound Interfaces Ensures Data Is Delivered at the Desired QoS*

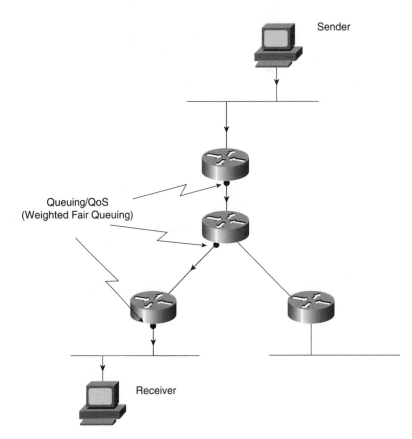

To configure RSVP on an interface, simply issue the **bandwidth** and **ip rsvp bandwidth**
commands, like this:

```
2503#conf t
Enter configuration commands, one per line.   End with CNTL/Z.
2503(config)#int s0
2503(config-if)#bandwidth 768
2503(config-if)#ip rsvp bandwidth
2503(config-if)#^Z
```

By default, the router limits the amount of bandwidth that can be reserved for RSVP sessions
to 75% of the interface bandwidth. This prevents RSVP sessions from hogging all of the
bandwidth on the interface and allows non-RSVP traffic at least 25% of the bandwidth. Note
that the **bandwidth** command is used to specify the amount of bandwidth in kilobits per second

available on this interface. Configuring this is very important because the router will use the number configured with this command to calculate the maximum bandwidth RSVP can reserve (75% of the number configured with the **bandwidth** command). Without this command, most serial interfaces default to a bandwidth equal to 1544 kbps (T1), which might not be a proper representation of the real bandwidth on the interface.

You can look at the router configuration to see what RSVP bandwidth was calculated. The following is a partial listing of a router configuration, using the **show running-config** command:

```
interface Serial0
 ip address 192.168.1.2 255.255.255.0
 ip rsvp bandwidth 576 576
 bandwidth 768
```

In the preceding example configuration, you can verify that 75 percent of 768 kbps is 576 kbps. The first number after **ip rsvp bandwidth** is the maximum amount of bandwidth RSVP can reserve for RSVP sessions. The second number is the maximum amount of bandwidth that any one session (a single reservation) can reserve. If you want to change these numbers, you can issue the command with different bandwidth numbers:

```
2503(config-if)#ip rsvp bandwidth 400 200
```

The preceding configuration restricts RSVP to a maximum of 400 kbps on this interface and states that no single reservation may exceed 200 kbps.

Verifying RSVP Configuration

To verify that RSVP is enabled on the interface, issue the command **show ip rsvp interface**, which presents the following output:

```
2503#sh ip rsvp int
interfac allocate i/f max  flow max per/255 UDP  IP   UDP_IP   UDP M/C
Et0      50K      7500K    7500K   1   /255 0    1    0        0
Se0      0M       400K     200K    0   /255 0    1    0        0
```

This output is read like a simple table:

- The first column indicates that two interfaces have RSVP enabled: Ethernet0 and Serial0.

- The **allocate** column shows that Ethernet0 has one or more active reservations, totaling 50 kbps of bandwidth. This bandwidth was allocated by RSVP on behalf of RSVP clients. Serial0 has no active reservations, as indicated by **0M** (zero Mbps allocated).

- The next two columns indicate the maximum bandwidth per interface (**i/f max**) and maximum bandwidth per reservation (**flow max**) that can be reserved by RSVP. These numbers should match the values set by the **ip rsvp bandwidth** command.

- The **per/255** column shows what fraction of the bandwidth is currently reserved on the interface, using 255 as the maximum.

- Finally, the last four columns denote the number of RSVP neighbors (routers and clients) seen on the interface, based on the type of protocol.

Configuring IOS as a Proxy for Path and Resv Messages

Cisco IOS can send Path and Resv messages on behalf of clients. This proxy capability is useful for testing RSVP when you don't have any RSVP-enabled clients available. Figure 5-8 depicts such a scenario.

Figure 5-8   *Router A Can Proxy Path Messages for a Non-RSVP Client (Client A)*

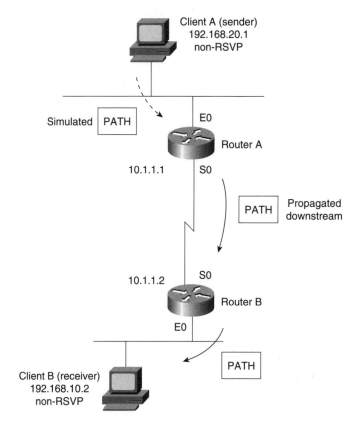

Client A does not support RSVP, so it cannot generate any Path messages and send them to the network. For the purpose of testing RSVP, you can configure Router A to proxy for Client A and send Path messages to the network on Client A's behalf. Other devices in the network then interpret the Path messages as originating from Client A, even though they are actually sourced by Router A.

To enable the proxy function, you configure one or more static RSVP senders on Router A. This causes Router A to generate Path messages and forward them downstream as normal RSVP Path messages. While Path messages are flowing, you can verify the mechanics of RSVP by observing what happens on Router A and other devices in the network.

The **ip rsvp sender** command (global configuration mode) configures a static RSVP sender. The following example coincides with Figure 5-8 and configures a static sender on Router A:

```
ip rsvp sender 192.168.10.2 192.168.20.1 TCP 0 0 192.168.20.1 Et0 10 5
```

The preceding command configures all the data that make up a Path message:

- The first IP address (192.168.10.2) is the receiver's address (Client B). The receiver can be an IP multicast address for multicast sessions. The second IP address (192.168.20.1) is the sender's IP address (Client A).

- Next, **TCP** tells the router that this is a TCP session. Alternatively, you can configure **UDP** or an IP protocol number.

- The two zeros tell the router to ignore the source and destination TCP port numbers when it considers packets part of this session. If you want the reservation to apply to a specific TCP session (instead of any TCP session from the sender), configure the destination port number in place of the first zero and the source port number in place of the second zero.

- The next entry is the *previous hop* address and is part of a standard RSVP Path message. The previous hop is the router that is one hop upstream in the direction of the sender; in this case, the upstream hop is the sender itself (Client A). In a different network, it could be an upstream router.

- **Et0** (Ethernet0) is the interface on this router that points to the previous hop.

- Finally, the last two numbers are descriptions of the session flow itself. This session is configured for a bandwidth of 10 kbps with a burst of 5000 bytes. The burst is the number of bytes that should be held in a queue when traffic from a session exceeds 10 kbps.

With Router A generating Path messages on behalf of Client A, you can verify that Router B is receiving them. Issuing the command **show ip rsvp sender** on Router B confirms that Router B (the downstream router) is receiving the static Path message configured on Router A:

```
RTB#sh ip rsvp sender
To              From          Pro DPort Sport Prev Hop    I/F  BPS  Bytes
192.168.10.2    192.168.20.1  TCP 0     0     10.1.1.1    Se0  10K  5K
```

In the preceding output, the **To** column is the receiver's address and the **From** column is the sender's address. The previous hop address is 10.1.1.1 (Router A), and Serial0 (Se0) is the interface that points to the previous hop. The other fields match the parameters of the static sender configured on Router A (protocol, ports, bandwidth, and burst).

In addition to Path messages, you can also proxy Resv messages with IOS. To proxy Resv messages on a router, configure one or more static RSVP receivers with the **ip rsvp reservation** global configuration command. The following line is configured in Router B, which is downstream of Router A (refer to Figure 5-8 for the topology):

```
ip rsvp reservation 192.168.10.2 192.168.20.1 TCP 0 0 192.168.10.2 Et0 FF RATE 10 5
```

Note the following in this configuration:

- The first IP address (192.168.10.2) is the receiver's address (Client B). The second IP address (192.168.20.1) is the sender's IP address (Client A).

- **TCP** tells the router that this is a TCP session. Alternatively, you can configure **UDP** or an IP protocol number.

- The two zeros tell the router to ignore the source and destination TCP port numbers when it considers packets part of this session. If you want the reservation to apply to a specific TCP session (instead of any TCP session from the sender), configure the destination port number instead of the first zero and the source port number instead of the second zero.

- The next entry is called the next hop address and is part of a standard RSVP Resv message. The next hop is the router that is one hop downstream in the direction of the receiver. In this example, the downstream hop is the receiver itself (Client B); in a different network, it could be a downstream router.

- **Et0** (Ethernet0) is the interface on this router that points to the next hop.

- **FF** stands for *fixed filter* and is an RSVP reservation *style*. Reservations can be dedicated to a single sender or shared by multiple senders. A reservation for a single sender is a fixed filter reservation, whereas a reservation shared by multiple senders is either a wildcard filter (WF) or a shared explicit (SE) reservation. For the purpose of testing, the fixed filter style should suffice.

NOTE   A WF reservation is shared by all upstream senders, but an SE reservation is shared by a selected group of upstream senders. Consult RFC 2205 for more information.

- **RATE 10 5** defines the QoS that is requested by the receiver in the Resv message. This example requests bandwidth of 10 kbps and a burst size of 5000 bytes.

With Router B configured to send Resv messages upstream on behalf of Client B, you can verify that Router A is receiving those messages. Issuing the command **show ip rsvp request** on Router A confirms that Router A (the upstream router) is receiving the static Resv message configured on Router B:

```
RTA#sh ip rsvp request
To            From         Pro DPort Sport Next Hop    I/F   Fi Serv BPS Bytes
192.168.10.2  192.168.20.1 TCP 0      0     10.1.1.2   Se0   FF RATE 10K   5K
```

In the preceding output, the **To** column is the receiver's address and the **From** column is the sender's address. The next hop address is 10.1.1.2 (Router B), and Serial0 (Se0) is the interface that points to the next hop. The other fields match the parameters of the static receiver configured on Router B (protocol, ports, style, bandwidth, and burst).

After the Path and Resv messages are flowing and the configured reservation is in place (confirm with the **allocate** column of **show ip rsvp interface**), you can test the QoS throughput and latency over the reserved path from sender to receiver.

TIP   Use the **debug ip rsvp** enable mode command to observe the Path and Resv messages generated by your routers.

RSVP Scaling Considerations

A consideration for your RSVP deployment is the issue of scaling RSVP in large networks. As mentioned earlier, routers keep track of information contained in Path and Resv messages and maintain stateful information for each reservation. It is possible in large networks for a high number of active reservations to adversely affect router resources such as memory and the CPU. As such, consider the current capacity of your routers as you plan deployments of RSVP applications. As with so much in networking, there are no golden rules—networks, goals, and applications vary. Consider getting Cisco involved in your particular project for design and planning assistance.

Random Early Detection

Chapter 4 discussed various queuing strategies you can use to manage traffic when the network is congested. *Random Early Detection (RED)* on a router also helps manage traffic, but takes the approach of avoiding congestion by taking advantage of flow control features in the TCP protocol. Thus, RED's strategy is *congestion avoidance* rather than congestion management (queuing, discussed in Chapter 4, is an example of congestion management).

This section covers

- Dynamics of Network Congestion and Tail Drops
- Global Synchronization

- TCP Slow Start
- Ill Effects of Global Synchronization and TCP Slow Start
- How RED Works
- RED and IP Precedence
- Configuring RED
- Verifying RED Configuration

Dynamics of Network Congestion and Tail Drops

As traffic increases on a router's output interface, the queues on that interface start to fill with packets. As mentioned in Chapter 4, the interface fills because the bandwidth of the output link cannot keep up with the amount of traffic scheduled to go out that link. If the traffic continues to pass through the router at a rate that exceeds the speed of the output link, it is possible for the queue system to fill to its maximum capacity. When this happens, the router has no choice but to drop all subsequent packets until the queue has more room. This is called a *tail drop* condition (some packets are in the queue, but trailing packets are dropped) and is depicted in Figure 5-9.

Figure 5-9 *When an Interface's Queue System Is Full, the Router Has No Choice But to Cause a Tail Drop*

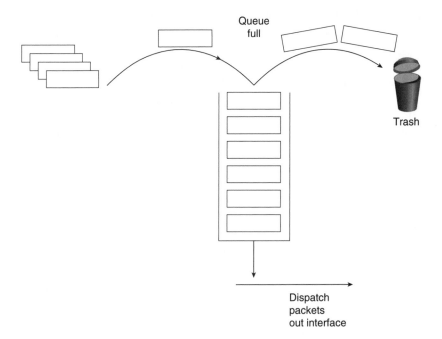

The interface in Figure 5-9 is configured with first-in, first-out (FIFO) queuing, but any other queuing system can be used in a similar manner and experience a tail-drop condition.

Tail drops are undesirable because packets from *all flows* are dropped at the same time and continue to drop until the queue system drains below its maximum capacity. Flows using a reliable protocol such as TCP will retransmit the packets that were dropped. Flows from unreliable protocols such as UDP might never retransmit those lost packets or might rely on an upper-layer application to retransmit the packets.

NOTE   Some application flows do not need to retransmit the data lost in their dropped packets. Real-time audio or video streams, for example, can tolerate some lost data and still be intelligible to a person on the receiving end. Additionally, retransmitting real-time data might not make sense if it causes the data to arrive too late on the receiving end.

Global Synchronization

It's common for an IP network to have many TCP flows—so many flows that the TCP flows make up the majority of the traffic on the network. Web, FTP, Telnet, and many other client-server applications transport their data with the TCP protocol. When these TCP flows experience a tail drop, all of the senders associated with the flows trigger retransmission at the same time. This *global synchronization* of retransmissions is an undesirable situation that can wreak havoc on the network (see "Ill Effects of Global Synchronization and Slow Start").

TCP Slow Start

An important part of the TCP protocol is the unique way it performs a retransmission. TCP senders retransmit packets and subsequently resume their flows, using a process called *TCP slow start*.

In TCP slow start, an endstation sends very few packets at the beginning of a TCP session or retransmission and gradually increases the throughput of the flow as packets are delivered to the destination without any packet drops.

NOTE   Explaining TCP slow start in detail is outside the scope of this book, but you can think of TCP as a cautious protocol that intentionally starts slowly and gains speed as packets successfully reach the destination of the flow. When an endstation detects that a packet was dropped, it abruptly slows down its transmission rate and starts the slow-start process again. Two references that explain TCP slow start in detail are Stevens and Comer (see the Bibliography).

III Effects of Global Synchronization and TCP Slow Start

Global synchronization combined with TCP slow starts can lead to some very undesirable results. When many TCP flows have one or more packets dropped in a tail drop, they all go through TCP slow start at the same time. This means these flows all slow down at the same time, and traffic on the network as a whole drops abruptly. The network gets significantly quieter than it was before the tail drop (again, this assumes most of the traffic is TCP). Next, because the flows are synchronized, they all start to speed up at the same time. This continues until the aggregate rate of the flows once again climbs to a maximum rate, at which time congestion causes another tail drop and the cycle repeats.

From a link-utilization standpoint, this cycle of traffic rising to saturation and crashing down looks like a sawtooth-shaped graph. This effect is depicted in Figure 5-10.

Figure 5-10   *Synchronized TCP Slow Starts Cause a Sawtooth Pattern of Network Utilization*

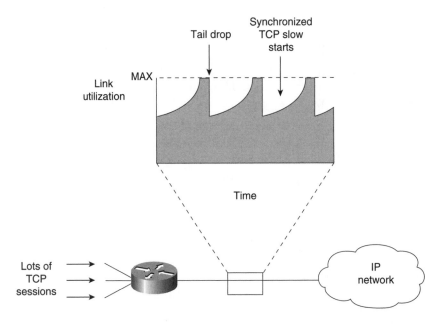

Utilization of the link climbs to 100 percent, drops sharply when the TCP flows go into slow start, and starts climbing back up to 100 percent, only to crash down again. Although there is nothing fundamentally wrong with TCP (slow start is a useful flow-control mechanism that throttles endstations for the good of the network), you can observe from the sawtooth pattern the following problems:

- Link utilization is not 100 percent the entire time, and overall throughput is less than the optimal rate you can get out of the link.

- Transmission rates start and stop; throughput is inconsistent. This could cause problems for applications and users.

- Recognizing bandwidth oversubscription and planning for network upgrades is difficult because average link utilization measures short of full capacity.

How RED Works

RED randomly drops packets based on the number of packets queued on an interface: As a queue reaches its maximum capacity, RED drops packets more aggressively to avoid a tail drop.

RED throttles back flows and takes advantage of TCP slow start. Rather than tail-dropping *all* packets when the queue is full, RED manages queue depth by randomly dropping *some* packets as the queue fills (past a certain threshold). As packets drop, the applications associated with those dropped packets slow down and go through TCP slow start. This reduces the traffic destined for the link and provides relief to the queue system.

NOTE	To carry over the funnel analogy introduced in Chapter 4: RED is analogous to pouring the water into the funnel more slowly because you see the funnel starting to fill up.

If the queue system continues to fill, RED drops more packets to slow down additional applications—again, to avoid a tail drop. The net result is that RED avoids global synchronization and increases overall utilization of the line (eliminating the sawtooth utilization pattern).

NOTE	On WAN lines of 2.048 Mbps and lower, RED might keep utilization and queues undesirably low. On such low-speed WAN lines, utilizing all of the available bandwidth is usually desirable. RED might throttle back traffic too much on low-speed lines and counteract this goal.

RED and IP Precedence (Weighted RED)

As a mechanism for QoS, RED drops low-precedence packets before high-precedence packets. This means high-priority applications are less likely to experience a packet drop (and TCP slow start) than low-priority applications. RED achieves QoS by maintaining thresholds at various queue depths—one threshold for each precedence level. As a queue fills and exceeds a threshold, the precedence level associated with that threshold is eligible for random drops. A high-precedence level correlates to a high threshold in the queue. This combination of RED and IP precedence is known as *Weighted RED (WRED)*.

WRED can also be configured for distributed processing on routers such as the Cisco 7500 with VIP modules. Known as *Distributed WRED (DWRED)*, this strategy can handle higher bandwidth links than nondistributed WRED/RED.

Configuring WRED

To configure WRED on an interface, use the **random-detect** command in interface configuration mode:

```
RTA#conf t
Enter configuration commands, one per line.  End with CNTL/Z.
RTA(config)#int s1
RTA(config-if)#random-detect
RTA(config-if)#^Z
```

This enables WRED on the interface and automatically defines queue thresholds for different IP precedence levels.

NOTE   Don't be overly concerned with the difference between RED and WRED. WRED is simply RED with the added feature of IP precedence and QoS. When all of your traffic is at same precedence level, you have RED. Otherwise, the precedence levels signal to WRED the different priorities of traffic. WRED, in turn, drops lower priority traffic before higher priority traffic as the interface queue fills up.

In general, you will not need to change WRED's default parameters. However, if you or Cisco determine that some tuning is required in your network, employ the **random-detect precedence** command (IOS 11.1CC, 12.0, and later releases). The following is an example:

```
interface Serial0
 random-detect
 random-detect precedence 0 15 35 10
```

Where **0** specifies IP precedence level 0. Traffic of this precedence is subject to this command. Acceptable values for precedence are 0 through 7 and **rsvp** for RSVP traffic. **15** and **35** define the *minimum* and *maximum thresholds* in number of packets. WRED maintains a statistic on the average queue depth (in number of packets) of an interface. When the average queue depth is below the minimum threshold, no packets are dropped. When the average queue depth is above the minimum threshold, WRED starts dropping packets. As the average climbs, due to increasing congestion, WRED drops packets more aggressively. Above the maximum threshold, all packets pertaining to the precedence level are dropped. The last parameter (**10**, in this example) is the *mark probability denominator*. It specifies how fast packets are dropped when the average queue depth is at the maximum threshold. 10 means one out of every 10 packets is dropped when the average queue depth is at the maximum threshold. So, to summarize:

- Below the minimum threshold: No packets are dropped.

- Above the minimum threshold and heading up to the maximum threshold: Some number of packets are dropped. This depends on the average queue depth at the time and the value of the mark probability denominator. When the denominator specifies an aggressive drop policy, packets are dropped more frequently. As the average queue depth climbs, so does the frequency of drops—up to the value of the denominator itself. The drops throttle-back TCP flows to control queue depth (as more packets get dropped, more traffic should be throttled-back).

- Exactly at the maximum threshold: Packets are dropped at the frequency specified by the denominator. This is the maximum drop rate before all packets are dropped.

- Above the maximum threshold: All packets of the precedence level are dropped. This is like a tail drop, but just for a precedence level.

NOTE IOS also allows you to tune WRED's *exponential weighting constant* (whose default value is 9) with the **random-detect exponential-weighting-constant** command. This parameter affects the sensitivity of WRED's average queue depth statistic. Consult Cisco if you think you need to change this; otherwise, don't worry about it.

Verifying WRED Configuration

To verify that WRED is active on an interface, issue the **show interface** command:

```
RTA#sh int s1/0
Serial1/0 is up, line protocol is up
  Hardware is M4T
  MTU 1500 bytes, BW 1544 Kbit, DLY 20000 usec,
     reliability 255/255, txload 80/255, rxload 6/255
  Encapsulation FRAME-RELAY, crc 16, loopback not set
  Keepalive set (10 sec)
  LMI enq sent  23, LMI stat recvd 23, LMI upd recvd 0, DTE LMI up
  LMI enq recvd 0, LMI stat sent  0, LMI upd sent  0
  LMI DLCI 1023  LMI type is CISCO  frame relay DTE
  Broadcast queue 0/64, broadcasts sent/dropped 63/0, interface broadcasts 57
  Last input 00:00:00, output 00:00:00, output hang never
  Last clearing of "show interface" counters 00:03:48
  Input queue: 0/75/0 (size/max/drops); Total output drops: 1160
  Queueing strategy: random early detection (RED)
    mean queue depth: 29
    drops: class   random    tail      min-th    max-th    mark-prob
           0       1141      9         15        35        1/10
           1       10        0         22        40        1/10
           2       0         0         24        40        1/10
           3       0         0         26        40        1/10
           4       0         0         28        40        1/10
           5       0         0         31        40        1/10
```

continues

```
          6     0      0      33     40     1/10
          7     0      0      35     40     1/10
       rsvp     0      0      37     40     1/10
<lines deleted for brevity>
```

The preceding output confirms that RED in enabled on Serial1/0. The **mean queue depth** is the average queue depth on the interface. The table following **drops: class** is a record of the number of packets that WRED dropped (**random** and **tail**) by precedence level (**class**). The minimum threshold, maximum threshold, and mark probability denominator are displayed in the **min-th**, **max-th**, and **mark-prob** columns, respectively.

NOTE   The format of the WRED data in the output of **show interface** might vary between IOS releases.

Committed Access Rate

Committed Access Rate (CAR) is used to control bandwidth coming into or going out of an interface. This bandwidth control is called *rate limiting* and is also known as *policing*. For example, you might choose to limit the bandwidth coming from a particular source or application. Traffic exceeding the threshold limit you specify can be dropped or reclassified (using IP precedence), based on the policy you define.

CAR can also be used to classify packets into IP precedence levels without rate-limiting them at all. For example, you might use CAR to classify packets based on application and rely on some other mechanism such as WFQ to deliver the QoS for those packets.

You can use a flexible criteria of access lists, IP precedence, or incoming interface (the interface on which the packet arrived) to specify the exact packets you want to rate-limit or classify.

This section covers

- Rate Policies
- Configuring Cisco Express Forwarding
- Configuring CAR
- Validating CAR Configuration

Rate Policies

To rate-limit or classify packets, you must first define a *rate policy*. This rate policy defines the bandwidth thresholds and actions to take when traffic exceeds (or conforms to) your thresholds. For example, you can configure an interface to drop all FTP traffic exceeding 240 kbps.

The rate policy contains *rate limits* that define the bandwidth thresholds and the exceed or conform actions. Some of the exceed and conform actions you can define are

- **Drop**—Drop the packet.
- **Transmit**—Transmit the packet.
- **Continue**—Go to the next rate limit in the list.
- **Set precedence and transmit**—Set the precedence of the packet to a value and then transmit it.
- **Set precedence and continue**—Set the precedence of the packet to a value and then go to the next rate limit in the list.

To define a rate limit, you must specify three numbers:

- **Average rate (in bps)**—The bandwidth throughput allowed before traffic is subject to the exceed action. All traffic below the average rate is said to *conform*. Traffic above the average rate is allowed to burst or is said to *exceed* (this depends on how you configure the normal and excess burst sizes, described in the following two paragraphs).
- **Normal burst size (in bytes)**—The number of bytes allowed in a burst before some traffic is subject to the exceed action. Traffic is allowed to burst this many bytes above the average rate before the router applies the exceed action to *some* of the packets (drops the packet, reclassifies the packet, or another action you define). Why "some" of the packets? Because traffic that bursts between the normal burst size and the excess burst size is dropped randomly in a RED-like manner (see "Random Early Detection," earlier in this chapter), helping to throttle back TCP-based flows before the excess burst size is reached.
- **Excess burst size (in bytes)**—The number of bytes allowed in a burst before all traffic is subject to the exceed action. Traffic is allowed to burst this many bytes above the average rate before the router applies the exceed action to *all* of the packets (drops the packet, reclassifies the packet, or another action you define). If the excess burst size is zero, the router applies the exceed action to all traffic that exceeds the average rate (no bursts allowed).

NOTE   CAR might not be compatible with all router interfaces, such as PRI and tunnel interfaces. Check with Cisco for the most current restrictions.

Configuring Cisco Express Forwarding

At the time of this writing, *Cisco Express Forwarding (CEF)* must be enabled on VIP-equipped routers before you can configure CAR. Other Cisco routers, such as the smaller access routers, might not need CEF configured (see the section "Configuring CAR"). CEF is a scalable, high-performance switching mode designed for large networks and dynamic traffic patterns. To enable CEF, configure the **ip cef switch** command in global configuration mode (the router must also run an IOS image that includes CEF support):

```
Cisco7513#conf t
Enter configuration commands, one per line.  End with CNTL/Z.
Cisco7513(config)#ip cef switch
Cisco7513(config)#^Z
```

To enable distributed CEF (DCEF) for processing on a distributed processor such as a VIP in a Cisco 7500 router, use the **ip cef distributed switch** command:

```
Cisco7513#conf t
Enter configuration commands, one per line.  End with CNTL/Z.
Cisco7513(config)#ip cef distributed switch
Cisco7513(config)#^Z
```

TIP   To verify that CEF is enabled on an interface, issue the **show cef interface** command.

Configuring CAR

To apply a rate policy on an interface, you configure by using the **rate-limit** command in interface configuration mode. The following example limits all inbound FTP traffic on Hssi0/0/0 to 240 kbps of bandwidth with 32 KB of burst. Inbound FTP traffic that exceeds the average rate (240 kbps) and the excess burst size (32 KB) is dropped.

```
interface Hssi0/0/0
rate-limit input access-group 101 240000 32000 32000 conform-action transmit exceed-
    action drop
!
access-list 101 permit tcp any any eq ftp-data
access-list 101 permit tcp any eq ftp-data any
```

Notice these in the preceding example:

- The command **rate-limit input access-group 101 240000 32000 32000 conform-action transmit exceed-action drop** applies an input rate policy to the interface Hssi0/0/0. To configure a rate policy for outbound traffic, use the keyword **output** instead of **input**.

- The rate policy applies to packets received on the interface that match the criteria defined by access list 101 (FTP traffic to or from any source or destination). For more information on access lists, see Chapter 6, "Deploying Basic Security Services."

- Throughput is limited to 240 kbps of bandwidth and is allowed to burst above this average rate for 32 KB. Traffic that falls below 240 kbps is said to conform and is allowed through the interface (conform-action transmit). Traffic that exceeds 240 kbps and bursts more than 32 KB is said to exceed and is dropped (**exceed-action drop**).

Note   Although the preceding example configures the exceed action as **drop**, a better drop policy is to use CAR to reclassify the non-conformant traffic to a lower precedence (**exceed-action set-prec-transmit**) and then use WRED to drop the lower precedence packets.

- The normal burst size and the excess burst size are equal, meaning all traffic below 32 KB of burst is said to conform and all traffic above 32 KB of burst is said to exceed.

You can configure CAR on a VIP module (Cisco 7500 routers) and run it in distributed processing mode. Called distributed CAR (DCAR), this feature improves performance by moving CAR processing off of the router's main CPU and onto the VIP module. At the time of this writing, DCAR can scale to DS-3 (45 Mbps) and OC-3 (155 Mbps), depending on the VIP model. You must have DCEF enabled on the interface to enable DCAR (see "Configuring Cisco Express Forwarding," earlier in this chapter).

Defining Multiple Rate Policies

You can define more than one rate policy per interface. The following example sets rate policies for FTP traffic at 240 kbps, Web traffic at 600 kbps, and all other traffic at 160 kbps. Web traffic conforming to the rate policy is transmitted with precedence level 4, and Web traffic that exceeds the rate policy is transmitted to precedence level zero (it is not dropped):

```
interface Hssi0/0/0
  rate-limit input access-group 101 240000 32000 32000 conform-action transmit exceed-
      action drop
  rate-limit input access-group 102 600000 24000 32000 conform-action set-prec-transmit
      4 exceed-action set-prec-transmit 0
  rate-limit input 160000 16000 24000 conform-action transmit exceed-action drop
!
access-list 101 permit tcp any any eq ftp-data
access-list 102 permit tcp any any eq www
```

Notice these in the preceding example:

- The command **rate-limit input access-group 101 240000 32000 32000 conform-action transmit exceed-action drop** sets the same rate policy for FTP traffic as the previous example.

- The command **rate-limit input access-group 102 600000 24000 32000 conform-action set-prec-transmit 4 exceed-action set-prec-transmit 0** sets an input rate policy for web traffic of 600 kbps with a normal burst size of 24 KB and an excess burst size of 32 KB. Web traffic conforming to this rate policy is transmitted with precedence level 4, and web traffic that exceeds this rate policy is transmitted with a precedence level zero. Here, instead of dropping the packets that exceed the policy, you are reclassifying them.

- The command **rate-limit input 160000 16000 24000 conform-action transmit exceed-action drop** is a catchall for all other input traffic and sets the rate policy to 160 kbps with a normal burst size of 16 KB and an excess burst size of 24 KB. Traffic conforming to the policy is transmitted, and traffic that exceeds the policy is immediately dropped at the interface.

Using CAR Rate-Limit Access Lists

In addition to standard and extended access lists, you can match traffic by using two CAR-specific access lists called *rate-limit access lists*.

- IP precedence rate-limit access lists simply match packets that have a precedence value you define. The command is

  ```
  access-list rate-limit <1-99> <precedence value>
  ```

  This access list, in conjunction with a rate policy, enables you to rate-limit traffic based on precedence values.

- MAC address rate-limit access lists match traffic that has a MAC address you define. The command for MAC address rate-limit access lists is

  ```
  access-list rate-limit <100-199> <MAC address>
  ```

- With MAC address rate-limit access lists, you can rate-limit traffic from a specific host or neighboring router. This can be useful when your router accepts traffic from a device outside of your control (at Internet exchange points, for example).

Using CAR to Classify Traffic

To classify packets (and not rate-limit them), configure both the conform action and the exceed action to set the precedence and transmit the packet. Here is an example:

```
interface Hssi0/0/0
  rate-limit input access-group 101 240000 32000 32000 conform-action set-prec-
    transmit 3 exceed-action set-prec-transmit 3
!
access-list 101 permit tcp any any eq www
```

The command **rate-limit input access-group 101 240000 32000 32000 conform-action set-prec-transmit 3 exceed-action set-prec-transmit 3** classifies all traffic matching access list 101 (all Web traffic) to precedence level 3, regardless of the traffic rate. Because the conform and exceed actions are the same, the bandwidth and burst numbers are unimportant.

Validating CAR Configuration

To validate that CAR is enabled on an interface, issue the **show interfaces rate-limit** command:

```
Cisco7513# show interfaces hssi0/0/0 rate-limit

Hssi0/0/0
  Input
    matches: access-group 101
      params: 240000 bps, 32000 limit, 32000 extended limit
      conformed 728331 packets, 445031609 bytes; action: transmit
      exceeded 62607 packets, 36710379 bytes; action: drop
      last packet: 473ms ago, current burst: 0 bytes
      last cleared 01:02:05 ago, conformed 256000 bps, exceeded 311000 bps
  Output
    matches: access-group 101
      params: 240000 bps, 32000 limit, 32000 extended limit
      conformed 672193 packets, 392055184 bytes; action: transmit
      exceeded 57203 packets, 30198131 bytes; action: drop
      last packet: 473ms ago, current burst: 0 bytes
      last cleared 01:02:05 ago, conformed 248000 bps, exceeded 293000 bps
```

The output confirms that a rate policy is configured on Hssi0/0/0 in both the inbound and outbound directions. The policy applies to packets matching access list 101 (**matches: access-group 101**) and defines a rate limit of 240 kbps with 32 KB of normal (**limit**) and excess (**extended**) burst (line starting with **params:**). The output also shows the statistics and conform or exceed actions for the rate policy (lines starting with **conformed** and **exceeded**).

Class-Based WFQ

Class-based WFQ (CBWFQ) is a follow-on to regular WFQ (refer to Chapter 4) and supports the concept of user-defined traffic classes. Instead of queuing on a per-conversation (per-flow) basis, with CBWFQ you define groups or classes of traffic and then control the QoS for each class. While CBWFQ is not automatic like WFQ, it gives you greater control over traffic queuing and bandwidth allocation. Additionally, CBWFQ incorporates the WRED mechanism covered earlier, in the section "Configuring WRED." You can enable WRED within a class for finer control than regular WRED. This is like activating WRED within individual queues on an interface rather than on the entire interface.

This section covers:

- Configuring CBWFQ
- Verifying CBWFQ

NOTE   There is a version of class-based WFQ that runs in a distributed processing mode on VIP-equipped routers like the 7500. Called *Distributed WFQ (DWFQ)*, this flavor of WFQ is designed for high speed links and has a different configuration syntax than CBWFQ. Consult the IOS documentation for DWFQ commands.

Configuring CBWFQ

Configuring CBWFQ comprises three basic steps:

Step 1   Separate your traffic into classes with class maps.

Step 2   Define the QoS for each class using policy maps.

Step 3   Apply the policy map to an interface.

The following sections demonstrate each of these steps using an example.

Separate Your Traffic Into Classes with Class Maps

The first step in CBWFQ is to separate your traffic into different classes so you can later apply QoS to those classes. Class maps define the names of your classes and the traffic associated with each class.

Consider an example. Suppose you need to define two classes with different QoS characteristics. One class of traffic is for high-priority, intranet Web (HTTP) traffic, and another class is for low-priority, "casual surfing" Web traffic. You might configure your class map like so:

```
Router(config)#class-map CLASS-HTTP-HI
Router(config-cmap)#match access-group 101
Router(config-cmap)#exit
Router(config)#class-map CLASS-HTTP-LO
Router(config-cmap)#match access-group 102
Router(config-cmap)#exit
```

NOTE   Cisco began CBWFQ support in IOS release 12.0(5)T.

The command **class-map CLASS-HTTP-HI** creates a class called CLASS-HTTP-HI.

The command **match access-group 101** defines the match criteria for CLASS-HTTP-HI. All packets that meet the criteria in access list 101 belong to this class. Because this is the high-priority Web class, you would write list 101 such that it matches all of the Web traffic in your intranet—HTTP packets to or from your major nets, for example. See Chapter 6 for access list information.

Similarly, the commands **class-map CLASS-HTTP-LO** and **match access-group 102** configure a class and match criteria for the low-priority Web traffic. Access list 102 would simply be the inverse of access list 101 and represent all other Web traffic (non-intranet Web traffic).

NOTE   In addition to access lists, you can match based on the protocol and the input (arrival) interface with the commands **match protocol** and **match input-interface**, respectively.

Define the QoS for Each Class Using Policy Maps

With the classes defined, you next configure the QoS for each class using policy maps. The **policy-map** command and its supporting commands accomplish this:

```
Router(config)#policy-map MYPOLICY
Router(config-pmap)#class CLASS-HTTP-HI
Router(config-pmap-c)#bandwidth 5000
Router(config-pmap-c)#random-detect
Router(config-pmap-c)#exit
Router(config-pmap)#class CLASS-HTTP-LO
Router(config-pmap-c)#bandwidth 1000
Router(config-pmap-c)#queue-limit 40
Router(config-pmap-c)#exit
```

The command **policy-map MYPOLICY** creates a policy map called MYPOLICY that will later be applied to an interface.

The command **class CLASS-HTTP-HI** specifies the previously defined class for which you want to define QoS parameters. Notice the prompt change to **config-pmap-c**.

The command **bandwidth 5000** assigns 5000 Kbps of the link bandwidth for the class, CLASS-HTTP-HI. During congestion, this class is allocated a 5000 Kbps share of the link.

NOTE   Just like regular WFQ, CBWFQ uses weights to determine QoS. But, you don't see any weight parameters here because CBWFQ automatically calculates weight values behind the scenes, based on the interface bandwidth (set by the interface **bandwidth** command) and the value you supply with the policy map **bandwidth** command.

The command **random-detect** activates WRED within the class CLASS-HTTP-HI. This provides WRED's congestion avoidance scheme (and all its benefits) within the class.

NOTE   As with interface-based WRED, you can change CBWFQ's WRED behavior within a class with the **random-detect precedence** command. You also can alter the exponential weighting constant with the **random-detect exponential-weighting-constant** command. See "Configuring WRED" for more information.

The command **class CLASS-HTTP-LO** enables configuration of the other previously defined class, CLASS-HTTP-LO.

The command **bandwidth 1000** allocates 1000 Kbps of bandwidth to CLASS-HTTP-LO.

Each class has an associated queue. The command **queue-limit 40** specifies the maximum depth of the queue belonging to the class. Here, up to 40 packets belonging to CLASS-HTTP-LO may be enqueued at any one time. The default value is 64.

NOTE   CBWFQ is quite similar to custom queuing. In CBWFQ, you classify traffic into user-defined classes and then specify the bandwidth each class receives. This is the same approach as custom queuing, but without the hassle of figuring out byte-counts. There are other differences: Custom queuing does not support WRED and CBWFQ is a newer technology (CBWFQ could undergo future enhancements).

CBWFQ has a default class called **class-default**. Packets that do not match the criteria specified in your user-defined classes fall into this catch-all class. You configure it like other classes:

```
Router(config)#policy-map MYPOLICY
Router(config-pmap)#class class-default
Router(config-pmap-c)#bandwidth 2000
Router(config-pmap-c)#random-detect
Router(config-pmap-c)#exit
```

The preceding configuration allocates 2000 Kbps to **class-default** and enables WRED within the class.

The default class (class-default) has a unique feature of fair queuing within the class. It's like having conversation queues within class-default—or "queues within a queue." This is useful for ensuring fairness to all application flows with the default class. To enable fair queuing within class-default, issue the **fair-queue** command:

```
Router(config)#policy-map MYPOLICY
Router(config-pmap)#class class-default
Router(config-pmap-c)#fair-queue 20
Router(config-pmap-c)#random-detect
Router(config-pmap-c)#exit
```

Where **fair-queue 20** enables fair-queuing within **class-default** using 20 conversation queues. See Chapter 4 for more on conversation queues and fair queuing.

Apply the Policy Map to an Interface

Finally, nothing happens until you apply the policy map to an interface:

```
Router(config)#int e0/0
Router(config-if)#service-policy output MYPOLICY
Router(config-if)#end
```

The command **service-policy output MYPOLICY** applies the policy map, MYPOLICY, to the interface and activates CBWFQ as defined by the policy map on Ethernet0/0.

Verifying CBWFQ

To verify CBWFQ configuration, simply issue the **show policy-map** enable mode command:

```
r3#sh policy-map
 Policy Map MYPOLICY
  Weighted Fair Queueing
   Class CLASS-HTTP-HI
    Bandwidth 5000 (kbps)
    exponential weight 9
    class   min-threshold   max-threshold   mark-probablity
    -----------------------------------------------------------

    0         -               -               1/10
    1         -               -               1/10
    2         -               -               1/10
    3         -               -               1/10
    4         -               -               1/10
    5         -               -               1/10
    6         -               -               1/10
    7         -               -               1/10
    rsvp      -               -               1/10

   Class CLASS-HTTP-LO
    Bandwidth 1000 (kbps)
    exponential weight 9
    class   min-threshold   max-threshold   mark-probablity
    -----------------------------------------------------------

    0         -               -               1/10
    1         -               -               1/10
    2         -               -               1/10
    3         -               -               1/10
    4         -               -               1/10
    5         -               -               1/10
    6         -               -               1/10
    7         -               -               1/10
    rsvp      -               -               1/10
```

```
Class class-default
  Flow Based Fair Queueing
  Number of Hashed Queues 20
  exponential weight 9
  class    min-threshold    max-threshold    mark-probablity
  ---------------------------------------------------------------

  0          -                -               1/10
  1          -                -               1/10
  2          -                -               1/10
  3          -                -               1/10
  4          -                -               1/10
  5          -                -               1/10
  6          -                -               1/10
  7          -                -               1/10
  rsvp       -                -               1/10
```

The **show policy-map interface** command validates the association between the policy map and the interface, and also displays queue statistics:

```
r3#sh pol int e0/0
 Ethernet0/0  output : MYPOLICY
  Weighted Fair Queueing
    Class CLASS-HTTP-HI
      Output Queue: Conversation 73
        Bandwidth 5000 (kbps) Packets Matched 1524
        mean queue depth: 4
        drops: class  random    tail    min-th    max-th    mark-prob
                0      67        26      20        40        1/10
                1      17        0       22        40        1/10
                2      0         0       24        40        1/10
                3      0         0       26        40        1/10
                4      0         0       28        40        1/10
                5      0         0       30        40        1/10
                6      0         0       32        40        1/10
                7      0         0       34        40        1/10
                rsvp   0         0       36        40        1/10
<lines deleted for brevity>
```

Summary

Although queuing strategies are fundamental building blocks of QoS, queuing alone does not provide enough controls for achieving end-to-end QoS for all situations. Your network (or parts of your network) might require additional services such as admission control and rate limiting to satisfy the QoS your applications require.

The following are the key concepts of this chapter:

- RSVP is a signaling protocol between applications and the network for QoS guarantees (called reservations) across a network.

- RSVP's admission control enables the network to reject QoS requests to protect existing QoS reservations.

- RSVP relies on WFQ as the queuing mechanism for the bulk data flows.
- RED is a congestion-avoidance strategy that randomly drops packets, prevents global synchronization of TCP slow starts, and increases overall link utilization.
- RED inspects IP precedence and provides multiple levels of QoS.
- CAR is a form of rate-limiting bandwidth control. User-defined rate policies describe bandwidth thresholds for traffic flows and conform or exceed actions to take against those thresholds.
- CAR can also set IP precedence and classify traffic.
- CBWFQ is a follow-on to regular WFQ and supports user-defined traffic classes. With CBWFQ, you define classes and then control the QoS for each class.

PART III

Managing Security

CHAPTER 6

Deploying Basic Security Services

Your ability to leverage the security services of IOS is crucial to running a highly effective and robust Cisco network. Security services enforce your organization's policies and safeguard your network against misuse.

Proper deployment of IOS security increases the utility and improves the stability of the network. Remote access security, for example, enables your network to reach mobile users and telecommuters securely, and services that guard against hacking attacks preserve the integrity of networking devices and increase reliability of the network service. In the end, enhancing security increases the trust users have in the network and enables your organization to deploy applications over the network with greater confidence.

This chapter explains some basic concepts and common practices that are key to maintaining security on a Cisco network. Chapter 7, "Advanced Security Services, Part I: IPsec," and Chapter 8, "Advanced Security Services, Part II: IOS Firewall Feature Set," extend the discussion with more advanced security services.

The main topics of this chapter are

- Controlling Traffic with Access Control Lists
- Securing Access to the Router
- Deploying Authentication, Authorization, and Accounting
- Other IOS Commands for Basic Security

Controlling Traffic with Access Control Lists

The *access control list (ACL)*, or *access list*, is a key IOS feature whose programming syntax is used across many Cisco features. As the name implies, access lists are commonly used as security filters to block traffic from entering or exiting parts of the network. Over the years, however, Cisco has extended the access list syntax to other features, such as

- Routing and routing filters (see Chapter 3, "Managing Routing Protocols")
- Packet classification for QoS and queuing (see Chapter 4, "Deploying Basic Quality of Service Features," and Chapter 5, "Deploying Advanced Quality of Service Features")

- Encryption (see Chapter 7)
- Dial-on-demand routing (see the IOS Configuration Guides)

An understanding of access lists is fundamental to designing and maintaining a Cisco network.

This section covers

- Filtering Traffic with Access Lists
- Standard IP Access Lists
- Important Points for Designing Access Lists
- The Invisible Rule in Every Access List
- Extended IP Access Lists
- Access Lists for Combating Spoofing Attacks

Filtering Traffic with Access Lists

The most popular use of an access list is for filtering traffic on a router interface. As a traffic filter, the access list defines the traffic you want to permit and deny through an interface. After writing an access list that meets your filtering criteria, you apply it to the appropriate router interface (or multiple router interfaces). The router inspects traffic flowing through the interface and rejects the packets that are denied by your access list. Packets are filtered in either the inbound or outbound direction on an interface. (To filter in both directions, apply two access lists; see "Important Points for Designing Access Lists" later in this chapter.)

Figure 6-1 shows a simple application of an access list that inspects traffic inbound on interface Serial0. The purpose of this access list is to deny traffic from Company B.

Figure 6-1   *A Simple Application of an Inbound Access List*

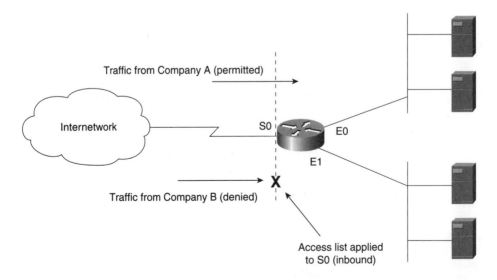

Company A's traffic is allowed through the interface and can reach the two network segments to the right of the router (assuming no other access lists are in effect), but Company B is denied access. Traffic not originating from Company A or Company B will be denied or permitted depending on the policy and how the access list was written. For example, the policy might dictate that only Company A's traffic should be allowed through the router and all other traffic (including Company B's) must be denied. On the other hand, if Company B is the real concern, the policy might allow everyone *except* Company B through the router. The syntax of access lists allows for flexible rules to cover these and more complex criteria. The access list in Figure 6-1 is an example of an *inbound access list*, which inspects packets entering a router's interface.

Figure 6-2 is an application of an *outbound access list* applied to an interface. The outbound access list filters traffic *exiting* a router interface.

Figure 6-2   *A Simple Application of an Outbound Access List*

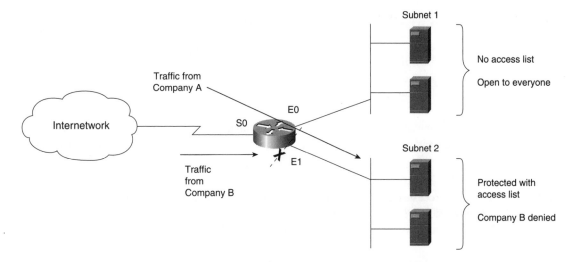

In this example, the outbound access list is applied to the router's Ethernet1 interface. Now, Company B's traffic is denied to subnet 2 only. All traffic, including traffic from Company B, is allowed to subnet 1 because there are no access lists denying traffic into Serial0 or out of Ethernet0.

Figure 6-3 is a conceptual view of a fictitious access list and illustrates the internal logic. An access list is a sequential progression of rules that describe your filtering policy.

Figure 6-3   *Conceptual View and Internal Logic of an Access List*

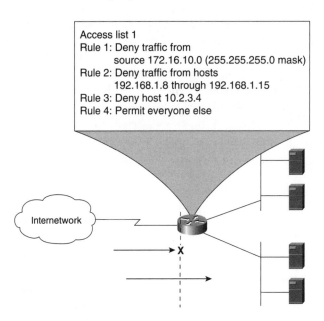

Each rule in the access list describes a pattern to match (an IP address, a protocol type, or other packet trait) and an instruction to the router to either permit (transmit) or deny (drop) the packet.

NOTE   Rules are processed in sequential order. When a packet matches a rule, the router takes the prescribed action (permits or denies the packet) and stops access-list processing for that packet. See "Important Points for Designing Access Lists" later in this chapter.

Access lists are very flexible; you can configure them to be granular or broad, depending on your requirements. For example, you can define an access list to deny a specific protocol from a single host, an entire network address space, or even all packets.

When you create an access list, you must give it a number (or a name in the case of named access lists—see the IOS Configuration Guides for named access lists). The number identifies the access list as a single entity in the router so it can be conveniently applied to one or more interfaces. This means you create an access list only once and then apply it to as many interfaces as needed.

There are restrictions on what numbers you can use, depending on the protocol being filtered. For IP, two types of access lists exist, each with its own number range:

- **Standard IP access lists**—To which you may assign numbers 1–99.
- **Extended IP access lists**—To which you may assign numbers 100–199.

Other number ranges for access lists (600–699, 800–899, and so on) are reserved for filtering such protocols as IPX, AppleTalk, DECnet, and XNS. The scope of this book is IP and so will focus on IP access lists: the standard IP access list and the extended IP access list. See the IOS Configuration Guides for configuring access lists for other protocols.

Standard IP Access Lists

The standard IP access list filters packets based on their *source* address. Each rule in the access list contains a bit pattern (expressed in dotted decimal notation like an IP address) that the router compares to source addresses. When a packet's source address matches the bit pattern, the router takes your prescribed action to either permit or deny the packet. Using a very flexible syntax, you can define granular rules that match a single source IP address or broad rules that match ranges of addresses (from multiple hosts, subnets, or networks, for example).

To create a standard IP access list, you must choose a number from 1–99 that will identify the access list in the router. The number range 1–99 is defined by Cisco and is reserved for standard IP access lists only. It doesn't matter which number you choose to identify your access list as long as it's in the range and unique from other access lists in the router.

Creating an Access List

To create your access list, you start with a rule. You include in this initial rule (and subsequent rules if there are any) the number of the access list. To create a standard access list that permits traffic from host 172.16.1.1, for example, configure the following:

```
MyRouter#conf t
Enter configuration commands, one per line.  End with CNTL/Z.
MyRouter(config)#access-list 1 permit 172.16.1.1 0.0.0.0
MyRouter(config)#exit
```

where **access-list 1 permit 172.16.1.1 0.0.0.0** adds a rule to access list 1 that permits packets with source address 172.16.1.1.

0.0.0.0 is the *wildcard* (also called the *mask* or *wildcard mask*) for the pattern 172.16.1.1. The wildcard tells the router which bits of the pattern to match and which to ignore. Like IP addresses, wildcards are 32 bits written in dotted decimal notation, like this:

0.0.0.0 equals 0000-0000.0000-0000.0000-0000.0000-0000

A zero in a bit position tells the router to match the bit; that is, to compare the bit in the packet's source address to the same bit in the pattern. Conversely, a one tells the router to ignore the bit— to skip a comparison of the bit in the packet to the same bit in the pattern. The one bit is often called the *don't care* bit because it indicates a bit position in the pattern that you want to ignore—you don't care if the bit is a one or a zero. Therefore, a wildcard 0.0.0.0 applied to the pattern 172.16.1.1 tells the router to match all 32 bits of the pattern 172.16.1.1. Because the wildcard has no don't care bits, the packet's source address must match 172.16.1.1 exactly for it to be permitted.

Using Wildcards to Match Address Ranges

Using one bits (don't care bits) in the wildcard is convenient for matching ranges of addresses. Consider the following access list, which permits addresses 192.169.1.128 through 192.169.1.159, inclusive:

```
access-list 2 permit 192.169.1.128 0.0.0.31
```

A good way to see what's going on is to convert the last octet of the pattern and wildcard to binary, line up the bits, and examine the don't care bits. You don't need to convert the other octets to binary in this example, because the first three octets of the wildcard are all zeros (to match all eight bits in each octet). Focusing on the last octet, the wildcard 0.0.0.31 tells the router to match the first three bits and ignore the last five bits.

Pattern: 192.169.1.128 equals 192.169.1.1000-0000
Wildcard: 0.0.0.31 equals 0.0.0.0001-1111

Lining up the pattern to the wildcard, the criteria to match is 192.169.1.100*x-xxxx*, where *x* indicates a don't care bit—the bit may be a zero or a one.

Line up the pattern with the wildcard:

```
192.169.1.100| 0-0000
    0.0.0.000| 1-1111
```

The pattern to match is 192.169.1.100*x-xxxx*.

If the last five bits can be any combination of zeros and ones, the rule permits addresses 192.169.1.1000-**0000**, 192.169.1.1001-**1111**, and everything between:

- Lowest address that matches (last 5 bits all zeros): 192.169.1.1000-**0000** (192.169.1.128)
- Highest address that matches (last 5 bits all ones): 192.169.1.1001-**1111** (192.169.1.159)

This bit-level analysis is how you determine that 192.169.1.128 with wildcard 0.0.0.31 matches the range 192.169.1.128 through 192.169.1.159, inclusive.

As you configure wildcards, consult Table 6-1 for assistance (or memorize it). Table 6-1 provides a handy reference for mapping wildcards that cover ranges to their binary equivalents. Notice that each wildcard contains binary zeros (match bits) on the left and binary ones (don't care bits) on the right.

Table 6-1   *Common Octets Used for Wildcards and Their Binary Equivalents*

Octet in Decimal[1]	Binary Equivalent
1	0000-0001
3	0000-0011
7	0000-0111
15	0000-1111
31	0001-1111
63	0011-1111
127	0111-1111
255	1111-1111

1.   For example, the octet *x* in 0.0.0.*x* or the octet *y* in 0.0.*y*.255.

The previous example used a wildcard of 0.0.0.31. Using Table 6-1, you can verify that the binary expansion of 31 is indeed 0001-1111.

NOTE   Masking addresses with access list wildcards is typically the reverse of subnet masking (see Chapter 1, "Managing Your IP Address Space"). Wildcards usually begin with a series of zeros and end with a series of ones (0.0.255.255, for example). Subnet masks begin with ones and end with zeros (255.255.0.0, for example).

Adding Rules to an Access List

If one pattern-wildcard pair is all you need to define the traffic you wish to filter, all you need is a one-rule access list like the previous example. However, you'll often need to add rules to your access list to permit or deny more types of traffic (from multiple addresses, for example).

To add more rules to an access list, you simply continue entering one-line rules with the same access list number. For instance, you could add more rules to the first example (access list 1) like this:

```
MyRouter(config)#access-list 1 deny 172.16.1.0 0.0.0.255
MyRouter(config)#access-list 1 permit 192.168.2.8 0.0.0.3
```

By issuing the **show running-config** command, you can view all three rules in the access list:

```
MyRouter(config)#exit
MyRouter#sh run
Building configuration...
Current configuration:
[partial listing, some lines not shown]

access-list 1 permit 172.16.1.1      (prior existing rule)
access-list 1 deny   172.16.1.0 0.0.0.255    (new rule)
access-list 1 permit 192.168.2.8 0.0.0.3     (new rule)
!
line con 0
line 1 8
 transport input all
line aux 0
line vty 0 4
 exec-timeout 0 0
 password cisco
 login
!
end
```

There is also a **show access-lists** enable mode command:

```
2503#sh access-l
Standard IP access list 1
    permit 172.16.1.1
    deny   172.16.1.0, wildcard bits 0.0.0.255
    permit 192.168.2.8, wildcard bits 0.0.0.3
```

Notice that the output doesn't include the wildcard 0.0.0.0 even though it was typed in during configuration. This is a shorthand notation; for access lists that match an address exactly, you do not have to type the wildcard 0.0.0.0. In fact, the three following commands are equivalent:

```
2503(config)#access-list 3 deny 192.168.1.1 0.0.0.0
2503(config)#access-list 3 deny 192.168.1.1
2503(config)#access-list 3 deny host 192.168.1.1
```

In the last line, the **host** keyword tells the router that the next parameter is an exact host address to match.

The following frequently used rule matches *any* address:

```
2503(config)#access-list 4 permit 0.0.0.0 255.255.255.255
```

The wildcard 255.255.255.255 contains all ones and means to ignore all 32 bits of the address pattern. The pattern 0.0.0.0 isn't very interesting because the pattern doesn't matter. Because the wildcard includes 32 don't care bits, the meaning of **access-list 4 permit 0.0.0.0 255.255.255.255** is "permit all packets" and all 32 bits will be ignored. This is commonly called the *permit-any* rule. The shorthand notation for 0.0.0.0 255.255.255.255 is simply the keyword **any**; thus, the following commands are equivalent:

```
2503(config)#access-list 4 permit 0.0.0.0 255.255.255.255
2503(config)#access-list 4 permit 123.123.123.123 255.255.255.255
2503(config)#access-list 4 permit any
```

NOTE   The permit-any rule often follows one or more deny rules. In other words, it's typical to write an access list that denies certain addresses but permits all others. See "Important Points for Designing Access Lists" later in this chapter for more design considerations.

Applying the Access List to an Interface

An access list is just a collection of rules occupying router memory and doesn't do anything until you tell the router how to use it. For example, you can write an access list that denies all traffic from host 172.16.1.1, but until you apply the access list to an interface, the access list will just sit on the router in a *ready for use* state.

To apply an access list to an interface and put it into action, use the **ip access-group** interface command:

```
RTA#conf t
Enter configuration commands, one per line.  End with CNTL/Z.
RTA(config)#interface s0
RTA(config-if)#ip access-group 1 in
```

The command **interface s0** selects an interface for configuration and changes the prompt to interface configuration mode. The command **ip access-group 1 in** applies access list number 1 to interface Serial0 (s0). The **in** keyword tells the router to use the access list to filter inbound traffic. Alternatively, you can use the **out** keyword to filter outbound traffic—that is, traffic leaving the router through this interface.

There's no harm in writing an access list and never applying it, but it would be a waste of time because the access list would sit on the router passively without inspecting a single packet. Therefore, remember these two tasks when deploying access lists:

- Write the access list with the rules you want.
- Apply the access list to the appropriate interface to begin filtering packets with it.

Also, don't forget to specify whether the access list should inspect *inbound* or *outbound* packets when you apply it to the interface.

To verify that the access list is properly applied to an interface, issue the **show ip interface** command:

```
RTA#sh ip int e0
Ethernet0 is up, line protocol is up
  Internet address is 192.168.80.138/30
  Broadcast address is 255.255.255.255
  Address determined by non-volatile memory
  MTU is 1500 bytes
  Helper address is not set
  Directed broadcast forwarding is enabled
  Outgoing access list is not set
  Inbound  access list is 1
```

The output **Inbound access list is 1** confirms that access list number 1 is active on this interface and is filtering inbound traffic.

Important Points for Designing Access Lists

You should be aware of some important points when designing your access lists:

- Rules are processed in sequential order. That is, the router compares a packet to the access list, starting with the first rule on the list, and—if the first rule does not match the packet—progresses down the list until it finds a rule that matches the packet. The first rule that matches the packet is the one the router uses to either permit or deny the packet.

- After permitting or denying the packet, the router stops access-list processing for that packet and does not continue down the rules list. When the next packet arrives on the interface, the router restarts the filtering process, beginning with the first rule on the access list.

- Try to write your access list so that the majority of traffic is matched in the first few rules at the top of your access list. This way, most of the packets will be quickly matched and fewer packets will be compared against all of the rules in the access list. This will improve access-list processing on your router.

- As you write rules for your access list, each rule is added to the end of the access list in the order you enter it. You cannot insert rules between two rules that already exist in your access list. If you need to insert a rule, you must delete the entire access list and rewrite it in its new form; therefore, a good idea is to save your router configurations and use copy-and-paste editing techniques when your access lists are long.

  If you are using a terminal emulation program, issue the **show running-config** command and paste the old access list into a text editor. Make the changes offline in the editor. Then, in IOS, delete the old access list with the **no access-list** command and paste the modified access list from the editor to the IOS configuration prompt.

TIP   To delete an access list, use the **no access-list** command:

```
RTA(config)#no access-list 1
```

- You cannot edit rules that already exist in an access list. As with inserting rules, you must delete the access list and reenter the list in its new form. Again, use copy-and-paste editing to avoid lengthy reconfiguration.

- When adding a rule that denies a particular packet, be certain that no preceding rules in the list match and undesirably permit that same packet. Remember, the *first* rule with a match is the one that is used.

- All packets will match at least one rule in the access list, because the last rule is a default, invisible, catchall rule that denies *all* packets. See "The Invisible Rule in Every Access List" later in this chapter for details.

- Access lists are unidirectional. When you apply an access list to an interface, you should specify whether the list is for matching inbound or outbound packets. If you do not specify the direction, outbound is the default. If you want to filter traffic both inbound and outbound on an interface, you must apply two access lists: one for inbound and another for outbound. You may apply the same access list for both the inbound and outbound directions.

- You may apply the same access list to multiple interfaces.

- Access list numbers are unique only within a router. An access list on one router is meaningless to another router.

- Try not to make your access lists too long. If they contain many rules, performance of the router might be slowed because the router must compare each packet to each rule in the access list (this is a minimal concern on routers that use hardware-based access lists). How long is too long depends on the horsepower of your router, the amount of throughput you need to sustain on a link, and the acceptable trade-off you can handle between security and performance.

NOTE   Enabling services such as Cisco's NetFlow™ switching can minimize the performance impact of long access lists. Consult the IOS Configuration Guides for NetFlow switching information.

- Try to write access lists with as few rules as possible while still meeting your filtering requirement. You might be able to consolidate multiple rules into one by leveraging the don't care bits to match ranges of addresses.

- Standard IP access lists can only match on bit patterns in the source address of packets. To match on the destination address and other fields of a packet, see the "Extended IP Access Lists" section later in this chapter.

The Invisible Rule in Every Access List

You need to be keenly aware that IOS automatically adds a default rule at the end of every access list. This terminating rule is invisible: It does not appear in outputs of **show running-config** or **show access-lists**, but it's there and you cannot disable it. The invisible rule is a *deny-any* rule that denies all packets that haven't matched the user-defined rules in your access list. For example, consider that you have configured an access list like this:

```
2509(config)#access-list 1 permit 172.16.1.1 0.0.0.0
2509(config)#access-list 1 deny 172.16.1.0 0.0.0.255
2509(config)#access-list 1 permit 192.168.2.8 0.0.0.3
```

The access list looks like this logically:

```
access-list 1 permit 172.16.1.1 0.0.0.0
access-list 1 deny 172.16.1.0 0.0.0.255
access-list 1 permit 192.168.2.8 0.0.0.3
(access-list 1 deny any)
```

where **(access-list 1 deny any)** is the invisible terminating rule at the end of this and every other access list, including extended access lists (covered later in "Extended IP Access Lists").

The invisible rule is a safety measure to prevent accidental leakage through the access list in case you make a configuration mistake—that is, in case you inadvertently missed some packets in your rules that should be denied by the access list. Because you most likely configured the access list for security, Cisco decided that denying packets that don't match your rules is the way to be safe. In a sense, better safe than sorry. If you find that packets are undesirably blocked by the invisible deny-any rule, you can configure a permit rule that matches the packets that should be allowed through.

TIP

When you're configuring access lists, don't forget that routing protocol packets (such as OSPF hellos) and other control packets are circulating on the network and might be blocked by your access list. If an access list undesirably blocks these packets because of the invisible deny-any rule, go back and add rules to your access list that permit them. You might have to use extended access lists for more granular matching rules (see the following section, "Extended IP Access Lists").

Extended IP Access Lists

Extended access lists enable you to build more elaborate rules for filtering than do standard access lists. Although standard access lists only match on source address, extended access lists can match on

- Source address
- Destination address
- Protocol (ICMP, TCP, UDP, EIGRP, IGRP, OSPF, and others)
- Protocol-specific options (Telnet, FTP, HTTP, SMTP, Echo, SNMP, and others)
- Precedence level
- Type of service (TOS)

Extended Access List Syntax

The syntax for extended access lists is

```
access-list access-list-number {deny¦permit} protocol source source-wildcard
destination destination-wildcard [precedence precedence] [tos tos]
```

That rule looks like quite a lot because you have more options, but it's really not much more than a standard access list. Consider the following example:

```
access-list 100 permit ip 172.16.1.0 0.0.0.255 192.168.25.0 0.0.0.31
```

where 100 is the access list number that for extended access lists must lie in the range 100–199, inclusive. Any number in the range will work as long as it does not conflict with other extended access lists in the router. 172.16.1.0 0.0.0.255 is the source-matching criteria and has the same meaning and syntax as standard access lists. To quickly review:

- **172.16.1.0 0.0.0.255** means the router will compare the first three octets of the pattern 172.16.1.0 to the source address of the packet—the last octet contains don't care bits, as indicated by the 0.0.0.255 wildcard.

- **192.168.25.0 0.0.0.31** is the destination matching criteria and also follows the same pattern-wildcard syntax.

For a packet to match this rule and be permitted, it must match both the source and destination criteria.

TIP   You must specify both source and destination matching criteria in rules for extended access lists.

As with standard access lists, the shorthand notations for **any** and **host** matching are allowed. Here's an example:

```
access-list 101 permit ip any host 192.168.25.10
```

Here, the source criteria is **any** (from any source) and the destination criteria is **host 192.168.25.10** (an exact match of the address 192.168.25.10). In more human terms, the previous rule might read:

Permit packets from any source to host 192.168.25.10.

To filter packets based on protocol information, you build on the source or destination criteria. To block Telnet sessions from one range of addresses to another, for example, you might configure an access list similar to this one:

```
access-list 102 deny tcp 192.168.25.0 0.0.0.31 172.16.1.0 0.0.0.255 eq telnet
access-list 102 permit ip any any
```

where the keyword **tcp** in the first rule tells the router that the rule filters TCP packets only.

TIP   To get a listing of other protocol options, use the question mark key and context-sensitive help:

```
MyRouter(config)#access-list 102 deny ?
  <0-255>  An IP protocol number
  eigrp    Cisco's EIGRP routing protocol
  gre      Cisco's GRE tunneling
  icmp     Internet Control Message Protocol
  igmp     Internet Gateway Message Protocol
  igrp     Cisco's IGRP routing protocol
  ip       Any Internet Protocol
  ipinip   IP in IP tunneling
  nos      KA9Q NOS compatible IP over IP tunneling
  ospf     OSPF routing protocol
  tcp      Transmission Control Protocol
  udp      User Datagram Protocol
```

The source criteria is **192.168.25.0 0.0.0.31** and is a straightforward match on an address pattern. The destination criteria is **172.16.1.0 0.0.0.255 eq telnet**, where the keywords **eq telnet** impose an additional requirement for a destination match: The destination port number must be equal to Telnet (port 23). The keyword **eq** is a logical operand and is short for "equal to." The operands you can use for matching port numbers are

- **eq**—equal to

- **neq**—not equal to

- **gt**—greater than

- **lt**—less than

- **range**—to specify the starting and ending port numbers in a range

To get a listing of well-known port numbers and their names, use the question mark key and context-sensitive help built into IOS. Here's a listing for TCP:

```
RTA(config)#access-list 101 deny tcp 192.168.25.0 0.0.0.31 172.16.1.0 0.0.0.255 eq ?
  <0-65535>  Port number
  bgp        Border Gateway Protocol (179)
  chargen    Character generator (19)
  cmd        Remote commands (rcmd, 514)
  daytime    Daytime (13)
  discard    Discard (9)
  domain     Domain Name Service (53)
  echo       Echo (7)
  exec       Exec (rsh, 512)
  finger     Finger (79)
  ftp        File Transfer Protocol (21)
  ftp-data   FTP data connections (used infrequently, 20)
  gopher     Gopher (70)
  hostname   NIC hostname server (101)
  ident      Ident Protocol (113)
```

```
irc       Internet Relay Chat (194)
klogin    Kerberos login (543)
kshell    Kerberos shell (544)
login     Login (rlogin, 513)
lpd       Printer service (515)
nntp      Network News Transport Protocol (119)
pop2      Post Office Protocol v2 (109)
pop3      Post Office Protocol v3 (110)
smtp      Simple Mail Transport Protocol (25)
sunrpc    Sun Remote Procedure Call (111)
syslog    Syslog (514)
tacacs    TAC Access Control System (49)
talk      Talk (517)
telnet    Telnet (23)
time      Time (37)
uucp      Unix-to-Unix Copy Program (540)
whois     Nicname (43)
www       World Wide Web (HTTP, 80)
```

TIP   You can type port numbers instead of the keywords **telnet**, **ftp**, **www**, and so on.

Look again at the previous two-line example (access list 102):

```
access-list 102 deny tcp 192.168.25.0 0.0.0.31 172.16.1.0 0.0.0.255 eq telnet
access-list 102 permit ip any any
```

The rule **access-list 102 permit ip any any** at the end of the list permits all other IP traffic—that is, traffic not matching the first rule. This *permit-any-any* rule is necessary because the invisible terminating rule would deny all other traffic, which is undesirable in this example. Refer to "The Invisible Rule in Every Access List," earlier in this chapter.

Examining the list whole lines at a time, the first rule, **access-list 102 deny tcp 192.168.25.0 0.0.0.31 172.16.1.0 0.0.0.255 eq telnet**, translates into human terms like this:

Deny TCP packets *from* source 192.168.25.0 (match first 27 bits) with any source port number *to* destination 172.16.1.0 (match first 24 bits) with destination port number equal to Telnet (port 23).

NOTE   The wildcard 0.0.0.31 is 0000-0000.0000-0000.0000-0000.0001-1111 in binary (see Table 6-1).

And the last rule, **access-list 102 permit ip any any**, translates to

Permit IP packets from any source to any destination.

Applying this access list 102 as an inbound list on Router A's Ethernet0 (see Figure 6-4) prevents Telnet sessions initiated from the finance clients to the engineering servers. However, engineering clients can Telnet to the engineering servers successfully.

Figure 6-4   *Using the Example Access List 102 to Deny Telnet Sessions*

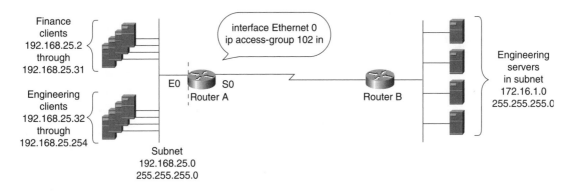

Applying the Extended Access List to an Interface

As with standard access lists, extended access lists do not filter traffic until you apply them to an interface with the **ip access-group** command. The following example applies access list 102 to Ethernet0 and specifies the inbound direction:

```
RTA(config)#int e0
RTA(config-if)#ip access-group 102 in
```

Logging Access List Activity

Sometimes it's useful to log the activity of traffic that is denied by an extended access list. This is especially true when you are using an access list for security and intentionally blocking conversations that shouldn't be happening. To log when packets match an access list rule, simply append the **log** keyword to the rule (logging is not available on standard access lists). For example, to log every time a packet is denied from sources matching 172.16.1.0 0.0.0.255, the access list might look like this:

```
access-list 103 deny ip 172.16.1.0 0.0.0.255 any log
<other access list rules>
access-list 103 permit ip any any
```

To view the log, issue the **show logging** command or check your syslog server if the router is sending output to a syslog server (see Appendix E, "A Crash Course in Cisco IOS," for syslog configuration):

```
2503#sh log
Syslog logging: enabled (0 messages dropped, 0 flushes, 0 overruns)
    Console logging: level debugging, 49 messages logged
    Monitor logging: level debugging, 0 messages logged
    Trap logging: level informational, 53 message lines logged
    Buffer logging: level debugging, 49 messages logged
        Log Buffer (4096 bytes):

%LINK-3-UPDOWN: Interface BRI0, changed state to up
%LINK-3-UPDOWN: Interface Ethernet0, changed state to up
<lines deleted>
*Apr 14 07:11:50: %SEC-6-IPACCESSLOGDP: list 103 denied icmp 172.16.1.1 -> 1
92.168.1.1 (0/0), 1 packet
*Apr 14 07:11:54: %SEC-6-IPACCESSLOGP: list 103 denied udp 172.16.1.1(0) ->
172.16.10.1(0), 23 packets
*Apr 14 07:12:23: %SEC-6-IPACCESSLOGP: list 103 denied tcp 172.16.1.1(0) ->
192.168.1.2(0), 1 packet
```

TIP	If you aren't getting timestamps in your log messages, configure the router with the **service timestamps log datetime** command:

```
RTA(config)#service timestamps log datetime
```

Monitoring Extended Access List Counters

Extended access lists maintain packet counters for each rule. These are useful when you're troubleshooting and verifying the operation of your access lists. You can view these statistics by issuing the **show access-lists** command:

```
RTA#sh access-l
Extended IP access list 103
    deny ip 172.16.1.0 0.0.0.255 any log (16 matches)
    permit ip any any (7703 matches)
```

TIP	Reset the counters with the **clear counters** enable mode command:

```
RTA#cle count
```

Access Lists for Combating Spoofing Attacks

IP address *spoofing* is an attack in which the hacker pretends to be a trusted computer by using an address within your range of acceptable internal addresses. Although spoofing is only one of many attacks practiced in the hacker world, it is one of the most popular and therefore should be on your list of attacks to thwart.

This section describes some basic anti-spoofing filters that are useful for almost any router connected to an untrusted network—for example, the Internet. The access list techniques in this section are generally considered good practices and a starting point for more sophisticated defenses.

An anti-spoofing access list is a defense against one style of attack, so it obviously cannot defend against all attacks and therefore should be used in conjunction with a dedicated firewall such as Cisco's PIX Firewall or a router running Cisco's IOS Firewall Feature Set (covered in Chapter 8). Dedicated firewalls also improve on the anti-spoof prevention performed by regular access lists. For more types of attacks and defenses, see the rest of this chapter, Chapter 7, and Chapter 8.

NOTE   Few will claim there's a 100 percent hacker-proof network out there on the Internet—to do so would probably attract the best hackers to their door. Even with an infinite budget and the best security technology available, organizations cannot ignore the fact that new vulnerabilities are found and more attacks invented regularly. Luckily, remedies are usually quick and published by vendors such as Cisco; still, preventing attacks is key to maintaining confidence in the network and its effectiveness for the users. The IOS-based techniques in this chapter, Chapter 7, and Chapter 8 will get you started and build on your current security practices. You can find some security references in the Bibliography.

The router in Figure 6-5 is configured with an anti-spoofing access list on interface Serial0, pointing to the public Internet.

Figure 6-5   *Deploying Anti-spoofing Access Lists to Increase Security*

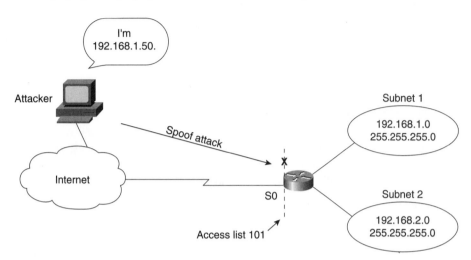

The access list configuration for the router in Figure 6-5 is as follows:

```
interface Serial0
ip address 172.16.1.1 255.255.255.252
ip access-group 101 in
!
access-list 101 deny   ip 192.168.1.0 0.0.0.255 any
access-list 101 deny   ip 192.168.2.0 0.0.0.255 any
access-list 101 deny   ip 127.0.0.0 0.255.255.255 any
access-list 101 permit ip any any
!
<lines deleted for brevity>
```

Access list 101 filters inbound traffic from the Internet on Serial0. The rule **access-list 101 deny ip 192.168.1.0 0.0.0.255 any** denies traffic from the Internet that has a source address belonging to the internal network, subnet 1 (with a subnet mask of 255.255.255.0). The filter is there because you wouldn't expect any inside address to *arrive* on the outside interface (Serial0) that points to the Internet. Any packets that come from the Internet with a source address from the internal network are highly suspicious of a spoofing attacker— that is, someone who looks like an internal computer but is coming from the Internet. If the attacker succeeds in masquerading as one of the internal clients, internal servers might think communicating with him is safe—a classic spoof job.

The rule **access-list 101 deny ip 192.168.2.0 0.0.0.255 any** is similar to the first rule. It ensures no packets are permitted from the Internet with a source address that belongs to subnet 2. This example has just two internal class C address ranges. With a larger internal network, you need to configure enough rules in your anti-spoofing access list to cover all of your internal addresses.

The rule **access-list 101 deny ip 127.0.0.0 0.255.255.255 any** denies packets that start with octet 127: IP loopback addresses for hosts. These packets should never appear on a physical link and certainly not from the Internet. Some spoof attacks use these reserved addresses as the source address. In these attacks, the hacker does not need to know what your addressing is on the inside.

Securing Access to the Router

The IOS command prompt is the primary place where you monitor and configure the router. By now, you have configured the router in IOS configuration mode and used some **show** commands, such as **show running-config** and **show access-lists**, to validate your work. For a quick start on basic IOS navigation and configuration, see Appendix E.

Without a doubt, you want to control who can access the command prompt, not only to control who can alter the behavior of your router but also to protect the information the router collects from your network. Configurations and statistics gleaned from a router tell a lot about your network's policies, topologies, traffic patterns, and attached systems. Therefore, controlling who can access a router is more than just protecting one device, it's protecting an intertwined operation of computer systems and policies.

These are the two main ways to access a router and get to the IOS prompt (also called the EXEC prompt):

- Connecting to the console port
- Initiating a Telnet session

NOTE   The most common way to connect to the console port is with an EIA/TIA-232 (RS-232) serial cable and client software with terminal emulation, but sometimes remotely dialing a modem connected to an AUX or other asynchronous serial port on the router is convenient. Detailed information is currently located at http://www.cisco.com/warp/public/701/6.html, or you can search for "modem, aux port" on Cisco's Web site (http://www.cisco.com). See also Appendix E.

After connecting to the router, you are placed into user mode and allowed some basic commands such as **ping**, **telnet**, **traceroute**, and so on. However, more useful administrator and configuration commands require enable mode.

This section covers

- Securing the Enable Mode of a Router
- Securing Telnet Access
- Securing Access to the Console Port

Securing the Enable Mode of a Router

The first thing you should do when configuring a router is set a password that protects the *enable mode* (the administrator level) of the router. You can think of the enable mode, also called the *privileged EXEC mode*, as the superuser level that is allowed to monitor and modify everything in the router. For basic information on navigating to and from enable mode, see Appendix E.

By default, no password is assigned to the enable mode, so you can get to it with a connection to the console port and the **enable** command:

```
RTA>enable
RTA#
```

You are not allowed into enable mode, however, when there is no enable password and you are connected to the router with Telnet. The following output is an attempt to initiate enable mode from a Telnet session on a router without an enable password. Notice that the message **No password set** is displayed and the prompt returns to user EXEC mode as indicated by the **>** character:

```
MyRouter>enable
% No password set
MyRouter>
```

To set the enable password, use the **enable secret** global command:

```
RTA#conf t
Enter configuration commands, one per line.  End with CNTL/Z.
RTA(config)#enable secret foo!enable
```

where **enable secret foo!enable** sets the enable password in this example to foo!enable (the exclamation point was used to make the password harder to guess). Attempts to change from user mode to enable mode now require the enable password:

```
RTA>en
Password: <Type the password here. Text is not displayed.>
RTA#
```

TIP

The **enable secret** command uses a one-way cryptographic hashing function to store the password securely. Another command, **enable password**, also sets the enable password but is not recommended because it is less secure.

Cisco IOS supports a total of 16 configurable modes called *privilege levels*. The idea is that you can configure privilege levels with different allowable commands and with different passwords. Then, based on the passwords people type, they are put into the corresponding level with IOS commands you allow for that level. For more information on privilege levels, consult the *Security Configuration Guide* IOS manual. By default, a router has two modes: the user EXEC mode (upon login) and the enable mode.

Securing Telnet Access

By default, Cisco routers support five simultaneous Telnet sessions, allowing up to five people to log into the router at the same time. The router treats these sessions as logical interfaces called *virtual terminal (or vty) lines*.

The router doesn't have any passwords configured on its vty ports by default. Trying to Telnet to the router without vty passwords will be unsuccessful. The router will respond with a message **Password required, but none set** and immediately terminate the attempt:

```
myserver#telnet 192.168.1.2
Trying...
Connected to 192.168.1.2.
Escape character is '^]'.

Password required, but none set

Connection closed by remote host.
```

To enable Telnet sessions to the router, you must at a minimum configure a password on the vty lines—or you can configure vty lines with the **no login** command and disable password checking entirely (not recommended). The following is an example:

```
RTA#conf t
Enter configuration commands, one per line.  End with CNTL/Z.
RTA(config)#service password-encryption
RTA(config)#line vty 0 4
RTA(config-line)#login
RTA(config-line)#password foo!pass
```

In this configuration:

- The command **service password-encryption** enables a feature that encrypts passwords in the router so you cannot see them in plaintext when viewing the configuration with the **show running-config** command.

- The command **line vty 0 4** tells the router that you want to simultaneously configure all five of the vty lines numbered 0-4. This changes the prompt to line configuration mode, as indicated by the text **config-line**.

- The command **login** enables password checking for vty (Telnet) connections. This should already be enabled by default, but it doesn't hurt to enter the command and ensure password checking is on.

- The last command, **password foo!pass**, sets the password for the vty lines to foo!pass.

NOTE   Cisco IOS passwords are case sensitive.

With passwords on the vty lines, you can now Telnet to the router and use the password:

```
myserver#telnet 192.168.1.2
Trying...
Connected to 192.168.1.2.
Escape character is '^]'.

User Access Verification

Password: <Type the password here. Text is not displayed.>
RTA>
```

TIP

If you worry that five active Telnet sessions by other people will prevent you from accessing the router, you can create more vty lines, or you can configure a common password for vty lines 0 through 3 and a different password for vty 4 for "emergency purposes only." Use the **line vty 4** command to configure line 4 only. To create more vty lines, simply issue the **line vty** command with numbers greater than 4. The command **line vty 5 9**, for example, creates five more vty lines, numbered 5 through 9. Telnet sessions consume vty lines in the order they are numbered, starting with 0.

Additional login options allow the router to check usernames and leverage RADIUS and TACACS+ servers. See "Deploying Authentication, Authorization, and Accounting (AAA)," later in this chapter.

Controlling vty Access with Access Lists

If you want to restrict who can Telnet to a router, apply access lists to the logical vty lines that permit only authorized addresses. Here's a partial configuration listing:

```
access-list 10 permit 192.168.1.0 0.0.0.255
!
line vty 0 4
 access-class 10 in
```

The command **access-class 10 in** applies access list number 10 to all five vty lines (vty lines 0–4). Only users matching the source criteria **192.168.1.0 0.0.0.255** are allowed to Telnet to the router. See "Controlling Traffic with Access Control Lists" earlier in this chapter for more information on access lists.

Securing Access to the Console Port

If you have a direct connection to the console port, you can break into a router by using password recovery techniques. This is to recover from forgotten passwords (see Appendix D, "Password Recovery"). Still, configuring the console port with a password to discourage the casual hacker is a good idea.

To set the console port password, configure the following and replace **foo!console** with your password:

```
RTA#conf t
Enter configuration commands, one per line.  End with CNTL/Z.
RTA(config)#line console 0
RTA(config-line)#password foo!console
```

NOTE   Password recovery requires a direct physical connection to the console port (see Appendix D). A hacker who has physical access to your router can do worse things than circumventing the password, so lock the router in a secure place.

Deploying Authentication, Authorization, and Accounting

Providing service to road warriors, telecommuters, and other remote users greatly extends the effective reach of the network. With the option to make the network available anytime from anywhere, organizations see opportunities for convenience, productivity, and cost savings.

Critical to these gains is ensuring that the network can extend to remote areas with sufficient security. If the network is available anytime from anywhere—perhaps just a phone call away—you must make sure it's still not accessible to *anyone*.

Some popular methods to reach a private network from the outside world include dialup modems over basic telephone service, telecommuter ISDN routers, cable modems or xDSL devices over the public Internet, wireless modems, and so on. These types of access methods can liberate new applications and new ways of doing business, but can also bring new challenges in securing a private service that is publicly accessible.

This section covers

- Authentication, Authorization, and Accounting
- Configuring Authentication for Network Access over PPP
- Using the Default Authentication List
- Configuring Authentication for Router Logins
- The Local Username Database
- Configuring Authorization
- Configuring Accounting
- Pointing the Router to the RADIUS or TACACS+ AAA Server

Authentication, Authorization, and Accounting

The networking industry has adopted three principles that address the basic needs of remotely accessible networks. They are *authentication, authorization, and accounting (AAA or "triple A")*.

Authentication validates a user's identity. This is the heart of remote access security and grants a user access to the network based on an assurance that the system knows the person. Authentication is typically done with user login names and passwords.

To improve the probability that a password is known only by the owner, *one-time password (OTP)* systems are often used. OTP systems usually consist of a server that authenticates passwords generated by electronic *token cards* the size of a credit card. Users type their personal identification number (PIN) into their token cards, and the token card dynamically generates and displays a password that can be used for one login only. At the time of this writing, the CiscoSecure™ AAA product for UNIX includes an OTP system.

Authorization limits what a user is allowed to do on the network, usually defined by a profile for the user or a group to which the user belongs. Some examples of what you can authorize
to a user are permitted hours of the day (or days of the week) to access the network, protocols (IP, IPX) allowed, areas of the network to access, maximum number of concurrent sessions to the network, services (Telnet, FTP, SNMP) allowed, and date of account expiration.

Accounting tracks what the user is doing or has done on the network. This usually involves recording such information as start and stop time of the user's session, duration of a session, number of bytes or packets transmitted, commands the user issued, caller line identification (CLID), and others. These records are important for usage billing and auditing.

NOTE   Security software on servers and clients works in conjunction with IOS to deliver the AAA capabilities discussed here. One such product is the CiscoSecure AAA server offered by Cisco.

AAA is just one building block in the security infrastructure that makes your internal network available over the public switched telephone network (PSTN), Internet, or other widely accessed network. AAA is necessary but might not be sufficient. Your security policy might require more layers of network security, such as encryption, per-packet authentication, or nonrepudiation. Advanced security services, covered in Chapter 7, address such needs.

In a Cisco IOS network, the following popular services are supported by AAA:

- Connectivity for remote users who want to join the private network with functionality similar to what they have "in the office." As an example, this could be a road warrior user who dials the private network with a modem to run e-mail and Web applications.

- Logins for networking service personnel (and other people) who need to access the IOS command prompt (EXEC prompt) and monitor or configure Cisco devices.

Figure 6-6 illustrates these AAA services.

Figure 6-6   *IOS-based AAA Supports Remote Access Connectivity and Router Logins*

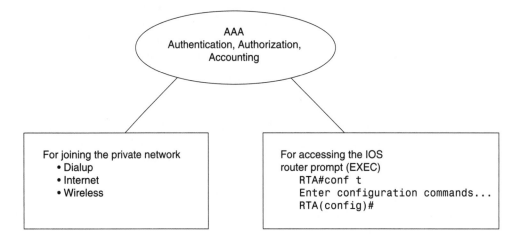

Centralized AAA Servers

A key AAA strength is a centralized security database residing on a AAA server that stores the usernames, passwords, profiles, policies, and accounting information for the organization. Centralizing the information eases administration for networks that have multiple points of access. For example, consider a network like Figure 6-7 that has multiple access points around the country.

With a centralized AAA server, each of the access routers—for example, in Chicago, Miami, and San Francisco—can consult the same database when authenticating passwords and authorizing users. This has obvious advantages in consistency and manageability because only one database needs to be maintained. Likewise, having one repository for accounting data simplifies reporting and billing.

Figure 6-7   *A Centralized AAA Server Supporting Access Routers at Multiple Branch Offices*

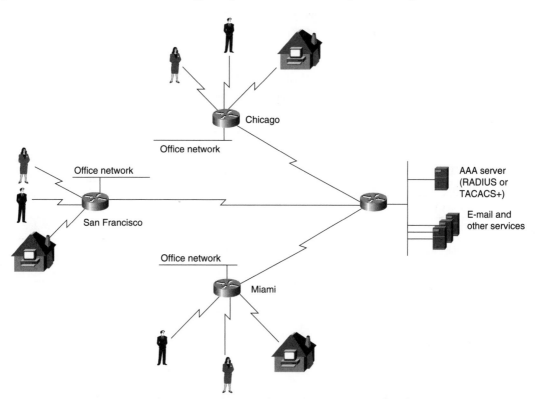

The alternative to the centralized AAA server model is a distributed model with separate, distributed databases on each router. Although feasible on a small network, having multiple databases on every router is cumbersome to build and maintain. Also, a distributed database approach does not deliver the variety of authorization and accounting features found in AAA servers.

Security Protocols—RADIUS and TACACS+

The AAA server and the routers converse over the network with a protocol specially designed for exchanging security information. The two most prevalent security protocols are *Remote Access Dial-In User Service (RADIUS)* and *Terminal Access Controller Access Control System (TACACS+—pronounced "tack-acks plus")*. There are technical differences in how the two protocols work, but their purpose is the same: They pass queries and responses between clients (the routers) and the AAA server for authentication, authorization, and accounting. Table 6-2 lists some of the main differences between RADIUS and TACACS+. Cisco IOS supports both protocols.

Table 6-2   *Distinctions Between RADIUS and TACACS+*

RADIUS	TACACS+
UDP: Connectionless transport without acknowledgements	TCP: Connection-oriented, reliable full-duplex transport
Encrypts password portion of packet only	Encrypts the entire packet
Primarily IP only	Multiprotocol
Standards-based	Proprietary

NOTE   Some vendors add their own extensions to RADIUS. This effectively makes the RADIUS implementation proprietary.

Configuring Authentication for Network Access over PPP

The *Point-to-Point Protocol (PPP)* is widely used to connect remote users and branch offices over dialup links. PPP is an OSI Layer 2 (link layer) encapsulation protocol that, in addition to IP, supports other protocols such as IPX and DECnet.

Built within PPP are two authentication methods called *Password Authentication Protocol (PAP)* and *Challenge Handshake Authentication Protocol (CHAP)*. CHAP sends a cryptographic hash of the password over the network and is therefore more secure than PAP, which sends passwords in cleartext.

Figure 6-8 illustrates a simple scenario with dialup road warriors and telecommuters connecting to an office network for their e-mail, Web, and other applications.

Figure 6-8   *Remote Users Connecting to an Office LAN over a PSTN*

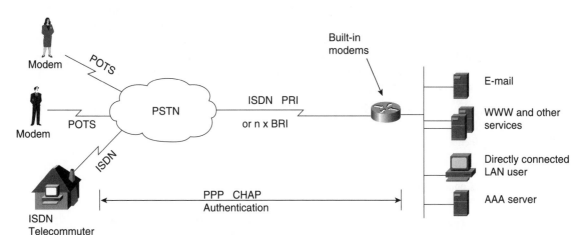

The idea is that the remote users join the network and appear as normal IP nodes with the same functionality as a user directly connected to the office LAN. Of course, performance over their remote link (modem, ISDN, and the like) will most likely lag behind the throughput of a direct LAN connection.

The steps a remote user goes through to connect to the network are the following:

1   User dials the office router over the PSTN.

2   Office router answers the call from the user. This establishes a physical (Layer 1) connection between the endpoints.

3   The two endpoints establish a data link (Layer 2) connection, using the PPP Link Control Protocol (LCP). LCP establishes, configures, and tests the link.

4   After link establishment, the router sends a packet called a *challenge* to the user.

5   PPP in the user's device formulates a packet called a *response* and sends it to the router. The response consists of a cryptographic hash value of the password and the user's login name.

6   The router checks the response against its own calculation of the hash value. If the response matches the router's calculation, the user is authenticated.

7   The two endpoints proceed to the Network Control Protocol (NCP) phase of PPP, where the network layer protocol (IP) is established and configured.

8   After NCP, the user is connected to the network at the IP layer (Layer 3).

Consult RFC 1994 for more information on CHAP and RFC 1661 for more information on PPP.

Authenticating Inbound Callers with Authentication Lists

To authenticate inbound callers on a router, you first define an *authentication list* that defines a sequence of *methods* to tell the router how it should attempt authentication of the user's password. For example, an authentication list might tell the router to try the RADIUS protocol first, and if the RADIUS protocol fails (because the AAA server is offline, for example), to use the router's local username database. After creating an authentication list, you apply it to the router interface that accepts the inbound caller.

Figure 6-9 describes the relationship between authentication lists and router interfaces.

Figure 6-9   *Two Example Authentication Lists*

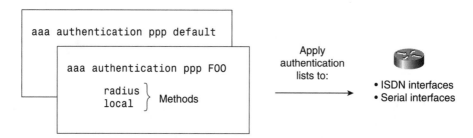

FOO is a user-defined authentication list with two methods: **radius** and **local**. The **default** authentication list is described in "Using the Default Authentication List," later in this chapter.

TIP   When a router is conversing with the AAA server, it is a RADIUS or TACACS+ client. When you configure RADIUS or TACACS+, you enable an IOS software process in the router that handles the client-side tasks of the RADIUS or TACACS+ protocol.

Configuring Authentication Lists on Routers

Here's an example that configures an authentication list on a router:

```
RTA#conf t
Enter configuration commands, one per line.  End with CNTL/Z.
RTA(config)#aaa new-model
RTA(config)#aaa authentication ppp FOO tacacs+ local
```

where **aaa new-model** enables AAA configuration on the router. This is a required step that disables some legacy login commands on the router and enables AAA commands.

The command **aaa authentication ppp FOO tacacs+ local** creates an authentication list called FOO. This particular authentication list specifies that TACACS+ is the first authentication method. If TACACS+ authentication fails for any reason, the router will attempt to authenticate the user with its local username database as indicated by the keyword **local** following **tacacs+**. See "The Local Username Database," later in this chapter.

After creating the authentication list, you apply it to interfaces that receive the inbound callers.

For asynchronous serial interfaces (or *async* for short):

```
RTA(config)#int async 1
RTA(config-if)#ppp authentication chap FOO
```

For ISDN BRI interfaces:

```
RTA(config)#int bri 0
RTA(config-if)#ppp authentication chap FOO
```

For ISDN PRI interfaces:

```
RTA(config)#int serial 0:23
RTA(config-if)#ppp authentication chap FOO
```

NOTE   Depending on the type of Cisco router, the numbering syntax for interfaces can vary slightly. Consult the documentation for your particular router for the exact numbering convention.

Additionally, your configuration might define logical interfaces that group multiple async interfaces. In the following example, async interfaces 1 through 24 are grouped as one logical interface **group-async1**, and configured as one entity for convenience:

```
RTA(config)#int group-async1
RTA(config-if)#group-range 1 24
RTA(config-if)#ppp authentication chap FOO
```

The **group-async** interface is commonly used on Cisco access servers. These routers aggregate high volumes of remote access users.

Using the Default Authentication List

Instead of creating named authentication lists (like FOO), you can define a default authentication list. The following configures the default authentication list with two methods (**tacacs+** and **local**) and enables CHAP on an interface:

```
RTA#conf t
Enter configuration commands, one per line.  End with CNTL/Z.
RTA(config)#aaa new-model
RTA(config)#aaa authentication ppp default tacacs+ local
RTA(config)#int async 1
RTA(config-if)#ppp authentication chap
```

Cisco routers use the default authentication list when CHAP is configured on an interface and no authentication list is defined.

TIP	With named authentication lists, you can configure multiple lists and assign them to different interfaces.

Configuring Authentication for Router Logins

AAA is not just for remote users who want to connect to your network. Network administrators, engineers, and managers can leverage the benefits of AAA in managing a router network.

A common problem with managing a network with a team of people is tracking who makes configuration changes and when those changes happened. To solve this, you can use a common AAA database to authenticate each person, authorize IOS commands, and log changes. Even if the logging task is unimportant in your particular environment, allowing users to use their own passwords instead of the enable mode password is a good policy for secure router administration. AAA makes these capabilities possible. (Enforcing that people change those passwords on a periodic basis might also be a good idea; AAA enables this too.)

TIP	AAA for IOS logins is also useful when using routers as terminal servers. Users connect to a router acting as a terminal server and, when authenticated, use the IOS prompt as a launch point to view console (tty) ports of other devices such as servers, LAN switches, modems, or other routers. See Appendix E for details on configuring a router as a terminal server (also called a *communications server*).

You configure login authentication similarly to PPP authentication by defining an authentication list and applying the list to the router's console port, vty lines, and line interfaces. Figure 6-10 illustrates the relationship between login authentication lists and router logins.

Figure 6-10 *Two Example Login Authentication Lists*

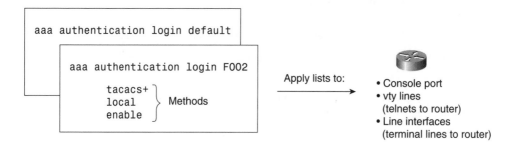

The following example configures a login authentication list and applies it to vty lines 0–4:

```
RTA#conf t
Enter configuration commands, one per line.  End with CNTL/Z.
RTA(config)#aaa new-model
RTA(config)#aaa authentication login FOO2 radius line enable
RTA(config)#line vty 0 4
RTA(config-line)#login authentication FOO2
```

where **aaa new-model** enables AAA on the router.

The command **aaa authentication login FOO2 radius line enable** creates an authentication list for logins called FOO2. This list tells the router to try RADIUS authentication first, and if that method fails for any reason, to use the password assigned to the vty line second. If no password is assigned to the vty line, the router will use the enable password as a last resort.

TIP   Configuring **enable** as a backup method in a login authentication list is highly recommended. This prevents you from being locked out of the router if your AAA server is down or unreachable for some other reason.

The Local Username Database

You have the option to configure a local security database in each router, containing usernames and passwords. This is useful when you have a small set of users and a few routers that don't warrant the convenience of a AAA server. The local database can also act as a backup for usernames and passwords if the AAA server is unavailable or unreachable. To use the local database as a backup to your AAA server, configure an authentication list with the **local** keyword following the **radius** or **tacacs+** keyword:

```
RTA(config)#aaa authentication ppp FOO radius local
```

To populate the local username database, use the **username** global configuration command:

```
RTA(config)#service password-encryption
RTA(config)#username donn password apple2
RTA(config)#username shirley pass tequila55
RTA(config)#username terry pass bigvan!
RTA(config)#username wes pass parson3
RTA(config)#username alex pass toonman21
```

where **service password-encryption** (if it's not already enabled) ensures that all passwords are stored in the encrypted format.

The command **username donn password apple2** creates a user whose login name is **donn** and password is **apple2**.

The remaining lines continue to populate the local database with the **username** command and login-password pairs.

Configuring Authorization

As mentioned earlier, the authorization task of AAA limits what a user is allowed to do on the network. Your ability to control time-of-day access, destination addresses, protocols, or other privileges depends on your AAA server and the features it supports. Profiles configured in the AAA server contain the access privileges of your users. Your router then consults the AAA server over the RADIUS or TACACS+ protocol and applies those privileges to users as they log in.

To configure a router to consult a AAA server for authorization of PPP sessions, use the **aaa authorization network** command. The following example uses the TACACS+ protocol (for RADIUS, use the keyword **radius** instead of **tacacs+**):

```
RTA(config)#aaa authorization network tacacs+ none
```

where the keyword **none** is a backup for TACACS+ and tells the router to allow authorization to succeed if the TACACS+ server is unavailable.

NOTE   The command **aaa authorization network** is also used to authorize Serial Line IP (SLIP) and Apple Remote Access Protocol (ARAP) sessions with AAA.

To configure authorization of router logins (EXEC prompt), use the **aaa authorization exec** global configuration command. The following example uses the TACACS+ protocol (for RADIUS use the keyword **radius** instead of **tacacs+**):

```
RTA(config)#aaa authorization exec tacacs+ none
```

Configuring Accounting

Like authorization, the accounting capabilities you have are largely dictated by the features of your AAA server. Still, you must instruct the AAA client in the router to use either RADIUS or TACACS+ for these accounting transactions.

Cisco IOS supports three kinds of accounting methods:

- **Stop-only**—The router sends a RADIUS or TACACS+ accounting record to the AAA server only when a user's session ends. This provides a minimal level of accounting.

- **Start-stop**—The router sends a RADIUS or TACACS+ accounting record to the AAA server at the start and end of a user's session.

- **Wait-start**—The router sends a RADIUS or TACACS+ accounting record to the AAA server at the start of the session and waits for an acknowledgment from the server before starting the user's service. As in start-stop, the router also sends an accounting record at the end of the session.

Accounting records typically contain information about the session such as when the session started or stopped, the duration of the session, the number of bytes and packets transmitted, CLID information, and commands that were issued.

To enable accounting on a router, use the **aaa accounting** global configuration command. The following example configures RADIUS accounting for network sessions such as PPP:

```
RTA(config)#aaa accounting network start-stop radius
```

where the keyword **start-stop** tells the router to use the start-stop accounting method mentioned earlier. For TACACS+ use the keyword **tacacs+** instead of **radius**, and for router logins use the keyword **exec** instead of **network**. For stop-only or wait-start accounting, replace the keyword **start-stop** with **stop-only** or **wait-start**.

TIP	To view the accounting information for active sessions, issue the **show accounting** command.

Pointing the Router to the RADIUS or TACACS+ AAA Server

You must configure the router with the IP address (or DNS name) and security key of your AAA server. Without these two pieces of data, the router will not communicate with the server over the RADIUS or TACACS+ protocol.

The security key is a password used to authenticate the router to the AAA server and to encrypt data exchanges between them.

The following example configures Router A with the RADIUS server's IP address and security key:

```
RTA(config)#radius-server host 192.168.60.1
RTA(config)#radius-server key Xj3lZtc8P9
```

In place of the IP address (**192.168.60.1** in the example), you can type the DNS name of the RADIUS server if your router is using DNS. See Appendix E for configuring a DNS server on a router. The key (**Xj3lZtc8P9** in the example) must match the key configured in the RADIUS AAA server.

NOTE	The key is a shared secret between the RADIUS clients (the routers) and the RADIUS server and must be kept confidential.

Pointing a router to a TACACS+ server follows a similar logic. Here's an example:

```
RTA(config)#tacacs-server host 192.168.70.2
RTA(config)#tacacs-server key g7P9v23W1b
```

where **192.168.70.2** is the IP address of the TACACS+ server and **g7P9v23W1b** is the security key. The keys **Xj3lZtc8P9** and **g7P9v23W1b** in these examples were chosen so that they are hard to guess.

NOTE   You can use multiple **tacacs-server host** commands to specify additional servers. IOS searches for hosts in the order in which you specify them. This also applies to the **radius-server host** command.

Other IOS Commands for Basic Security

The commands presented in this section enhance network security and are recommended for routers connected to untrusted networks such as the Internet.

Cisco routers have several minor TCP/IP services that might be abused by hackers. This section covers some common attacks and illustrates how to defend against them.

The topics of this section are

- Disable TCP and UDP Small Servers
- Disable IP Source Routing
- Disable CDP on Public Links
- Disable Directed Broadcasts on Interfaces

Disable TCP and UDP Small Servers

By default, so-called TCP and UDP *small servers* are enabled. These are relatively simple protocol services required for standards compliance. However, hackers can abuse these services, so unless you have a compelling reason for their existence, disable them as follows:

```
RTA(config)#no service tcp-small-servers
RTA(config)#no service udp-small-servers
```

TIP   The TCP small servers are Echo, Discard, Chargen, and Daytime. The UDP small servers are Echo, Discard, and Chargen.

Disable IP Source Routing

IP source routing is rarely used. On occasion, it's used for troubleshooting. However, a hacker might attempt to communicate with one of your hosts by inserting himself or herself as an intermediary stop between two legitimate host addresses. Figure 6-11 illustrates the scheme.

Figure 6-11   *A Hacker Attacking with IP Source-Routing*

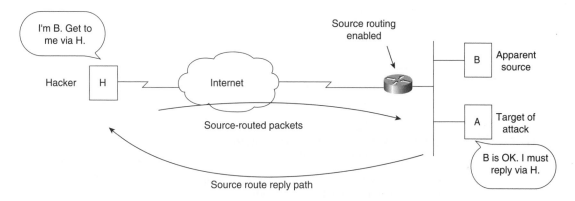

The hacker, H, pretends to be an intermediary hop in a source-routed path from Host B to Host A. H creates a request and a fictitious source-route path with B as the source and H as the middle hop. H sends this to A. Host A looks at the source address of the packet, sees that it's Host B, decides that B is friendly because it's on the same subnet, and sends a reply back to B along the source-routed path with H as the next hop. H is now communicating with A.

The hacker could do this if both the router and Host A have IP source-routing enabled. To comply with the standards, Cisco routers and just about all TCP/IP hosts have IP source-routing on by default. To disable IP source-routing on a router, issue the **no ip source-route** global configuration command:

```
RTA#conf t
Enter configuration commands, one per line.  End with CNTL/Z.
RTA(config)#no ip source-route
```

TIP   See RFC 1122 for the details of IP source routing.

Disable CDP on Public Links

Cisco Discovery Protocol (CDP) is a feature that gives you useful information about other Cisco devices (called *neighbors*) attached to a router. CDP information is helpful for determining the topology of a network and for troubleshooting. This information could also be useful to a hacker, however, so disabling it on interfaces that point to an untrusted network is a good idea. CDP packets travel only between neighboring Cisco devices; they do not span multiple hops or roam around the network, so you can safely keep CDP enabled between trusted devices in a private network.

To disable CDP on an interface:

```
RTA(config)#int s1
RTA(config-if)#no cdp enable
```

To disable CDP on the whole router (all interfaces):

```
RTA(config)#no cdp run
```

TIP   View the CDP information with the **show cdp neighbors** command.

Disable Directed Broadcasts on Interfaces

Directed broadcasts are IP-based broadcasts sent over a routed network to a destination subnet. When the directed broadcast reaches the destination subnet, the last router in the path issues a data link layer broadcast that is processed by all nodes on that subnet. Hosts and routers might suffer from processing overload if a flood of broadcasts storm their subnet. Therefore, if you do not have a compelling reason to use directed broadcasts it is recommended that you disable them to prevent problems from misconfigured hosts and abuse by hackers. Disabling directed broadcasts does not affect normal local broadcasts necessary for host-to-host and host-to-router communication. See RFC 1812 for more information on directed broadcasts.

Here's an example that disables directed broadcasts on an Ethernet interface:

```
RTA(config)#int e0
RTA(config-if)#no ip directed-broadcast
```

The command **no ip directed-broadcast** disables directed broadcast processing on the interface and protects the subnet on Ethernet0 from directed broadcasts.

Summary

Security is a significant area of concern for network engineers and managers. This chapter covered some basic security principles fundamental to maintaining a secure Cisco network. Although this chapter is by no means a complete set of all the network security you need, it is a good foundation for building more advanced security services. Chapter 7 and Chapter 8 cover some of these advanced services.

The following are the key concepts of this chapter:

- The most common use of access lists is for filtering traffic, but the access list syntax is also used in other IOS features because of its flexibility.
- Standard access lists match on source address only.
- Extended access lists can match on several more aspects of the packet (destination address, protocol, port number, IP precedence, and so on).
- Access list rules consist of an address bit pattern and a wildcard that defines the match and don't care bits.
- Access list rules are processed in sequential order. List processing for a packet stops when the router reaches the first matching rule.
- You need to consider several things when designing an access list. One that you should always remember is the invisible deny-any rule at the end of every access list.
- Extended access lists maintain statistics on their rules and can be configured to log activity.
- You can deploy access lists to combat spoofing attacks.
- Securing access to a router involves protecting the enable mode password, securing Telnet access, and securing the console port.
- AAA provides secure remote access for both network connections (such as PPP) and router logins.
- Centralized AAA servers simplify the management of passwords, policies, and billing.
- Cisco routers support RADIUS and TACACS+ and are clients of AAA servers.
- Cisco routers have several minor TCP/IP services that can be disabled to prevent abuse by hackers. These services are TCP/UDP small servers, IP source routing, CDP, and directed broadcasts.
- There are no 100 percent hacker-proof networks because new attacks are invented every day. Good network security is a continuous process of deploying defenses, auditing activity, and keeping current with new attacks.

CHAPTER 7

Advanced Security Services, Part I: IPsec

The Internet provides a wealth of services for any organization that chooses to connect to it. No longer are organizations confined to the connectivity and information available in their private networks. Instead, a huge infrastructure and vast repositories of data can be tapped into simply by connecting to a local service provider. In a sense, the Internet becomes an extension, a very large extension, of the private network.

On the other hand, the Internet is a very public place. Data exchanged between the private network and the Internet is generally nonconfidential, public information. Internal data generally stays confined to the private network because to send it through the Internet would make it available for the public to see.

But what if you could securely send internal data *through* the Internet to another private location (like a branch office)? Then, you could capitalize on the size and reach of the Internet and make the Internet *your* infrastructure for interconnecting your private locations. Instead of building your own worldwide network, you could use the worldwide network of the Internet. You would then be using the Internet as a *virtual* private network or VPN. This can significantly save on monthly line costs, offload operations to the service provider, and free up resources for more strategic projects.

This chapter covers the IP Security (IPsec) standard that enables such a solution: the capability to connect your private offices and users, using any untrusted IP network for the secure interconnections.

The main topics of this chapter are

- IPsec Enables Virtual Private Networks
- Benefits of IPsec's Layer 3 Service
- Basic IPsec Security Concepts and Cryptography
- IPsec Concepts
- Internet Key Exchange
- Tying All of the Pieces Together: A Comprehensive Example with IPsec and IKE
- Configuring IKE
- Configuring IPsec
- Troubleshooting IPsec and IKE

NOTE   You might notice from the preceding topic list that configuring IKE (Internet Key Exchange) is covered *before* configuring IPsec—even though the background on IKE follows IPsec. This is because IKE is a parent protocol of IPsec. This will be more apparent after the section "Tying All of the Pieces Together: A Comprehensive Example with IPsec and IKE."

IPsec Enables Virtual Private Networks

The IPsec standard is an architecture for transporting data securely on an untrusted network, using encryption and other services. Although IPsec can be used on any IP network, its most popular use by far is for building virtual private networks (VPNs) over the public Internet. RFC 2401 defines the general architecture of IPsec, and RFCs 2402 through 2412 define specific technologies within the IPsec framework.

A VPN is a network service over a public infrastructure (like the Internet or other untrusted network) with the privacy and security policies of a private network. There are three main categories of VPNs:

- *Remote access VPNs* or *access VPNs* provide connectivity for remote users such as road warriors and telecommuters. They are an alternative to direct-dial access and ISDN. The benefits include universal access, remote access outsourcing, and lower costs.

- *Intranet VPNs* provide internal, site-to-site connectivity for organizations—connections between private branch offices, for example. They are an alternative to leased lines and other WAN links. The benefits include wide-reaching connectivity and lower costs.

- *Extranet VPNs* provide connectivity for business partners, customers, and suppliers. They are an alternative to FAX, mail, and electronic data interchange (EDI). They enable collaboration, application sharing, and electronic commerce.

To achieve a level of privacy and security on a public infrastructure equal to that of a private network, many things need to happen:

- You need to identify and authenticate trusted parties (network devices) with whom you want to communicate.

- Data must be exchanged so that it is infeasible for an unauthorized person to intercept, record, and extract the contents of the data.

- The data should not be altered in transit and trusted parties on a VPN must be able to detect this. An attacker should not be able to change your bank deposit of $1000 to $100, for example.

- Data exchanged between trusted parties must be protected against replay attacks. That is, an attacker should not be able to record you withdrawing $1000 from your bank account and then replay that transaction at a later time so that an additional $1000 gets withdrawn.

To address these requirements and make VPNs possible, IPsec provides encryption, authentication, and integrity-checking services. These services are covered in this chapter.

Benefits of IPsec's Layer 3 Service

IPsec works at the IP layer (Layer 3) and integrates with your existing IP network. You might, for example, replace a costly leased line connection between two international offices with an intranet VPN that connects the offices through an Internet Service Provider (ISP). The rest of your network can be left unchanged.

The IP layer approach gives IPsec advantages over more traditional security strategies such as link-layer and application-layer encryption. The following are some key IPsec benefits:

- To transfer data securely between any two sites, you need IPsec only at the endpoints: The network in between (the Internet, for example) does not have to be IPsec-aware, just IP-enabled. This differs from the link-layer (Layer 2) approach, which requires encryption devices on every network link between the sites.

- IPsec can be deployed transparent of clients and servers. You do not have to reconfigure workstations or applications to work with IPsec. This differs from application-layer encryption. With application-layer encryption, each client program must have its own security implementation, and little can be done to secure a program that does not have such built-in services as encryption.

- Offloading IPsec to routers (and other networking devices) simplifies deployment: The routers are responsible for applying such services as encryption, and the clients and servers remain as they are for easier management.

- Applying IPsec services at key network points makes it easier to enforce and maintain a consistent security policy across the organization.

- IPsec is flexible. With IPsec you can selectively protect certain types of traffic and let other non-secret traffic circulate in the clear (without any IPsec service) to save system resources.

- From a QoS standpoint, IPsec packets are just like regular IP packets: They carry an IP precedence value. This means you can apply QoS to IPsec packets with the same services used to control normal packets (see Chapters 4, "Deploying Basic Quality of Service Features," and 5, "Deploying Advanced Quality of Service Features").

Figure 7-1 depicts a simple intranet VPN with routers providing IPsec secure networking on behalf of clients and servers at two sites.

Figure 7-1 *IPsec-Enabled Routers Provide IP Layer Security for Clients and Servers*

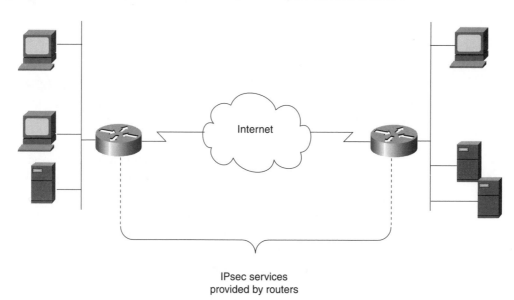

IPsec services
provided by routers

In Figure 7-1, the routers apply IPsec services (encryption, authentication, and so on) to traffic that is exchanged between the two sites. Because IPsec is an IP layer function, no modification is required for the Internet (it simply forwards IP packets) or to the clients and servers at each site. Because it is a trusted network, the traffic on the LAN within each site is not protected, but data exchanged between the sites is protected to maintain privacy over the Internet. Finally, rules are configured on each router so that traffic not destined to the other site—for example, traffic to public Web sites on the Internet—is transmitted normally, that is, without any IPsec handling.

NOTE   To *protect* data with IPsec means to apply encryption, integrity checking, authentication, and other security services to the data so it can be transported securely over an untrusted network.

Basic IPsec Security Concepts and Cryptography

IPsec is a fairly large collection of technologies that encompasses network and security protocols, cryptographic algorithms, and recommendations. IPsec is an architecture for building secure communications over untrusted networks and provides the security services listed in the following sections. These services are *confidentiality*, *integrity*, *origin authentication*, and *anti-replay*. The following sections cover these services and introduce basic security and cryptographic principles as they apply to IPsec.

Confidentiality (Encryption)

Confidentiality provides privacy for the data being exchanged— only the intended recipient can easily read the data. This is achieved through encryption algorithms that scramble plaintext data into an unintelligible form called *ciphertext*. As part of the scrambling process, an encryption algorithm requires a *key* (or more than one key in the case of public key cryptography). The key is nothing more than a string of bits usually written in ASCII or hexadecimal notation. For example, the key 01111000011001100011010101110 1110111101000110011 is written as xf5wz3 (ASCII) or 786635777A33 (hexadecimal). Keys are used by algorithms to encrypt plaintext and subsequently decrypt ciphertext. When encryption is used effectively, it is infeasible (see "Cryptographic Security: Infeasible, Not Impossible") to deduce the original plaintext from the ciphertext without the proper key. The key is like a password: If you know the key, you can decrypt the message and read the data, but if you don't know the key, you'll have great difficulty discovering the original message.

Some popular encryption algorithms include DES (Data Encryption Standard), Triple-DES (often written as 3DES), IDEA (International Data Encryption Algorithm), and Blowfish. The IPsec standard defines mandatory encryption algorithms (DES and null) and allows for 3DES, IDEA, Blowfish, and future algorithms. Consult RFC 2406 for more details.

Cryptographic Security: Infeasible, Not Impossible

Cryptography, a branch of mathematics and the science of secret writing, often calls a trusted security service *infeasible* to subvert (rather than *impossible* to subvert) because mathematically, any algorithm can be compromised if an attacker has enough computing power, know-how, and time to crack it. The security of an algorithm lies in the *amount* of computing power and time required to break it. If descrambling a ciphertext without the key takes years and millions of dollars of computing power, an algorithm is generally considered secure—that is, secure enough to protect most kinds of data for most users.

Another popular phrase in cryptographic circles is *believed to be secure* or *considered to be secure*. A security algorithm is believed to be secure (and *believed to be difficult to subvert*) if there is no easy way to crack it at the present time. The possibility always exists, however, that some smart person will come up with a mathematical breakthrough that makes an algorithm easy to compromise—a way to solve a difficult mathematical problem that is a feature and the basis of a security algorithm. If this happens, everyone will have to cease use of the once-believed secure algorithm and resort to other algorithms that are believed to be secure.

Applying Cryptographic Security to Your Data

There's simply no such thing as a security algorithm that is impossible to break. There are only algorithms that in practice, and depending on the type of data that needs to be protected, are considered secure and secure enough for general VPN applications.

At the time of this writing, Triple-DES is considered a secure encryption algorithm. DES (a precursor of Triple-DES), on the other hand, has reportedly been cracked within a few hours or less with specialized cracking hardware—hardware designed by and accessible to the crypto-elite. More information on the security provided by DES can be found in RFC 2405.

NOTE   Governments such as the United States of America often restrict the exportation and use of encryption algorithms. Violations of such laws can be a serious offense, so it is important to be familiar with the laws and involve the exportation policy expert in your organization (if you have one).

Ultimately, you and your organization determine which algorithms are secure enough for your application. Concluding that an algorithm is secure enough for your data depends on the sensitivity of data you are protecting. Protecting top-secret corporate strategies or formulas for example, might require a more secure encryption algorithm than one for encrypting general office e-mail.

Typically, encryption algorithms follow one of two approaches: shared key encryption or public key encryption. Shared key encryption algorithms are the most familiar and are covered in the following section. IPsec employs both encryption strategies.

Shared Key Encryption

In shared key encryption, a single key is used for both encryption and decryption of the data. Only the trusted parties must know the shared key (also called a *shared secret* or *secret key*). DES, 3DES, IDEA, and Blowfish are examples of shared key encryption.

Consider the following communication sequence between two parties, Alice and Bob, using shared key encryption:

1   Alice and Bob agree on a shared key encryption algorithm and a shared key to use for their session.

2   Alice takes the plaintext she wants to send to Bob and encrypts it into ciphertext by using the algorithm and the shared key.

3   Alice sends the ciphertext to Bob.

4   Bob decrypts the ciphertext by using the algorithm and shared key. This results in the original plaintext.

5   Bob can now read the original message from Alice.

Alice and Bob represent any two parties that need to communicate securely over an untrusted infrastructure. Depending on the implementation, they can be people with PCs (or other client devices) or they can represent networking devices such as servers, routers, and firewalls (for instance, router *Alice* communicating with firewall *Bob*).

NOTE   Shared key algorithms are also called *symmetric algorithms* because the same key is used for both encryption and decryption.

Agreeing on a Shared Key

Confidentiality ensures that communication is private between the trusted parties, Alice and Bob, but in a shared key encryption scenario, Alice and Bob must agree to use the same key before secure communication can commence. This is a problem, because Alice has to tell Bob what the shared key is without an attacker eavesdropping on the conversation and learning the shared key. Alice could tell Bob what the shared key is over a prior-existing secure session, but if Alice and Bob already have a secure means of communicating, they could use that to communicate and not bother with the shared key. Another thing Alice can do is communicate the shared key to Bob over a secure out-of-band channel—a direct telephone call or a registered letter. This might be feasible if Alice and Bob only have to do this a few times, but if Alice and Bob need to change keys frequently, or if Alice has to communicate with many more people than Bob, the out-of-band method becomes cumbersome.

Using Diffie-Hellman to Agree on a Shared Key

Clearly, the out-of-band method of establishing shared keys does not scale to the size needed for large networks and does not allow easy renegotiation of shared keys that have grown stale. To address this, the *Diffie-Hellman key exchange* algorithm allows two parties to exchange non-secret (publicly readable) data and calculate a unique shared key that is only known by them.

NOTE   The Internet Key Exchange (IKE) protocol, used in conjunction with IPsec, leverages Diffie-Hellman key exchange to establish shared keys. See section "Internet Key Exchange" later in this chapter for more information. IKE is defined in RFC 2409.

Diffie-Hellman is not an encryption algorithm but an algorithm for establishing a shared key over an unsecured medium. After a shared key is established with Diffie-Hellman, that shared key can be used with the shared key encryption algorithms mentioned earlier: DES, Triple-DES, IDEA, Blowfish, and so on.

It is outside the scope of this book to explain exactly how Diffie-Hellman works—to do so requires a fair bit of mathematics involving discrete logarithms, modulus arithmetic, prime numbers, and other good things (see Bibliography for references). Without getting into too much math, Diffie-Hellman gets its security from the property that raising a number to a power (exponentiation) is much easier than calculating the logarithm (the reverse operation of exponentiation). With Diffie-Hellman, the calculations are performed with large numbers and modulus arithmetic. This does not make exponentiation more difficult, but it makes the reverse operation, calculating the logarithm and cracking the security, infeasible. That is, it's *believed* to be infeasible. The difficult problem of calculating the logarithm is a security feature of Diffie-Hellman and is known as the problem of finding a *discrete logarithm in a finite field*.

NOTE   You do not have to know the mathematical gears of Diffie-Hellman to successfully deploy IPsec or IKE. Diffie-Hellman is working behind-the-scenes and is automatically invoked in IPsec/IKE implementations like Cisco's. It does not hurt to understand what is going on, though. Thus, the information in this section is provided for understanding how Diffie-Hellman solves the problem of establishing shared keys.

In brief, a Diffie-Hellman key exchange between two parties, Alice and Bob, looks like this (here comes some math):

- Alice and Bob are given numbers g and n. These are non-secret, publicly available numbers.

- Alice picks a large random number, x, calculates $A=g^x$ mod n, and sends this value, A, to Bob over an untrusted network. The value x is known only to Alice and is called Alice's *secret*.

- Bob picks a large random number, y, calculates $B=g^y$ mod n, and sends this value, B, to Alice over the untrusted network. The value y is known only to Bob and is Bob's secret.

- Alice computes $K_a = B^x$ mod n.

- Bob computes $K_b = A^y$ mod n.

- By virtue of an algebraic property of exponents, K_a and K_b are equal because

    — B^x mod $n = g^{xy}$ mod $n = A^y$ mod n

- Alice and Bob have successfully negotiated a shared key $K=K_a=K_b$ that is known only to them.

Diffie-Hellman Security Details: Discrete Logarithms

An attacker knows g and n and can intercept non-secret values A and B, but will find it infeasible to calculate secret values x or y (assuming numbers g, n, x, and y are selected properly). Either x or y is needed to arrive at the shared key, K, but to find x or y the attacker must calculate a discrete logarithm in a finite field. This is difficult to do when x, y, and n are very large numbers (several hundred bits long).

The following is a simple example in which the attacker must find secret value y. This is for illustration purposes. In real-world Diffie-Hellman implementations, larger numbers are used to make the problem infeasible to solve.

> $g^y \bmod n = B$
>
> $g = 2$
>
> $n = 124798787687687643873593$
>
> $B = 87733227500518975093493$
>
> Attacker must find secret value y (the discrete logarithm of B, modulus n). This is hard to do with large numbers.
>
> Answer: $y = 23874239847329847238472398$

To find the answer, the attacker cannot simply calculate the logarithm of B base g and arrive at secret value y because of complications introduced by modulus arithmetic. For more information, see the sources listed in the Bibliography.

Subverting Diffie-Hellman

Although it is infeasible to find the secret values (x and y) owned by Alice and Bob, an attacker could launch a different attack against Diffie-Hellman called a *man-in-the-middle* attack. The following describes the attack:

- The attacker intercepts a Diffie-Hellman exchange between Alice and Bob.

- The attacker pretends to be Bob and exchanges Diffie-Hellman messages with Alice. Alice is unaware that she is communicating with the attacker.

- Alice and the attacker complete their Diffie-Hellman exchange and compute a shared secret.

- The attacker turns to Bob, pretends to be Alice, and exchanges Diffie-Hellman messages with Bob. Bob is unaware that he is communicating with the attacker.

- Bob and the attacker complete their Diffie-Hellman exchange and compute a shared secret. This is a different shared secret than the one the attacker shares with Alice.

- The attacker now acts as an intermediary in the transfer of data between Alice and Bob by decrypting from one side and encrypting to the other. All the while, Alice and Bob are unaware of the fact that an attacker exists and is reading the data transferred between them.

As a countermeasure to the man-in-the-middle attack, the IKE protocol uses digital signatures to authenticate the origin of Diffie-Hellman exchanges. See "Digital Signatures," later in this chapter.

Public Key Encryption

With public key encryption, the parties that wish to communicate (Alice and Bob) each create a pair of keys and each own the key pair they create. One key, the *private key*, is kept secret and known only by the owner. The other key, the *public key*, is non-secret information and is given to anyone who wishes to send confidential information to the owner of the public key.

NOTE   One of the most popular public key encryption algorithms is *RSA*, which is named after its inventors: Rivest, Shamir, and Adleman. In the Cisco implementation, RSA encryption is part of the IKE protocol that works in conjunction with IPsec. IKE is covered in the "Internet Key Exchange" section later in this chapter.

The advantage of using public key encryption is that you do not have to transmit any secret information to have someone communicate with you securely. You can openly publish your public key and anyone can use your public key to send you an encrypted message. You keep your private key secret (known only to you) and use it to decrypt messages that were encrypted with your public key. Likewise, to send an encrypted message to someone, all you need is that person's public key.

The following sequence illustrates how public key encryption works. Bob wishes to send Alice an encrypted message:

1   Alice sends Bob her public key.

2   Bob encrypts the message destined for Alice, using Alice's public key.

3   Bob sends the encrypted data to Alice.

4   Alice receives the encrypted data and, through some fancy math built into the encryption algorithm, decrypts the data by using her private key.

5   Alice and Bob switch roles for communication in the opposite direction (when Alice sends an encrypted message to Bob).

Unlike shared key encryption, in which there is one key known by Alice and Bob, public key encryption involves four keys (assuming bidirectional communication): Alice's public and private keys, and Bob's public and private keys.

This system has scaling advantages because people only need to exchange public keys to securely communicate with one another. Public keys can also be held in a widely accessible, central repository (because they are non-secret, public information) for better management.

The following are some notable properties of public key encryption:

- Decrypting by using the public key is infeasible. Because of clever mathematical tricks (called *one-way trapdoor functions*) built into the system, the public key is useful for only encryption, not decryption. (The logic is reversed with digital signatures: The private key can be used to encrypt/sign and the public key used to decrypt/verify. See "Digital Signatures.")

- Deducing the private key by knowing only the public key and the encrypted data is infeasible. As long as the private key is known only by the owner, only the owner can decrypt the data.

- Public key encryption is slow—public key algorithms are commonly 1,000 times slower than shared key encryptions. As such, public key encryption is often used to exchange small pieces of information and shared key encryption is used to encrypt bulk data such as traffic flows between two points on the Internet.

NOTE   Public key encryption is one application of *public key cryptography*, which is the broader study of systems that use the concept of a public and private key. Another popular application of public key cryptography is *digital signatures*, which are covered in the "Digital Signatures" section later in this chapter.

Integrity

Integrity (also called *data integrity*) provides a guarantee that data has not been altered in transit. Two parties that are communicating over an untrusted network must be able to verify that the data received is exactly the same as the data originally sent.

Integrity is achieved through cryptographic hashing algorithms that calculate a unique value when given a piece of data or *message* as input. The unique value (called a *hash value* or *message authentication code*) is like a fingerprint. Given a message and its calculated hash value, it is infeasible to find another message with the same hash value (assuming the implementation is done properly). This is analogous to the idea that it is infeasible to find another person with a fingerprint that matches one on your hand.

Therefore, if someone sends you a message and its associated hash value (fingerprint), you can do your own calculation of what the hash value for the message should be and compare it to the hash value from the other person. If the hash values match, you can be reasonably certain that the message was not altered in transit, because any alteration would change the message and result in a different hash value.

The following sequence illustrates how Bob can validate the integrity of a message sent by Alice:

1 Alice and Bob agree to use a hashing algorithm for integrity checking of data sent between them.

2 Alice and Bob agree on a shared key known only to them. See the "Agreeing on a Shared Key" earlier in this chapter for more information.

3 Alice needs to send Bob a message, "Hello!"

4 Alice calculates a hash value for the message. This is done by inputting the message "Hello!" and the shared key into the hashing algorithm. The output of the algorithm is the hash value.

5 Alice sends the message and her calculated hash value to Bob.

6 Bob calculates his own hash value for the received message. This is done by inputting the message and the shared key into the hashing algorithm. The output of the algorithm is Bob's hash value.

7 Bob compares his hash value with the hash value from Alice. If the hash values match, Bob knows the message was not altered in transit. Any alteration of the data would cause Bob's hash value to be different from Alice's hash value.

If the hash values match, Bob is also certain that the message came from Alice because they are the only ones who know the shared key. A different key would produce a different hash value even if the message were the same. Both the key and the message affect the outputted hash value because they are inputs to the hashing algorithm.

The use of a shared key with a hashing algorithm is a form of authentication (as described previously) and is called *keyed-hashing for message authentication,* or *HMAC* for short (MAC stands for Message Authentication Code and H signifies the use of a hashing function). HMAC is detailed in RFC 2104.

Hashing Algorithms: Examples with Message Digest 5

To illustrate the security provided by cryptographic hashing algorithms, consider the hash values computed by a popular algorithm, Message Digest 5 (MD5), in the following examples.

NOTE	Another popular hashing algorithm used with IPsec is Secure Hash Algorithm (SHA-1), which was designed by the National Institute of Standards and Technology (NIST), a division of the U.S. Department of Commerce, and the National Security Agency (NSA), the official security organization of the U.S. government.

The MD5 hashing algorithm takes an input message and outputs a 128-bit hash value. The resulting hash value, written in hexadecimal format, is considered a unique fingerprint of the message. Consider the following input messages and their calculated hash values:

Case 1 MD5 Input: The quick brown fox jumped over the lazy dog.

MD5 Output: 5c6ffbdd40d9556b73a21e63c3e0e904

Case 2 MD5 Input: the quick brown fox jumped over the lazy dog.

MD5 Output: bb0fa6eff92c305f166803b6938dd33a

Although the two message inputs for Case 1 and Case 2 are very similar (only differing by an uppercase *T* and a lowercase *t* in the first word), their hash values are very different. This is a feature of a good hashing algorithm: For all practical purposes, every input (message) should have a unique output (hash value).

A value of 128 bits provides for 2^{128} unique combinations. The security of MD5 lies in infeasibility of altering a message (or substituting the message with a different one) so it passes undetected through the recipient's integrity check. This means, for the attack to succeed, the altered message has to produce the same hash value as the original message—a very difficult thing to do when a good hashing algorithm is used.

No matter how big (or how small) the input message is, the output of MD5 is always a 128-bit hash value. Consider the following examples where a single word is the input (Case 3) and a 100 KB file is the input (Case 4):

Case 3 MD5 Input: Shirley

MD5 Output: 257f4d1a26d393d41524ad7e83e7c524

Case 4 MD5 Input: <100 KB file>

MD5 Output: 5058f1af8388633f609cadb75a75dc9d

The preceding cases highlight the compressive nature of hashing algorithms like MD5. Hashing algorithms are flexible enough to generate hash values for short and long messages alike.

Origin Authentication

Origin authentication provides the assurance that the person you are communicating with is who he or she claims to be. Consider again Bob and Alice: An attacker could masquerade as Bob and attempt to communicate with Alice. If Alice has no means of authenticating Bob, Alice might then communicate with the attacker, thinking she's communicating with Bob. Alice needs a way to know for certain that a message claiming to be from Bob was indeed sent by Bob.

Digital signatures and digital certificates provide the origin authentication for which Alice is looking. IPsec leverages both digital signatures and digital certificates.

Digital Signatures

Digital signatures provide a mechanism for guaranteeing the authenticity of a message. A digital signature is the electronic equivalent of a written signature in that the digital signature can be used to prove that the message was indeed signed by the originator.

RSA signatures and *Digital Signature Standard (DSS)* are two common digital signature algorithms used in IPsec and IKE. Both are based on public key cryptography: An owner keeps a private key confidential and openly publishes a public key (see the related section on "Public Key Encryption" earlier in this chapter). An originator signs a message using his or her private key and sends the message, along with its associated signature, to the recipient. The recipient then verifies the signature by using the originator's public key.

The following sequence describes the basic idea behind digital signatures, using an exchange between Alice and Bob. In this example, Bob sends Alice a signed message using an RSA signature (other algorithms vary, but the concept is the same):

1 Bob sends Alice his public key.

2 Bob encrypts the message with his private key. This produces a unique, encrypted message that only Bob could have made, because he alone is the keeper of his private key. The encrypted message is considered a digitally signed message.

3 Bob sends the signed message to Alice.

4 Alice decrypts the message with Bob's public key. This verifies the digitally signed message. If Alice cannot decrypt the message, the digital signature is invalid. Only the private key can properly sign (encrypt) a message that can be verified (decrypted) with the matching public key.

Digital Certificates and Certification Authorities

A *digital certificate* is an electronic message that binds a public key to a real person (or organization). This association is needed to address some potential problems with public key cryptography (signatures or encryption), namely:

- When Alice receives Bob's public key, how does she know with certainty that the key really belongs to Bob? An attacker could easily generate a bogus private/public key pair and send the public key to Alice, pretending to be Bob.

- Bob could send a legitimately signed message to Alice but repudiate at a later time that the transaction took place. That is, he could deny signing the message that Alice received. Bob could do this by generating a temporary private/public key pair just for his transaction with Alice. When Alice attempts to prove she has a message signed by Bob, Bob could claim he never owned that particular public key.

To address these problems, a third party that Alice trusts needs to be involved. The trusted third party, called a *certification authority (CA)*, creates and signs a digital certificate containing Bob's name (and other identification data) and Bob's public key. The CA is responsible for verifying that the public key belongs to Bob. This is usually done through some manual, out-of-band (non-network) procedure. After a digital certificate is created and signed by the CA, Bob can distribute his certificate to anyone who wants his public key. Digital certificates can also be stored in centralized repositories (centralized servers or *CA servers*) because they are non-secret, public information. This helps to scale the distribution of public keys in large networks.

Obtaining a Digital Certificate

The following is a typical sequence of how Bob obtains a digital certificate from a CA:

1 Bob creates his key pair (private and public keys).

2 Bob sends his public key to the CA over the network and includes personal information (his name, his IP address, the serial number of his device, and so on). This is a request for certificate.

3 The request sits on the CA's server in a pending status until someone at the CA begins processing Bob's request.

4 A person at the CA verifies Bob's identity and confirms that Bob was the one who submitted the public key. For a trustworthy binding of Bob to the key, this verification step is done via some person-to-person, out-of-band procedure.

5 Bob periodically queries the CA server, hoping his certificate is complete and ready for retrieval.

6 The CA creates and signs a certificate containing Bob's public key and personal information, thereby guaranteeing the authenticity of the key.

7 Bob queries the CA server, discovers the certificate is ready, downloads the certificate, and stores the certificate.

8 Bob can now distribute his public key, using the certificate, and other people can validate the authenticity of the certificate by checking the CA's signature (checking the signature requires the CA's public key).

Trust and Nonrepudiation

If Alice trusts the CA who signed Bob's certificate, she has an assurance that the key contained in Bob's certificate has a binding to Bob's identity. Armed with Bob's certificate, Alice can prove that data she received with Bob's signature is authentic. The digital certificate (and the trusted third party behind it) can vouch for the fact that the key contained in the certificate belongs to Bob. This security feature is called *nonrepudiation*; in other words, Bob cannot repudiate or dismiss a digital signature as having no binding force. This addresses the problem of repudiation and public key cryptography stated earlier in this section.

Security of Digital Certificates

The binding of Bob's identity to the public key is only as good as the CA's manual verification step: A CA that requires Bob to visit one of its offices and present a valid passport along with his public key has a stronger binding certificate than a CA that merely requires Bob to submit his public key in an e-mail application. A digital certificate is like an ID card or passport—the level of trust you have in the document is determined by the reputation of the issuer and the lengths to which the issuer validates the identity of the individual.

What if a certificate is altered in transit? The CA's digital signature on the certificate protects against such an attack. If the certificate is modified in any way, a check of the CA's signature will fail. This is a property of digital signatures: The signature is derived from a combination of the certificate's contents *and* the CA's private key. Anyone can check the signature with the CA's public key and detect an alteration. (See also "Digital Signatures," earlier in this chapter.)

Anti-Replay

Anti-replay provides the assurance that past transactions cannot be replayed by an attacker. In spite of taking the precautions mentioned earlier (encryption, hashing, digital signatures, and certificates), an attacker might simply try to record and replay a transaction and not bother with subverting the security defenses.

IKE provides anti-replay security for IPsec by using sequence numbers combined with authentication. With anti-replay, senders and receivers can detect and reject data that is old or duplicate.

Consider Bob and Alice again: Bob invests in the stock market and places an order with Alice to buy 100 shares of some company. Somewhere between Bob and Alice, a lurking attacker records this transaction (with a packet analyzer or other capture device) and replays the captured transaction as another order from Bob to Alice. If Alice has anti-replay protection, she will detect and discard the replayed order from the attacker. On the other hand, if Alice does not have anti-replay protection, she might think Bob placed two orders—each for 100 shares, or 200 shares combined.

IPsec Concepts

The preceding sections of this chapter covered some basic principles of security and cryptography; the following sections introduce concepts specific to IPsec. These are

- Peers
- Transform Sets
- Security Associations
- Transport and Tunnel Modes
- Authentication Header (AH) and Encapsulating Security Payload (ESP)

Peers

A *peer* of an IPsec device is another device participating in IPsec. A peer can be a router, a firewall, a server, or a remote access device such as a PC with IPsec support. Peering between two IPsec devices is typically a point-to-point relationship. Going back to the example of two IPsec devices, Alice and Bob, Bob is a peer of Alice (and Alice a peer of Bob) when the two of them communicate with IPsec.

Transform Sets

A *transform set* is a list of IPsec protocols and cryptographic algorithms that a peer can accept. Because IPsec allows for the use of different protocols and algorithms, a peer needs to declare and negotiate with other peers what it can support. Peers communicate the protocols and algorithms they support by exchanging transform sets. For two peers to communicate successfully, they must share a common transform set. If they do not, their attempt to establish a peering will fail and they will not be able to communicate.

The following situation highlights transform sets in action. Consider a case where Alice and Bob are two IPsec devices on the Internet, but they were made by different manufacturers. Suppose Alice's implementation of IPsec supports an optional encryption algorithm (one that is supported but not mandated by the standard) that Bob does not support. If Alice sends Bob a transform set that includes the optional encryption algorithm, Bob will reject it because he has no way of encrypting or decrypting with that algorithm. What Alice could do to make things easier is send Bob two or three transform sets she thinks Bob might accept and have Bob pick a transform set acceptable to him.

A transform set typically contains the following information:

- An IPsec security protocol (AH or ESP—see "Authentication Header and Encapsulating Security Payload," later in this chapter) that is supported by the peer. Using AH and ESP together is also supported.

- An integrity/authentication algorithm supported by the peer (a hashing algorithm such as MD5 HMAC or SHA-1 HMAC, for example).

- An encryption algorithm supported by the peer (DES or Triple-DES, for example). A *null* encryption algorithm (no encryption) is also supported.

NOTE You may use authentication alone if encryption is not required. Encryption without authentication is also supported but is not recommended because of a potential security risk (see Bibliography for a reference).

An important point to know is that a transform set defines a set of protocols and algorithms to be used for *peering* with another device. It does not define a list of *all* the protocols and algorithms a peer supports. In other words, a transform set lists the rules for a session and is session-focused, not device-focused. A transform set is a proposal for communication: Alice might support DES, Triple-DES, IDEA, and Blowfish, but *propose* to Bob by way of a transform set that their session use DES.

Security Associations

A *security association (SA)* is a logical connection that protects data flowing from one peer to another by using a transform set. Security associations are like logical tunnels between peers: Traffic entering an SA is protected and transported to the other side (the other peer).

SAs are unidirectional—an SA protects data flowing in one direction only. Therefore, for secure bidirectional communication between peers, a pair of SAs is required.

IPsec maintains many pieces of data needed to support an SA between two peers. These parameters include

- The identity of the remote peer participating in IPsec (an IP address or hostname).

- The security protocol (AH or ESP), hashing algorithm (if one is used), and encryption algorithm (if ESP is used). This information is negotiated when the peers exchange transform sets.

- The shared keys used by the hashing and encryption algorithms for the duration of the SA (called the *lifetime* of the SA).

- A description of the traffic flow protected by the SA. Typically, this specifies the IP addresses and port numbers protected by the SA. The description can be fine-grained, such as a single TCP session between two hosts, or it can be broad, such as all traffic flowing from Subnet X to Subnet Y.

Note	In the Cisco implementation, this flow description is equivalent to an extended access list (see Chapter 6, "Deploying Basic Security Services," for access list information).

- A unique number that identifies the SA (called the *Security Parameter Index*, or *SPI*).
- Timers and counters that record the lifetime of an SA. This is used to detect when an SA and its associated keys get old and need to be refreshed. SAs and keys can be refreshed only when IKE is used with IPsec.
- Sequence numbers for detecting replay attacks when IKE is used.

Multiple SA pairs are allowed between peers. For example, one pair of SAs can protect Telnet traffic with Triple-DES and MD5, and another pair of SAs can protect all other traffic with DES and SHA-1.

SAs are established by manual user configuration or dynamically by IKE. IKE is the recommended method, especially for large implementations, because of its scalability and enhanced security services (dynamic rekeying and anti-replay). See "Internet Key Exchange," later in this chapter.

Transport and Tunnel Modes

IPsec defines two kinds of SAs: transport and tunnel mode SAs. A *transport mode SA* is an association between two hosts. In transport mode, the IP payload is protected by IPsec and the original IP header is left intact. Additionally, an IPsec header is inserted after the IP header. This is illustrated in Figure 7-2.

Figure 7-2   *Transport Mode SA*

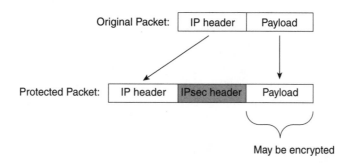

Transport mode protects traffic between two IPsec hosts (between a PC and a server, for example) and does not afford any *traffic flow confidentiality*. That is, the volume of traffic transmitted from one host to another can easily be observed, even if encryption is used, because the original source and destination addresses are left intact. An attacker could use this data to determine where servers are located, with the assumption that servers transmit and receive more data than clients.

A tunnel mode SA is an association between two routers (also called *security gateways*) or between a router and a host. In tunnel mode, the entire IP packet is protected by and becomes the payload of a new packet. The IPsec header is inserted after the IP header of the new packet. This is illustrated in Figure 7-3.

Figure 7-3   *Tunnel Mode SA*

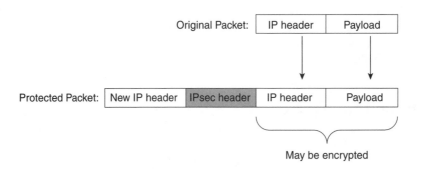

Tunnel mode is the basis for enabling dedicated VPNs between routers, as well as VPDNs that involve remote users terminating their SAs on routers to gain access to hosts within a network. With tunnel mode you do not have to equip every PC and server with IPsec; instead, you can activate IPsec on routers and use the routers to provide IPsec services on behalf of those computers. For example, you might establish an IPsec peering over the Internet between two branch office routers and use tunnel mode SAs between the routers to protect all interoffice traffic. This is a scenario depicted in Figure 7-1.

The source and destination addresses contained in the new IP header are that of the tunnel mode SA endpoints. Thus, tunnel mode SAs provide a level of traffic flow confidentiality because the IP addresses of the original packet are carried within the secure payload of an IPsec packet (assuming encryption is used).

Authentication Header and Encapsulating Security Payload

IPsec defines two security protocols called *Authentication Header (AH)* (RFC 2402) and *Encapsulating Security Payload (ESP)* (RFC 2406). Each protocol defines its own format for the IPsec header that follows the IP header of an IPsec packet (see Figures 7-2 and

7-3). Both protocols use the concept of an SA; therefore, SAs can be either AH SAs or ESP SAs (an SA cannot be both an AH *and* ESP SA). Additionally, both AH and ESP support transport and tunnel mode.

NOTE   A device might send a transform set to its peer that specifies use of both AH *and* ESP. If the peer agrees, four SAs will be established: two for AH and two for ESP (assuming bidirectional traffic flow).

AH provides integrity and authentication, using shared key hashing algorithms such as MD5 HMAC and SHA-1 HMAC. AH does not provide confidentiality (encryption).

ESP provides confidentiality and, optionally, integrity and authentication. For confidentiality, ESP supports shared key encryption algorithms such as DES and Triple-DES. Like AH, ESP supports shared key hashing algorithms such as MD5 HMAC and SHA-1 HMAC for integrity and authentication.

Because ESP provides everything that AH does (integrity and authentication), you might not have a need for AH at all. However, there is a slight difference between the integrity and authentication provided by AH and the integrity and authentication provided by ESP. This is illustrated in Figure 7-4.

Figure 7-4   *Differences Between AH and ESP Integrity Checking*

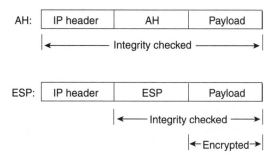

ESP does not check the integrity of the entire IP packet—it protects everything but the IP header. AH on the other hand, checks the integrity of the entire IPsec packet, including the IP header (technically, some fields in the IP header are subject to change during transit and AH cannot protect these values).

Is this difference between AH and ESP significant enough to dismiss ESP's integrity and authentication service? Probably not for most implementations; however, if the integrity of the IP header is important, you can use AH and ESP together. This comes at the price of having twice as many SAs as when using ESP alone: An SA can support either AH or ESP, but not both.

Internet Key Exchange

The Internet Key Exchange (IKE) protocol (RFC 2409) is a management protocol used in conjunction with IPsec and is based on three key management protocols: Internet Security Association and Key Management Protocol (ISAKMP) (RFC 2408), Oakley (RFC 2412), and SKEME (simply called "A Versatile Secure Key Exchange Mechanism for Internet" in a paper by Hugo Krawczyk).

IKE is an important protocol that provides IPsec with the following services:

- Establishes IPsec SAs dynamically as they are needed. Without IKE, you must manually configure all SAs required between all of the peers.

- Enables dynamic rekeying. With IKE, keys are expired after a period of time and new keys are dynamically created. This enhances IPsec security by limiting the amount of data protected by any one key and ever increasing the number of keys an attacker has to crack. Some security aspects of key lifetimes are discussed in RFC 2405.

- Enables anti-replay protection. Without IKE, IPsec peers cannot detect a replay attack. See "Anti-Replay," earlier in this chapter.

- Enables origin authentication with digital certificates and CA servers. Without IKE, there is no CA support, and origin authentication must be done person-to-person (manually and out-of-band).

- Optionally provides *Perfect Forward Secrecy (PFS)*. This is a cryptographic characteristic of shared keys and means that the compromise of a key does not help an attacker discover other keys. In other words, each key is secure on its own merits and is not derived from any other key. Use PFS for enhanced security. (See also "Configuring Perfect Forward Secrecy," later in this chapter.)

For the preceding reasons, deploying IPsec with IKE is highly recommended. IKE adds security features, increases scalability, and simplifies configuration.

When two IPsec devices need to communicate by using IPsec, they first authenticate one another by using IKE and then establish an IKE SA between them for management. The IKE SA is secure and acts as a control channel for exchanging keys and negotiating IPsec SAs (the SAs that protect *user* data flowing between the peers). Unlike IPsec SAs, which are unidirectional, the IKE SA is bidirectional. Only one IKE SA is needed between two IPsec peers to support multiple IPsec SAs, as shown in Figure 7-5.

Figure 7-5   *A Single IKE SA Acts as a Secure Management Channel for IPsec SAs*

Tying All of the Pieces Together: A Comprehensive Example with IPsec and IKE

The sections up to this point have covered the building blocks of IPsec, but how do all of these technologies work together? The following sequence between Alice and Bob incorporates the concepts covered in the preceding sections and describes how IPsec's cryptographic techniques can achieve secure communication over an untrusted network.

In this example, assume that no prior communication has occurred between Alice and Bob. To make the example more concrete, further assume that Alice needs to establish a secure FTP session with Bob:

1   Alice initiates an IKE SA with Bob and proposes a transform set they should use. The transform set specifies the encryption, hashing, and authentication algorithm for the IKE SA as well as such other information as the SA lifetime (the lifetime sets an expiration time for the SA). If Bob can support the transform set, the negotiation continues. Otherwise, the IKE SA fails and no other communication occurs. See "Transform Sets," earlier in this chapter.

2   Alice sends her digital certificate to Bob. The certificate contains her public key and guarantees the authenticity of the key. Bob does the same thing so that Alice has his public key. See "Digital Certificates," earlier in this chapter.

3   Alice and Bob exchange digitally signed Diffie-Hellman numbers for the purpose of establishing a shared secret. The Diffie-Hellman numbers are signed so that each peer can validate the identity of the other peer. Otherwise, an attacker could masquerade as Bob and perform a Diffie-Hellman exchange with Alice—a man-in-the-middle attack (see "Subverting Diffie-Hellman," earlier in this chapter).

4   Alice verifies the signature on Bob's Diffie-Hellman number with Bob's public key (this authenticates Bob). Bob does the same thing and verifies the signature on Alice's Diffie-Hellman number, using Alice's public key.

5   Alice and Bob calculate a shared key known only to them by using the Diffie-Hellman key exchange algorithm. See "Using Diffie-Hellman to Agree on a Shared Key," earlier in this chapter.

6   At this point, the IKE SA is established between Alice and Bob: Data can be sent securely between the peers, using the shared key from Step 5 and the algorithms specified in the IKE transform set.

7   Alice initiates an IPsec SA, which is needed to support the packets for the FTP session (recall that the IKE SA is used for management only, not for user data). Using the IKE SA as a secure channel, Alice proposes one or more transform sets for the IPsec SA. Each of her transform sets specifies a security protocol (AH or ESP) and algorithms (hashing and/or encryption) for the SA. If Bob can support a transform set, negotiation continues. Otherwise, the IPsec SA fails and no other communication occurs (no FTP packets can be sent).

8 Alice and Bob calculate a shared key for the IPsec SA, using the Diffie-Hellman key exchange algorithm. This provides PFS: The key for the IPsec SA is not derived from the key for the IKE SA.

9 Alice can now send FTP packets securely to Bob over the IPsec SA, using the shared key from Step 8 and the algorithms specified in the transform set for the IPsec SA (Step 7).

10 The IPsec SA is maintained by IKE. A short time before the IPsec SA expires, a new SA with new keys is created and communication is rolled over to the new SA transparently. This is the rekeying service provided by IKE.

11 When Bob needs to send data, he must initiate and establish an IPsec SA with Alice because IPsec SAs are unidirectional. See "Security Associations," earlier in this chapter.

Configuring IKE

Cisco's implementation of IKE supports three authentication methods. They are

- **Pre-shared keys**—Two peers are configured with a predetermined shared key. Peers are authenticated if they both possess the same key. This is a simple configuration, does not use public key cryptography or digital certificates, and might be suitable for small networks.

- **RSA encryption**—RSA encryption uses public key cryptography to authenticate peers but does not use digital certificates (does not provide nonrepudiation). Each device must be manually configured with the public key of its peer. This has the advantage of not relying on a shared key and might be suitable for small networks.

- **RSA signatures with digital certificates**—This uses public key cryptography and provides nonrepudiation in conjunction with a CA. A peer obtains a digital certificate from a CA server and distributes its public keys, using the digital certificate. This provides the scalability needed for larger networks.

Configuring IKE with Pre-Shared Keys

Authentication with pre-shared keys is the simplest implementation of IKE and might be suitable for small networks (10 routers and fewer, perhaps). As mentioned previously, this configuration does not have the scaling advantages of public key cryptography and digital certificates. Instead, two peers are manually configured with the same key (a shared key). How the keys are determined and programmed into the routers is the responsibility of the router administrators. When a pre-shared key needs to change, human intervention is needed again.

NOTE	The shared key is confidential information and therefore needs to be exchanged and configured out-of-band, never across an untrusted network. This makes key management more cumbersome than IKE using RSA encryption and IKE using RSA signatures with digital certificates.

Consider the network in Figure 7-6 with two routers that peer over an untrusted network and provide tunnel mode SAs for their local clients.

Figure 7-6   *Two Routers Peering with IKE and Pre-Shared Keys*

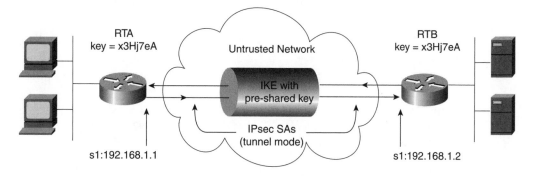

The following IOS commands configure Router A so it can establish an IKE SA with Router B, using pre-shared keys. For clarity, these commands include the context of the IOS prompt.

```
RTA#conf t
Enter configuration commands, one per line. End with CNTL/Z.
RTA(config)#crypto isakmp policy 10
RTA(config-isakmp)#authentication pre-share
RTA(config-isakmp)#hash md5
RTA(config-isakmp)#encryption des
RTA(config-isakmp)#lifetime 43200
RTA(config-isakmp)#exit
RTA(config)#crypto isakmp key x3Hj7eA address 192.168.1.2
```

The command **conf t** (short for **configure terminal**) changes the prompt from enable mode to configure mode.

The command **crypto isakmp policy 10** creates an IKE transform set (called a *policy*) whose priority is 10 and changes the command mode to ISAKMP policy configuration. The keyword **isakmp** in IOS commands refers to IKE (recall that IKE is a hybrid protocol of ISAKMP, Oakley, and SKEME). A router can have multiple IKE transform sets. When a router peers with another IKE device, it negotiates an IKE transform set. It checks each of its IKE transform sets in the order of priority (1 is the highest priority) until a match with the other device is found.

The next four lines configure the parameters of the IKE transform set:

- **authentication pre-share** dictates that the transform set use pre-shared keys for authenticating the remote peer.
- **hash md5** configures MD5 hashing as the transform set's integrity-checking algorithm. Instead of **md5**, you can use the keyword **sha** to define SHA-1 (Secure Hash Algorithm).
- **encryption des** configures the transform set for DES (56-bit) encryption. At the time of this writing, the other option available to most routers is Triple-DES (keyword **3des**). More algorithms might be added by Cisco in the future.
- **lifetime 43200** sets the lifetime for the IKE SA to 43,200 seconds (12 hours). The default is 86,400 seconds (24 hours). After the IKE SA reaches the age specified by this command, it is removed until IKE is needed again to establish new IPsec SAs (existing IPsec SAs have their own lifetimes and are not disturbed when the IKE SA expires).

The command **exit** changes the mode from ISAKMP policy configuration back to global config mode.

Finally, the command **crypto isakmp key x3Hj7eA address 192.168.1.2** sets the pre-shared key used by Router A to peer with Router B to the string **x3Hj7eA**. The string can be any user-defined text (no spaces) as long as it matches the string configured in Router B (see the following configuration for Router B). The keywords **address 192.168.1.2** specify the IP address of Router B's Serial1 interface.

The following is the matching configuration for Router B. For brevity, only the output of **show running-config** relevant to IKE is shown.

```
RTB#sh run

crypto isakmp policy 10
 hash md5
 authentication pre-share
 lifetime 43200
crypto isakmp key x3Hj7eA address 192.168.1.1
```

where **address 192.168.1.1** specifies the IP address of Router A's Serial1 interface.

The command **encryption des** does not appear in the output of **show running-config** because it is the default encryption algorithm for IKE.

NOTE   Router A and Router B must share at least one common IKE transform set; otherwise, IKE negotiation will fail. The pre-shared keys must also match, or authentication will fail.

Configuring IKE with RSA Encryption

A router using IKE with RSA encryption (RSA public key cryptography) is configured with the non-secret, public keys of its peers. This makes the exchanging of keys less problematic than authentication with secret, pre-shared keys. However, a device must be manually configured with the public key of every peer with which it builds an IKE SA. This means RSA encryption does not scale well in large networks. Also, RSA encryption lacks the nonrepudiation that is available when using digital certificates (see "Configuring IKE with RSA Signatures and Digital Certificates," later in this chapter).

Consider the network in Figure 7-7 with two routers peering over an untrusted network with IKE and RSA encryption.

Figure 7-7   *Two Routers Peering with IKE and RSA Encryption*

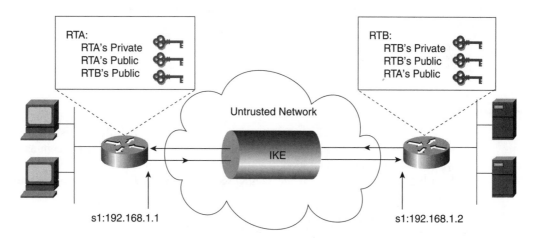

In the preceding figure, Router A owns a private and public key pair and is configured with Router B's public key. Router A uses Router B's public key to authenticate IKE sessions with Router B. Likewise, Router B owns its key pair and is configured with Router A's public key. The IP addresses assigned to the serial interfaces of Router A and Router B are 192.168.1.1 and 192.168.1.2, respectively.

Configure IKE Transform Sets

The following IOS commands configure Router A so that it can establish an IKE SA with Router B, using RSA encryption (for clarity, these commands include the context of the IOS prompt):

```
RTA#conf t
Enter configuration commands, one per line. End with CNTL/Z.
RTA(config)#crypto isakmp policy 9
RTA(config-isakmp)#authentication rsa-encr
```

continues

```
RTA(config-isakmp)#hash sha
RTA(config-isakmp)#encryption des
RTA(config-isakmp)#lifetime 43200
RTA(config-isakmp)#exit
RTA(config)#_
```

The preceding commands create an IKE transform set with the following characteristics:

- Priority is 9.

- Authentication method is RSA encryption (**rsa-encr**).

- Hashing algorithm is SHA-1 (**sha**).

- Encryption algorithm is 56-bit DES (**des**).

- Lifetime is 43,200 seconds (12 hours).

You must configure Router B with the same IKE transform set; otherwise, authentication with RSA encryption will fail. The following is a partial output of Router B's configuration (the default IKE parameters do not appear):

```
crypto isakmp policy 9
 authentication rsa-encr
 lifetime 43200
```

Generate RSA Key Pair

Router A and Router B must each generate a private and public key pair. To do this, you run a small program within global config mode by issuing the **crypto key generate rsa** command, as shown in the following configuration. Before you issue this command, ensure that your router has a hostname and a domain name (configured with the **hostname** and **ip domain-name** global config commands).

```
RTA(config)#crypto key generate rsa
The name for the keys will be: RTA.cisco.com
Choose the size of the key modulus in the range of 360 to 2048 for your
  General Purpose Keys. Choosing a key modulus greater than 512 may take
  a few minutes.

How many bits in the modulus [512]: 1536
Generating RSA keys ...
<This takes some time>
[OK]

RTA(config)#_
```

As shown in the preceding output, the key generation program requires you to input the modulus (or key length). Longer key lengths provide greater security but take more time to generate.

NOTE During key generation you might see system messages that begin with **%SYS-3-CPUHOG**. These messages indicate that the router is experiencing high CPU utilization—expected, because key generation is CPU-intensive. Other tasks in the router might be adversely affected by the high utilization; therefore, generate the keys before you put the router into service.

Depending on the size of the key and the CPU power of your router, the time to generate the key pair can range from 1 second (Cisco 4700 router and a 512-bit length) to over an hour (Cisco 2500 router and a 2048-bit length). RSA keys smaller than 512 bits are not recommended. Bruce Schneier (see Bibliography) has theorized that a 1536-bit public key length will be reasonably secure for protecting the data of a typical corporation through the year 2010. This takes into account some assumptions on the advance of computing power and mathematics.

After the keys are generated, you can view the public key with the enable command **show crypto key mypubkey rsa** (this is Router A):

```
RTA#sh crypto key mypubkey rsa
% Key pair was generated at: 10:06:46 PST Mar 2 1999
Key name: RTA.cisco.com
 Usage: General Purpose Key
 Key Data:
  305C300D 06092A86 4886F70D 01010105 00034B00 30480241 00CE23D4 4C3CB0E9
  4C44DB1B E29F1F20 53E64550 1A832B8A A439EBFE ACD24C5B 6E6CAB70 CE03048F
  8BFA0F00 C87CD8A7 756EA2D4 A387CA30 628DBC14 22903286 D3020301 0001
```

The hexadecimal data after the line **Key Data**: is the public key.

NOTE For security purposes, you cannot view the private key. The private key is stored in a nonviewable portion of the router's nonvolatile RAM (NVRAM) and is not stored when the configuration is backed up to another device.

Here's the key generation step and display of the public key for Router B (refer to Figure 7-7):

```
RTB(config)#crypto key generate rsa
The name for the keys will be: RTB.cisco.com
Choose the size of the key modulus in the range of 360 to 2048 for your
  General Purpose Keys. Choosing a key modulus greater than 512 may take
  a few minutes.

How many bits in the modulus [512]: 1536
Generating RSA keys ...
[OK]

RTB(config)#^Z
```

continues

```
RTB#sh cry key mypub rsa
% Key pair was generated at: 19:08:18 UTC Mar 2 1999
Key name: RTB.cisco.com
 Usage: General Purpose Key
 Key Data:
  305C300D 06092A86 4886F70D 01010105 00034B00 30480241 00A62A0B 2376E4EC
  CB8E21B7 FFD405E8 BE36BC5B AE39FE9F BB57A830 CAFE6A51 E6A14427 191056F1
  5611F624 081CCD3F 73FCD337 8EA14F27 95634B9F 367BDCF4 E5020301 0001
```

Configure the Router with the Public Key of the Other Device

Router A must now be configured with the public key of Router B (and vice versa). If you own Router A and someone else owns Router B, you might not have visibility to Router B's public key. In such a case, the owner of Router B has to send you the output of Router B's **show crypto key mypubkey rsa**. Again, public keys are non-secret information so they do not have to be sent out-of-band—e-mail and Telnet are viable methods. However, you must be certain that the public key you are given is genuine (owned by the remote peer, not by an attacker pretending to be the remote peer).

The following configuration commands configure Router A with Router B's public key (Router B's configuration is similar):

```
RTA(config)#crypto key pubkey-chain rsa
RTA(config-pubkey-chain)#addressed-key 192.168.1.2
RTA(config-pubkey-key)#key-string
Enter a public key as a hexadecimal number ....

RTA(config-pubkey)# 305C300D 06092A86 4886F70D 01010105 00034B00 30480241 00A62A0B
    2376E4EC
RTA(config-pubkey)# CB8E21B7 FFD405E8 BE36BC5B AE39FE9F BB57A830 CAFE6A51 E6A14427
    191056F1
RTA(config-pubkey)# 5611F624 081CCD3F 73FCD337 8EA14F27 95634B9F 367BDCF4 E5020301
    0001
RTA(config-pubkey)#quit
RTA(config-pubkey-key)#^Z
RTA#
```

The command **crypto key pubkey-chain rsa** changes the command mode from global config mode to public key chain configuration mode (indicated by prompt changing to **config-pubkey-chain**). The public key *chain* is the set of all public keys this router possesses—it's similar to a real-world key chain.

The command **addressed-key 192.168.1.2** tells the router that you wish to enter a public key for remote peer 192.168.1.2 (Router B's Serial1 interface). This command changes the command mode to public key configuration mode as indicated by the next prompt **config-pubkey-key**.

You use the command **key-string** (followed by a carriage return) to begin entry of the remote peer's public key. The hexadecimal data of the public key (the next three lines) is cut and pasted into the router to avoid making typographical mistakes. After the key data is entered, the command **quit** is issued on its own line and the mode reverts to public key configuration mode.

Finally, typing `Ctrl-Z` (or `end`) exits configure mode completely and returns the prompt to enable mode.

To verify that the public key has been configured correctly, issue **show running-config** on Router A:

```
RTA#sh run
Building configuration...

Current configuration:
<lines deleted for brevity>
!
crypto key pubkey-chain rsa
 addressed-key 192.168.1.2
  address 192.168.1.2
  key-string
   305C300D 06092A86 4886F70D 01010105 00034B00 30480241 00A62A0B 2376E4EC
   CB8E21B7 FFD405E8 BE36BC5B AE39FE9F BB57A830 CAFE6A51 E6A14427 191056F1
   5611F624 081CCD3F 73FCD337 8EA14F27 95634B9F 367BDCF4 E5020301 0001
  quit
```

TIP

When there are multiple peers, add the public keys of the other devices.

After Router B is configured with Router A's public key (similar method), the IKE configuration for the network in Figure 7-7 is complete.

Configuring IKE with RSA Signatures and Digital Certificates

IKE authentication with digital certificates uses RSA digital signatures and provides scalability for larger networks. As mentioned previously, digital certificates provide nonrepudiation through the service of a CA.

NOTE

Your organization might administer a CA server and act as the CA for all of the devices and people that belong to your organization. Also, you might be the CA for third parties (suppliers, partners, customers) that do business with your organization.

With digital certificate support, a router does not need to be configured with the public keys of each of its peers; instead, a router only needs to obtain its digital certificate from the CA. The digital certificate contains the router's public key (and other identity information) and the CA's signature for the certificate. When building an IKE SA with a peer, the router offers its digital certificate to the peer. The peer can then validate the authenticity of the certificate (by checking the CA's signature) and extract the public key contained within the certificate. See "Digital Signatures" and "Digital Certificates," earlier in this chapter.

CAs and supporting systems that provide digital certificates and public key management are collectively called the *public key infrastructure (PKI)*. PKI standards come from the IETF, International Telecommunication Union (ITU), RSA Data Security, and other organizations. IOS supports standards for PKI elements such as certificates, keys, and CAs. Consult Cisco
for a current list of supported PKI systems and standards.

NOTE   A particularly relevant PKI document is RFC 2510.

The example configurations presented in this section on certificates are based on the network depicted in Figure 7-8. This figure describes two routers peering over an untrusted network with IKE and digital certificates with RSA signatures.

Figure 7-8 *Two Routers Peering with IKE and Digital Certificates with RSA Signatures*

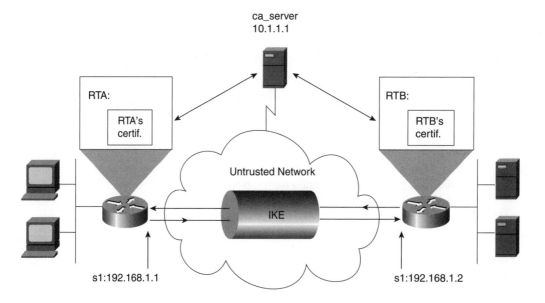

In the preceding figure, both Router A and Router B store their own certificates locally in their IOS configurations. Both have already obtained their certificates at a prior time by following the certificate request, verification, and retrieval process with the CA server called **ca_server**. When Router A and Router B need to build an IKE SA, they exchange certificates as part of the IKE authentication process. Refer to "Tying All of the Pieces Together: A Comprehensive Example with IPsec and IKE" for a sequence including IKE and digital certificates.

Configure the IKE Transform Set for RSA Signature

As with pre-shared keys and RSA encryption, you must configure matching IKE transform sets in the routers to support RSA signature. The following IOS commands configure Router A so it can establish an IKE SA with Router B using RSA signature (for clarity, these commands include the context of the IOS prompt):

```
RTA#conf t
Enter configuration commands, one per line. End with CNTL/Z.
RTA(config)#crypto isakmp policy 7
RTA(config-isakmp)#authentication rsa-sig
RTA(config-isakmp)#hash sha
RTA(config-isakmp)#encryption des
RTA(config-isakmp)#lifetime 43200
RTA(config-isakmp)#exit
RTA(config)#_
```

The preceding commands create an IKE transform set with the following characteristics:

- Priority is 7.
- Authentication method is RSA signature (**rsa-sig**).
- Hashing algorithm is SHA-1 (**sha**).
- Encryption algorithm is 56-bit DES (**des**).
- Lifetime is 43,200 seconds (12 hours).

You must configure Router B with the same IKE transform set; otherwise, IKE negotiation will fail.

Configure CA Information

Both Router A and Router B need to be configured with the identity of the CA server so that they can communicate with it. The following commands configure the CA server information in Router A (Router B's configuration is similar):

```
RTB(config)#ip host ca_server 10.1.1.1
RTB(config)#crypto ca identity myca
RTB(ca-identity)#enrollment url http://ca_server
RTB(ca-identity)#enrollment mode ra
RTB(ca-identity)#query url ldap://ca_server
RTB(ca-identity)#crl optional
RTB(ca-identity)#exit
```

The command **ip host ca_server 10.1.1.1** adds an entry in the router's host table so that it can resolve the name **ca_server** to **10.1.1.1**. This command can be skipped if the router is configured with the **ip name-server** command and can resolve the name with DNS.

The command **crypto ca identity myca** adds an entry for the CA, names the CA **myca** (this can be any string), and begins CA identity config mode as indicated when the prompt changes to **ca-identity** in the next line.

The command **enrollment url http://ca_server** configures the router with the Uniform Resource Locator (URL) of the CA. This is required and should match the hostname configured by the preceding **ip host** command. The URL in this example assumes the script directory of the CA server is in a default location. This should apply to most cases; however, if the script directory is in a nonstandard location, include the full path to the script directory in the URL (for example, **enrollment url http://ca_server/cgi-bin/subdir1/subdir2**). Consult your CA for assistance in determining the correct URL.

The command **enrollment mode ra** is necessary only if the router is communicating with a *Registration Authority (RA)*. Some PKI systems split administration tasks across two servers: a CA that signs certificates and an RA that handles the certificate enrollment transactions. Consult your CA. If your CA does not use an RA, you should skip this command.

The command **query url ldap://ca_server** configures the router to use the Lightweight Directory Access Protocol (LDAP) for retrieving certificates from this server. This is usually configured in conjunction with an RA that supports the LDAP protocol. If your CA does not use LDAP, you should skip this step.

NOTE　　At the time of this writing, IOS interoperates with CA servers from Entrust Technologies and Verisign, using the Certificate Enrollment Protocol (CEP). The Entrust CA server requires the commands **enrollment mode ra** and **query url**; the Verisign CA server does not. See a bulletin at http://www.cisco.com/warp/public/778/security/821_pp.htm or search for "certificate authority support" on Cisco's Web site. Consult Cisco for a current list of supported PKI systems.

The command **crl optional** allows the router to accept a peer's certificate even if the *certificate revocation list (CRL)* is not available. Routers and other devices use the CRL to check for certificates that have been revoked. Certificates expire over time and can be retracted by the owner of the certificate or the CA. To ensure that a certificate is still valid, a device downloads a CRL from its CA and rejects certificates that are on the CRL. If the CRL is not available (if the CA server is down and the CRL is not stored on the router), **crl optional** enables the router to accept a peer's certificate and continue.

Without the **crl optional** command, the security policy is more strict: The router must possess and check the CRL before accepting a peer's certificate. This might be desirable for enhanced security, but it adds an additional step that might require troubleshooting.

Finally, **exit** ends CA identity mode and returns to global configure mode.

Retrieve the Certificate of the CA

Each device participating in authentication with digital certificates needs to retrieve the CA's certificate. This provides the device with the CA's public key that is used to verify certificates the CA has signed.

The following command instructs Router A to contact the CA and retrieve the CA's certificate (Router B also requires this command). The administrator commands are highlighted in boldface. Refer to Figure 7-8 for the topology.

```
RTA(config)#crypto ca authenticate myca
Certificate has the following attributes:
Fingerprint: B60065B9 63EC9373 D33B4548 CAEF52B9

% Do you accept this certificate? [yes/no]: y
RTA(config)#
```

The command **crypto ca authenticate myca** is a global config command and tells a router to get the certificate of the server **myca**.

In the next lines, the router retrieves the *fingerprint* of the CA's certificate and asks you to verify it. The fingerprint is a cryptographic number calculated by the CA and is used to verify the integrity of the certificate. Check the fingerprint your router receives against the fingerprint provided by your CA. Matching fingerprints validates the CA's certificate and ensures that the certificate was not altered in transit.

After accepting the certificate, you can view it with the **show crypto ca certificates** command:

```
RTA#sh cry ca certificates

CA Certificate
  Status: Available
  Certificate Serial Number: 3654B2FF
  Key Usage: Not Set
```

Generate Public and Private Keys

After configuring the CA information, you need to generate the router's public and private keys. This is performed with the command **crypto key generate rsa** introduced in the section "Configuring IKE with RSA Encryption" earlier in this chapter.

Some PKI servers (CA or RA) require each device to have two public/private key pairs—a total of four keys. One key pair is used for encryption and the other key pair is used for digital signatures. The following command generates two such key pairs. Before you issue this command, ensure that your router has a hostname and a domain name (configured with the **hostname** and **ip domain-name** global config commands):

```
RTA(config)#crypto key generate rsa usage-keys
The name for the keys will be: RTA.cisco.com
Choose the size of the key modulus in the range of 360 to 2048 for your
  Signature Keys. Choosing a key modulus greater than 512 may take
  a few minutes.

How many bits in the modulus [512]: 1536
Generating RSA keys ...

%SYS-3-CPUHOG: Task ran for 2812 msec (109/109), process = Key Proc, PC = 72B1EE.
[OK]
Choose the size of the key modulus in the range of 360 to 2048 for your
  Encryption Keys. Choosing a key modulus greater than 512 may take
  a few minutes.

How many bits in the modulus [512]: 1536
Generating RSA keys ...

%SYS-3-CPUHOG: Task ran for 2048 msec (17/9), process = Key Proc, PC = 72A3A8.
[OK]

RTA(config)#_
```

The command **crypto key generate rsa usage-keys** runs a small program within global configure mode that creates *two* RSA key pairs. These key pairs are submitted to the PKI server (CA or RA) with a request for a certificate. See "Send Public Keys to the CA and Get Your Certificate," later in this chapter.

If your PKI server (CA or RA) requires only one public/private key pair, use the command **crypto key generate rsa** instead of **crypto key generate rsa usage-key**.

NOTE   The system message **%SYS-3-CPUHOG** in the preceding output indicates that the router is experiencing high CPU utilization. This is expected because key generation is CPU-intensive. As mentioned in an earlier note, generate keys before putting the router into service.

Send Public Keys to the CA and Get Your Certificate

To submit the router's public key (or keys) to the PKI server and request a certificate, issue the **crypto ca enroll** command:

```
RTA(config)#crypto ca enroll myca
% Start certificate enrollment ..
% Create a challenge password. You will need to verbally provide this
    password to the CA Administrator in order to revoke your certificate.
    For security reasons your password will not be saved in the
configuration.
    Please make a note of it.

Password: <type a password here>
Re-enter password: <re-enter password>

% The subject name in the certificate will be: RTA.cisco.com
% Include the router serial number in the subject name? [yes/no]: yes
% Include an IP address in the subject name? [yes/no]: no
Request certificate from CA? [yes/no]: yes
% Certificate request sent to Certificate Authority
% The certificate request fingerprint will be displayed.
% The 'show crypto ca certificate' command will also show the
fingerprint.

RTA(config)#
    Signing Certificate Request Fingerprint:
    AABB1FD9 594B3209 39D9058C 2A19205C
  Encryption Certificate Request Fingerprint:
    6289344E AEFDC0AE BCB06E1B ECD62171
```

The command **crypto ca enroll myca** initiates a request for a certificate and prompts you for the following (indicated by boldface in the preceding output):

- **Password**—You need to supply a password to the CA with your request. If you ever have to revoke a certificate, the CA will ask for this password to prevent fraudulent revocation requests.

- **Include router serial number**—You may include your router's serial number in the certificate. This is not required by IPsec or IKE, but might be required by your CA.

- **Include IP address**—You may include your router's IP address in the certificate. Generally, you will not include this because IP addresses can change and such a change would require a new certificate.

- **Request certificate from CA**—When you are ready to submit the request, answer **yes** to this prompt to send the request.

Next, the router displays the fingerprints associated with the certificate requests and periodically queries the PKI server until the CA fulfills the request. By default, the router queries the server every minute until the certificate is ready for retrieval. The query interval can be adjusted by the **enrollment retry-period** command (CA identity config mode).

The following output of **show crypto ca certificates** indicates that a certificate request is still pending:

```
RTA#sh cr ca certificates
Certificate
  Subject Name
    Name: RTA.cisco.com
    IP Address: 192.168.1.1
  Status: Pending
  Key Usage: Signature
    Fingerprint: AABB1FD9 594B3209 39D9058C 2A19205C
```

A status of **Pending** means the CA server has not yet completed the processing of the certificate request. As mentioned in the earlier section, "Digital Certificates and Certification Authorities," the CA should manually verify that the public key and the owner are legitimate before issuing a certificate.

When the router queries the server, discovers that the certificate is ready, and downloads the certificate, the following system message is displayed:

```
RTA(config)#
%CRYPTO-6-CERTRET: Certificate received from Certificate Authority
RTA(config)#
```

The router now has its certificate. You can verify this by issuing the **show crypto ca certificates** command:

```
RTA#show crypto ca certificates
Certificate
  Subject Name
    Name: RTA.cisco.com
    IP Address: 192.168.1.1
  Status: Available
  Certificate Serial Number: 3654B3B6
  Key Usage: Signature
```

A status of **Available** confirms that the router has its certificate and is ready to distribute it to peers.

When both routers, Router A and Router B in Figure 7-8, have their certificates, IKE configuration for this example is complete.

Additional Commands for IKE

The following paragraphs provide some additional commands for IKE configuration.

The command **group 2** configures the IKE transform set for Diffie-Hellman group 2 (1024-bit numbers). The default is group 1 (768-bit numbers). Group 2 provides greater security but takes longer to compute (the computational time can make a difference on routers with smaller CPUs):

```
RTA(config)#crypto isakmp policy 10
RTA(config-isakmp)#group 2
```

The command **crypto isakmp identity hostname** applies to IKE with pre-shared keys and tells the router to use its hostname (RTA.cisco.com, for example) when it identifies itself to peers:

```
RTA(config)#crypto isakmp identity hostname
```

This might be necessary if the router uses multiple interfaces to peer with other devices. By default, routers identify themselves with their IP address (**crypto isakmp identity address**). It is recommended that peers identify themselves to each other the same way: with addresses or with hostnames.

The command **crypto key zeroize rsa** erases the router's RSA keys (public and private) from the configuration:

```
RTA(config)#crypto key zeroize rsa
```

The command **no addressed-key** removes a peer's public key from the router's public key chain. The following example removes the public key for peer 192.168.1.2:

```
RTA(config)#cry key pubkey-chain rsa
RTA(config-pubkey-chain)#no addressed-key 192.168.1.2
```

The command **no certificate** removes a certificate from the router's configuration. The following example removes a certificate with serial number **3654B30A**:

```
RTA(config)#cry ca certificate chain myca
RTA(config-cert-chain)#no certificate 3654B30A
```

NOTE   The enable mode command **show crypto ca certificate** displays certificates and their associated serial numbers.

The command **crypto ca crl request myca** tells the router to contact the CA server **myca** (configured by **crypto ca identity myca**) and download a CRL:

```
RTA(config)#crypto ca crl request myca
```

Skip this command if your CA does not support CRLs. See also "Configure CA Information," earlier in this chapter.

With the **crypto ca certificate query** command, the router downloads certificates and CRLs directly from the CA as they are needed and does not store the data to NVRAM:

```
RTA(config)#crypto ca certificate query
```

By default, when a router initially receives certificates and CRLs, it stores them locally in NVRAM (data in NVRAM is always available to the router even after a power-down). The **crypto ca certificate query** command conserves NVRAM space, but might result in loss of service if the CA is unavailable and the router cannot download certificates and CRLs.

Validating IKE Configuration

To view the IKE transform sets (policies) and verify IKE configuration, issue the **show crypto isakmp policy** command. The following is an example output:

```
RTA#sh cry isakmp pol
Protection suite of priority 7
        encryption algorithm:   DES - Data Encryption Standard (56 bit keys).
        hash algorithm:         Secure Hash Standard
        authentication method:  Rivest-Shamir-Adleman Signature
        Diffie-Hellman group:   #1 (768 bit)
        lifetime:               43200 seconds, no volume limit
Protection suite of priority 9
        encryption algorithm:   DES - Data Encryption Standard (56 bit keys).
        hash algorithm:         Secure Hash Standard
        authentication method:  Rivest-Shamir-Adleman Encryption
        Diffie-Hellman group:   #1 (768 bit)
        lifetime:               43200 seconds, no volume limit
Protection suite of priority 10
        encryption algorithm:   DES - Data Encryption Standard (56 bit keys).
        hash algorithm:         Message Digest 5
        authentication method:  Pre-Shared Key
        Diffie-Hellman group:   #1 (768 bit)
        lifetime:               180 seconds, no volume limit
Default protection suite
        encryption algorithm:   DES - Data Encryption Standard (56 bit keys).
        hash algorithm:         Secure Hash Standard
        authentication method:  Rivest-Shamir-Adleman Signature
        Diffie-Hellman group:   #1 (768 bit)
        lifetime:               86400 seconds, no volume limit
```

The default transform set (line **Default protection suite**) is always present, is listed last, and has the lowest priority.

When Are IKE SAs Established?

After you configure IKE, the router does not initiate an IKE SA until it is needed for establishing the IPsec SAs that protect user traffic. This means you need to configure IPsec before you can see an IKE SA and know with certainty that IKE is working. The following section covers how to configure IPsec.

NOTE

IKE uses UDP port number 500. Make sure you do not have any access lists configured on interfaces that might be undesirably blocking UDP port 500.

Configuring IPsec

After IKE is configured, the next step is to configure policies called *crypto maps* that tell a router how to build IPsec SAs within the IKE SA.

This section covers

- Crypto Maps
- Crypto Map Configuration Overview
- Configuring Crypto Access Lists
- Crypto Access Lists: An Example
- Configuring IPsec Transform Sets
- Configuring and Applying Crypto Maps
- When Are SAs Established?
- Configuring IPsec SA Lifetimes
- Configuring Perfect Forward Secrecy
- Configuring Dynamic Crypto Maps
- Tunnel Endpoint Discovery
- Validating IPsec Configuration

Crypto Maps

A crypto map defines the IPsec policies on a router. These policies include:

- The traffic that is protected by IPsec
- The transforms that are applied to the IPsec SAs
- The identity of peers to which the protected traffic should be sent
- Additional rules, such as SAs lifetimes and PFS

Crypto maps are applied to router interfaces and can contain one or more *entries*. An entry defines a policy for packets that match an extended access list (called a *crypto access list*). By configuring multiple entries, you can define different protection schemes (IPsec transform sets) for different types of traffic, based on IP address, application port, or anything else that can be matched with an extended access list (see also Chapter 6 on access lists).

NOTE   An interface can have only one crypto map. Use multiple entries within a crypto map to assign different policies for different types of traffic.

Figure 7-9 is a conceptual view of a crypto map.

Figure 7-9 *Conceptual View of a Crypto Map Applied to Router A's Serial1 Interface*

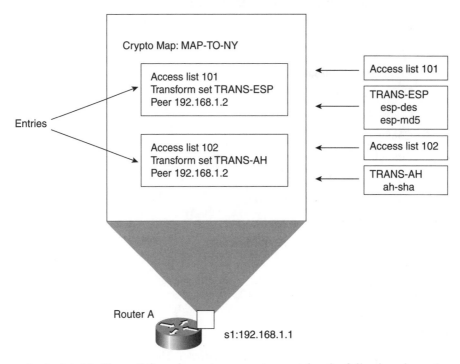

As depicted in Figure 7-9, each crypto map entry contains the following elements:

- **Crypto access list**—An extended access list that defines the packets protected by the entry.

- **Transform set**—A list of one or more transforms considered acceptable for protecting the traffic covered by the crypto access list. See "IPsec Concepts" earlier in this chapter for more information.

- **Peer's identity**—The IP address or hostname of the remote peer that the router sends the protected traffic to.

- **Additional parameters**—The lifetime of the IPsec SAs and PFS (on or off). If IKE is not implemented (not recommended), the session's keys and SPIs are manually configured in the entry as well.

Crypto Map Configuration Overview

Your goal is to configure the router so it protects the data you want with the security protocols and algorithms you want. This entails the following:

- Creating the crypto map elements (crypto access lists and transform sets)

- Configuring the crypto map
- Applying the crypto map to a router interface
- Validating the configuration

The following sections describe these steps.

Configuring Crypto Access Lists

As mentioned previously, crypto access lists define the scope or set of packets that need protection of an IPsec SA.

You configure crypto access lists no differently than regular extended access lists. However, crypto access lists have a different purpose and meaning than regular extended access lists. The following list describes the unique characteristics of crypto access lists:

- Unlike regular access lists, crypto access lists do not specify the traffic to filter on an interface, but rather the outbound traffic that is to be protected with IPsec. In crypto access lists, the keyword **permit** means protect. For example, the rule **access-list 101 permit ip host 192.168.10.3 host 10.1.1.4** means "protect all IP traffic from 192.168.10.3 to 10.1.1.4" (when this access list is used as a crypto access list).

- IPsec processing is skipped when a packet is denied by a crypto access list. This means the router simply processes the packet normally, as if IPsec never existed. Recall from Chapter 6 that there is an invisible deny-any rule at the end of every access list. This includes crypto access lists.

- Each rule in a crypto access list defines the traffic to be protected by a single IPsec SA. This means a single SA will protect a large set of packets if the rule is broad (permit all traffic from Subnet X to Subnet Y, for example). On the other hand, an SA might protect a small set of packets if the rule is narrow (permit Telnet traffic from Host A to Host B).

- A crypto access list not only defines the outbound traffic that requires IPsec protection but also checks *inbound* traffic to enforce consistent policies. When a router sends a protected flow to a peer, it expects the flow in the return direction to also be protected. The router checks this by comparing inbound packets to its crypto access lists but with the logic reversed. The reversed logic means the source and destination criteria are swapped. Packets that arrive from a remote peer and match the reverse logic of a crypto access list will be dropped if they are *not* protected by IPsec. This is a safety measure and ensures that traffic the router expects to be protected is indeed protected.

NOTE   Because a router checks inbound traffic against its crypto access list, configuring peers with matching, mirror-image access lists is crucial. See the following section, "Crypto Access Lists: An Example."

Crypto Access Lists: An Example

Consider the scenario depicted in Figure 7-10 with two routers that must peer across an untrusted network and provide IPsec services on behalf of devices located in multiple subnets.

Figure 7-10 *Scenario for Configuring Crypto Access Lists*

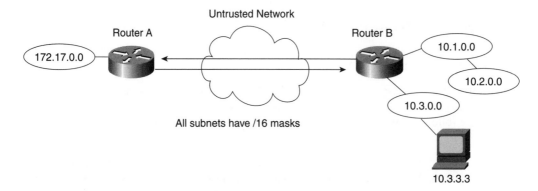

Suppose all subnets have a /16 mask and you are given the following requirements:

- Traffic between subnets 172.17.0.0 and 10.1.0.0 requires IPsec.
- Traffic between subnets 172.17.0.0 and 10.2.0.0 requires IPsec.
- Traffic between subnet 172.17.0.0 and host 10.3.3.3 requires IPsec.
- All other traffic between subnets 172.17.0.0 and 10.3.0.0 does not require IPsec.

To simplify the overall task at hand, you can draw a simple logical diagram like Figure 7-11. This figure depicts the protection required between the subnets.

Figure 7-11 *Protection Required Between the Subnets in Figure 7-10*

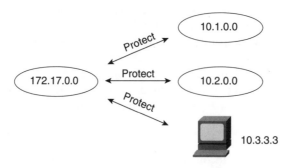

The following crypto access lists for Router A and Router B define the traffic that needs to be protected based on the stated requirements.

For Router A:

```
hostname RTA
<lines deleted for brevity>
!
access-list 101 permit ip 172.17.0.0 0.0.255.255 10.1.0.0 0.0.255.255
access-list 101 permit ip 172.17.0.0 0.0.255.255 10.2.0.0 0.0.255.255
access-list 101 permit ip 172.17.0.0 0.0.255.255 host 10.3.3.3
```

For Router B:

```
hostname RTB
<lines deleted for brevity>
!
access-list 102 permit ip 10.1.0.0 0.0.255.255 172.17.0.0 0.0.255.255
access-list 102 permit ip 10.2.0.0 0.0.255.255 172.17.0.0 0.0.255.255
access-list 102 permit ip host 10.3.3.3 172.17.0.0 0.0.255.255
```

First, notice that crypto access lists are nothing more than extended access lists—except their purpose is different and they are applied with crypto maps. As mentioned previously, the router applies IPsec services (encryption, integrity, and the like) to outbound traffic that is permitted by the crypto access list. *Permit* means *protect*.

You write crypto access lists from the perspective of traffic exiting the router and destined to the remote peer. Therefore, Router A matches all packets *from* subnet 172.17.0.0/16 *to* destination subnets 10.1.0.0/16 and 10.2.0.0/16, plus the destination host 10.3.3.3.

Router B matches the same traffic as Router A but has the reverse criteria. From Router B's perspective, the source traffic is subnets 10.1.0.0/16 and 10.2.0.0/16 plus host 10.3.3.3 and the destination subnet is 172.17.0.0/16.

Notice that every access list rule in Router B is a mirror-image of a corresponding rule in Router A. The two access lists 101 and 102 are called *mirror-image crypto access lists*. Mirror-image crypto access lists are crucial to the proper operation of IPsec. If Router B's crypto access list is not a mirror-image of Router A's list, communication problems might occur.

Without mirror-image crypto access lists, problems occur because the access lists do not agree and do not protect the same set of traffic. IPsec packets might flow in one direction but not the other. A modified (and incorrect) configuration for Router B follows and describes the problem (Router A's list is unchanged):

```
hostname RTB
<lines deleted for brevity>
!
access-list 102 permit ip 10.1.0.0 0.0.255.255 172.17.0.0 0.0.255.255
access-list 102 permit ip 10.2.0.0 0.0.255.255 172.17.0.0 0.0.255.255
access-list 102 permit ip 10.3.0.0 0.0.255.255 172.17.0.0 0.0.255.255
```

Notice that the last rule in access list 102 is not a mirror-image of the last rule in access list 101. The criteria **10.3.0.0 0.0.255.255** in list 102 matches all addresses in subnet 10.3.0.0/16, but the criteria **host 10.3.3.3** in list 101 matches just one address in the subnet. Access list 102 covers a wider range of addresses than list 101. This will cause problems when Router A sends packets destined for 10.3.0.0/16 other than 10.3.3.3.

To demonstrate the problem with Router B's modified and incorrect list, suppose a host in subnet 172.17.0.0/16 sends a packet to host 10.3.3.10 (not 10.3.3.3). The following sequence assumes that the crypto access lists have been added to active crypto maps.

NOTE   Like regular access lists, crypto access lists do not do anything until they are applied to interfaces. The section "Configuring and Applying Crypto Maps" later in this chapter covers how to add crypto access lists to crypto maps that then get applied to interfaces.

---

1 Router A receives the packet and determines that packets to 10.3.3.10 need to be forwarded to Router B.

2 Router A checks its crypto access list and finds that the packet does not match any of the permit statements. Router A's list matches packets from 172.17.0.0/16 to host 10.3.3.3, but not to host 10.3.3.10.

3 Because the packet does not match the crypto access list, the router transmits the packet normally without any IPsec services (no AH or ESP headers, no encryption).

4 The packet arrives at Router B.

5 Router B checks the inbound packet against every rule in its crypto access list while reversing the logic of each rule (recall that reversing the logic means the source and destination criteria are swapped). The packet does not match the first two rules of the list but *does* indeed match the third rule (source criteria is 172.17.0.0 0.0.255.255 and destination criteria is 10.3.0.0 0.0.255.255 by reverse logic).

6 Router B drops the packet, because it expects the packet to be protected with IPsec but it is not.

7 The unfortunate result: Hosts in 172.17.0.0/16 cannot contact hosts in 10.3.0.0/16 with or without IPsec. The exception is host 10.3.3.3, which is included in the lists of both Router A and Router B.

NOTE   The use of the keyword **any** in crypto access lists can cause problems and is strongly discouraged. The **any** criterion is broad and requires protection for all inbound packets. Thus, inbound packets that lack protection (such as routing protocol updates and other control packets) might be undesirably dropped. You should always explicitly define the traffic that needs IPsec protection.

Configuring IPsec Transform Sets

A transform set (also called a *transform proposal*) defines the security protocols and algorithms that protect traffic for a given IPsec SA. Before two devices can establish an IPsec SA, they must negotiate and agree on a common transform set.

To configure a transform set, use the **crypto ipsec transform-set** global configuration command:

```
RTA(config)#crypto ipsec transform-set TRANS-ESP esp-des esp-md5-hmac
RTA(cfg-crypto-trans)#mode tunnel
RTA(cfg-crypto-trans)#exit
```

The command **crypto ipsec transform-set TRANS-ESP esp-des esp-md5-hmac** creates a transform set called **TRANS-ESP**. This transform set includes two ESP transforms: 56-bit DES encryption (**esp-des**) and MD5 HMAC integrity/authentication (**esp-md5-hmac**).

The command **mode tunnel** dictates that all SAs created with this transform set will be tunnel mode SAs. The other choice is **mode transport**. See "Transport and Tunnel Modes," earlier in this chapter.

NOTE   The command **mode transport** is useful for secure router management—that is, for communicating with the router as an IPsec host. You can, for example, use a transport mode SA to Telnet to the router securely. Transport mode can also be used to secure SNMP traffic to and from the router.

NOTE   After creating the transform set, you must add it to a crypto map to put it to use. See "Configuring and Applying Crypto Maps," later in this chapter.

Here's another example. The following commands create a transform set that uses both the AH and ESP protocols:

```
RTA(config)#crypto ipsec transform-set TRANS-AH-ESP ah-sha-hmac esp-des
RTA(cfg-crypto-trans)#mode tunnel
RTA(cfg-crypto-trans)#exit
```

The command **crypto ipsec transform-set TRANS-AH-ESP ah-sha-hmac esp-des** creates a transform set called **TRANS-AH-ESP**. This transform set includes an AH transform and an ESP transform: AH with SHA-1 hashing for integrity and authentication and ESP with 56-bit DES for encryption.

NOTE   As mentioned earlier in "Authentication Header and Encapsulating Security Payload,"
        protecting bidirectional traffic with both AH and ESP requires two pairs of SAs: an SA pair
        for AH and another SA pair for ESP (a total of four unidirectional IPsec SAs).

Configuring and Applying Crypto Maps

After configuring crypto access lists and transform sets, you can add them to a crypto map.

Consider the network in Figure 7-12 with two routers that peer over an untrusted network.
Assume that IKE, crypto access lists, and transform sets are configured and a crypto map
is now needed.

Figure 7-12   *A Network with a Basic Crypto Map Configuration*

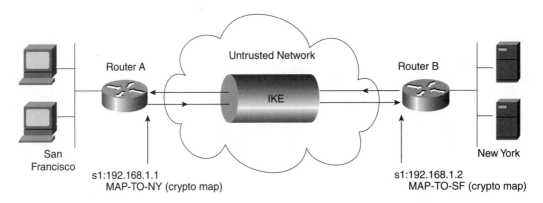

In the preceding diagram, Router A's serial interface to the untrusted network is
192.168.1.1.
A crypto map named MAP-TO-NY is applied to this interface (the configuration
commands follow). Likewise, Router B's serial interface is 192.168.1.2 and has a crypto
map called
MAP-TO-SF.

The following commands create a crypto map on Router A (for clarity, the context of the
IOS prompt is included):

```
RTA#conf t
Enter configuration commands, one per line. End with CNTL/Z.
RTA(config)#crypto map MAP-TO-NY 20 ipsec-isakmp
RTA(config-crypto-map)#match address 101
RTA(config-crypto-map)#set transform-set TRANS-ESP TRANS-AH-ESP
RTA(config-crypto-map)#set peer 192.168.1.2
RTA(config-crypto-map)#exit
RTA(config)#int s1
RTA(config-if)#crypto map MAP-TO-NY
```

The command **crypto map MAP-TO-NY 20 ipsec-isakmp** creates a crypto map entry with a sequence of 20 for a crypto map called **MAP-TO-NY** (the crypto map is created when its first entry is created). Although this example contains just one entry, crypto maps may contain multiple entries to designate multiple peers, transform sets, and access lists. The sequence number prioritizes the crypto map entries. As the router compares packets to the crypto map, it examines entries in the order of their sequence number (lower sequence numbers are examined first). For this example, a sequence of **20** was chosen so that future entries may be placed before or after this entry. The keyword **ipsec-isakmp** indicates that IKE is used to manage the SAs for this entry.

NOTE   In addition to IKE, which is specified by the **ipsec-isakmp** keyword, crypto maps support two other options: **ipsec-manual** (IPsec without IKE) and **cisco** (Cisco's pre-IPsec encryption feature called Cisco Encryption Technology, or CET). Consult the IOS documentation for configuring **ipsec-manual** or **cisco**.

The command **match address 101** assigns crypto access list 101 to this entry. Outbound packets that match this list are protected with IPsec. Inbound packets that match the reverse logic of the list are expected to be protected.

The command **set transform-set TRANS-ESP TRANS-AH-ESP** defines the transform sets that are acceptable for protecting the traffic covered by the crypto access list. When negotiating IPsec SAs with the remote peer (Router B), the router proposes transform sets in the order listed by this command (this router's first choice is the transform set TRANS-ESP). Router A and Router B must agree to use a common transform set (a common set of protocols and algorithms) before an SA can be established. **TRANS-ESP** and **TRANS-AH-ESP** are the names of transform sets previously created by the **crypto ipsec transform-set** command. The transform set *names* (TRANS-ESP, TRANS-AH-ESP) are locally significant and do not have to be the same on both routers.

The command **set peer 192.168.1.2** defines the remote peer, Router B, with which this router builds the IPsec SA and to which it subsequently sends the protected traffic. Multiple peers can be configured by repeating the **set peer** command. This provides a level of redundancy for when SAs are established: If the first peer is not reachable, the router attempts to establish the SA with the next peer in the entry.

The interface configuration command **crypto map MAP-TO-NY** applies the crypto map to the router's Serial1 interface (selected by the command **int s1**). Like access lists, crypto maps do not do anything until you apply them to an interface. The proper place to apply the crypto map is the interface where the protected traffic *exits* the router: the interface that points in the direction of the remote peer. In this example, Router A's Serial1 interface is the exit point (refer to Figure 7-12).

The following is the corresponding configuration on Router B (only the relevant crypto map lines are shown):

```
RTB#sh run
Current configuration:
hostname RTB
<lines deleted for brevity>
!
crypto map MAP-TO-SF 20 ipsec-isakmp
 match address 102
 set transform-set B-TRANS1 B-TRANS2
 set peer 192.168.1.1
!
interface Serial1
 ip address 192.168.1.2 255.255.255.0
 crypto map MAP-TO-SF
!
```

The crypto access list **102** must be a mirror image of list 101 on Router A, and at least one of the transform sets (**B-TRANS1** or **B-TRANS2**) must match one of Router A's transform sets (TRANS-ESP and TRANS-AH-ESP). A match means the transform sets share the same protocols (AH, ESP) and algorithms (DES or MD5, for example).

NOTE Crypto access lists are crypto map elements and interoperate with regular packet-filtering access lists that might exist on an interface. Packets blocked by regular access lists are not processed by IPsec.

When Are SAs Established?

The following list describes the logic of a router as it pertains to the setup of IPsec and IKE SAs:

- When a packet requiring IPsec needs to be transmitted, the router checks for an existing IPsec SA suitable for protecting the packet. An SA is suitable if its source and destination criteria (as defined by a crypto access list rule) match the packet. If a suitable IPsec SA exists, the packet is sent using the transform set and peer parameters associated with the SA.

- If a suitable IPsec SA does not exist for the packet, the router needs to set up a new SA. When IKE is configured, the router first checks for an existing IKE SA before creating the IPsec SA. If the router has an existing IKE SA with the destination peer, the IPsec SA is created, using the IKE SA as a secure channel.

- If the router does not have an existing IKE SA with the destination peer, the router needs to set it up. After the IKE SA is in place, the IPsec SA is created, using the IKE SA as a secure channel.

TIP   IKE uses UDP port number 500. Make sure you do not have any regular, packet filtering access lists that might be undesirably blocking UDP port 500.

Configuring IPsec SA Lifetimes

The following commands modify the lifetimes associated with IPsec SAs:

```
RTA(config)#crypto map MAP-TO-NY 20 ipsec-isakmp
RTA(config-crypto-map)#set security-association lifetime seconds 2700
RTA(config-crypto-map)#set security-association lifetime kilobytes 2000000
```

The command **set security-association lifetime seconds 2700** sets the lifetime of IPsec SAs created by this crypto map entry to 2700 seconds (45 minutes). The default is 3600 seconds (60 minutes).

The command **set security-association lifetime kilobytes 2000000** sets the *volume* lifetime of IPsec SAs created by this crypto map entry to 2,000,000 kilobytes (approximately 10 Mbps per second for one half hour). This means that after 2,000,000 kilobytes have been transmitted over an SA, the SA will expire. The default is 4,608,000 kilobytes (10 Mbps per second for one hour).

An IPsec SA expires when the first of the two lifetimes (seconds or kilobytes) is reached.

NOTE   Shorter lifetimes provide better security because the keys associated with the SAs change more frequently. However, rekeying more frequently results in an increased load on the router's CPU.

Shortly before an IPsec SA expires, the router builds a new SA (called a *rollover SA*) to ensure an SA is ready to use when the old one expires. This provides a smooth transition and minimal disruption to the users. Rollover SAs are created approximately 30 seconds before the **seconds** lifetime or approximately 256 kilobytes less than the **kilobytes** lifetime (whichever comes first).

NOTE   When two Cisco routers propose different lifetimes during IPsec SA negotiation, they will agree to use the shorter lifetime.

Configuring Perfect Forward Secrecy

The following commands configure a crypto map entry for PFS:

```
RTA(config)#crypto map MAP-TO-NY 20 ipsec-isakmp
RTA(config-crypto-map)#set pfs group1
```

The command **set pfs group1** tells the router to use PFS on all IPsec SAs created with this entry. By default, PFS is off. The keyword **group1** specifies Diffie-Hellman group 1 (768-bit numbers). The other option, **group2**, specifies Diffie-Hellman group 2 (1024-bit numbers). Group 2 provides greater security but requires more time to compute. See "Internet Key Exchange" earlier in this chapter for more on PFS.

NOTE   PFS provides better security than the alternative, which is the exchange of encrypted *nonces*. A nonce is a randomly generated number meant for one-time use. For instance, Alice and Bob can establish a new shared key by exchanging nonces that are encrypted with a shared key they already know. This is considered less secure than PFS because the new key is derived from the old key—discovering the old key helps an attacker find the new key too. With PFS, on the other hand, the new key is created on its own with the Diffie-Hellman algorithm. The downside of PFS is the computational overhead required to generate a new Diffie-Hellman key each time.

Configuring Dynamic Crypto Maps

When a router has numerous remote peers, configuring a crypto map entry for every peer can be laborious. This is especially true when remote access users dial into a central router: Manually configuring each user as a peer in the router's crypto map is impractical. Remote users typically have dynamically assigned IP addresses, so there's no way to predict a remote peer's address and program that into a crypto map.

Dynamic crypto maps simplify large peering configurations by providing templates of basic IPsec requirements. The dynamic crypto map mandates a set of basic requirements and leaves other parameters, such as the peers' IP addresses, undefined. If a peer can authenticate and establish an IKE SA, and if the peer meets the basic requirements defined by the dynamic crypto map, the peer is allowed an IPsec SA with the router.

NOTE   Dynamic crypto maps require IKE. IKE establishes dynamic IPsec SAs and authenticates the remote peer.

Dynamic crypto maps are nothing more than crypto maps that are missing some parameters. The missing parameters represent the information that the router does not know about the other peer and does not require from the peer to successfully establish an IPsec SA. Typically, the missing parameter is the peer's IP address (normally configured with the **set peer** command). This provides scalability when there are many peers because the router does not need to know and does not require the peers' IP addresses ahead of time.

The following is an example configuration of a dynamic crypto map:

```
crypto dynamic-map DYN-MAP-DIALIN 20
 match address 101
 set transform-set TRANS-ESP TRANS-AH-ESP
!
crypto map MYMAP 500 ipsec-isakmp dynamic DYN-MAP-DIALIN
!
interface Serial1
 ip address 192.168.1.1 255.255.255.0
 crypto map MYMAP
```

The command **crypto dynamic-map DYN-MAP-DIALIN 20** creates an entry with a sequence of **20** for a dynamic crypto map called **DYN-MAP-DIALIN**. As with regular crypto maps, the sequence number prioritizes the map's entries.

The command **match address 101** assigns crypto access list 101 to this entry. As with regular crypto maps, the list defines the traffic that requires IPsec protection and checks inbound packets to ensure consistent policy. Inbound packets that match the reverse logic of the list are expected to be protected—if they are not, the packets are dropped.

The command **set transform-set TRANS-ESP TRANS-AH-ESP** defines the transform sets accepted by this router. When a remote peer initiates an IPsec SA with this router, it must propose a matching transform set or the negotiation will fail.

Notice that the dynamic crypto map lacks the **set peer** command found in regular crypto maps. This means the map accepts any peer that passes IKE negotiation (the authentication step) and proposes a matching transform set. This eliminates the task of having to configure each peer manually (the main benefit of dynamic crypto maps).

NOTE   Recall that the choices for IKE authentication are pre-shared keys, RSA encryption, and RSA signatures with digital certificates.

The command **crypto map MYMAP 500 ipsec-isakmp dynamic DYN-MAP-DIALIN** binds the dynamic crypto map to an entry (sequence of 500) in a regular crypto map called MYMAP. This syntax allows you to configure multiple dynamic crypto maps in a single crypto map or to mix dynamic crypto maps with regular, static map entries.

NOTE	When mixing dynamic crypto map entries with regular entries in a crypto map, set the dynamic crypto map entries to be the highest sequence numbers (lowest priority). This is why the example uses a sequence of 500 for the dynamic crypto map entry.

The command **crypto map MYMAP** applies MYMAP, which includes the dynamic crypto map, to interface Serial1.

NOTE	By default, dynamic crypto maps can only answer *incoming* peer requests for IKE and IPsec SAs. They cannot initiate outbound SAs to remote peers. The exception to this is dynamic crypto maps with Cisco's *Tunnel Endpoint Discovery* service (covered in the following section).

Tunnel Endpoint Discovery

Tunnel Endpoint Discovery (TED) is a Cisco feature that improves the scalability and availability of IPsec VPNs by extending the capabilities of dynamic crypto maps. As mentioned in the preceding section, "Configuring Dynamic Crypto Maps," dynamic crypto maps greatly reduce your work by eliminating the configuration of specific IPsec peers. However, dynamic crypto maps (by default) are only *receivers* of IKE negotiation requests. That is, unlike regular crypto maps, they cannot initiate outbound SAs to remote peers—dynamic crypto maps rely on other peers to first contact them.

The listen-only behavior of dynamic crypto maps is acceptable in most *access* VPN environments where a central router accepts IKE requests from lots of dial-in users. However, in an *intranet* VPN environment, the listen-only approach isn't very useful because you want to give each peer the ability to initiate IKE with any other peer. This means you have to use regular, static crypto maps.

When you have a large intranet VPN—say over 20 or 30 routers—configuring static crypto maps to connect to all possible peers becomes laborious and difficult to manage. When it's time to add a new peer, you have to revisit all other peers and modify each configuration to accommodate the addition—that's a lot of work.

TED Improves IPsec Scalability

So here comes TED. With TED, a dynamic crypto map can probe for and discover remote peers dynamically. With TED, this means that a dynamic crypto map *can* be used to initiate SAs to multiple peers automatically, on demand, and with minimal configuration (the remote peers must also have TED enabled). Thus, many-to-many (mesh topology) peering is possible without a need to configure huge static crypto maps.

TED works by sending a probe packet and listening for a response to determine the other end of an IKE SA. When an outbound packet requires IPsec protection, TED dispatches a probe packet. The probe gets routed over the untrusted network toward the ultimate destination of the data until it reaches the remote, TED-enabled peer. When the remote peer responds to the originator of the probe, the remote peer is "discovered" and the two devices establish an IKE SA. The rest of the IPsec process then continues as usual.

TIP TED is handy when you're deploying backup peers for high-availability VPNs. If the remote peer goes down, TED will dynamically discover a new remote peer (assuming you deployed one as a backup). When you add a backup peer, you do not have to reconfigure the other routers in the network—the new backup is automatically discovered by TED.

Configuring TED

To enable TED, you simply configure dynamic crypto maps as described in the preceding section, "Configuring Dynamic Crypto Maps," and add the keyword **discover** to the **crypto map ipsec-isakmp dynamic** command. The following is an example:

```
crypto dynamic-map DYN-TED-MAP 20
 match address 101
 set transform-set TRANS-ESP TRANS-AH-ESP
!
crypto map MYMAP 500 ipsec-isakmp dynamic DYN-TED-MAP discover
!
interface Serial1
 ip address 192.168.1.1 255.255.255.0
 crypto map MYMAP
```

The preceding TED-enabled configuration is syntactically the same as the configuration for dynamic crypto maps except the keyword **discover** is appended to the crypto map entry.

NOTE IPsec in IOS releases before 12.0(5)T and 12.0(5)XE do not support TED.

Validating IPsec Configuration

The following enable mode commands are useful for validating the IPsec configuration:

- **show crypto isakmp policy** returns the router's active IKE transform sets (policies) in order of priority.

- **show crypto isakmp sa** displays the status of the router's IKE SAs. A state of **QM_IDLE** means the IKE SA is up and functioning properly. Recall that both IKE and IPsec SAs are built only when they are needed and are triggered by traffic that matches a crypto map.

- **show crypto map** displays the crypto maps configured in the router. Here you can find the details of a crypto map, including its elements (crypto access lists, transform sets, peers, PFS setting, and so on).

- **show crypto ipsec transform-set** displays the transform sets configured in the router.

- **show crypto ipsec sa** displays a detailed list of the router's active IPsec SAs. Here you can find information on each SA, including the lifetime remaining, transforms, mode (tunnel or transport), SPI, and packet counters. Clear the packet counters with **clear crypto sa counters**.

- **show crypto engine connections active** displays a list of active SAs with their associated interfaces, transforms, and counters.

- **show crypto dynamic-map** displays the dynamic crypto maps in the router.

Troubleshooting IPsec and IKE

To communicate successfully with IPsec, two devices must successfully negotiate many steps. The slightest misconfiguration of a protocol, key, lifetime, transform set, or other parameter will result in failed IKE or IPsec negotiations and SAs will not be established.

The next couple of sections offer some hints for isolating and troubleshooting IKE and IPsec.

Check Configurations and Show Commands

Examine the configuration of each peer (issue the **show running-config** command) and double-check the following:

- IKE SA transform sets (policies) agree on both peers including the lifetime parameter.

- IKE pre-shared keys, public keys, or certificates are correct.

- Crypto maps on both routers share a common IPsec transform set.

- Crypto access lists on both routers are mirror images of each other and are included in the crypto maps.

- Crypto maps are configured with the peer's correct and reachable IP address.

- Crypto maps are applied to the proper interfaces (the exiting interface that points to the remote peer).

Also, use the **show** commands from the section "Validating IPsec Configuration" earlier in this chapter and check if any IKE or IPsec SAs have been successfully established (**show crypto isakmp sa** and **show crypto ipsec sa**). If the routers are not establishing SAs when they should, investigate the situation in more detail with the debugging commands in the following section.

NOTE	Before you configure any IPsec, it's a good idea to verify you have normal IP connectivity between peers—a regular ping or Telnet from one peer to the other does the trick. After you know the IP layer works, you can configure IPsec.

Enable Debugging and Clearing Existing SAs

To get more detailed information and observe IKE and IPsec negotiations, enable debugging with these commands:

```
RTA#debug crypto isakmp
RTA#debug crypto ipsec
```

With debugging enabled, the router displays the status of IKE and IPsec events in detail. See the following section "Messages for IKE Negotiation and CA Servers."

To debug CA events, issue these additional commands:

```
RTA#debug crypto pki messages
RTA#debug crypto pki transactions
```

To observe IKE negotiation, you might want to clear any existing IKE SAs with the command **clear crypto isakmp**. This allows you to observe IKE negotiation on the router from the beginning.

To clear existing IPsec SAs, issue the command **clear crypto sa**. This clears all IPsec SAs on the router and might be undesirable if there are active SAs transporting live traffic. Alternatively, you can clear existing IPsec SAs by crypto map name, peer, or SPI (issue the command **clear crypto sa ?** for help).

Messages for IKE Negotiation and CA Servers

The following messages indicate that IKE negotiation failed and an IKE SA cannot be established. This is caused by one or more mismatching IKE parameters (lifetime, hashing algorithm, encryption algorithm, authentication method, or Diffie-Hellman group). *Main mode* is the negotiation step that establishes the IKE SA.

```
%CRYPTO-6-IKMP_MODE_FAILURE: Processing of Informational mode failed with peer at
    192.168.1.1
ISAKMP (215): no offers accepted!
ISAKMP (212): SA not acceptable!
%CRYPTO-6-IKMP_MODE_FAILURE: Processing of Main mode failed with peer at 192.168.1.1
```

The following messages appear when a peer is configured with the wrong pre-shared key (IKE authentication with pre-shared keys):

```
ISAKMP: reserved not zero on payload 5!
%CRYPTO-4-IKMP_BAD_MESSAGE: IKE message from 192.168.1.2 failed its sanity check or is
    malformed
```

Any one of the following messages appears when a peer is configured with the wrong public key of the remote peer (IKE with RSA encryption and manually configured public keys):

```
%CRYPTO-6-IKMP_CRYPT_FAILURE: IKE (connection id 127) unable to encrypt (w/peers RSA
    public key) packet
%CRYPTO-6-IKMP_MODE_FAILURE: Processing of Main mode failed with peer at 192.168.1.1
%CRYPTO-4-IKMP_BAD_MESSAGE: IKE message from 192.168.1.1 failed its sanity check or is
    malformed
```

The following messages indicate a communication problem between the router and the CA server:

```
CRYPTO_PKI: socket connect error.
CRYPTO_PKI: 0, failed to open http connection
CRYPTO_PKI: 65535, failed to send out the pki message
```

Ensure that nothing on the network is preventing the router from communicating with the CA server (perhaps an access list).

The following messages indicate that the router submitted a certificate request to the CA server and is waiting for the CA to grant the certificate:

```
CRYPTO_PKI: status = 102: certificate request pending
CRYPTO_PKI: resend GetCertInitial
```

The following messages indicate that the CA granted the certificate and the router received it:

```
CRYPTO_PKI: status = 100: certificate is granted
%CRYPTO-6-CERTRET: Certificate received from Certificate Authority
```

The following messages indicate that IKE negotiation was successful. *Quick mode* is the negotiation step that establishes IPsec SAs.

```
ISAKMP (96): SA has been authenticated with 192.168.1.1
ISAKMP (96): beginning Quick Mode exchange
```

After the IKE SA Is in Place: Messages for IPsec Negotiation

The following messages appear when the two peers cannot negotiate a common IPsec transform set:

```
IPSEC(key_engine): request timer fired: count = n,
ISAKMP (269): SA not acceptable!
%CRYPTO-6-IKMP_MODE_FAILURE: Processing of Quick mode failed with peer at 192.168.1.2
```

Check the transform sets in the crypto maps of both peers and ensure that they propose the same protocols and algorithms (**esp-des** with **esp-md5-hmac**, for example).

The following messages indicate that the peers have successfully negotiated an IPsec transform set:

```
ISAKMP (288): Checking IPSec proposal n
ISAKMP: transform 1, <name>
<lines deleted for brevity>
ISAKMP (288): atts are acceptable.
```

The following messages appear when IPsec SAs are starting up:

```
ISAKMP (264): Creating IPSec SAs
IPSEC(initialize_sas):
```

The following message indicates that an IPsec SA was successfully created:

```
IPSEC(create_sa): sa created
```

The following messages indicate that the router received an IPsec packet but is unable to decrypt it because it does not match a crypto access list:

```
%CRYPTO-4-RECVD_PKT_INV_IDENTITY_ACL: ipsec check access: identity not allowed by
    ACL
00:31:27: IPSEC(epa_des_crypt): decrypted packet failed SA identity check
00:31:41: IPSEC(epa_des_crypt): decrypted packet failed SA identity check
```

This usually happens when the router and its remote peer are not configured with mirror-image access lists. See "Crypto Access Lists: An Example" earlier in this chapter for more information on mirror-image access lists.

The following messages appear when a router receives a non-IPsec packet and expects the packet to be protected with IPsec:

```
%CRYPTO-4-RECVD_PKT_NOT_IPSEC: Rec'd packet not an IPSEC packet.
        (ip) dest_addr= 172.16.2.137, src_addr= 192.168.10.4, prot= 6
```

The packet matches a crypto access list in the crypto map but is not an IPsec packet. This usually happens when the router and its peer are not configured with mirror-image access lists (or when the router receives a non-IPsec packet for some other reason). See "Crypto Access Lists: An Example" earlier in this chapter for more information on mirror-image access lists.

Summary

This chapter covered the basic principles of security and cryptography necessary for understanding and implementing VPNs with IPsec. The IPsec standard embodies a broad range of security protocols, algorithms, and practices that work together to provide secure communication over an untrusted network.

The following are the key concepts of this chapter:

- IPsec is a security architecture that uses many technologies to secure IP traffic across an untrusted network.
- The most popular use of IPsec is for building VPNs.
- Confidentiality is achieved by encrypting plaintext with an algorithm to create ciphertext.

- Shared key encryption requires trusted parties to agree on a common, confidential key. Some common algorithms are DES, Triple-DES, IDEA, and Blowfish. The Diffie-Hellman key exchange algorithm provides a way of establishing a shared key by exchanging non-secret information.

- With public key encryption (or public key cryptography), each party generates and owns a pair of keys: a private key that is kept secret and a public key (non-secret information) that is given to anyone who wishes to send confidential data to the owner of the public key. RSA is a common algorithm.

- Integrity provides a guarantee that data has not been altered in transit. Hashing algorithms such as MD5 and SHA-1 provide the mechanics for delivering integrity.

- Origin authentication provides an assurance that the person (or device) you are communicating with is who he or she claims to be. Digital signatures guarantee authenticity of messages using public key cryptography. Digital certificates (issued by CAs) bind a public key to an identity, thereby establishing trust and nonrepudiation.

- Anti-replay provides the assurance that past transactions cannot be replayed by an attacker. IKE enables this service.

- The main elements of IPsec are peers, transform sets, security associations, modes (transport and tunnel), and protocols (AH and ESP).

- The IKE protocol works hand-in-hand with IPsec and performs many important functions. IKE dynamically establishes IPsec SAs as they are needed, supports the exchange of digital certificates, and enables dynamic rekeying, anti-replay, and perfect forward secrecy.

- In the Cisco implementation, IKE can authenticate peers by using pre-shared keys, RSA encryption, and RSA signatures with digital certificates.

- A router does not initiate an IKE SA until it is needed to establish the IPsec SAs that protect user traffic.

- A crypto map can contain multiple entries. Each entry contains a crypto access list, a list of acceptable transform sets, the address of the remote peer (or multiple addresses if redundancy is desired), and other information (lifetime and PFS).

- Crypto access lists do not specify the traffic to filter on an interface, but rather the outbound traffic that is to be protected with IPsec.

- Crypto access lists also check inbound traffic to enforce consistent security policies.

- Mirror-image crypto access lists are crucial to the proper operation of IPsec. Without them, problems occur because the peers' access lists do not agree and do not protect the same set of traffic.

- Dynamic crypto maps simplify large peering configurations by providing templates of basic IPsec requirements.

- TED allows a dynamic crypto map to probe for and discover remote peers. With TED, a dynamic crypto map can be used to initiate SAs to multiple peers automatically, on demand, and with minimal configuration. This increases IPsec scalability in large intranet and extranet VPNs.

- Many steps have to happen before two peers can successfully communicate with IPsec. Typically, you will need to enable IOS debugging to observe and validate IKE/IPsec negotiations.

CHAPTER 8

Advanced Security Services, Part II: IOS Firewall Feature Set

As mentioned in the introduction of Chapter 7, "Advanced Security Services, Part I: IPsec," the public Internet is a wonderful extension of the private network, providing global reach to numerous services and vast repositories of data. However, the openness and public nature of the Internet requires you to take precautions. That is, you must protect your private world of users and information from the external swarm of chaos and hackers.

This chapter presents some strategies for defending the perimeter of your private network with two key IOS services: the Firewall feature set and the Intrusion Detection System.

The main topics of this chapter are

- IOS Firewall Fundamentals
- Defending the Perimeter Against Attacks
- How Context-Based Access Control Works
- Configuring CBAC
- Adjusting CBAC Timers and Thresholds
- Enabling Auditing of Sessions
- CBAC with a Demilitarized Zone
- Notes on CBAC Performance
- Configuring Java Applet Blocking for Security
- The IOS Intrusion Detection System

IOS Firewall Fundamentals

The IOS Firewall feature set is an optional, add-on software license for Cisco routers that provides firewall functionality integrated in an IOS router. This is useful for enhancing security at the perimeters of a network—for example, connections to the Internet and links to business partners. Also, because the feature set is IOS-based, it might be a convenient add-on for locations with existing routers or for organizations that need the integration of routing and firewalling in a single platform.

The IOS Firewall feature set provides the following security services:

- **Stateful, application-level filtering**—Called context-based access control (CBAC), this service dynamically examines and maintains application-layer protocol information. IOS uses this information to intelligently filter traffic flowing through the firewall router (the router running CBAC).

- **Denial of service detection and prevention**—Denial of service attacks attempt to cripple or disable an IP host by abusing certain vulnerabilities in the host's TCP/IP implementation. CBAC defends against these attacks and reports denial of service activity.

- **Real-time alerts**—CBAC detects certain application attacks and notifies you when they occur. Using the router's syslog reporting service (or console), you can collect and monitor these attacks as part of your security strategy.

- **Auditing of sessions (optional)**—You can enable transactional logging of every session that occurs through the firewall. As sessions end, CBAC reports these statistics via syslog or the console.

- **Java applet blocking (optional)**—CBAC can block Java applets from entering your network, based on a user-defined access list of friendly and hostile external sites.

- **Active auditing of the network with the Intrusion Detection System**—An independent service that you can run with or without CBAC.

Defending the Perimeter Against Attacks

The point where your network connects to the Internet (or other untrusted network) marks the end of your internal network, or the network *perimeter*. The perimeter defines the boundary between the generally controlled, stable internal network and the generally uncontrollable, chaotic outside world. At the perimeter, you must prevent unauthorized access to the internal network from the outside while allowing your internal users access to services on the Internet. This is the fundamental defense provided by a firewall: It allows internal users access to external services on the Internet and, at the same time, prevents external users from accessing the internal network. This defense is provided by CBAC and is depicted in Figure 8-1.

External users might need to access some of your internal resources. Web servers, for example, provide the public with information published by your organization. Other servers, such as Domain Name System (DNS), Simple Mail Transfer Protocol (SMTP), and File Transfer Protocol (FTP), must also be accessible from the outside. For these servers, the firewall must allow just enough access for the services to work and must defend the servers against denial of service attacks.

Figure 8-1   *CBAC (IOS Firewall Feature Set) Allows Outbound Internet Sessions but Blocks Incoming Sessions*

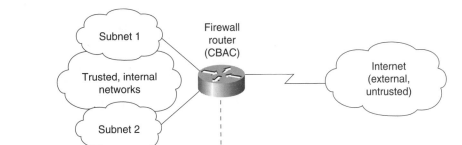

There are many kinds of denial of service attacks, and new attacks are invented on a regular basis. Typical denial of service attacks attempt to cripple or disable an IP host by flooding it with illegal or unusual traffic generated by a custom-made hacker program. That is, the attack *denies* others from using the services on the host for legitimate purposes. Some of the most common denial of service attacks are Teardrop, Land, SYN Flood, and FIN Flood. A firewall defends against these attacks by monitoring traffic to the servers, detecting certain characteristics of the attacks, and intercepting the attacks before they get a chance to overload the servers. Such a defense is provided by CBAC.

NOTE   The title *hacker* is traditionally given to a skillful software programmer—someone who masterfully hacks code. Over the years, however, it has become a derogatory name for troublemakers who break into computer systems and networks (and do other menacing activities).

How Context-Based Access Control Works

When an internal user initiates a session (for example, a Web page retrieval) to the Internet, CBAC allows return traffic for that session to pass through access lists that normally prevent external traffic from entering the internal network. CBAC allows the return traffic through to the internal network by dynamically adding temporary access list rules to existing access lists. These temporary CBAC rules are very specific and only permit traffic associated with the user's session—without the rules, the user's application session would fail because its return traffic would be blocked. You can think of the CBAC rules as "tiny holes" in an access list that normally blocks outside traffic. The concept is depicted in Figure 8-2.

Figure 8-2 *CBAC Creates Temporary Access List Rules*

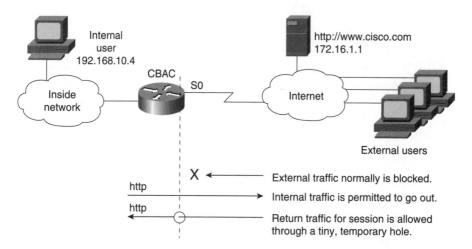

As shown in Figure 8-2, externally sourced packets not associated with the user's session (or other users' sessions also managed by CBAC) are blocked by the access list—this prevents anyone from initiating a session to the internal network from the outside.

As a security precaution, CBAC removes the temporary rules from access lists after the user's session ends, thereby sealing the tiny holes that were needed for the user's session.

Configuring CBAC

These are the basic steps for configuring CBAC:

1 Configure and apply extended access lists to block external traffic from entering the internal network.

2 Define a CBAC inspection rule that tells the router which applications require CBAC to function properly.

3 Apply the inspection rule to an interface.

The following sections cover these steps in more detail, starting with a simple two-port firewall example.

CBAC Example: A Basic Two-Port Firewall

Consider the scenario depicted in Figure 8-3 with a basic two-port firewall router.

Figure 8-3   *A Two-Port Firewall Example*

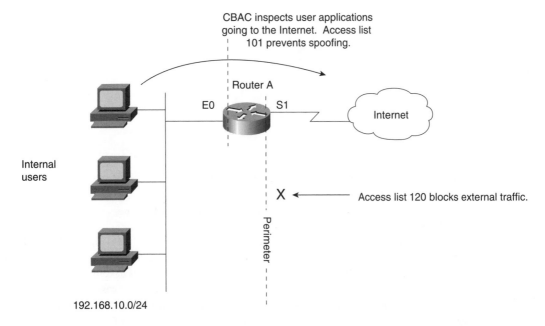

The network in Figure 8-3 is a straightforward application of CBAC. Router A is configured with CBAC and inspects application sessions that originate from the inside and are destined to the Internet. An inbound access list is applied to Router A's Serial1 interface that faces the public Internet; the access list guards against unauthorized entry from the Internet to the internal network. Finally, CBAC allows return traffic for internal user applications (Web, Telnet, FTP, and so on) through the access list—the return traffic must be permitted for the applications to function properly.

This two-port configuration is good for explaining basic CBAC configuration. This scenario might be appropriate for a home office or an organization that does not directly offer Web, FTP, DNS, or SMTP servers to the public. Such organizations might make their public servers available through an ISP that hosts the servers at an off-site location. See "CBAC with a Demilitarized Zone" later in this chapter for a CBAC example that makes servers available from the outside.

The following is the configuration for the firewall router, Router A (for brevity, only the lines relevant to security and CBAC are shown):

```
no service tcp-small-servers
no service udp-small-servers
service password-encryption
enable secret <my-password>
no ip source-route
no cdp run
!
```

continues

```
hostname RTA
!
ip inspect name INSPECT-RULE1 tcp
ip inspect name INSPECT-RULE1 udp
!
interface Ethernet0
 ip address 192.168.10.1 255.255.255.0
 ip access-group 101 in
 ip inspect INSPECT-RULE1 in
 no ip directed-broadcast
!
interface Serial1
 ip address 192.168.1.2 255.255.255.0
 ip access-group 120 in
 no ip directed-broadcast
!
logging 192.168.10.3
!
access-list 101 permit ip 192.168.10.0 0.0.0.255 any
access-list 101 deny   ip any any
access-list 120 permit icmp any 192.168.10.0 0.0.0.255 echo
access-list 120 permit icmp any 192.168.10.0 0.0.0.255 echo-reply
access-list 120 deny   ip any any
```

The first block of six lines consists of security measures covered in Chapter 6, "Deploying Basic Security Services." These commands increase security and are desirable because this router is directly connected to the Internet. More commands might be needed to reinforce the security of the router itself because this router is on the front line of attacks. Access lists, for example, might be required to prevent all possible external communication with the router itself. Passwords on the vty interfaces are highly recommended (see Chapter 6).

The command **ip inspect name INSPECT-RULE1 tcp** does two things:

- It creates a CBAC *inspection rule* called **INSPECT-RULE1**. An inspection rule defines the applications (HTTP, FTP, H.323, SQL*Net, and so on) that CBAC observes and manages. CBAC creates the temporary access list rules mentioned earlier for the applications listed in the inspection rule.

- It tells CBAC to inspect generic TCP applications as designated by the **tcp** keyword. Generic TCP applications include Web (http), Telnet, Usenet news (NNTP), Time (NTP), passive-mode FTP, and other applications that do not carry application-specific address or port information within the TCP packet. In other words, return packets for generic TCP applications have the same address and port number as the user-sourced packets that exited the network (with source and destination fields reversed). See "Configuring CBAC Inspection of Other Applications" later in this chapter for configuring applications that require application-layer CBAC inspection.

The command **ip inspect name INSPECT-RULE1 udp** adds to the rule **INSPECT-RULE1** and enables generic UDP application inspection. As with generic TCP inspection, UDP inspection supports applications that return packets over the same address and port numbers as exiting packets (with source and destination fields reversed). DNS is an example of a generic UDP application.

The next block of commands pertains to the router's Ethernet0 interface that connects to the internal LAN:

- The command **ip access-group 101 in** applies access list 101 to the interface and specifies the inbound direction. Access list 101 is an anti-spoofing access list that ensures all packets coming from the LAN (entering Ethernet0) have a valid source address from the 192.168.10.0/24 subnet. This is a good security policy: It prevents mischievous *internal* users (or attackers that have gained access to your network) from launching spoof attacks to the Internet and thereby causing potential legal problems for your organization. See Chapter 6 for more information on access lists and spoofing.

- The command **ip inspect INSPECT-RULE1 in** applies the previously configured inspection rule **INSPECT-RULE1** to the interface and specifies the inbound direction. The inspection rule does not do anything until you apply it to an interface with this command. The keyword **in** is very important and defines the *direction of inspection* for the applications defined in INSPECT-RULE1. It tells CBAC to inspect applications that are initiated from the internal LAN and *enter* Ethernet0. Alternatively, you could apply INSPECT-RULE1 to Serial1 in the *outbound* direction (keyword **out**) and accomplish the same thing because user-initiated packets flow out of Serial1. You can think of the direction of inspection as the direction of session initiation: Sessions originate at the internal users, enter Ethernet0, and exit out Serial1.

NOTE   For the technically inclined, direction of inspection is the path of the first TCP SYN packet (or the first UDP packet). From the router's point of view, it expects the first packet to arrive *inbound* on Ethernet0; thus, the keyword **in** is needed in this example.

- The command **no ip directed-broadcast** is a security measure and protects the internal LAN against attacks that generate floods with IP broadcasts. See Chapter 6 for more information.

The next block of commands pertains to the router's Serial1 interface that connects to the Internet:

- The command **ip access-group 120 in** applies access list 120 to the interface and specifies the inbound direction. Access list 120 is the heart of the protection provided by the firewall router. It blocks all traffic from the Internet except pings (ICMP echo) for troubleshooting purposes. CBAC dynamically adds temporary rules to this access list ("pokes holes" in the list) to permit return traffic of legitimate, internally initiated sessions.

NOTE   If ping flooding attacks are a concern, they can be denied—common ping attacks attempt to consume your bandwidth with floods of ping packets. Alternatively, if more types of packets need to be permitted, the access list can permit them. Other external packets you might consider permitting are ssh (secure shell, port 22) and the following ICMP messages: unreachable, traceroute, time exceeded, administratively prohibited, and packet-too-big (path MTU discovery).

- The command **no ip directed-broadcast** blocks outgoing IP broadcasts to the Internet. In the event an attacker gains access to your network and attempts to use it as a launch pad for attacking other networks, this command prevents the router from sending IP broadcasts to the Internet.

The command **logging 192.168.10.3** tells the router to send IOS system and error messages to a syslog server whose address is 192.168.10.3. This is useful for remotely monitoring CBAC alerts and all other router messages. See Appendix E, "A Crash Course in Cisco IOS," for more information on syslog.

The remaining commands configure access lists 101 and 120. Access list 101 is applied to Ethernet0 in the inbound direction:

- The rule **access-list 101 permit ip 192.168.10.0 0.0.0.255 any** permits source addresses from the internal subnet 192.168.10.0/24 only.

- The rule **access-list 101 deny ip any any** is not really necessary because it is the same as the invisible rule at the end of every IP access list (see Chapter 6). However, it is explicitly configured to make more visible and more obvious the denial of all packets not matching the preceding rule.

Access list 120 is applied to Serial1 in the inbound direction:

- The rules **access-list 120 permit icmp any 192.168.10.0 0.0.0.255 echo** and **access-list 120 permit icmp any 192.168.10.0 0.0.0.255 echo-reply** permit ping packets from the outside to the internal LAN. This is for troubleshooting purposes and might not be desirable if ping attacks are a concern.

- The rule **access-list 120 deny ip any any** makes obvious the denial of all other packets.

Validating CBAC Configuration

To validate that CBAC is working properly, issue the **show ip inspect all** enable mode command. The following is an output from the previous two-port firewall example:

```
RTA#sh ip ins all
Session audit trail is disabled
one-minute (sampling period) thresholds are [400:500] connections
max-incomplete sessions thresholds are [400:500]
max-incomplete tcp connections per host is 50. Block-time 0 minute.
```

```
tcp synwait-time is 30 sec -- tcp finwait-time is 5 sec
tcp idle-time is 3600 sec -- udp idle-time is 30 sec
dns-timeout is 5 sec
Inspection Rule Configuration
 Inspection name INSPECT-RULE1
    tcp timeout 3600
    udp timeout 30

Interface Configuration
 Interface Ethernet0
 Inbound inspection rule is INSPECT-RULE1
    tcp timeout 3600
    udp timeout 30
 Outgoing inspection rule is not set
 Inbound access list is 101
 Outgoing access list is not set

Established Sessions
 Session B0893C (192.168.10.4:1148)=>(172.16.224.209:23) tcp SIS_OPEN
 Session AF7C4C (192.168.10.4:1147)=>(172.16.10.72:53) udp SIS_OPEN
```

The preceding output of **show ip inspect all** displays

- The current CBAC settings, such as various timers and thresholds covered in "Adjusting CBAC Timers and Thresholds" later in this chapter.

- The names of inspection rules and the applications that are defined for each rule. In this example, the router has just one rule, called **INSPECT-RULE1**, and this rule is inspecting generic TCP and UDP applications only.

- The interfaces configured with CBAC, along with inspection rule names and access list numbers.

- The active sessions that CBAC is inspecting and managing. **Session B0893C** displays a unique number that the router uses to identify the session. **(192.168.10.4:1148)=>** is the internal address and port number that initiated the session. **(172.16.224.209:23)** is the external destination address and port number. **tcp** indicates this is a generic TCP application, and **SIS_OPEN** means the connection status is open and active. Other status messages you'll typically see are **SIS_OPENING** (connection half-open) and **SIS_CLOSING** (connection closing).

To verify that CBAC is indeed adding temporary rules to access lists that block external traffic, issue the **show access-lists** command. Recall that, in the previous two-port firewall example, access list 120 is filtering inbound on Serial1.

```
RTA#sh access-l
Extended IP access list 101
    permit ip 192.168.10.0 0.0.0.255 any (31970 matches)
    deny ip any any (4 matches)
Extended IP access list 120
    permit tcp host 172.16.224.209 eq telnet host 192.168.10.4 eq 1148 (19 matches)
```

continues

```
permit udp host 172.16.10.72 eq domain host 192.168.10.4 eq 1147 (1 match)
permit icmp any 192.168.10.0 0.0.0.255 echo
permit icmp any 192.168.10.0 0.0.0.255 echo-reply (4 matches)
deny ip any any (2497 matches)
```

The first two rules in access list 120 were dynamically created by CBAC to permit return traffic for two very specific internally initiated applications: a Telnet session and a DNS query (keyword **domain**). Notice that CBAC inspection pinpoints the specific port numbers for both the source and destination and allows only these packets to pass through the interface.

NOTE   When the router has multiple access lists that block return traffic, CBAC adds temporary rules to the lists that require them to make the application work successfully.

After the Telnet session terminates, CBAC promptly removes the temporary access list rules. This stateful operation is verified by issuing **show access-lists** again:

```
RTA#sh access-l
Extended IP access list 101
    permit ip 192.168.10.0 0.0.0.255 any (32043 matches)
    deny ip any any (4 matches)
Extended IP access list 120
    permit icmp any 192.168.10.0 0.0.0.255 echo
    permit icmp any 192.168.10.0 0.0.0.255 echo-reply (4 matches)
    deny ip any any (2497 matches)
```

The preceding output shows that the temporary rules no longer exist in access list 120 after the Telnet session has ended. List 120 is back to its original rule list.

NOTE   Because of the connectionless nature of UDP applications, CBAC has no definitive way of determining the end of a UDP session. Therefore, CBAC approximates the end of a UDP session by expiring a configurable period of inactivity before declaring the session over. See also "Adjusting CBAC Session Timers," later in this chapter.

Configuring CBAC Inspection of Other Applications

In addition to generic TCP and UDP applications, CBAC supports some popular applications that require inspection of application-layer protocols to function properly. To get a current list of supported application-layer protocols, check the Cisco documentation or boot up a recent release of IOS with CBAC and look at the context-sensitive help for the **ip inspect name** global config command:

```
RTA#conf t
Enter configuration commands, one per line. End with CNTL/Z.
RTA(config)#ip inspect name MY-RULE ?
  cuseeme      CUSeeMe Protocol
  fragment     IP fragment inspection
  ftp          File Transfer Protocol
  h323         H.323 Protocol (e.g, MS NetMeeting, Intel Video Phone)
  http         HTTP Protocol
  rcmd         R commands (r-exec, r-login, r-sh)
  realaudio    Real Audio Protocol
  rpc          Remote Procedure Call Protocol
  smtp         Simple Mail Transfer Protocol
  sqlnet       SQL Net Protocol
  streamworks  StreamWorks Protocol
  tcp          Transmission Control Protocol
  tftp         TFTP Protocol
  udp          User Datagram Protocol
  vdolive      VDOLive Protocol
  <cr>
```

To add support for H.323 and FTP applications in the previous two-port firewall example, add the necessary lines to the inspection rule **INSPECT-RULE1**:

```
hostname RTA
!
ip inspect name INSPECT-RULE1 tcp
ip inspect name INSPECT-RULE1 udp
ip inspect name INSPECT-RULE1 ftp
ip inspect name INSPECT-RULE1 h323
```

The commands **ip inspect name INSPECT-RULE1 ftp** and **ip inspect name INSPECT-RULE1 h323** enable CBAC support for FTP and H.323 applications, respectively. Internal users can now successfully communicate through the firewall to the Internet with these applications.

NOTE   The command **ip inspect name *<rule-name>* ftp** permits the use of regular FTP sessions, but most FTP clients and servers support an option called *passive mode* that works fine with CBAC's generic TCP inspection.

CBAC provides some additional security benefits for application-protocols such as SMTP by watching for suspicious application-layer commands. Also, Cisco routinely updates CBAC with new defenses; however, as mentioned in Chapters 6 and 7, there is no such thing as a hacker-proof network. A service such as CBAC can enhance security and defend against common attacks, but cannot defend against yet-to-be-invented attacks.

Keep Your Security Systems Current

It is highly recommended that you maintain a constant process of staying current with security advisories, implementation of defenses, and auditing of the effectiveness of your security systems. Here are some security resources that will get you started:

— **Cisco security advisories mailing list**—To subscribe to the advisories mailing list, send a message to majordomo@cisco.com. In the body of the message, include the single line "info cust-security-announce" (without the quotation marks).

— **Cisco security discussion mailing list**—To subscribe to the discussion mailing list, send a message to majordomo@cisco.com. In the body of the message, include the single line "info cust-security-discuss" (without the quotation marks).

— **CERT**®—http://www.cert.org

— **CIAC (Computer Incident Advisory Capability)**—http://ciac.llnl.gov

— **Bugtraq**—This e-mail discussion list reports security holes in operating systems and applications. To subscribe, send a message to listserv@securityfocus.com. In the body of the message include the single line "subscribe bugtraq" (without the quotation marks). Go to http://www.securityfocus.com for archives of the list and other security information.

— **FIRST (Forum of Incident Response and Security Teams) mailing list**—Another good security mailing list. To subscribe, send a message to first-majordomo@first.org. In the body of the message, include the single line "subscribe first-info" (without the quotation marks).

— **RFC 2196, "Site Security Handbook"**

Adjusting CBAC Timers and Thresholds

CBAC maintains several timers and thresholds that define how long the temporary access list rules are active and how aggressively CBAC combats denial of service attacks. The following sections cover CBAC's adjustable parameters in detail.

Adjusting CBAC Session Timers

To change the default timers associated with CBAC, issue one or more of the following global config commands (you need to issue these commands only if you want to change the built-in CBAC defaults):

- **ip inspect tcp synwait-time** *<seconds>* configures the number of seconds CBAC waits for a half-open TCP session to be established before dropping it. The default is 30 seconds. In most cases, you will not have to modify this value.

NOTE	A half-open session is a session that has not yet completed TCP's *three-way handshake* process. A complete handshake between two hosts consists of a SYN (synchronization) packet from the initiator, followed by a SYN+ACK (SYN plus acknowledgement) packet from the destination, and then a final ACK packet from the initiator.

- **ip inspect tcp finwait-time** *<seconds>* configures the number of seconds CBAC continues to manage a TCP session after observing a TCP FIN-exchange (a FIN-exchange between two hosts terminates the TCP session). The default is 5 seconds. In most cases, you will not have to modify this value.

- **ip inspect tcp idle-time** *<seconds>* configures the number of seconds a TCP session may remain idle before CBAC terminates the session and removes it from its state table. The default is 3,600 seconds (1 hour). It might be desirable to lower this value and close CBAC's temporary holes for inactive sessions sooner (to increase security and reduce the number of stale CBAC rules in an access list). As a possible downside of lowering this timer, your users might complain that their sessions get disconnected after they leave their computers for a while. This idle timer can be overridden on a per-application basis by defining timeout values in an inspection rule (see the following section, "Overriding Global Timers with Inspection Rules").

- **ip inspect udp idle-time** *<seconds>* configures the number of seconds a UDP session may remain idle before CBAC declares the session over. Because of the connectionless nature of UDP, CBAC approximates the end of a UDP session by expiring this period of inactivity. The default is 30 seconds. You might have to increase this value slightly if CBAC is undesirably closing UDP applications too aggressively. This idle timer can be overridden on a per-application basis by defining timeout values in an inspection rule (see the following section, "Overriding Global Timers with Inspection Rules").

- **ip inspect dns-timeout** *<seconds>* configures the number of seconds a DNS session may remain idle before CBAC declares the session over and removes the temporary access list rule. Because DNS queries are quick and short-lived, CBAC maintains a short idle timer just to guard against attacks on DNS servers. The default is 5 seconds. You should not have to modify this value.

Overriding Global Timers with Inspection Rules

You can override the global TCP and UDP idle timers for certain applications by defining timeout values as you configure inspection rules with the **ip inspect name** command.

The following example configures inspection rule **INSPECT-RULE1** with SQL*Net support and defines a specific idle timeout for SQL*Net sessions only:

```
RTA(config)#ip inspect name INSPECT-RULE1 sqlnet timeout 900
```

This command tells CBAC to close SQL*Net sessions after 900 seconds of inactivity. Other applications may have different timeouts or may inherit the global values set by **ip inspect tcp idle-time** and **ip inspect udp idle-time** (see the preceding section, "Adjusting CBAC Session Timers").

Adjusting CBAC Denial of Service Thresholds

CBAC detects and prevents common denial of service attacks as part of its inspection process. As mentioned earlier, denial of service attacks attempt to cripple or disable a server by flooding it with illegal or unusual traffic.

You can tune the default thresholds that govern how aggressively CBAC combats these attacks with the following global config commands (you need to issue these commands only if you want to change the built-in CBAC defaults):

- **ip inspect max-incomplete high** *<number>* configures the number of half-open sessions that will trigger CBAC to start deleting half-open sessions. If you do not issue this command, the default number is 500. A high number of half-open sessions is suspicious and might mean a denial of service attack is happening (see "Adjusting CBAC Session Timers," earlier in this chapter). When the number of half-open sessions reaches the threshold defined by this command, CBAC deletes half-open sessions until the number of half-open sessions falls below the threshold defined by the following command, **ip inspect max-incomplete low**. CBAC does this so that the number of half-open sessions is limited and manageable and so that existing half-open sessions are deleted to accommodate new, and possibly legitimate, session requests.

NOTE   For TCP applications, half-open means the session has not yet completed the TCP three-way handshake (see "Adjusting CBAC Session Timers," earlier in this chapter). For UDP applications, half-open means the session was initiated but hasn't experienced any return traffic.

- **ip inspect max-incomplete low** *<number>* configures the number of half-open sessions that causes CBAC to stop deleting half-open sessions. This command works in conjunction with the preceding command, **ip inspect max-incomplete high**. After CBAC begins deleting half-open sessions as a result of reaching the upper threshold defined by

ip inspect max-incomplete high, it stops deleting when the number of half-open sessions reaches the number defined by **ip inspect max-incomplete low**. The default for this lower threshold is 400 half-open sessions.

- **ip inspect one-minute high** *<number>* configures the upper threshold for the number of new half-open sessions per minute. This measures the *rate* of new half-open sessions per minute instead of the absolute number of half-open sessions that exist in the router. It's the same idea as **ip inspect max-incomplete high** but takes into account the added dimension of time. By default the number is 500, which means CBAC will start deleting half-open sessions when the rate of new half-open sessions reaches 500 per minute.

- **ip inspect one-minute low** *<number>* configures the lower threshold for the number of new half-open sessions per minute. This threshold, like the **ip inspect max-incomplete low** command, tells CBAC when to stop deleting half-open sessions—except this command takes into account the rate of new half-open sessions per minute. After CBAC begins deleting half-open sessions as a result of reaching the upper threshold defined by **ip inspect one-minute high**, it stops deleting when the rate of half-open sessions reaches the number defined by **ip inspect one-minute low**. The default for this lower threshold is 400 half-open sessions per minute.

- **ip inspect tcp max-incomplete host** *<number>* configures the number of half-open TCP sessions that will trigger CBAC to start deleting half-open sessions *per destination host*. This protects hosts by limiting the number of half-open TCP sessions any one host can have (of course, CBAC must be inspecting the sessions to the host). The default limit is 50 half-open TCP sessions. When this limit is reached, CBAC deletes an old half-open session for every new session that is passed to the host. Optionally, you can specify a *block time* that temporarily shields hosts from new session requests after the limit is reached. For example, the command **ip inspect tcp max-incomplete host 50 block-time 2** tells CBAC to drop all new session requests to a host for 2 minutes after the host has 50 half-open sessions. The block time protects hosts from denial of service storms and is recommended when you need to protect against high-rate, high-bandwidth denial of service attacks.

- **ip inspect name** *<rule-name>* **fragment** adds a feature to your inspection rule that protects against IP fragmentation attacks. These attacks attempt to consume and freeze server resources by sending packets that are illegally fragmented or intentionally incomplete. With this command, CBAC detects and prevents certain fragmentation attacks within the traffic it inspects. Consult the IOS command reference for specifics and tunable parameters.

NOTE   Just about every workstation, server, and operating system vendor has issued software updates to defend against common denial of service attacks. It is highly recommended that you check with the manufacturers of your host systems and implement these updates. The security Web sites and mailing lists mentioned in "Keep Your Security Systems Current" also have information on software updates.

Enabling Auditing of Sessions

An option is available in CBAC that enables you to audit the sessions inspected by CBAC. Issue the **ip inspect audit-trail** global config command to do this:

```
RTA(config)#ip inspect audit-trail
```

Now, when a session ends you will receive a system message like this:

```
%FW-6-SESS_AUDIT_TRAIL: tcp session initiator (192.168.10.4:1246) sent 109 bytes -
- responder (172.17.24.20:23) sent 22806 bytes
```

If you want more granular control of audit trail messages, use the keyword **audit-trail** when you define the applications in your inspection rule:

```
RTA(config)#no ip inspect audit-trail
RTA(config)#ip inspect name INSPECT-RULE1 tcp
RTA(config)#ip inspect name INSPECT-RULE1 udp
RTA(config)#ip inspect name INSPECT-RULE1 ftp
RTA(config)#ip inspect name INSPECT-RULE1 h323 audit-trail on
```

where **no ip inspect audit-trail** turns off auditing by default and **ip inspect name INSPECT-RULE1 h323 audit-trail on** enables auditing for H.323 applications only. No audit messages will be displayed for the other applications: generic TCP, generic UDP, and FTP.

NOTE   Auditing on a per-application basis with **ip inspect name audit-trail on** is not available in some older releases of the IOS Firewall feature set.

CBAC with a Demilitarized Zone

A simple two-port firewall was presented earlier in this chapter to explain the basics of CBAC configuration (see "CBAC Example: A Basic Two-Port Firewall"). Now consider a more complex CBAC configuration that includes a third network port to connect a *demilitarized zone (DMZ)*—a publicly accessible network that provides public Web, SMTP (e-mail), DNS, and other servers. Suppose a company, Widget, Inc., has the firewall and DMZ topology depicted in Figure 8-4.

Figure 8-4 *A More Complex CBAC Example: Firewall and DMZ*

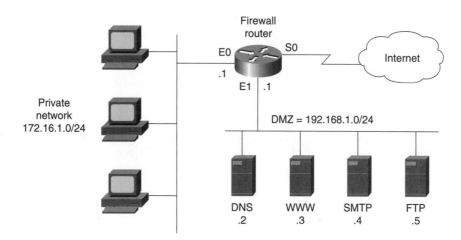

Widget, Inc., has the following security requirements:

- No traffic is permitted from the Internet to the private network except return traffic for sessions initiated by the internal users.

- Traffic is permitted from the Internet to the DMZ for accessing public DNS, Web, e-mail, and FTP servers. This traffic is inspected for denial of service attacks.

- Traffic is permitted from the private network to the Internet and to the DMZ.

- ICMP echo (ping) traffic is permitted to the private network and DMZ for troubleshooting network reachability.

- No traffic is permitted from the DMZ to the Internet except return traffic for sessions initiated by users on the Internet.

The following sections walk through the IOS configuration of the firewall router and demonstrate how CBAC is used to meet the security objective.

Basic Security Commands for the Firewall Router

The following portion of the firewall router's configuration implements basic IOS security principles (these are covered in Chapter 6):

```
no service tcp-small-servers
no service udp-small-servers
service password-encryption
enable secret <my-password>
no ip source-route
no cdp run
!
```

continues

```
interface Ethernet0
 no ip directed-broadcast
!
interface Ethernet1
 no ip directed-broadcast
!
line 0 6
 login
 password <my-password>
```

Configuring the Inspection Rule

Widget, Inc., next configures its inspection rule to support generic TCP, generic UDP, FTP, H.323, RealAudio, SMTP (e-mail), StreamWorks, and VDOLive applications:

```
ip inspect name FW-RULE tcp
ip inspect name FW-RULE udp
ip inspect name FW-RULE ftp
ip inspect name FW-RULE h323
ip inspect name FW-RULE realaudio
ip inspect name FW-RULE smtp
ip inspect name FW-RULE streamworks
ip inspect name FW-RULE vdolive
ip inspect name FW-RULE fragment
```

The last line in the preceding list, **ip inspect name FW-RULE fragment**, enables protection against fragmentation-based denial of service attacks. See "Adjusting CBAC Denial of Service Thresholds," earlier in this chapter.

Configuring the Private Network Interface

The following portion of the Widget, Inc., configuration implements access control and CBAC inspection for the private network interface Ethernet0:

```
interface Ethernet0
 description Interface to the Private Network
 ip address 172.16.1.1 255.255.255.0
 ip access-group 101 in
 ip access-group 121 out
 ip inspect FW-RULE in
!
access-list 101 permit ip 172.16.1.0 0.0.0.255 any
access-list 101 deny ip any any
access-list 121 permit icmp any any echo
access-list 121 permit icmp any any echo-reply
access-list 121 deny ip any any
```

The command **ip access-group 101 in** applies an inbound anti-spoofing access list to Ethernet0, thus ensuring that packets entering the router from the private network have legitimate source addresses (addresses from subnet 172.16.1.0/24). See Chapter 6 for more information on anti-spoofing access lists.

The command **ip access-group 121 out** applies an outbound access list that blocks all traffic to the private network except ICMP echo (ping) packets. CBAC will add temporary access list rules to this access list to permit return traffic for sessions that are initiated by the internal clients.

The command **ip inspect FW-RULE in** applies the inspection rule **FW-RULE** and specifies the inbound direction. All application sessions entering the router through this interface will be inspected by CBAC. Then, CBAC will create the necessary access list rules to permit return traffic for those sessions.

The remaining lines are the global config commands that define the anti-spoofing access list 101 and the firewall access list 121. As mentioned earlier, the command **access-list <#> deny ip any any** is not necessary but makes the meaning of the access list more obvious.

Configuring the DMZ Network Interface

The next portion of the Widget, Inc., configuration implements access control on the DMZ network interface Ethernet1:

```
interface Ethernet1
  description Interface to the DMZ
  ip address 192.168.1.1 255.255.255.0
  ip access-group 102 in
  ip access-group 122 out
```

Access list 102 is an anti-spoofing access list that ensures all packets entering the router from the DMZ network have legitimate source addresses (addresses from subnet 192.168.1.0/24). Here are the lines that define access list 102:

```
access-list 102 permit ip 192.168.1.0 0.0.0.255 any
access-list 102 deny ip any any
```

Access list 122 controls the traffic that can enter the DMZ (exit Ethernet1). First, the list must allow Internet users access to the DNS, Web, SMTP, and FTP servers on the DMZ. This is defined by the following access list rules:

```
access-list 122 permit udp any host 192.168.1.2 eq domain
access-list 122 permit tcp any host 192.168.1.3 eq www
access-list 122 permit tcp any host 192.168.1.4 eq smtp
access-list 122 permit tcp any host 192.168.1.5 eq ftp
```

TIP   To allow DNS zone transfers, add a rule to permit DNS over TCP. Opening DNS servers to zone transfers is sometimes considered a security risk: The information stored in your DNS server could be useful to an attacker.

Next, list 122 must permit traffic from the private network to the DMZ. This was one of the requirements of Widget, Inc., and allows the internal users to use the public services on the DMZ. The following rule accomplishes this:

```
access-list 122 permit ip 172.16.1.0 0.0.0.255 192.168.1.0 0.0.0.255
```

The list then permits ICMP echo traffic to the DMZ:

```
access-list 122 permit icmp any any echo
access-list 122 permit icmp any any echo-reply
```

Finally, the list denies all other traffic:

```
access-list 122 deny ip any any
```

Configuring the Internet Interface

The final portion of the Widget, Inc., configuration implements access control and CBAC inspection on the Internet interface Serial0:

```
interface Serial0
 description Interface to the ISP
 ip unnumbered ethernet 1
 ip access-group 103 in
 ip access-group 123 out
 ip inspect FW-RULE in
!
access-list 103 deny ip 172.16.0.0 0.0.255.255 any
access-list 103 deny ip 192.168.1.0 0.0.0.255 any
access-list 103 deny ip 127.0.0.0 0.255.255.255 any
access-list 103 permit ip any any
access-list 123 deny ip 192.168.1.0 0.0.0.255 any
access-list 123 permit ip any any
```

The command **ip unnumbered ethernet 1** is covered in Chapter 1, "Managing Your IP Address Space." It configures the interface without a subnet assignment.

The command **ip access-group 103 in** applies an inbound anti-spoofing access list to Serial0 to ensure that packets entering the router from the Internet *do not* have a source address from the Widget, Inc., address space. This protects against spoofing attacks originating from the Internet. See Chapter 6 for more information about spoofing attacks.

The command **ip access-group 123 out** applies an outbound access list that permits all traffic to the Internet except packets from the DMZ. In the event an attacker gains access to the DMZ, this access list prevents the attacker from using the DMZ as a launch pad for attacks to other parts of the Internet.

The command **ip inspect FW-RULE in** applies the inspection rule **FW-RULE** and specifies the inbound direction. The command tells the router to inspect all sessions entering the router from the Internet. With this command, CBAC detects and prevents denial of service attacks coming from the Internet and destined to the servers on the DMZ. Widget, Inc., can optionally tune CBAC's denial of service parameters to suit its taste (see "Adjusting CBAC Denial of Service Thresholds," earlier in this chapter). CBAC also adds temporary access list rules to outbound access list 123 so traffic from the DMZ is permitted to the Internet if it belongs to an inspected session. This is a reverse logic of the inspection occurring on the private interface Ethernet0. On this interface (Serial0), the sessions are initiated from *external* users on the Internet and the "return traffic" is traffic from the DMZ to the Internet.

Notes on CBAC Performance

Sizing CBAC performance and selecting the router for your network perimeter depends on many factors: for example, the bandwidth of the WAN link you need to support, the average packet size of your traffic, and the IOS services you need to run on the router. Although there are no hard and fast rules, Table 8-1 offers some general guidelines—you might find that your particular environment is more or less forgiving. These guidelines assume the firewall router is dedicated to CBAC processing.

Table 8-1 *General Guidelines for CBAC Routers*

Router Platform	Typical CBAC Capability
Low-end (Cisco 1600, 2500)	Up to T1 (1.544 Mbps)
Mid-range (Cisco 2600, 3600)	Up to 5 Mbps
High-end (Cisco 7200)	Up to T3 (45 Mbps)

NOTE Cisco also manufactures a dedicated firewall appliance called the PIX Firewall, suited for securing networks at higher bandwidth rates. The PIX also supports some unique features not found in the IOS Firewall. Check with Cisco for the most recent performance enhancements and features.

Configuring Java Applet Blocking for Security

You can configure CBAC to inspect Web (HTTP) traffic for Java applets and prevent some or all applets from entering your private network. Blocking of the applets is based on a user-defined list of Web sites—that is, you can define a Web site as hostile and block all applets from that site. This might be useful for protecting internal users from sites known to have malicious Java applets.

The following example configuration blocks Java applets coming from two sites, 172.16.206.33 and 192.168.171.65 (only the lines relevant to configuring the inspection rule are shown):

```
ip inspect name FW-RULE tcp
ip inspect name FW-RULE udp
ip inspect name FW-RULE ftp
ip inspect name FW-RULE h323
ip inspect name FW-RULE realaudio
ip inspect name FW-RULE smtp
ip inspect name FW-RULE streamworks
ip inspect name FW-RULE vdolive
ip inspect name FW-RULE fragment
ip inspect name FW-RULE http java-list 10
!
access-list 10 deny host 172.16.206.33
access-list 10 deny host 192.168.171.65
access-list 10 permit any
```

The command **ip inspect name FW-RULE http java-list 10** adds another line to the inspection rule **FW-RULE** and tells CBAC to block Java applets based on user-defined access list **10**. This access list defines the sites that are deemed to house hostile applets.

The last three lines configure access list 10, which defines (with the **deny** keyword) the addresses known to have hostile applets. This must be a standard, not extended, access list. The last line of access list 10, **access-list 10 permit any**, allows applets from all other sites to pass through the firewall router. Alternatively, you could reverse the logic of the access list and permit applets from approved sites only and deny applets from all other sites.

NOTE   CBAC cannot block Java applets that are packaged or "wrapped" in files, such as ZIP and JAR archives. Also, CBAC looks for applets in HTTP port 80 traffic streams and therefore cannot filter applets transferred via other means, such as FTP or HTTP over a nonstandard port.

The IOS Intrusion Detection System

An important part of any good security policy is active auditing of applications on the network and timely detection of hacker activity. It is simply not enough to implement a few perimeter defenses and consider it a job well done. Nor is it wise to sit back and wait for an attacker to foil your defenses and then do something blatant enough to be noticed—many attackers are quiet and hope to roam your network undetected.

Active auditing or *intrusion detection* is a security service offered with the IOS Firewall feature set and acts as a watchdog for your believed-to-be-secure network. This security service provides constant surveillance, detection, termination, and alerting of suspicious network activity.

The IOS Intrusion Detection System (IDS) contains a database of hacking patterns called *signatures*. Each signature describes the characteristics of a particular hacker attack. For example, hackers who gain access to UNIX hosts often try to download the */etc/passwd* file (a system file that, in some versions of UNIX, contains user login and password information). The IDS signature for this attack could be written in human terms as follows:

Issuing the string *passwd* during an FTP session is an attack.

The preceding is an attack signature because under normal circumstances, no legitimate user would issue an FTP command containing the word *passwd*. IDS examines the application sessions flowing through the router and looks for matches to this and other signatures. If a hacker types the FTP command **GET /etc/passwd** (or *any* command containing the word **passwd**), IDS immediately detects this, closes the suspicious session, and sends you an alert. You can then review the incident, correct any alterations, and implement appropriate countermeasures.

NOTE   The database of signatures is administered by a team of security experts at Cisco. This team follows developments in the hacker community and creates new signatures as they are needed.

The IOS version of IDS is a subset of the technology found in Cisco's standalone intrusion detection product, NetRanger™. NetRanger is a dedicated active audit appliance that provides a full suite of signatures, high performance, and central management. NetRanger also supports a feature called *shunning*: the application of dynamic access lists when an attack is detected to block further hacking. Consult Cisco for more information on NetRanger.

You can deploy the IOS version of IDS standalone or in conjunction with a comprehensive NetRanger system. The following sections describe how to configure IDS on IOS router platforms.

Configuring IDS

Typically, you use IDS to examine traffic at the perimeter of your network and on DMZs. However, nothing prevents you from applying IDS anywhere you need to audit suspicious network activity.

The following is a basic IDS configuration and audits traffic coming from the Internet (interface Serial0):

```
ip audit notify log
ip audit smtp spam 30
ip audit name MY-AUDIT info action alarm
ip audit name MY-AUDIT attack action alarm drop reset
!
interface Serial0
 description Interface to the Internet
 ip audit MY-AUDIT in
```

The command **ip audit notify log** tells the router to send IDS messages in syslog format. Optionally, you can send messages to a NetRanger Director central monitoring station (this is the management server for standalone NetRanger devices). Consult the IOS documentation for NetRanger Director configuration.

The command **ip audit smtp spam 30** configures a parameter for the SMTP (e-mail) anti-spam signature. IDS monitors SMTP traffic and suspects a spam attack (junk e-mail sent to many people) if the number of recipients in a mail message exceeds this threshold (in this case, 30 recipients).

The command **ip audit name MY-AUDIT info action alarm** creates an audit rule called **MY-AUDIT** and configures IDS to send alarm messages in response to traffic matching informational signatures. Informational signatures identify suspicious, but not necessarily hostile activity.

The command **ip audit name MY-AUDIT attack action alarm drop reset** configures the action to be taken by **MY-AUDIT** when traffic matches an attack signature. The keywords **alarm drop reset** define a three-step action: Send an alarm, drop the packet, and reset the connection. Reset applies to TCP connections—IDS will send TCP packets with the reset (RST) flag set to both members of the session. Attack signatures identify suspicious and potentially hostile activity.

NOTE   The IOS documentation section for IDS includes a complete list of the informational and attack signatures with descriptions.

Finally, the command **ip audit MY-AUDIT in** applies the audit rule **MY-AUDIT** to the Internet interface and specifies the inbound direction. Traffic entering Serial0 from the Internet is examined by IDS and scrutinized for suspicious activity.

TIP   You can run IDS alone, CBAC alone, or IDS and CBAC together. Because IDS is an additional router task, you should evaluate your router's performance with and without it and consult Cisco for implementation assistance.

Additional Commands for IDS

Here are some additional commands for IDS configuration:

- **ip audit signature** *<sig#>* **disable** enables you to exclude a particular signature from the auditing process. This command disables detection of the signature identified by the signature number you specify. Cisco assigns a 4- or 5-digit number to every signature in the signature database (consult the IOS documentation section on IDS for a list of signatures). You use this command if a particular signature alarms repeatedly (becomes an annoyance) and is not a security concern in your environment. This is called a *benign trigger.*

- **ip audit signature 1234 list 11** allows IDS to compare traffic permitted by access list **11** to signature number **1234**. Traffic denied by the access list is not compared to this signature. Use this to reduce false alarms and benign triggers. The default is to compare all traffic to each signature (unless the signature was disabled by **ip audit signature** *<sig#>* **disable**).

- **ip audit name MY-AUDIT info list 12** configures IDS to compare traffic permitted by access list **12** to the audit rule **MY-AUDIT**. Traffic denied by the access list is not subject to this audit rule (bypasses IDS). This keyword **list** is an optional add-on to the **ip audit name** command covered earlier. The default is to compare all traffic to the audit rule.

- Useful **show** commands: **show ip audit statistics**, **show ip audit configuration**, and **show ip audit interface**.

- Debugging commands: **debug ip audit ?** shows you a list of IDS debugging commands.

Summary

This chapter has extended the discussion on Cisco's advanced security services to the IOS Firewall feature set and Intrusion Detection System. Both of these services are generally deployed at the network perimeter, although nothing prevents you from using them in other parts of the network to bolster security.

The following are the key concepts of this chapter:

- The IOS Firewall feature set provides stateful application-level filtering, denial of service detection and prevention, real-time alerts, auditing of sessions, and Java applet blocking.

- The firewall service (CBAC) prevents unauthorized access to the internal network from the outside and still allows your internal users access to services on the Internet.

- CBAC allows return traffic of legitimate sessions to pass through access lists that normally prevent external traffic from entering the internal network.

- CBAC allows legitimate return traffic through to the internal network by dynamically adding temporary access list rules to existing access lists.

- The basic CBAC configuration steps: Configure and apply extended access lists to protect the internal network, define a CBAC inspection rule, apply the inspection rule to an interface.

- Security is a constant process of staying current with security advisories, implementing defenses, and auditing the effectiveness of your security systems.

- Intrusion detection provides constant surveillance, detection, termination, and alerting of suspicious network activity.

Appendixes

Obtaining IETF RFCs

The Internet Engineering Task Force (IETF) is a large organization of network designers, operators, vendors, and researchers. It is an open, self-organized community that makes recommendations and develops standards for the operation and evolution of the Internet.

Requests for Comments (RFCs) started in 1969 as notes between network architects about experiments on the early Internet (called the Advanced Research Projects Agency Network or ARPANET). Along with the evolution of the Internet, RFCs have become more formal and more influential over the years. Now, they are an ever-growing collection of IETF standards, procedures, and recommendations for the Internet community.

If you want to gain a better understanding of a particular protocol or application, the RFC is a good place to start.

For detailed information about the IETF and RFCs, go to the IETF's Web site at http://www.ietf.org.

Via the World Wide Web

A good starting point for browsing and retrieving RFCs is the Web site of the *RFC Editor*, where you can find overviews, search engines, directories, and other sources of RFC information. To get there, point your Web browser to http://www.rfc-editor.org.

To get a complete directory of all RFCs, point your Web browser to ftp://ftp.isi.edu/in-notes. This provides a list of every RFC by number and is useful when you know the number of the RFC you want to retrieve. However, when you are looking for RFCs on a particular subject, try one of the RFC search engines listed on the Web site of the *RFC Editor*, http://www.rfc-editor.org.

You can also browse any of the indexes available on the *RFC Editor's* Web site or retrieve the RFC index located at ftp://ftp.isi.edu/in-notes/rfc-index.txt.

Other RFC repositories around the world can be found at the Web site of the *RFC Editor* or at http://www.isi.edu/in-notes/rfc-retrieval.txt.

Via FTP

When using an FTP client, connect to ftp.isi.edu and log in with *anonymous* as your username and your e-mail address as the password. Change to the *in-notes* directory and use the FTP **get** command to retrieve the RFC with a filename syntax of RFC*nnnn*.txt (where *nnnn* refers to the number of the RFC). The following output is from an FTP session on a UNIX host:

```
myserver% ftp ftp.isi.edu
Connected to venera.ISI.EDU.
220 venera.isi.edu FTP server (Version s/key wu-2.4(6) Mon Feb 26 09:43:41 PST 1
    996) ready.
Name (ftp.isi.edu:donnlee): anonymous
331 Guest login ok, send your complete e-mail address as password.
Password:
230-
230 Guest login ok, access restrictions apply.
Remote system type is UNIX.
Using binary mode to transfer files.
ftp> cd in-notes
250 CWD command successful.
ftp> get rfc0822.txt
```

Via E-Mail

You can also obtain RFCs via e-mail. Address a message to rfc-info@isi.edu with any text as the subject and a message body of

```
retrieve: rfc
doc-id: rfcnnnn
```

where *nnnn* is the four-digit number of the RFC. For example, the doc-id of RFC 822 is rfc0822.

To get a listing of all RFCs (this is a long list), formulate an e-mail message with a message body of

```
HELP: rfc_index
```

Finally, for other ways to retrieve RFCs via e-mail, using keywords, words of titles, and such, formulate an e-mail message with a message body of

```
HELP: help
```

Finding Current RFCs

When reading or citing an RFC, always check that a newer one does not make it obsolete. You can do this by viewing the index of RFCs and checking for the words "Obsoleted by RFC *nnnn*" (where *nnnn* refers to the number of the RFC). Also, look for any updates to the RFC, indicated by the words "Updated by RFC *nnnn*." The RFC index is located at ftp:// ftp.isi.edu/in-notes/rfc-index.txt.

Authoring RFCs

RFC 2223 (ftp://ftp.isi.edu/in-notes/rfc2223.txt) provides instructions for authors and describes the RFC process in detail.

Retrieving Internet Drafts

Internet Drafts are the working documents of the Internet Engineering Task Force (IETF). They document work-in-progress, projects, and proposals of current interest to the Internet community. Usually, Internet Drafts originate from IETF working groups and serve as rough drafts for candidate Requests for Comments (RFCs).

An Internet Draft is not a standard and should not be cited as one. In fact, few drafts become RFCs, and they can be updated, replaced, or made obsolete at any time. Still, these drafts are useful for learning the current activities and emerging technologies in the IETF.

Also, Internet Drafts are not archived. They expire after six months and must be formally submitted, reviewed, and approved to become formal RFCs.

Via the World Wide Web

Internet Drafts can be retrieved in several ways. The easiest is to point your Web browser to http://www.ietf.org/ID.html. This is a user-friendly Web site with a search engine and a hierarchical listing of drafts by subject matter (IETF working group).

Alternatively, you can jump to a complete directory of drafts at ftp://ftp.ietf.org/internet-drafts. This will give you the listing for the entire Internet Drafts directory. The file *1id-abstracts.txt* in this directory is an organized list with a short summary of every draft. Another file, *1id-index.txt*, is an abbreviated list without the summaries.

Via FTP

When using an FTP client, connect to ftp.ietf.org and log in with *anonymous* as your username and your email address as the password. Change to the *internet-drafts* directory and retrieve the draft of your choice by using its filename and the FTP **get** command. The following output is from an FTP session on a UNIX host:

```
myserver% ftp ftp.ietf.org
Connected to optimus.ietf.org.
220 optimus FTP server (Welcome to the IETF FTP server.) ready.
Name (ftp.ietf.org:donnlee): anonymous
331 Guest login ok, send ident as password.
Password:
```

continues

```
230 Guest login ok, access restrictions apply.
Remote system type is UNIX.
Using binary mode to transfer files.
ftp> cd internet-drafts
250 CWD command successful.
ftp> get 1id-index.txt
```

Internet Drafts are mirrored to FTP sites around the world. To find the site nearest you, refer to Table B-1.

Table B-1 *Mirrors for Internet Drafts*

Region	FTP Address
Africa	ftp.is.co.za
Northern Europe	ftp.nordu.net
Southern Europe	ftp.nis.garr.it
Pacific Rim	munnari.oz.au
U.S. East Coast	ftp.ietf.org
U.S. West Coast	ftp.isi.edu

Via E-Mail

You can also obtain Internet Drafts via e-mail by addressing a message to mailserv@ietf.org with any text as the subject. In the body of the message, type one or more of the following commands:

```
FILE /internet-drafts/file.txt
```

where **file.txt** is the complete name of the file you want to retrieve. For example, to retrieve the index file *1id-index.txt*, put the following command in the body of the e-mail message:

```
FILE /internet-drafts/1id-index.txt
```

If you have a MIME-compliant mail reader, you can insert the command **ENCODING mime** before the **FILE** command when formulating the message body:

```
ENCODING mime
FILE /internet-drafts/1id-index.txt
```

Authoring Internet Drafts

Prospective authors can get information on how to write Internet Drafts at ftp://ftp.ietf.org/ietf/1id-guidelines.txt.

RFC 2223 (ftp://ftp.isi.edu/in-notes/rfc2223.txt) provides instructions for authors and describes the Internet Draft and RFC process in detail.

APPENDIX **C**

Common TCP and UDP Ports

Common TCP Port Numbers

TCP Port	Service
7	Echo
9	Discard
11	Systat
13	Daytime
17	qotd, Quote of the Day
19	Chargen, Character Generator
20	FTP Data
21	FTP, File Transfer Protocol
22	ssh, Secure Shell
23	Telnet
25	SMTP, Simple Mail Transfer Protocol
37	Time
43	NICName/WhoIs
49	TACACS, Terminal Access Controller Access Control System
53	DNS, Domain Name System
70	Gopher
79	Finger
80	HTTP/WWW, Hypertext Transfer Protocol/ World Wide Web
101	Hostname (old)
109	POP v2, Post Office Protocol version 2
110	POP v3, Post Office Protocol version 3
111	Sunrpc, Sun Remote Procedure Call

continues

Common TCP Port Numbers (Continued)

TCP Port	Service
113	Indent, Identification Protocol
117	UUCP Path, UNIX to UNIX Copy Path Service
118	Sqlserv, SQL Services
119	NNTP, Network News Transfer Protocol
143	IMAP, Internet Message Access Protocol
179	BGP, Border Gateway Protocol
194	IRC, Internet Relay Chat Protocol (standard). See also 6667.
389	LDAP, Lightweight Directory Access Protocol
443	https, HTTP (Hypertext Transfer Protocol) over SSL (Secure Sockets Layer)
512	rexec, Remote Process Execution
513	rlogin, Remote Login
514	rsh, Remote Shell
515	LPR, Line Printer Daemon Protocol
540	UUCP, UNIX to UNIX Copy
563	nntps, NNTP (Network News Transfer Protocol) over SSL (Secure Sockets Layer)
636	ldaps, LDAP over SSL
989	ftps-data, FTP Data over SSL
990	ftps, FTP over SSL
992	telnets, Telnet over SSL
993	imaps, IMAP over SSL
994	ircs, IRC over SSL
995	pop3s, POP over SSL
829	PKIX, Public Key Infrastructure (X.509), Certification Authority/Registration Agent
1433	Microsoft SQL Server
2049	Sun NFS, Network File System
6667	IRC, Internet Relay Chat Protocol (default). See also 194.

Common UDP Port Numbers

UDP Port	Service
7	Echo
9	Discard
37	Time
42	IEN116 Name Service (old)
49	TACACS, Terminal Access Controller Access Control System
53	DNS, Domain Name System
67	BOOTP, Bootstrap Protocol Server; DHCP, Dynamic Host Configuration Protocol
68	BOOTP, Bootstrap Protocol Client; DHCP, Dynamic Host Configuration Protocol
69	TFTP, Trivial File Transfer Protocol
111	Sunrpc, Sun Remote Procedure Call
123	NTP, Network Time Protocol
137	NETBIOS Name Service
138	NETBIOS Datagram Service
161	SNMP, Simple Network Management Protocol
162	SNMP Traps
177	XDMCP, X Display Manager Control Protocol, X Window System
195	DNSIX Security Protocol Auditing
387	AURP, AppleTalk Update-Based Routing Protocol
434	Mobile IP Registration
500	IKE, Internet Key Exchange; ISAKMP, Internet Security Association Key Management Protocol
512	Biff, Mail system notification
513	who/rwho service, users, load, uptime
514	Syslog, System Logger
517	UNIX talk service
518	UNIX ntalk service
520	RIP, Routing Information Protocol
525	Time server
2049	Sun NFS, Network File System

Password Recovery

This appendix provides instructions for gaining access to a router's enable mode without the enable password. This is a necessary procedure when you inherit a router and do not know the enable or EXEC mode passwords or when you simply can't remember the passwords.

You must have *physical* access to the router to do this procedure. To prevent unauthorized users from using password recovery to break into a router, you must secure physical access to the router—keep it in a locked room or closet, for example. A malicious person with physical access to your router can do more harm than simply changing a password.

NOTE The password recovery procedure does not help you learn the enable password. (It is infeasible to learn the enable password if it is protected with the **enable secret** command, which uses a one-way cryptographic hash algorithm). Rather, the password recovery procedure gets you into enable mode without the password so you can *override* the old password with a new one.

You can use either of two methods to recover a password on a Cisco router. Most router models follow the steps outlined in "Recovering a Lost Password on Most Router Models" in this appendix. Some older, legacy models follow the steps outlined in "Recovering a Lost Password on Other Router Models." To determine the method you need to use, do the following on your router:

1 Connect to the router's console port via a direct serial connection. Use 9600 baud, 8 data bits, no parity, and 2 stop bits. See Appendix E for more information.

2 Attempt a login to user EXEC mode. If you succeed, issue the **show version** command and record the setting of the so-called configuration register (config register for short). The config register setting is listed last and highlighted in boldface in the following sample output (if you cannot get to user EXEC mode, go on to the next step):

```
3640-1#sh ver
Cisco Internetwork Operating System Software
IOS (tm) 3600 Software (C3640-IS-M), Version 12.0(3)T,  RELEASE SOFTWARE
    (fc1)
Copyright (c) 1986-1999 by cisco Systems, Inc.
Compiled Tue 23-Feb-99 18:58 by ccai
Image text-base: 0x600088F0, data-base: 0x60AD6000


ROM: System Bootstrap, Version 11.1(19)AA, EARLY DEPLOYMENT RELEASE SOFTWARE
    (f)


3640-1 uptime is 4 hours, 14 minutes
System restarted by reload
System image file is "flash:c3640-is-mz_120-3.T.bin"


cisco 3640 (R4700) processor (revision 0x00) with 28672K/4096K bytes of
    memory.
Processor board ID 10382988
R4700 CPU at 100Mhz, Implementation 33, Rev 1.0
Bridging software.
X.25 software, Version 3.0.0.
1 Ethernet/IEEE 802.3 interface(s)
5 Serial network interface(s)
2 Voice FXO interface(s)
2 Voice FXS interface(s)
2 Voice E & M interface(s)
DRAM configuration is 64 bits wide with parity disabled.
125K bytes of non-volatile configuration memory.
16384K bytes of processor board System flash (Read/Write)
```

Configuration register is 0x2102

— Consult your router's documentation or search the Cisco Web site with
keywords *configuration register* for detailed information on the config register.

3 Power off the router and then power it back on. If your terminal is properly connected, you
should see a startup banner similar to the following (the numerical data in the banner
varies from router to router):

```
System Bootstrap, Version 11.1(19)AA, EARLY DEPLOYMENT RELEASE SOFTWARE (fc1)
Copyright (c) 1998 by cisco Systems, Inc.
C3600 processor with 65536 Kbytes of main memory
```

4 Approximately 10 to 60 seconds after power-on, press the break key (typically Ctrl+Break) on your terminal. This interrupts the boot process and puts you into the *ROM Monitor* (ROMMON for short).

— The break keystroke is the Telnet or terminal break of your terminal emulation software (consult your software's documentation). For a list of common break key combinations, see http://www.cisco.com/warp/public/701/61.html on Cisco's Web site.

5 You should see the ROMMON prompt: > or rommon1>.

6 Type **?** at the prompt to view the ROMMON menu.

7 If the menu looks like the following output, continue with the steps in the section on "Recovering a Lost Password on Most Router Models."

```
rommon 1 > ?
alias              set and display aliases command
boot               boot up an external process
break              set/show/clear the breakpoint
confreg            configuration register utility
cont               continue executing a downloaded image
context            display the context of a loaded image
<lines deleted for brevity>
```

8 If the menu does not resemble the output in Step 7, continue with the steps in "Recovering a Lost Password on Other Router Models."

Recovering a Lost Password on Most Router Models

After following Steps 1 through 8, continue the password recovery procedure with the following steps:

9 At the ROMMON prompt, issue the command **confreg 0x2142** followed by the command **reset**. The **confreg** command sets the config register to a hex value (don't forget the hex identifier 0x that's part of 0x2142). Changing the register from 0x2102 to 0x2142 forces the router to ignore the startup config, which contains the enable password, during boot-up. The **reset** command reboots the router. The following is an example:

```
rommon 3 > confreg 0x2142
rommon 4 > reset
```

10 After the router reboots, answer **no** when the router asks to enter the initial configuration dialog:

```
        --- System Configuration Dialog ---

Would you like to enter the initial configuration dialog? [yes/no]: no

Press RETURN to get started!
```

11 Use the **enable** command to change from user EXEC mode to enable mode:

```
Router>ena
Router#
```

12 Now you are in enable mode with a mostly empty default configuration. Issue **show running-config** to view the current configuration (notice that the interfaces are in shutdown mode). Issue **show startup-config** to view the original configuration stored in NVRAM.

13 If you want to restore the original configuration in NVRAM, issue the **configure memory** command. This copies the commands in NVRAM to the current configuration (if you want to discard the original configuration, skip this command and go on to the next step):

```
Router#config mem

myrouter#
00:13:06: %SYS-5-CONFIG_I: Configured from memory by console
```

14 Configure the new enable password. Change **mypassword** in the following example to the password of your choice:

```
myrouter#conf t
Enter configuration commands, one per line.  End with CNTL/Z.
myrouter(config)#enable secret mypassword
```

15 Configure a new password for console logins, if necessary:

```
myrouter(config)#line con 0
myrouter(config-line)#password mypassword
```

16 Bring up the interfaces that should be online:

```
myrouter(config)#int e0
myrouter(config-if)#no shut
myrouter(config-if)#int s0
myrouter(config-if)#no shut
```

17 Exit interface configuration mode and change the config register to the value discovered in Step 2 or to the factory default of 0x2102:

```
myrouter(config-if)#exit
myrouter(config)#config-register 0x2102
```

18 Exit configuration mode and save the configuration to NVRAM with the **copy running-config startup-config** command:

```
myrouter(config)#end
myrouter#
00:29:00: %SYS-5-CONFIG_I: Configured from console by consolecopy
myrouter#copy runn star
```

19 Reload the router:

```
myrouter#reload
```

20 Log in to the router, using the new passwords.

Recovering a Lost Password on Other Router Models

After following Steps 1 through 8, continue the password recovery procedure with the following steps:

9 At the ROMMON prompt, issue the command **o/r 0x2142** followed by the command **i**. The command **o/r** sets the config register to a hex value. The command **i** reboots or initializes the router. The following is an example:

```
>o/r 0x2142
>i
```

10 Continue the procedure beginning with Step 10 in the previous section, "Recovering a Lost Password on Most Router Models."

A Crash Course in Cisco IOS

This appendix is a quick reference guide for the most common IOS commands and configuration tasks. If you are new to IOS, this appendix can also serve as a shotgun tutorial on the basics. For details on these and other commands, consult the IOS documentation.

NOTE   The massive IOS documentation library is freely available at http://www.cisco.com/univercd/home/home.htm on the Cisco Web site.

Connecting to the Router

Connecting to the router can be done through a direct serial cable to the console port, with a Telnet over the IP network, or through the AUX port. This section describes these connections in more detail.

Connect via Direct Serial Cable to the Console Port

The simplest way to start using IOS is to connect to the router's console port with an EIA/TIA-232 (RS-232) serial cable and a terminal (an ASCII terminal or terminal emulation software on a workstation). The console port is handy when you have physical access to the router and when you are configuring a brand-new router (or one that had its configuration erased).

Cisco usually ships a serial console cable kit with each router. Generally, this one console cable (and its detachable connectors) will allow you to connect to the console port of any Cisco router and other Cisco hardware such as switches and internet appliances. If you don't have a console cable, you can order one from Cisco or find a rollover serial cable with the right serial connectors to fit the console port. Connectors do vary across Cisco's products, so consult the particular router's installation manual for details.

Connect via Telnet over the IP Network

If your router is on the network and in operation, simply Telnet to the router (using an IP address or hostname). Depending on how the router is configured (see Chapter 6, "Deploying Basic Security Services"), the router asks you for a login/password before proceeding to IOS or immediately drops you at the IOS prompt (called *user EXEC mode*).

NOTE By default, IOS rejects Telnet attempts to the router. This is a security precaution. To permit incoming Telnet sessions, connect to the console port and configure a login password on the router's VTY interfaces. See "Securing Telnet Access" in Chapter 6 for details.

Connect via the AUX Port or Other Asynchronous Serial Port

Most Cisco routers have an auxiliary serial port called the AUX port. You can cable a regular modem to this port, dial up the router over a telephone line, and access user EXEC mode remotely.

Some routers, such as access servers, have multiple asynchronous serial ports in addition to the AUX port. You can also connect a modem to one of these ports.

As of this writing, you can find detailed information at http://www.cisco.com/warp/public/701/6.html or you can search "modem, aux port" on Cisco's Web site (http://www.cisco.com). Your router's installation guide should also have instructions on how to connect a modem to the AUX and other serial ports.

NOTE The console port is a serial DCE (data circuit-terminating equipment) port and the AUX port is a serial DTE (data terminal equipment) port.

Modes

IOS has several different command modes. For each administrator task that needs to be done, there is an appropriate command mode. Each mode has a unique command prompt that enables you to quickly identify the active mode while you navigate the IOS environment. This section describes each mode in more detail.

User EXEC Mode

By default, **user EXEC mode** is the first IOS prompt you see after connecting to the router and passing the login:

```
%telnet 192.168.1.2
Trying 192.168.1.2 ... Open

User Access Verification

Password: <type the vty login password here>
Router>
```

Notice that the command prompt **Router>** contains the router's name (in this case, simply **Router**) and the **>** character at the end. The **>** character indicates that you are in user EXEC mode. User EXEC mode has a limited set of fairly harmless IOS commands such as **ping** and **show version**. See "Common IOS Commands" later in this appendix for some common user EXEC mode commands.

NOTE   If the router is brand new or had its configuration erased, you will usually see the Setup utility prompt instead of the user EXEC prompt. See "The Setup Utility" later in this appendix for more on Setup.

Privileged EXEC Mode (Enable Mode)

Privileged EXEC mode, more commonly known as *enable mode*, is where the main configuration, control, and observation of the router take place. This is similar to the concept of a superuser on other operating systems.

Enter enable mode from user EXEC mode by issuing the **enable** command along with the correct password (if an enable password is set):

```
Router>enable
Password: <type the enable password here>
Router#
```

The **#** character at the end of the prompt indicates enable mode is active.

NOTE   To enter enable mode during a Telnet session, there must be an enable password configured on the router. The router will terminate the Telnet session if there is no enable password configured and the **enable** command is issued. This is a security precaution.

To set the enable password, see "Common Configuration Tasks" later in this appendix.

Global Configuration Mode

Global configuration mode (or global config mode, for short) is where you begin configuring the router. In this mode, you program IOS commands into the router's active configuration. The active configuration or (preferably) *running configuration* is a list of IOS commands that tells the router all the details of how it is programmed and how it behaves. In the configuration are the instructions on how the router manages itself and the traffic. Needless to say, the configuration is crucial to the behavior of your router and your network.

To enter global config mode, issue the **configure terminal** command from the enable mode prompt:

```
Router#configure terminal
Enter configuration commands, one per line.  End with CNTL/Z.
Router(config)#
```

The text **(config)#** at the end of the prompt designates global config mode.

To exit global config mode and return to enable mode, issue the **exit** command or type `Ctrl-Z`:

```
Router(config)#exit
Router#
```

Interface Configuration Mode

Interface configuration mode (or interface config mode, for short) is one of several modes within global config mode. You enter interface config mode from global config mode to program IOS commands that are specific to a router's interface (an ethernet, serial, or other interface).

To enter interface config mode, issue the **interface** command from global config mode and specify the interface on the router you wish to configure. The following example activates interface config mode for interface Ethernet0:

```
Router(config)#interface ethernet 0
Router(config-if)#
```

TIP   Shorthand notations for interfaces work too. For example, **interface e0** and **int e0** are equivalent to **interface ethernet 0**.

Issue the **exit** command to exit interface configuration mode and return to global configuration mode:

```
Router(config-if)#exit
Router(config)#
```

TIP   Ctrl-Z or **end** will exit completely out of any configuration mode and jump straight to
enable mode.

Subinterface Configuration Mode

Subinterfaces are logical interfaces within a physical interface and are commonly deployed
with such services as frame relay, ATM, X.25, and SMDS. You can think of subinterfaces
as multiple virtual interfaces nested inside a physical interface.

To enter subinterface config mode, issue the **interface** command from global config mode
and specify a subinterface on the router you wish to create and subsequently configure. The
following example creates subinterface 0.1 on serial interface 0 and drops the user into
subinterface config mode:

```
Router(config)#interface s0.1
Router(config-subif)#
```

MajorInterface.Subinterface is the naming convention for subinterfaces.

Line Configuration Mode

Line config mode is where you configure terminal lines (TTYs), virtual terminal lines
(VTYs, Telnet sessions), the AUX port, and the console port. Some examples follow.

To configure terminal lines 1 through 8 (all 8 lines at the same time):

```
2509(config)#line 1 8
2509(config-line)#
```

To configure VTYs 0 through 4:

```
2509(config)#line vty 0 4
2509(config-line)#
```

To configure the AUX port:

```
2509(config)#line aux 0
2509(config-line)#
```

To configure the Console port:

```
2509(config)#line console 0
2509(config-line)#
```

Other Configuration Modes

Router config mode is where you enter specific commands for routing processes such as RIP, EIGRP, OSPF, and so on. The following command begins router config mode for OSPF process number 100:

```
Router(config)#router ospf 100
Router(config-router)#
```

Route Map config mode is where you define route maps for policy-based routing. The following command creates a route map called MYMAP and drops the user into route map config mode:

```
Router(config)#route-map MYMAP permit 10
Router(config-route-map)#
```

See Chapter 3, "Managing Routing Protocols," for more on route maps and policy-based routing.

Controller config mode is where you enter specific commands for built-in T1 and E1 controllers, if they exist on your router. The following example begins configuration of a T1 controller in slot **4/2/0**:

```
Router(config)#controller t1 4/2/0
Router(config-cont)#
```

Crypto map config mode is where you enter specific commands about how data will be protected by encryption (IPsec or Cisco's pre-IPsec encryption technology). Crypto maps are key elements of router encryption. For more information on crypto maps, see Chapter 7, "Advanced Security Services, Part I: IPsec."

```
2509(config)#crypto map MYCRYPTO 10 ipsec-isakmp
2509(config-crypto-map)#
```

Context-Based Help, Navigation, and Line Editing

IOS provides features that help you learn commands, reduce repetitive typing, and fix mistakes. This section covers these features in more detail.

Context-Based Help

The question mark key provides help screens for IOS keywords. Use the **?** key whenever you need help with an IOS command. The following example shows a list of commands allowed in enable mode:

```
2509#?
Exec commands:
  <1-99>            Session number to resume
  access-enable     Create a temporary Access-List entry
  access-template   Create a temporary Access-List entry
  bfe               For manual emergency modes setting
```

```
clear          Reset functions
clock          Manage the system clock
configure      Enter configuration mode
connect        Open a terminal connection
copy           Copy configuration or image data
<listing truncated for brevity>
```

To get help on a specific command, such as what keywords follow the first word, use **?** in place of the keyword. The following example shows how context-based help can walk you through all the required keywords for setting the router's clock:

```
2509#clock ?
  set  Set the time and date

2509#clock set ?
  hh:mm:ss  Current Time

2509#clock set 11:25:00 ?
  <1-31>  Day of the month
  MONTH   Month of the year

2509#clock set 11:25:00 apr ?
  <1-31>  Day of the month

2509#clock set 11:25:00 apr 22 ?
  <1993-2035>  Year

2509#clock set 11:25:00 apr 22 1999 ?
  <cr>

2509#clock set 11:25:00 apr 22 1999
2509#
```

The **?** key is also helpful when you want to find keywords that start with the same letters. For example, to display all enable mode commands that start with the letter **c**:

```
2509#c?
clear  clock  configure  connect  copy
```

Navigation

The up-arrow key is invaluable for retrieving previously entered commands and reducing repetitive typing. You can edit retrieved commands with basic line editing (cursor positioning, backspacing, and insertion) and enter them as new commands. See "Line Editing" in this appendix for editing features.

The down-arrow key is the opposite of the up-arrow key and recalls commands that are more recent instead of farther back in time.

For example, here's the enable mode prompt before you use the up-arrow key:

```
Router#
```

After you press the up arrow once, the most recently entered command is displayed at the same prompt:

```
Router#show version
```

Pressing the up arrow a second time displays the *next* most recent command (the one that is desired):

```
Router#clock set 11:25:00 apr 22 1999
```

The recalled line is edited to reflect the correct day of the month and submitted with the Enter key:

```
Router#clock set 11:25:00 apr 23 1999
```

Alternatively, Ctrl+P and Ctrl+N can be used instead of the up- and down-arrow keys (respectively). This is handy if your terminal's arrow keys aren't recognized by the router, which can happen if your terminal isn't one of the ANSI-compatible terminals such as VT100.

The Tab key completes long IOS keywords after you provide the first few characters. After typing enough characters to uniquely identify the command, you can press the Tab key and IOS will fill in the rest for you.

For example, if you don't want to type the whole command **configure terminal**, you can type:

```
Router#conf<TAB> t<TAB>
```

IOS will fill in the rest and display:

```
Router#configure terminal
```

You don't even have to use the Tab key. The abbreviated command **conf t** is equivalent to **configure terminal** because **conf** is unique enough to identify the command **configure** (and **t** is unique enough to identify the keyword **terminal**). Tab and **?** just help you learn the minimal amount of characters needed to make an unambiguous shortcut.

For example, three commands start with **co**, so **co** is not a legitimate shortcut for **configure**. The keyword **con** is also not enough to substitute for **configure** because **connect** also starts with **con**. But **conf** is unique enough to act as a shortcut for **configure**:

```
2509#co?
configure  connect  copy

2509#conf ?
  memory             Configure from NV memory
  network            Configure from a TFTP network host
  overwrite-network  Overwrite NV memory from TFTP network host
  terminal           Configure from the terminal
  <cr>
```

Line Editing

IOS provides control keys that help you position the cursor, delete text, and control display output. Tables E-1, E-2, and E-3 describe these useful keys.

Table E-1   *Cursor Positioning*

Press:	To:
Left arrow or Ctrl+B	Move cursor back one character.
Right arrow or Ctrl+F	Move cursor forward one character.
Ctrl+A	Move cursor to the beginning of the line.
Ctrl+E	Move cursor to the end of the line.

Table E-2   *Deleting*

Press:	To:
Backspace or Delete	Delete character to the left of the cursor.
Ctrl+D	Delete character at the cursor.
Ctrl+K	Delete everything from the cursor to the end of the line.
Ctrl+U or Ctrl+X	Delete everything from the cursor to the beginning of the line.
Ctrl+W	Delete the word to the left of the cursor.

Table E-3   *Other Keys*

Press:	To:
Ctrl+L	Refresh/redisplay the current line.
Spacebar	Scroll down one screen.
Enter or Return	Scroll down one line.

Common IOS Commands

IOS commands have a few thousand permutations. Table E-4 and Table E-5 list the most commonly used IOS commands.

Table E-4   *Common User EXEC Commands*

Command	Purpose
ping [*hostname	IP address*]	Ping another host.
traceroute [*hostname	IP address*]	Find a path to another host.
telnet	Open a Telnet session to another host[1].
enable	Change from user EXEC mode to enable mode (see "Modes" earlier in this appendix).
q or **exit**	Log off the router.

1. Shortcut: Instead of typing **telnet myhost** or **telnet 172.168.1.1**, you can just type **myhost** or **172.168.1.1** at the IOS prompt.

Table E-5   *Common Enable Mode (Privileged EXEC) Commands*

Command	Purpose
All of the previous user EXEC Commands	See Table E-4, "Common User EXEC Commands"
show running-config or **write terminal**	Displays the current configuration.
configure terminal	Changes from enable mode to global config mode (see "Modes," earlier in this appendix).
copy running-config startup-config or **write memory**	Saves the current configuration (in DRAM) to NVRAM[1].
copy running-config tftp	Saves the current configuration to a TFTP (Trivial File Transfer Protocol) server on the network.[2]
copy startup-config tftp	Saves the configuration stored in NVRAM to a TFTP server on the network.
show commands	See "Common **show** Commands," later in this appendix.
clear counters	Resets the values of various counters in the router, such as the packet/error counters displayed in **show interfaces**.
clear arp-cache	Clears the ARP cache in the router.
clear line *line#*	Clears the line (TTY or VTY) you specify.
clear ip route *A.B.C.D* [*mask*]	Clears one or more routes from the routing table. Triggers routing updates with most routing protocols.
clear ip route *	Clears all routes from the routing table. Triggers routing updates with most routing protocols.

Table E-5   *Common Enable Mode (Privileged EXEC) Commands (Continued)*

Command	Purpose
debug	Enables various levels of system and network debugging. *Never* do a **debug all**.[3]
terminal monitor	Displays debug and system messages in the current terminal session.[4]
no debug all or **undebug all**	Turns off all debugging.
copy flash tftp	Copies an IOS image in flash memory to a TFTP server on the network.[5]
copy tftp flash	Copies an IOS image from a TFTP server to flash memory.
erase startup-config or **write erase**	Erases the router's configuration stored in NVRAM.
erase flash	Erases the contents of flash memory (for most router models with on-board flash memory).
format *flash-device*[6]	Formats or erases the contents of flash memory (for most router models with multiple flash devices).
delete *file*	Marks a file in flash deleted (for most router models with multiple flash devices).[7]
squeeze *file*	Permanently erases files from flash that are marked deleted. Reclaims flash memory space.
reload	Reboots the router.

1.   Unlike DRAM, the contents of NVRAM (nonvolatile RAM) are *not* lost when the router is powered off. Routers normally read their configuration from NVRAM when they boot up.

2.   Another popular way to save a router's config is to display the config with **show running-config** (or the legacy command **write terminal**) and then use the cut-&-paste feature of your terminal emulation software to save the config on your PC/workstation. Also, beginning in IOS 12.0, FTP (keyword **ftp**) can be used in place of TFTP. This enables you to save to an FTP server.

3.   **debug all** turns on all gadzillion debugging services on the router and can overload or cripple your router. Debug sparingly: Zero in and enable just enough debug to reveal the activity you are troubleshooting.

4.   Use this when you connect via Telnet and want to see debug and system messages.

5.   The IOS image is a large file that contains the router's operating system. Flash memory is where the image is stored on a router (you can think of flash as the "hard drive"). Routers can store more than one image in flash, but only one image can run on the router's CPU at a time. Also, beginning in IOS 12.0, FTP (keyword **ftp**) can be used in place of TFTP. This enables you to save to an FTP server.

6.   For a list of flash devices in your router, do **show flash devices**. Device names end with a colon (for example, **slot0:**).

7.   Does not actually erase the file. Files can be undeleted with the **undelete** command. See **squeeze** command.

Beginning in IOS release 11.0, Cisco introduced replacements for some IOS commands to make the commands more descriptive. The legacy (pre-11.0) commands are still supported and sometimes preferred because they require less typing. Table E-6 correlates the commands in 11.0 (and later) to their pre-11.0 equivalents.

Table E-6   *Commands in 11.0 (and Later) and Pre-11.0 Equivalents*

11.0 and Later	Pre-11.0 Equivalent
config term	**config term**
show running-config	**write terminal**
config memory	**config memory**
copy running-config startup-config	**write memory**
copy tftp running-config	**config network**
copy running-config tftp	**write net**
show startup-config	**show config**
erase startup-config	**write erase**

Extended Ping

Ping is a nickname for the Echo message in ICMP (RFC 792). Extended ping gives you control over more ICMP and IP parameters than regular ping. Extended ping is a helpful utility available in enable mode. The command is **ping** (with no other arguments).

The following example runs the extended ping utility (default values are displayed by the router in brackets):

```
Router#ping
Protocol [ip]:
Target IP address: 192.168.1.1
Repeat count [5]: 50
Datagram size [100]: 1500
Timeout in seconds [2]:
Extended commands [n]: y
Source address or interface: 192.168.10.1
Type of service [0]:
Set DF bit in IP header? [no]:
Validate reply data? [no]:
Data pattern [0xABCD]: 0xffff
Loose, Strict, Record, Timestamp, Verbose[none]:
Sweep range of sizes [n]:
Type escape sequence to abort.
Sending 50, 1500-byte ICMP Echos to 192.168.1.1, timeout is 2 seconds:
Packet has data pattern 0xFFFF
!!!!!!!!!!!!!!!!!!!!!!!!!!!!!!!!!!!!!!!!!!!!!!!!!!!!
Success rate is 100 percent (50/50), round-trip min/avg/max = 16/20/44 ms
```

The following describes the parameters in the preceding configuration:

- Protocol is IP. Your router can support IPX, AppleTalk, DECnet, and other protocols, depending on the IOS software running on the router.

- Destination/target to ping is 192.168.1.1.

- Number of pings to send is 50.

- Size of each ping is 1500 bytes (datagram size).

- Time to wait for a ping reply is 2 seconds (timeout)

- Source address in the pings will be 192.168.10.1 (one of the router's interfaces). Alternatively, you can enter interface names—Ethernet0, for example.

- Value of the TOS (type of service) field is 0 (can set to test quality of service based on IP precedence).

- "Don't fragment" bit (DF bit) in the packet is zero. Answer yes to set the bit (useful for troubleshooting and finding the smallest MTU in the path to the target).

- The **Validate reply data** option is off. This means the router will check ping replies against matching identifier numbers only—a number in ping (ICMP Echo, ICMP Echo Reply) packets used to match requests with replies (see RFC 792 for more information). Answer yes to this option to make the router check both the identifier number and the data payload in reply packets.

- The payload of the ping packets will contain FFFF (hex), which is a binary pattern of all ones. (The text **0x** in front of a number means the number is in hexadecimal format. For example, to indicate that 1234 is hexadecimal, type **0x1234**.) This can be useful when debugging problems that are data pattern–sensitive, especially with serial lines and CSU/DSUs. Another good pattern to use is all zeros: 0x0000.

- No IP options will be specified in the IP header. This is prompted by **Loose, Strict, Record, Timestamp, Verbose[none]**. For information on IP options, see RFC 791.

- The ping packets will be the same size. If you want to generate pings of varying lengths, answer **Y** to **Sweep range of sizes**.

Extended Traceroute

Like extended ping, *extended traceroute* is available in enable mode.

The following example shows an output of extended traceroute. A name server is configured on the router to get hostname information in the results instead of just IP addresses (see "Common Configuration Tasks" later in this appendix for configuring name servers).

```
Router#trace
Protocol [ip]:
Target IP address: www.yahoo.com
Translating "www.yahoo.com"...domain server (172.16.1.14) [OK]
```

continues

```
Source address: 192.168.1.2
Numeric display [n]:
Timeout in seconds [3]:
Probe count [3]:
Minimum Time to Live [1]:
Maximum Time to Live [30]:
Port Number [33434]:
Loose, Strict, Record, Timestamp, Verbose[none]:
Type escape sequence to abort.
Tracing the route to www1.yahoo.com (10.170.71.10)

 1 192.168.1.1 16 msec 12 msec 12 msec
 2 HQ-router-2.cisco.com (172.16.23.13) 16 msec 12 msec 12 msec
 3 172.16.23.1 64 msec 64 msec 64 msec
 4 blackcat.cisco.com (172.16.36.7) 64 msec 60 msec 64 msec
 5 zip-gate1.cisco.com (192.168.223.33) 68 msec 60 msec 64 msec
 6 rtr-2.cisco.com (192.168.8.161) 64 msec 60 msec 68 msec
 7 Inet-router.cisco.com (192.168.71.30) 60 msec 60 msec 64 msec
 8 j521.paloalto.bbnplanet.net (172.16.108.13) 64 msec 64 msec 68 msec
 9 h405.paloalto-3gw.bbnplanet.net (10.1.63.64) 64 msec 64 msec 68 msec
10 cb22.sanjose-622.bbnplanet.net (10.1.129.3) 64 msec 56 msec 64 msec
11 dc09.sanjose-55.bbnplanet.net (10.5.201.23) 64 msec 64 msec 72 msec
12 fd3-4.SanJ.globalcenter.net (192.168.129.2) 60 msec 60 msec 68 msec
13 hs87.SanJ.globalcenter.net (192.168.171.133) 64 msec 60 msec 72 msec
14 sonet7.SV.globalcenter.net (172.16.17.1) 60 msec 60 msec 64 msc
15 www1.yahoo.com (10.170.71.10) 64 msec 64 msec 72 msec
```

The following describes the parameters in the preceding configuration:

- **Numeric display** enables you to toggle the output between numeric IP addresses and hostnames.

- The **timeout** is the number of seconds to wait for a reply to each traceroute probe packet.

- The **probe count** is the number of probe packets to send to each router hop (Time To Live level, see RFC 791) along the path to the target.

- **Minimum Time to Live** specifies the TTL of the first set of probes.

- **Maximum Time to Live** specifies the largest TTL (the maximum router hops) to use. The trace stops when the target is reached or when the maximum TTL is reached.

- **Port Number** sets the UDP port number to use.

- The last prompt is for adding IP options to the probe packets.

The preceding traceroute output shows 15 router hops to the target. The latency of the three probes sent at each router hop is displayed in milliseconds. To abort the traceroute, type the IOS escape sequence: `Ctrl-Shift-6, x`. See "Using the Router as a Terminal Server (Communications Server)" later in this appendix for detailed instructions on the escape key sequence.

Common Configuration Tasks

A look at the IOS documentation library will tell you one thing: Cisco router configuration is a massive subject. This section provides a quick synopsis of the most frequently used IOS configuration commands.

The Setup Utility (Initial Configuration Dialog)

The *setup* utility (also called the *initial configuration dialog*) is a small program that the router runs at startup when its configuration is empty (that is, if the router is new or if someone erased the router's configuration with the command **erase startup-config**). Some people like this utility because it helps them quickly configure some basic parameters such as the name of the router, the enable password, the address on each interface, and so on. Other people would rather configure the router from scratch from global config mode. To skip the setup utility, answer no if the router asks:

```
Would you like to enter the initial configuration dialog? [yes]:
```

You can also type **Ctrl-C** at any prompt when you are inside the setup utility.

Here's what the setup utility looks like (some lines are removed for brevity):

```
Notice: NVRAM invalid, possibly due to write erase.
         --- System Configuration Dialog ---

At any point you may enter a question mark '?' for help.
Use ctrl-c to abort configuration dialog at any prompt.
Default settings are in square brackets '[]'.
Would you like to enter the initial configuration dialog? [yes]:
...

Configuring global parameters:

  Enter host name [Router]: MYROUTER

The enable secret is a one-way cryptographic secret used
instead of the enable password when it exists.

  Enter enable secret: cisco

The enable password is used when there is no enable secret
and when using older software and some boot images.

  Enter enable password: mypassword
  Enter virtual terminal password: mypassword
  Configure SNMP Network Management? [yes]: n
  Configure DECnet? [no]: n
  Configure AppleTalk? [no]: n
  Configure IPX? [no]: n
  Configure IP? [yes]: y
    Configure IGRP routing? [yes]: n
    Configure RIP routing? [no]: y
```

continues

```
Configure bridging? [no]: n
Enter ISDN BRI Switch Type [none]:

Configuring interface parameters:

Configuring interface Ethernet0:
  Is this interface in use? [yes]: y
  Configure IP on this interface? [yes]: y
    IP address for this interface: 192.168.10.1
    Number of bits in subnet field [0]: 0
    Class C network is 192.168.10.0, 0 subnet bits; mask is /24

Configuring interface Serial0:
  Is this interface in use? [yes]: n
...

The following configuration command script was created:

hostname MYROUTER
enable secret 5 $1$DOH8$xthIIdLx4/7L7VHko/INJ1
enable password today
line vty 0 4
password cisco
no snmp-server
!
no decnet routing
no appletalk routing
no ipx routing
ip routing
!
interface Ethernet0
ip address 192.168.10.1 255.255.255.0
no mop enabled
!
interface Serial0
shutdown
no ip address
!
router rip
redistribute connected
network 192.168.10.0
!
end

Use this configuration? [yes/no]: y
```

NOTE   You can run the setup utility at any time with the enable mode command **setup**.

Set the Enable Password

The enable password protects enable mode and is the equivalent to the superuser/root password on the router. To set the enable password, use the **enable secret** command in global config mode.

NOTE   Older versions of IOS (generally prior to release 11.0) might not support the **enable secret** command. Subsequently, you must use the **enable password** command instead. It is highly recommended that you use **enable secret** instead of **enable password** for better security. The **enable secret** command uses a secure, one-way cryptographic hash algorithm.

The following example sets the enable password to *mypassword*:

```
Router(config)#enable secret mypassword
```

Set the Router's Hostname

To set the hostname:

```
Router(config)#hostname Myrouter
Myrouter(config)#
```

Make a Banner

To configure a banner message that is displayed at console and Telnet logins:

```
Myrouter(config)#banner ~
Enter TEXT message.  End with the character '~'.

Unauthorized access and use of this device is prohibited.

~
Myrouter(config)#
```

All the text, including carriage returns, between the ~ (tilde) characters make up the banner message. Instead of ~, you can use any other character as long as it is not part of your banner.

NOTE   It is recommended that you write banners *without* friendly greetings. Do not, for example, write a banner that says "Welcome to the XYZ Inc. Router!" You do not want to give hackers a legal argument that you were "inviting" them to attack your site.

Set the System Clock and Date

To set the clock and date on the router, use the **clock set** command from enable mode (not global config mode):

```
Myrouter#clock set 15:53:00 Jun 13 1999
```

To view the clock:

```
Myrouter#show clock
*03:51:24.049 UTC Tue Jul 2 1999
```

NOTE   It is recommended that you set the clock by using NTP whenever possible. See "Point the Router to a Network Time Protocol (NTP) Server" later in this appendix.

Set the Domain Name

To tell the router the Internet domain it belongs to:

```
Myrouter(config)#ip domain-name cisco.com
```

Set the Name Server(s)

To configure the router to point to one or more DNS servers so it can resolve hostnames for IP addresses:

```
Myrouter(config)#ip name-server 172.16.100.10
Myrouter(config)#ip name-server 172.16.100.11
```

Populate the Router's Local Host Table

To configure a table of hostnames and their associated IP addresses in lieu of DNS:

```
Myrouter(config)#ip host sparky 172.16.50.25
Myrouter(config)#ip host tequila-cat 192.168.23.14
Myrouter(config)#ip host grumpy 10.15.1.100
```

Set SNMP Community Strings

To set the SNMP community strings, which are analogous to passwords (between SNMP servers and SNMP clients such as routers), for network management, use the **snmp-server community** command. The first line of the following example sets the read-only string to *public*, and the second line sets the read-write string to *MYPASSWORD*:

```
Myrouter(config)#snmp-server community public ro
Myrouter(config)#snmp-server community MYPASSWORD rw
```

Set SNMP Trap Hosts

To tell the router the address or hostname of an SNMP trap host (trap receiver) and the associated community string:

```
Myrouter(config)#snmp-server host 172.16.40.10 MYPASSWORD
```

Enable the Router to Send SNMP Traps

To permit the router to send SNMP traps to the trap hosts:

```
Myrouter(config)#snmp-server enable traps
```

To narrow the types of traps sent:

```
snmp-server enable traps ?
```

Point the Router to a Syslog Server

To configure the router to send system messages to one or more syslog servers for centralized monitoring:

```
Myrouter(config)#logging 192.168.10.4
```

The **logging** command sends system console messages to a syslog daemon on a host (192.168.10.4, in the example) via UDP port 514 (syslog). Use this in conjunction with the global configuration command **service timestamps**, which applies timestamps to system messages for aiding in troubleshooting.

Configure Timestamping of System and Debug Messages

To timestamp system messages using the router's date, time (with milliseconds), and time zone:

```
Myrouter(config)#service timestamps log datetime msec show-timezone
```

This is useful for correlating messages from routers in different time zones and tracking network problems. Use the keyword **debug** instead of **log** to enable timestamping of debug messages.

Point the Router to a Network Time Protocol (NTP) Server

To set the router's clock using NTP (highly recommended):

```
Myrouter(config)#ntp server sundial.columbia.edu
```

The preceding example uses a host name instead of an IP address (DNS is configured on this router). Search the Internet for "NTP" to find time servers (see also RFC 1305). Use the enable commands **show ntp associations** and **show ntp status** to verify NTP configuration.

Set the Time Zone

To configure the router with time zone information (useful when correlating system messages across routers that are geographically spread apart):

```
Myrouter(config)#clock timezone PST -8
```

In the preceding configuration:

- **PST** is the name of the time zone displayed when standard time is in effect—Pacific Standard Time (PST) in this example.

- **-8** is the number of hours the time zone differs from Coordinated Universal Time (UTC), also known as Greenwich Mean Time (GMT) or Zulu time.

Set Daylight Saving Time Information

To tell the router the start and end of summer Daylight Saving Time (DST):

```
7206(config)#clock summer-time PDT recurring 1 Sun Apr 2:00 last Sun Oct 2:00
```

In the preceding configuration:

- **PDT** is the name of the time zone displayed when DST is in effect—Pacific Daylight Time (PDT) in this example.

- **1 Sun Apr 2:00** sets the beginning of DST for 2:00 a.m. on the first Sunday of April.

- **last Sun Oct 2:00** sets the end of DST for 2:00 a.m. on the last Sunday of October.

NOTE   The start and end of DST presented in this example apply to regions of the USA observing DST (set forth by the Uniform Time Act of 1966 and later amended in 1986).

You can also use the **clock summer-time** *zone* **date** command to configure absolute dates that define DST in a region.

Configure a Static Route

To configure a static route that tells the router how to reach a network:

```
Myrouter(config)#ip route 172.16.192.0 255.255.255.0 192.168.33.1
```

This overrides dynamic routing protocols (unless the administrative distance of the static route is configured higher than that of the routing protocol). In this configuration:

* **172.16.192.0 255.255.255.0** specifies the prefix and mask for the destination subnet.
* **192.168.33.1** specifies the next-hop router. Packets destined for 172.16.192.0/24 are forwarded to the next-hop router. Alternatively, you can configure an interface such as **serial0** instead of a next-hop router address.

To set the administrative distance of a static route, append the administrative distance value to the **ip route** command:

```
Myrouter(config)#ip route 172.16.192.0 255.255.255.0 192.168.33.1 180
```

The distance of the preceding static route is 180. See Chapter 3 for information on administrative distances.

Configure a Default Route

To configure a default route that the router will use if it has no other route to a destination:

```
Myrouter(config)#ip route 0.0.0.0 0.0.0.0 172.16.1.1
```

NOTE   Typically, you will want a router, such as one that connects to the Internet, configured with the default route. Then, have that router propagate the default route to other routers in your network, using OSPF, EIGRP, RIP, or other routing protocol. Default routing strategies are covered in Chapter 3.

In this configuration:

* **0.0.0.0 0.0.0.0** is a special address that means this route is the default route.
* **172.16.1.1** is the next-hop router address. Packets that Myrouter doesn't have a route for are sent to 172.16.1.1.

Consult Chapter 3 for default routing information and strategies.

Configure an IP Address on an Interface

To configure an IP address on an interface:

```
Myrouter(config)#int e0
Myrouter(config-if)#ip address 192.168.1.2 255.255.255.0
```

In this configuration:

- **int e0** (short for **interface ethernet0**) changes from global config mode to interface config mode.

- **192.168.1.2 255.255.255.0** is the interface's IP address and subnet mask.

Other Interface Configuration Tasks

To write a brief description of an interface:

```
Myrouter(config-if)#description Fractional T1 to Cincinnati sales office
```

To configure the bandwidth that is used by routing protocols to compute route metrics:

```
Myrouter(config-if)#bandwidth 512
```

NOTE   This does *not* set the actual bandwidth of the physical link. You set this to accurately describe the bandwidth of the link to routing protocols such as OSPF, EIGRP, and IGRP. The actual bandwidth depends on the physical media (ethernet, FDDI, OC-12, serial line clockrate, and so on.)

In the preceding configuration, **512** is the bandwidth in kilobits per second (512 kbps).

To set the link layer encapsulation on the interface (you cannot set the encapsulation on some interfaces such as Ethernet):

```
Myrouter(config-if)#encapsulation frame-relay
```

For encapsulation types other than frame relay, type **encapsulation ?** at the prompt.

To administratively shut down the interface:

```
Myrouter(config-if)#shutdown
```

Confirm that the interface is in shutdown with the **show interfaces** enable mode command.

To administratively bring the interface online:

```
Myrouter(config-if)#no shutdown
```

Configure the Location of the Boot Image

By default, a router boots with the first available IOS image stored in flash memory. When you have multiple images stored in flash, you should specify which image the router will load with the **boot system flash** command:

```
Myrouter(config)#boot system flash c2500-dos-l.112.12_P.bin
```

Here, **c2500-dos-l.112.12_P.bin** is the filename of the image stored in flash for this particular router.

NOTE   On routers that have multiple flash devices such as PCMCIA flash card slots, you must also provide the flash device name. Check your router for multiple flash devices with the **show flash devices** command.

To configure the router to boot from the network with an image stored on a TFTP server (you can use rcp, as well):

```
Myrouter(config)#boot system tftp c2500-d-l.112.15_P.bin 192.168.77.10
```

You can also configure multiple image locations from which the router tries to boot. This is highly recommended, especially if the router is trying to boot from the network or if you are testing an image that hasn't been loaded on the router before. The router attempts to load IOS from each location in sequence until it successfully loads and activates an operating system.

The following example configures a router to boot with an image in the **slot0:** flash device. If that fails, the router will try a backup image stored in **slot1:**. And if that second try fails, the router will attempt to boot from the network with an image stored on a TFTP server called **hugo**.

```
7206(config)#no boot system
7206(config)#boot system flash slot0:c7200-p-mz_111-18_CA.bin
7206(config)#boot system flash slot1:c7200-j-mz.111-14.CA1.bin
7206(config)#boot system tftp c7200-j-mz.111-11.CA.bin hugo
```

In this example, **no boot system** clears the boot system list so you can configure a new one from scratch.

In IOS releases 12.0 and later, you can also use the URL (Uniform Resource Locator) syntax:

```
7206(config)#boot system tftp://172.16.55.5/c7200-j-mz.111-11.CA.bin
```

Retract (undo) Configuration Commands

To undo a command that you configured in the router (or to disable a default command), simply enter the command again with the word **no** in front of it:

```
Myrouter(config)#ip name-server 192.168.44.8
Myrouter(config)#no ip name-server 192.168.44.8
```

TIP   This is where the up arrow (recall previous command) and Ctrl+A (move cursor to the beginning of line) come in handy.

Some commands, such as **ip address** *x.y.z.t* (configure an IP address on an interface), simply overwrite the prior value, so you don't have to use the **no** command to undo the value if you just want to reconfigure it.

Common Show Commands

The group of enable mode commands called the **show** commands are essential to validating configuration and monitoring the router. This section describes some of the most commonly used **show** commands. Use the command **show ?** and context-based help to discover other **show** commands or consult the IOS documentation.

General Show Commands

This section provides some general and widely used IOS **show** commands along with their corresponding sample outputs.

show version Command

show version displays IOS software version information, hardware, memory, uptime, and other vital information:

```
2509>show ver
Cisco Internetwork Operating System Software
IOS (tm) 2500 Software (C2500-JS40-L), Version 11.2(12), RELEASE SOFTWARE (fc1)
Copyright (c) 1986-1998 by cisco Systems, Inc.
Compiled Mon 23-Feb-98 18:31 by tlane
Image text-base: 0x030410AC, data-base: 0x00001000

ROM: System Bootstrap, Version 4.14(9.1), SOFTWARE

2509 uptime is 6 weeks, 4 days, 20 hours, 58 minutes
System restarted by power-on at 08:07:16 UTC Thu Mar 11 1999
```

```
System image file is "c2500-js40-l.112-12.bin", booted via flash

cisco 2509 (68030) processor (revision C) with 16384K/2048K bytes of memory.
Processor board ID 01500480, with hardware revision 00000000
Bridging software.
SuperLAT software copyright 1990 by Meridian Technology Corp).
X.25 software, Version 2.0, NET2, BFE and GOSIP compliant.
TN3270 Emulation software.
1 Ethernet/IEEE 802.3 interface(s)
2 Serial network interface(s)
8 terminal line(s)
32K bytes of non-volatile configuration memory.
16384K bytes of processor board System flash (Read ONLY)

Configuration register is 0x2102
```

show running-config and show startup-config Commands

show running-config and **show startup-config** display the router's active config in DRAM and saved config in NVRAM, respectively:

```
Myrouter#sh running-config (or sh startup-config)
Building configuration...

Current configuration:
!
version 11.2
service timestamps debug datetime msec
no service password-encryption
service udp-small-servers
service tcp-small-servers
!
hostname Myrouter
!
enable secret 5 $1$LLd7$aGK1Cqtj6oo5e4r3Z2mjQ0
!
ip domain-name cisco.com
ip name-server 172.16.100.10
ip name-server 172.16.100.11
<lines deleted for brevity>
```

show logging Command

show logging displays the contents of the system management log:

```
Myrouter#sh log
Syslog logging: enabled (0 messages dropped, 0 flushes, 0 overruns)
    Console logging: level debugging, 74 messages logged
    Monitor logging: level debugging, 0 messages logged
    Trap logging: level informational, 40 message lines logged
    Buffer logging: level debugging, 74 messages logged
```

continues

```
Log Buffer (4096 bytes):
%LINK-3-UPDOWN: Interface Ethernet0, changed state to up
%LINK-3-UPDOWN: Interface Serial0, changed state to down
%LINK-3-UPDOWN: Interface Serial1, changed state to up
%LINEPROTO-5-UPDOWN: Line protocol on Interface Ethernet0, changed state to up
%LINEPROTO-5-UPDOWN: Line protocol on Interface Serial1, changed state to up
%LINK-5-CHANGED: Interface Serial0, changed state to administratively down
%SYS-5-CONFIG_I: Configured from memory by console
%SYS-5-RESTART: System restarted --
Cisco Internetwork Operating System Software
IOS (tm) 2500 Software (C2500-DOS-L), Version 11.2(12)P, RELEASE SOFTWARE (fc1)
Copyright (c) 1986-1998 by cisco Systems, Inc.
Compiled Tue 03-Mar-98 07:00 by dschwart
%SYS-5-CONFIG_I: Configured from console by console
```

show debug Command

show debug displays the current levels of debugging that are in effect:

```
Myrouter#sh debug
IP routing:
  OSPF adjacency events debugging is on
  IP routing debugging is on
Frame Relay:
  Frame Relay events debugging is on
```

show clock Command

show clock displays the date and time:

```
Myrouter#show clock
*03:51:24.049 UTC Tue Jul 2 1999
```

show users Command

show users displays who's logged into the router:

```
Myrouter#sh users
    Line       User       Host(s)                  Idle Location
   0 con 0                192.168.1.1         00:00:00
*  2 vty 0                idle                00:00:00 192.168.1.1
```

show tech-support Command

show tech-support dumps the output of several important show commands. This is handy when you need to send baseline data to Cisco for technical support.

The output of **show tech-support** includes the outputs of:

- **show version**
- **show running-config**
- **show controllers**
- **show stacks**
- **show interfaces**
- **show process memory**
- **show process cpu**
- **show buffers**

Resource Show Commands

This section provides resource-related **show** commands along with their corresponding sample outputs.

show process cpu Command

show process cpu displays the router's CPU utilization and a list of processes running on the router. Pay attention to the top line (shown in boldface), which displays the CPU load over various intervals of time:

```
2509#sh proc cpu
CPU utilization for five seconds: 20%/6%; one minute: 7%; five minutes: 4%
 PID  Runtime(ms)  Invoked  uSecs  5Sec   1Min   5Min TTY Process
   1      644316   810587    794  0.00%  0.00%  0.00%   0 Load Meter
   2      414212   810337    511  0.00%  0.00%  0.00%   0 OSPF Hello
   3     7656708    82779  92496  0.00%  0.26%  0.20%   0 Check heaps
   4          96       54   1777  0.00%  0.00%  0.00%   0 Pool Manager
   5           0        2      0  0.00%  0.00%  0.00%   0 Timers
   6       28700    72149    397  0.00%  0.00%  0.00%   0 ARP Input
   7           0        1      0  0.00%  0.00%  0.00%   0 SERIAL A'detect
   8     1863988  1299311   1434  1.31%  0.60%  0.27%   0 IP Input
   9      288612   472965    610  0.00%  0.00%  0.00%   0 CDP Protocol
<lines deleted>
```

On most routers and in most situations, you will not want your router's CPU utilization to run over 60% for long periods of time. An undesirably high CPU utilization indicates that the router is busy with too many process-intensive services or is undersized for the bandwidth flowing through it.

show ip cache Command

show ip cache displays the statistics of the fast switching cache, if one exists on your router:

```
Myrouter#sh ip cache
IP routing cache 3 entries, 492 bytes
    251 adds, 248 invalidates, 0 refcounts
Minimum invalidation interval 2 seconds, maximum interval 5 seconds,
    quiet interval 3 seconds, threshold 0 requests
Invalidation rate 0 in last second, 0 in last 3 seconds

Prefix/Length        Age        Interface    Next Hop
10.0.0.0/8           05:56:29   Serial1      192.168.1.1
192.168.1.1/32       00:21:45   Serial1      192.168.1.1
192.168.10.4/32      00:03:03   Ethernet0    192.168.10.4
```

show buffers Command

show buffers displays statistics for the router's buffer pools (chunks of memory used to temporarily hold packets). The output shows you the buffers that are available and a performance history.

```
2509#sh buffers
Buffer elements:
     499 in free list (500 max allowed)
     5562939 hits, 0 misses, 0 created

Public buffer pools:
Small buffers, 104 bytes (total 50, permanent 50):
     50 in free list (20 min, 150 max allowed)
     1307500 hits, 0 misses, 0 trims, 0 created
     0 failures (0 no memory)
Middle buffers, 600 bytes (total 25, permanent 25):
     23 in free list (10 min, 150 max allowed)
     954012 hits, 0 misses, 0 trims, 0 created
     0 failures (0 no memory)
Big buffers, 1524 bytes (total 179, permanent 50):
     9 in free list (5 min, 150 max allowed)
     339534 hits, 168 misses, 9 trims, 138 created
     51 failures (0 no memory)
VeryBig buffers, 4520 bytes (total 10, permanent 10):
     10 in free list (0 min, 100 max allowed)
     0 hits, 0 misses, 0 trims, 0 created
     0 failures (0 no memory)
Large buffers, 5024 bytes (total 0, permanent 0):
     0 in free list (0 min, 10 max allowed)
     0 hits, 0 misses, 0 trims, 0 created
     0 failures (0 no memory)
```

```
Huge buffers, 18024 bytes (total 0, permanent 0):
    0 in free list (0 min, 4 max allowed)
    0 hits, 1 misses, 2 trims, 2 created
    0 failures (0 no memory)

Interface buffer pools:
Ethernet0 buffers, 1524 bytes (total 32, permanent 32):
    8 in free list (0 min, 32 max allowed)
    24 hits, 0 fallbacks
    8 max cache size, 8 in cache
Serial0 buffers, 1524 bytes (total 32, permanent 32):
    7 in free list (0 min, 32 max allowed)
    25 hits, 0 fallbacks
    8 max cache size, 8 in cache
Serial1 buffers, 1524 bytes (total 32, permanent 32):
    0 in free list (0 min, 32 max allowed)
    143455 hits, 65248 fallbacks
    8 max cache size, 0 in cache
CD2430 I/O buffers, 1524 bytes (total 40, permanent 40):
    0 in free list (0 min, 40 max allowed)
    40 hits, 0 fallbacks
```

Routers have multiple pools (small, middle-size, big, and so on), each with its own set of buffers of a specific size. When a router receives a packet, it stores the packet in a buffer whose size best matches the size of the packet. A *hit* is good and means a packet was successfully stored in a memory buffer. The *free list* is the number of available buffers in that pool. A *miss* means the router did not have an available buffer in the pool and had to create a new buffer to accommodate the packet. A *trim* means a buffer was released because it was no longer needed. A *failure* means the router could not create a buffer for a packet and subsequently had to drop the packet. This might happen if the router is too busy to create a buffer on the spot (it is the responsibility of protocols such as TCP to retransmit the packet). A *no memory* is a special kind of failure that happens when there's no more memory available to create a new buffer (this might indicate that the router needs a DRAM upgrade). A *fallback* happens when an interface attempts to allocate a buffer and falls back to one of the public buffers (small, middle, big, etc.).

In general, large counts of failures (when compared to hits plus misses) means the router is having some kind of performance problem. Get Cisco involved in pinpointing the issue and finding a remedy.

WARNING   Reconfiguring the buffer pools without the assistance of Cisco is highly discouraged. Do not attempt to tweak the buffer system unless you are a router performance expert.

---

show flash Commands

show flash devices—which is supported on routers with more than one flash device such as PCMCIA flash cards—and **show flash all** display flash memory and file information:

```
7200#sh flash dev
slot0, slot1, bootflash, tftp, rcp, nvram

7200#sh flash all
-#- ED --type-- --crc--- -seek-- nlen -length- -----date/time------ name
1   .. FFFFFFFF 6E22464D 3FF0AC 21   4059180  Oct 02 1997 10:26:12 c7200-j-mz.111-
    14.CA1
2   .. FFFFFFFF 67B4E28A 69E950 24   2750500  Apr 30 1998 09:30:31 c7200-p-mz_111-
    18_CA.bin

13768368 bytes available (6809936 bytes used)
```

Interface Show Commands

This section provides interface-related **show** commands along with their corresponding sample outputs.

show interfaces Command

show interfaces displays lots of good information about interfaces: whether they are up, how they are configured, the status of queues, queuing methods, throughput statistics, packet counters, and error statistics.

```
2509#sh int s1
Serial1 is up, line protocol is up
  Hardware is HD64570
  Internet address is 192.168.1.1/24
  MTU 1500 bytes, BW 2000 Kbit, DLY 20000 usec, rely 255/255, load 15/255
  Encapsulation HDLC, loopback not set, keepalive set (10 sec)
  Last input 00:00:00, output 00:00:00, output hang never
  Last clearing of "show interface" counters never
  Input queue: 0/75/51 (size/max/drops); Total output drops: 0
  Queueing strategy: weighted fair
  Output queue: 0/1000/0 (size/max total/drops)
    Conversations  0/3/64 (active/max active/threshold)
    Reserved Conversations 0/0 (allocated/max allocated)
  5 minute input rate 2000 bits/sec, 5 packets/sec
  5 minute output rate 122000 bits/sec, 11 packets/sec
    5059857 packets input, 1328529726 bytes, 51 no buffer
    Received 616671 broadcasts, 0 runts, 0 giants, 0 throttles
    0 input errors, 0 CRC, 0 frame, 0 overrun, 0 ignored, 0 abort
    6600958 packets output, 966554675 bytes, 0 underruns
    0 output errors, 0 collisions, 40 interface resets
    0 output buffer failures, 0 output buffers swapped out
    94 carrier transitions
    DCD=up  DSR=up  DTR=up  RTS=up  CTS=up
```

show ip interface Command

show ip interface displays IP-related information for an interface. This is useful when validating an IP configuration on an interface:

```
2509#sh ip interface s1
Serial1 is up, line protocol is up
  Internet address is 192.168.1.1/24
  Broadcast address is 255.255.255.255
  Address determined by non-volatile memory
  MTU is 1500 bytes
  Helper address is not set
  Directed broadcast forwarding is enabled
  Secondary address 192.168.20.1/24
  Multicast reserved groups joined: 224.0.0.5 224.0.0.6 224.0.0.9
  Outgoing access list is not set
  Inbound  access list is not set
  Proxy ARP is enabled
  Security level is default
  Split horizon is enabled
  ICMP redirects are always sent
  ICMP unreachables are always sent
  ICMP mask replies are never sent
  IP fast switching is enabled
  IP fast switching on the same interface is enabled
  IP multicast fast switching is enabled
  Router Discovery is disabled
  IP output packet accounting is disabled
  IP access violation accounting is disabled
  TCP/IP header compression is disabled
  Probe proxy name replies are disabled
  Gateway Discovery is disabled
  Policy routing is disabled
  Network address translation is enabled, interface in domain inside
```

show interfaces stat Command

show interfaces stat displays statistics for switching paths such as process switching and fast switching if they exist on your router. Depending on IOS release, switching paths are usually described in the "Switching Services Configuration Guide" (search the Cisco Web site with those title words). **show interfaces stat** is an undocumented command. It's useful for gathering statistics and ensuring traffic is switched the way you expect it to be:

```
2509#sh int stat
Ethernet0
        Switching path    Pkts In   Chars In  Pkts Out  Chars Out
            Processor      304854   46349259    745443   57745727
          Route cache     4955746  898448974   3644878 1289403919
                Total     5260600  944798233   4390321 1347149646
```

In the preceding output, the **Processor** line is for process switching and the **Route cache** line is for fast switching.

show controllers Command

show controllers displays statistics on physical and link layer communication devices embedded in the router such as Ethernet, serial, ATM, ISDN, and T1/E1 controllers. Most of this data is cryptic, but some good information such as the number of low layer errors can be gleaned and used to troubleshoot hardware problems:

```
2509#sh cont ethernet 0
LANCE unit 0, idb 0xE2C98, ds 0xE4770, regaddr = 0x2130000, reset_mask 0x2
IB at 0x4006DAC: mode=0x0000, mcfilter 0001/0004/8008/0000
station address 0000.0c34.ae5e  default station address 0000.0c34.ae5e
buffer size 1524
RX ring with 16 entries at 0x4006DF0
Rxhead = 0x4006E38 (9), Rxp = 0xE47B0 (9)
00 pak=0x0E795C ds=0x4011E56 status=0x80 max_size=1524 pak_size=74
01 pak=0x0E7CFC ds=0x4012BC6 status=0x80 max_size=1524 pak_size=74
<lines deleted>
0 missed datagrams, 0 overruns
0 transmitter underruns, 0 excessive collisions
49 single collisions, 43 multiple collisions
0 dma memory errors, 0 CRC errors

0 alignment errors, 0 runts, 0 giants
0 tdr, 0 spurious initialization done interrupts
0 no enp status, 0 buffer errors, 0 overflow errors
0 tx_buff, 0 throttled, 0 enabled
Lance csr0 = 0x73
```

show queue Command

show queue displays the status of queues on the interface you specify. This is handy for monitoring queue depths, packet drops, and quality of service on an interface.

```
2509#sh queue s1
  Input queue: 0/75/51 (size/max/drops); Total output drops: 0
  Queueing strategy: weighted fair
  Output queue: 7/1000/0 (size/max total/drops)
     Conversations  2/4/64 (active/max active/threshold)
     Reserved Conversations 0/0 (allocated/max allocated)

  (depth/weight/discards/tail drops) 2/4096/0/0
  Conversation 228, linktype: ip, length: 45
  source: 192.168.1.1, destination: 192.168.10.4, id: 0x00A9, ttl: 255,
  TOS: 0 prot: 6, source port 23, destination port 2271

  (depth/weight/discards/tail drops) 5/4096/0/0
  Conversation 198, linktype: ip, length: 1336
  source: 172.9.4.3, destination: 192.168.10.4, id: 0xBD36, ttl: 247,
  TOS: 0 prot: 6, source port 60980, destination port 2276
```

show line Command

show line displays the console, AUX, async, and VTY lines on the router:

```
2509#sh line
   Tty Typ     Tx/Rx       A Modem  Roty AccO AccI  Uses   Noise  Overruns
     0 CTY                  -   -     -    -    -      0       0      0/0
     1 TTY     9600/9600    -   -     -    -    -      0       0      0/0
     2 TTY     9600/9600    -   -     -    -    -      0       0      0/0
     3 TTY     9600/9600    -   -     -    -    -      0       0      0/0
     4 TTY     9600/9600    -   -     -    -    -      0       0      0/0
     5 TTY     9600/9600    -   -     -    -    -      0       0      0/0
     6 TTY     9600/9600    -   -     -    -    -      0       0      0/0
     7 TTY     9600/9600    -   -     -    -    -      0       0      0/0
     8 TTY     9600/9600    -   -     -    -    -      0       0      0/0
     9 AUX     9600/9600    -   -     -    -    -      0       0      0/0
 *  10 VTY                  -   -     -    -    -     22       0      0/0
 *  11 VTY                  -   -     -    -    -      5       0      0/0
 *  12 VTY                  -   -     -    -    -      8       0      0/0
 *  13 VTY                  -   -     -    -    -      9       0      0/0
 *  14 VTY                  -   -     -    -    -      4       0      0/0
```

Issue **show line** with the line number to view detailed information about a particular line:

```
2509#sh line 1
   Tty Typ     Tx/Rx       A Modem  Roty AccO AccI  Uses   Noise  Overruns  Int
     1 TTY     9600/9600    -   -     -    -    -      0       0      0/0     -

Line 1, Location: "", Type: ""
Length: 24 lines, Width: 80 columns
Baud rate (TX/RX) is 9600/9600, no parity, 2 stopbits, 8 databits
Status: Ready
Capabilities: None
Modem state: Ready
Modem hardware state: CTS* noDSR  DTR RTS
Special Chars: Escape  Hold  Stop  Start  Disconnect  Activation
               ^^x     none   -     -       none
Timeouts:      Idle EXEC     Idle Session   Modem Answer  Session   Dispatch
               00:10:00         never                      none     not set
                             Idle Session Disconnect Warning
                               never
                             Login-sequence User Response
                             00:00:30
                             Autoselect Initial Wait
                               not set
Modem type is unknown.
Session limit is not set.
Time since activation: never
Editing is enabled.
History is enabled, history size is 10.
DNS resolution in show commands is enabled
Full user help is disabled
Allowed transports are pad v120 telnet rlogin.  Preferred is telnet.
No output characters are padded
No special data dispatching characters
```

Network Show Commands

This section provides network-related **show** commands along with their corresponding sample outputs.

show ip traffic Command

show ip traffic displays lots of protocol statistics for the router as a whole:

```
2509#sh ip traf
IP statistics:
  Rcvd:  9850937 total, 875128 local destination
         1 format errors, 0 checksum errors, 32 bad hop count
         0 unknown protocol, 3 not a gateway
         0 security failures, 0 bad options, 0 with options
  Opts:  0 end, 0 nop, 0 basic security, 0 loose source route
         0 timestamp, 0 extended security, 0 record route
         0 stream ID, 0 strict source route, 0 alert, 0 cipso
         0 other
  Frags: 0 reassembled, 1 timeouts, 0 couldn't reassemble
         0 fragmented, 0 couldn't fragment
  Bcast: 146261 received, 146242 sent
  Mcast: 2 received, 405322 sent
  Sent:  1164881 generated, 8953546 forwarded
         1 encapsulation failed, 22226 no route

ICMP statistics:
  Rcvd: 0 format errors, 0 checksum errors, 0 redirects, 142550 unreachable
        4943 echo, 1020 echo reply, 0 mask requests, 0 mask replies, 0 quench
        0 parameter, 0 timestamp, 0 info request, 0 other
        0 irdp solicitations, 0 irdp advertisements
  Sent: 0 redirects, 14781 unreachable, 1520 echo, 4940 echo reply
        0 mask requests, 0 mask replies, 0 quench, 0 timestamp
        0 info reply, 33 time exceeded, 0 parameter problem
        0 irdp solicitations, 0 irdp advertisements

UDP statistics:
  Rcvd: 146337 total, 0 checksum errors, 52 no port
  Sent: 146315 total, 0 forwarded broadcasts

TCP statistics:
  Rcvd: 580266 total, 0 checksum errors, 72 no port
  Sent: 450389 total

ARP statistics:
  Rcvd: 4458 requests, 2 replies, 0 reverse, 0 other
  Sent: 5 requests, 4467 replies (0 proxy), 0 reverse
```

show access-lists Command

show access-lists displays the access list filters configured on the router:

```
2509#sh access-lists
Standard IP access list 1
    deny    192.168.1.0, wildcard bits 0.0.0.255
    deny    192.168.0.0, wildcard bits 0.0.255.255
    permit any
Standard IP access list 2
    permit 192.168.10.0, wildcard bits 0.0.0.255
    permit 192.168.0.0, wildcard bits 0.0.255.255
Extended IP access list 101
    deny    tcp any any eq telnet
    permit ip any any
```

show cdp neighbors Command

show cdp neighbors displays information about neighboring Cisco devices and can be useful during troubleshooting:

```
MVlab-7000-01#sh cdp nei
Capability Codes: R - Router, T - Trans Bridge, B - Source Route Bridge
                  S - Switch, H - Host, I - IGMP, r - Repeater

Device ID       Local Intrfce   Holdtme   Capability  Platform  Port ID
cat5500-02      ATM1/0.6        127         T B S     WS-C5500  5/1-2
4500-rtr        ATM1/0.5        135         R         4500      ATM0.5
Cat3000         Eth 0/0         151         T         CAT3000   1/1
LS1010          ATM1/0.1        152                   ASP       ATM13/0/0
```

show frame-relay pvc Command

show frame-relay pvc displays status information for frame-relay links:

```
7200#sh fram pvc

PVC Statistics for interface Serial6/0 (Frame Relay DTE)

DLCI = 200, DLCI USAGE = LOCAL, PVC STATUS = ACTIVE, INTERFACE = Serial6/0

    input pkts 14827        output pkts 24812       in bytes 7168356
    out bytes 14876307      dropped pkts 0          in FECN pkts 0
    in BECN pkts 0          out FECN pkts 0         out BECN pkts 0
    in DE pkts 0            out DE pkts 0
    pvc create time 1w3d, last time pvc status changed 1w3d
```

Other good frame-relay commands are **show frame-relay map** and **show frame-relay lmi**.

show tcp brief Command

show tcp brief displays the open TCP connections the router has with other devices:

```
2509#sh tcp br
TCB        Local Address        Foreign Address        (state)
001B853C   192.168.1.1.23       192.168.10.4.1052      ESTAB
0010A8FC   192.168.1.1.23       C2503.11002            CLOSEWAIT
001B8D70   192.168.1.1.23       192.168.10.4.1051      ESTAB
001D0C50   192.168.1.1.23       C2503.11006            ESTAB
001D2C58   192.168.1.1.23       192.168.10.4.2271      ESTAB
001D8C74   192.168.1.1.62989    C2503.23               ESTAB
```

Routing Show Commands

This section provides routing-related **show** commands along with their corresponding sample outputs.

show ip route Command

show ip route displays the active routing table:

```
Router01>sh ip ro
Codes: C - connected, S - static, I - IGRP, R - RIP, M - mobile, B - BGP
       D - EIGRP, EX - EIGRP external, O - OSPF, IA - OSPF inter area
       E1 - OSPF external type 1, E2 - OSPF external type 2, E - EGP
       i - IS-IS, L1 - IS-IS level-1, L2 - IS-IS level-2, * - candidate default

Gateway of last resort is 172.16.6.1 to network 0.0.0.0

     172.30.0.0 is variably subnetted, 2 subnets, 2 masks
D       172.30.254.227 255.255.255.255
           [90/409600] via 171.68.36.129, 6d08, Ethernet0
D       172.30.0.0 255.255.0.0 [90/2332160] via 171.68.36.129, 5d17, Ethernet0
     172.17.0.0 255.255.255.0 is subnetted, 1 subnets
D       172.17.59.0 [90/283648] via 171.68.36.136, 3d02, Ethernet0
     172.6.0.0 is variably subnetted, 7 subnets, 3 masks
D EX    172.6.157.81 255.255.255.255
           [170/46795776] via 171.68.36.129, 3d06, Ethernet0
D EX    172.6.157.80 255.255.255.248
           [170/46795776] via 171.68.36.129, 3d06, Ethernet0
C       172.16.6.0 255.255.255.128 is directly connected, Ethernet0
<lines deleted for brevity>
```

You can also get detailed information on a route to a destination with **show ip route**:

```
2509>sh ip ro 192.168.10.25
Routing entry for 192.168.10.0/24
  Known via "rip", distance 120, metric 1
  Redistributing via rip
  Last update from 192.168.1.2 on Serial1, 00:00:01 ago
  Routing Descriptor Blocks:
  * 192.168.1.2, from 192.168.1.2, 00:00:01 ago, via Serial1
      Route metric is 1, traffic share count is 1
```

show ip protocols Command

show ip protocols displays status information for IP routing protocols running in the router:

```
Myrouter#sh ip prot
Routing Protocol is "rip"
  Sending updates every 30 seconds, next due in 16 seconds
  Invalid after 180 seconds, hold down 180, flushed after 240
  Outgoing update filter list for all interfaces is not set
  Incoming update filter list for all interfaces is not set
  Redistributing: rip
  Default version control: send version 1, receive any version
    Interface       Send  Recv   Key-chain
    Ethernet0        1     1 2
    Serial1          1     1 2
  Routing for Networks:
    192.168.1.0
    192.168.10.0
  Routing Information Sources:
    Gateway         Distance        Last Update
    192.168.1.1          120        00:00:12
  Distance: (default is 120)
```

Routing **Show** Commands with EIGRP

When running the EIGRP routing protocol, **show ip eigrp neighbors** and **show ip eigrp topology** are notable commands (issue **show ip eigrp ?** for more commands).

```
2509#sh ip ei nei
IP-EIGRP neighbors for process 100
H   Address                 Interface   Hold Uptime   SRTT   RTO  Q  Seq
                                        (sec)         (ms)        Cnt Num
0   192.168.1.2             Se1           12 00:03:49   12    200  0  1

2509#sh ip ei topology
IP-EIGRP Topology Table for process 100

Codes: P - Passive, A - Active, U - Update, Q - Query, R - Reply,
       r - Reply status

P 192.168.10.0/24, 1 successors, FD is 1817600
        via 192.168.1.2 (1817600/281600), Serial1
P 192.168.1.0/24, 1 successors, FD is 1792000
        via Connected, Serial1
```

Refer to the IOS Command Reference for detailed information on the output of these **show ip eigrp** commands.

Routing **Show** Commands with OSPF

When running the OSPF routing protocol, **show ip ospf neighbor** and **show ip ospf interface** are notable troubleshooting commands (for more OSPF **show** commands, issue **show ip ospf ?** at the prompt).

```
2503#sh ip ospf nei

Neighbor ID     Pri   State          Dead Time   Address        Interface
10.20.1.1         1   FULL/  -       0:00:32     10.100.1.1     Serial0
10.2.1.3          1   FULL/  -       0:00:39     10.1.1.3       Serial1

Router02#sh ip osp int s 0.4
Serial0.4 is up, line protocol is up
  Internet Address 10.3.1.2 255.255.255.0, Area 0
  Process ID 10, Router ID 10.44.2.1, Network Type BROADCAST, Cost: 64
  Transmit Delay is 1 sec, State DR, Priority 1
  Designated Router (ID) 10.44.2.1, Interface address 10.3.1.2
  Backup Designated router (ID) 10.3.101.1, Interface address 10.3.1.1
  Timer intervals configured, Hello 10, Dead 40, Wait 40, Retransmit 5
    Hello due in 0:00:04
  Neighbor Count is 1, Adjacent neighbor count is 1
    Adjacent with neighbor 10.3.101.1  (Backup Designated Router)
```

Using the Router as a Terminal Server (Communications Server)

It is common to deploy Cisco routers with several asynchronous serial interfaces as *terminal servers*, also known as *communications servers*. A communications server (or comm server for short) connects to the console ports of other routers (or other devices) and then acts as a central point of access for the consoles.

Figure E-1 shows a user connecting with Telnet to comm server router (CS-RTR) and using CS-RTR to jump onto the console of seven other routers plus a UNIX workstation. This is a useful configuration for datacenter and lab setups where you want quick access to many router and server consoles.

To set up a router as a comm server, connect the async interfaces of the comm server to the console ports of the other devices.

If needed, configure the async lines in the comm server to match the serial parameters of the consoles. The Cisco defaults are 9600 baud, 8 bits, no parity, and 2 stop bits for both lines and console ports. So, usually no serial line configuration is needed when using a Cisco router as a comm server to connect to other Cisco router console ports.

Figure E-1   *A Comm Server Router Conveniently Reaches Multiple Consoles*

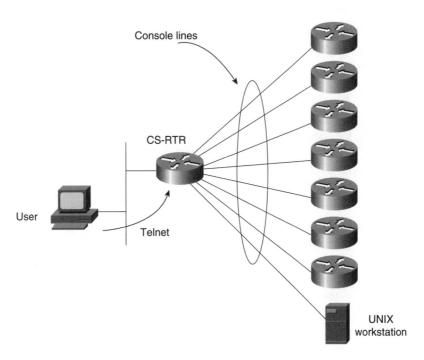

To change these settings, use one or more of the following commands in line config mode:

- **speed**
- **databits**
- **parity**
- **stopbits**
- **flowcontrol**

The following example configures lines 1 through 8 on a comm server router:

```
CS-RTR_2509#conf t
Enter configuration commands, one per line.  End with CNTL/Z.
CS-RTR_2509(config)#line 1 8
CS-RTR_2509(config-line)#speed 9600
CS-RTR_2509(config-line)#databits 8
CS-RTR_2509(config-line)#no exec
CS-RTR_2509(config-line)#transport input telnet
CS-RTR_2509(config-line)#transport output telnet
CS-RTR_2509(config-line)#end
```

In the preceding output **no exec** disallows outside connections to the comm server through the async lines. This effectively sets the lines for outbound EXEC sessions only, which is what we want on a comm server.

The commands **transport input telnet** and **transport output telnet** enable the Telnet protocol over the lines.

To connect to a console port hanging off the comm server, Telnet to port 2000+*n* of the comm server where *n* is the number of the async line (1 for line 1, 2 for line 2, 3 for line 3, and so on). As an example, suppose a router's console port is attached to line 5 of the comm server and 192.168.1.1 is the address of the comm server. To reach the router's console, simply Telnet to port 2005 of 192.168.1.1 (this is called a *reverse Telnet* through the comm server):

```
unix-server#telnet 192.168.1.1 2005
Trying 192.168.1.1, 2005 ... Open

Unauthorized access and use of this device is prohibited.

User Access Verification

Password:
RTA>
```

In the preceding output, the prompt **RTA>** belongs to the router attached to comm server, not to the comm server (192.168.1.1) itself.

NOTE   For each router console that attaches to the comm server, you usually need to permit reverse Telnets with the **transport input telnet** command, like so:

```
RTA#conf t
Enter configuration commands, one per line.  End with CNTL/Z.
RTA(config)#line con 0
RTA(config-line)#transport input telnet
RTA(config-line)#end
```

When switching between many consoles on one comm server, it is often convenient to Telnet to the comm server first, then use the comm server's prompt to jump from console to console.

From the comm server prompt, connect to a console by doing a Telnet to the comm server (a Telnet to itself) with the 2000+n port number:

```
CommSvr>192.168.1.1 2005
Trying 192.168.1.1, 2005 ... Open

Unauthorized access and use of this device is prohibited.

User Access Verification

Password:
RTA>
```

Improving on this, you can configure names for the consoles and do away with typing those IP addresses and 2000+n port numbers. Use the **ip host** command to populate a table of device names and their associated port/address pairs:

```
CommSvr#conf t
Enter configuration commands, one per line.  End with CNTL/Z.
CommSvr(config)#ip host RTA 2005 192.168.1.1
CommSvr(config)#ip host sparky 2006 192.168.1.1
CommSvr(config)#^Z
CommSvr#
```

TIP   The **show hosts** command displays the table of hostnames configured in the router.

Now you can connect to the device by typing **RTA** (case insensitive) instead of **192.168.1.1 2005**:

```
CommSvr>rta
Trying RTA (192.168.1.1, 2005)... Open

Unauthorized access and use of this device is prohibited.

User Access Verification

Password:
```

Now you are on RTA's console. But how do you get back to the comm server prompt and connect to more consoles?

To escape out of a console and return to the comm server's prompt, use the following IOS escape key sequence:

1   Depress **Ctrl** and **Shift**.

2   While keeping **Ctrl** and **Shift** depressed, depress and release the **6** key.

3   Release **Ctrl** and **Shift**.

4   Type the **X** key.

NOTE   Some Telnet clients do not pass special characters such as Ctrl-Shift-6. If the escape sequence doesn't seem to work, try it from a direct serial connection to the comm server's console port instead of a Telnet session. Also, try different Telnet and terminal emulation programs.

This sends you back to the comm server prompt and leaves the console session you escaped out of intact. Here's a sample output:

```
CommSvr>rta
Trying RTA (192.168.1.1, 2005)... Open

Unauthorized access and use of this device is prohibited.

User Access Verification

Password:
RTA> (Ctrl-Shift-6 and x sequence entered here)
CommSvr> (Now escaped backed to the comm server)
```

Now, from the comm server prompt connect to another console **sparky** that was also configured in the comm server with the **ip host** command:

```
CommSvr>sparky
Trying RTA (192.168.1.1, 2006)... Open

Unauthorized access and use of this device is prohibited.

User Access Verification

Password:
sparky>
```

This creates a second console session on the comm server.

Escape back to the comm server (**Ctrl-Shift-6**, **X**) and issue the **show sessions** command to view the open sessions you have:

```
CommSvr>sh ses
Conn Host              Address           Byte  Idle Conn Name
    1 rta              192.168.1.1          0    16 rta
  * 2 sparky           192.168.1.1          0     0 sparky
```

To flip back and forth between active console sessions, simply enter the number of the session you want to go to:

```
CommSvr>1
[Resuming connection 1 to rta ... ]

RTA> (Ctrl-Shift-6 and x escape sequence entered here)
CommSvr>2
[Resuming connection 2 to sparky ... ]

sparky>
```

To disconnect a session, issue the **disconnect** command along with the session number:

```
CommSvr>disc 2
Closing connection to sparky [confirm]y
CommSvr>sh ses
Conn Host              Address           Byte  Idle Conn Name
  * 1 rta              192.168.1.1          0     3 rta
```

NOTE   Instead of using the comm server to switch between consoles, you can simply open up multiple, simultaneous Telnet sessions to the comm server over different port numbers: 2001, 2002, 2003, and so on. Then, use your PC or workstation to switch between the sessions (where every session is a different console).

Enabling IOS Web-Based Management

Built into the IOS software is a simple Web server that can be used to monitor the router. Using a standard Web browser, you can view some basic statistics and issue enable mode commands from a Web page.

To enable the Web (http) server on a router use the **ip http server** command:

```
Myrouter(config)#ip http server
```

To view the home page of the router, use a Web browser pointed to http://x.y.z.t, where x.y.z.t is the IP address of your router. When prompted for a password, enter the enable password.

Figure E-2 is a sample router's home page.

Figure E-2   *A Web Server Inside IOS Offers Simple Web-Based Management*

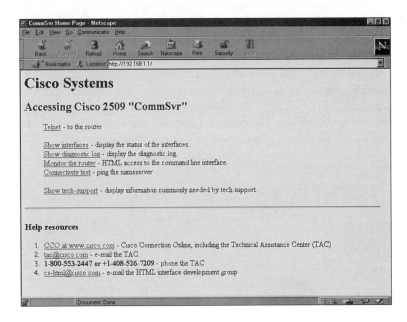

Click the *Monitor the router* link to load a page that enables you to enter IOS commands (see Figure E-3):

Figure E-3 *The Monitor the Router Page Enables You to Enter IOS Commands from a Web Browser*

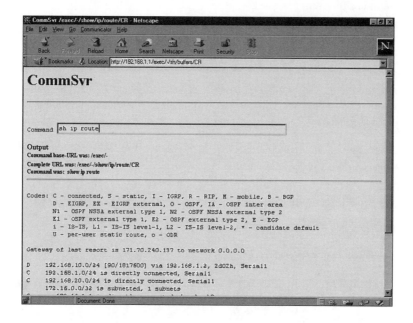

Instead of hunting laboriously through outputs of long **show** commands from the IOS prompt, consider issuing those commands from a Web browser. Then, use your browser's *find-in-page* function to zip to the text you are looking for.

BIBLIOGRAPHY

Chapter 1

Comer, Douglas E. *Internetworking with TCP/IP, Volume 1*, Third Edition. Upper Saddle River, NJ: Prentice-Hall, 1995.

> An authoritative book on TCP/IP. The third edition includes a chapter on IPv6.

Stevens, W. Richard. *TCP/IP Illustrated, Volume 1*. Reading, MA: Addison-Wesley, 1994.

> This is a good book on TCP/IP that illustrates how the protocols work with examples.

Chapter 2

Cisco Systems, Inc. "OSPF Design Guide." http://www.cisco.com/warp/public/104/1.html.

> A freely available primer on Open Shortest Path First (OSPF).

Downes, Kevin, H. Kim Lew, Steve Spanier, and Tim Stevenson. *Internetworking Technologies Handbook*, Second Edition. Indianapolis, IN: Cisco Press, 1998.

> A comprehensive reference on just about everything in the networking world.

Doyle, Jeff. *CCIE Professional Development: Routing TCP/IP, Volume 1*. Indianapolis, IN: Macmillan Technical Publishing, 1998.

> A recommended book that covers routing and all interior routing protocols in depth.

Halabi, Bassam. *Internet Routing Architectures*. Indianapolis, IN: New Riders Publishing, 1997.

> An in-depth book on Border Gateway Protocol (BGP).

Chapter 3

See sources listed for Chapter 2.

Chapter 4

Baker, Fred, ed. "Requirements for IP Version 4 Routers." RFC 1812, June 1995.

> Specifically referenced in this book for IP TOS field and precedence information, this RFC covers all requirements for IP routers.

Chapter 6

Kaeo, Merike. *Designing Network Security.* Indianapolis, IN: Macmillan Technical Publishing, 1999.

> A guide for security policies and implementations.

Kaufman, Charlie, Radia Perlman, and Mike Speciner. *Network Security: Private Communication in a Public World.* Upper Saddle River, NJ: Prentice-Hall, 1995.

> A resource on network security and cryptography.

Chapter 7

Bellovin, Steven M. "Problem Areas for the IP Security Protocols." *Proceedings of the Sixth USENIX Security Symposium.* San Jose: USENIX Association, 1996.

> Explains why authentication is required for secure encryption.

Krawczyk, Hugo. "SKEME: A Versatile Secure Key Exchange Mechanism for Internet." *Proceedings of the 1996 Symposium on Network and Distributed Systems Security.* San Diego: Internet Society (ISOC), 1996.

> A paper on SKEME, an influential part of the IKE protocol. Listed here because it is mentioned in the text along with ISAKMP (Internet Security Association and Key Management Protocol) and Oakley.

Schneier, Bruce. *Applied Cryptography,* Second Edition. New York, NY: John Wiley & Sons, Inc., 1996.

> A good source of cryptography theory and applications, although directed more to software programmers.

See also the sources listed for Chapter 6.

Symbols

Numerics

A

J-K-L

N

O

P

R

T

U

CCIE Professional Development

Advanced IP Network Design

Alvaro Retana, CCIE; Don Slice, CCIE; and Russ White, CCIE

1-57870-097-3 • **AVAILABLE NOW**

Network engineers and managers can use these case studies, which highlight various network design goals, to explore issues including protocol choice, network stability, and growth. This book also includes theoretical discussion on advanced design topics.

Routing TCP/IP, Volume I

Jeff Doyle, CCIE

1-57870-041-8 • **AVAILABLE NOW**

This book takes the reader from a basic understanding of routers and routing protocols through a detailed examination of each of the IP interior routing protocols. Learn techniques for designing networks that maximize the efficiency of the protocol being used. Exercises and review questions provide core study for the CCIE Routing and Switching exam.

CCIE Professional Development: Large-Scale IP Network Solutions

Khalid Raza, CCIE; Salman Asad, CCIE; and Mark Turner

1-57870-084-1 • **AVAILABLE SEPTEMBER 1999**

Network engineers can find solutions as their IP networks grow in size and complexity. Examine all the major IP protocols in-depth and learn about scalability, migration planning, network management, and security for large-scale networks.

Cisco CCIE Fundamentals: Network Design and Case Studies

Cisco Systems, Inc.

1-57870-066-3 • **AVAILABLE NOW**

This two-part reference is a compilation of design tips and configuration examples assembled by Cisco Systems. The design guide portion of this book supports the network administrator who designs and implements routers and switch-based networks, and the case studies supplement the design guide material with real-world configurations. Begin the process of mastering the technologies and protocols necessary to become an effective CCIE.

CISCO SYSTEMS

CISCO PRESS

www.ciscopress.com

Cisco Career Certifications

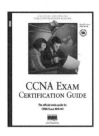

CCNA Exam Certification Guide
Wendell Odom, CCIE

0-7357-0073-7 • AVAILABLE NOW

This book is a comprehensive study tool for CCNA Exam #640-407 and part of a recommended study program from Cisco Systems. *CCNA Exam Certification Guide* helps you understand and master the exam objectives. Instructor-developed elements and techniques maximize your retention and recall of exam topics, and scenario-based exercises help validate your mastery of the exam objectives.

Advanced Cisco Router Configuration
Cisco Systems, Inc., edited by Laura Chappell

1-57870-074-4 • AVAILABLE NOW

Based on the actual Cisco ACRC course, this book provides a thorough treatment of advanced network deployment issues. Learn to apply effective configuration techniques for solid network implementation and management as you prepare for CCNP and CCDP certifications. This book also includes chapter-ending tests for self-assessment.

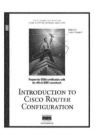

Introduction to Cisco Router Configuration
Cisco Systems, Inc., edited by Laura Chappell

1-57870-076-0 • AVAILABLE NOW

Based on the actual Cisco ICRC course, this book presents the foundation knowledge necessary to define Cisco router configurations in multiprotocol environments. Examples and chapter-ending tests build a solid framework for understanding internetworking concepts. Prepare for the ICRC course and CCNA certification while mastering the protocols and technologies for router configuration.

Cisco CCNA Preparation Library
Cisco Systems, Inc., Laura Chappell, and Kevin Downes, CCIE

1-57870-125-2 • AVAILABLE NOW • CD-ROM

This boxed set contains two Cisco Press books—*Introduction to Cisco Router Configuration* and *Internetworking Technologies Handbook,* Second Edition— and the *High-Performance Solutions for Desktop Connectivity* CD.

www.ciscopress.com

Cisco Press Solutions

Internetworking SNA with Cisco Solutions

George Sackett and Nancy Sackett

1-57870-083-3 • AVAILABLE NOW

This comprehensive guide presents a practical approach to integrating SNA and TCP/IP networks. It provides readers with an understanding of internetworking terms, networking architectures, protocols, and implementations for internetworking SNA with Cisco routers.

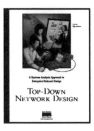

Top-Down Network Design

Priscilla Oppenheimer

1-57870-069-8 • AVAILABLE NOW

Building reliable, secure, and manageable networks is every network professional's goal. This practical guide teaches you a systematic method for network design that can be applied to campus LANs, remote-access networks, WAN links, and large-scale internetworks. Learn how to analyze business and technical requirements, examine traffic flow and Quality of Service requirements, and select protocols and technologies based on performance goals.

Internetworking Technologies Handbook, Second Edition

Kevin Downes, CCIE; Merilee Ford; H. Kim Lew; Steve Spanier; Tim Stevenson

1-57870-102-3 • AVAILABLE NOW

This comprehensive reference provides a foundation for understanding and implementing contemporary internetworking technologies, providing you with the necessary information needed to make rational networking decisions. Master terms, concepts, technologies, and devices that are used in the internetworking industry today. You also learn how to incorporate networking technologies into a LAN/WAN environment, as well as how to apply the OSI reference model to categorize protocols, technologies, and devices.

OSPF Network Design Solutions

Thomas M. Thomas II

1-57870-046-9 • AVAILABLE NOW

This comprehensive guide presents a detailed, applied look into the workings of the popular Open Shortest Path First protocol, demonstrating how to dramatically increase network performance and security, and how to most easily maintain large-scale networks. OSPF is thoroughly explained through exhaustive coverage of network design, deployment, management, and troubleshooting.

CISCO SYSTEMS

CISCO PRESS

www.ciscopress.com

Cisco Press Solutions

Internetworking Troubleshooting Handbook

Kevin Downes, CCIE; H. Kim Lew; Spank McCoy;
Tim Stevenson; Kathleen Wallace

1-57870-024-8 • AVAILABLE NOW

Diagnose and resolve specific and potentially problematic issues common to every network type with this valuable reference. Each section of the book is devoted to problems common to a specific protocol. Sections are subdivided into symptoms, descriptions of environments, diagnosing and isolating problem causes, and problem-solution summaries. This book aims to help you reduce downtime, improve network performance, and enhance network reliability using proven troubleshooting solutions.

IP Routing Primer

Robert Wright, CCIE

1-57870-108-2 • AVAILABLE NOW

Learn how IP routing behaves in a Cisco router environment. In addition to teaching the core fundamentals, this book enhances your ability to troubleshoot IP routing problems yourself, often eliminating the need to call for additional technical support. The information is presented in an approachable, workbook-type format with dozens of detailed illustrations and real-life scenarios integrated throughout.

Designing Network Security

Merike Kaeo

1-57870-043-4 • AVAILABLE NOW

Designing Network Security is a practical guide designed to help you understand the fundamentals of securing your corporate infrastructure. This book takes a comprehensive look at underlying security technologies, the process of creating a security policy, and the practical requirements necessary to implement a corporate security policy.

For the latest on Cisco Press resources and Certification and

Training guides, or for information on publishing opportunities, visit

www.ciscopress.com.

Cisco Press books are available at your local bookstore, computer store, and online booksellers.